SECURITY AFTER CHRISTENDOM

THEOPOLITICAL VISIONS

SERIES EDITORS:

Thomas Heilke
D. Stephen Long
and Debra Dean Murphy

Theopolitical Visions seeks to open up new vistas on public life, hosting fresh conversations between theology and political theory. This series assembles writers who wish to revive theopolitical imagination for the sake of our common good.

Theopolitical Visions hopes to re-source modern imaginations with those ancient traditions in which political theorists were often also theologians. Whether it was Jeremiah's prophetic vision of exiles "seeking the peace of the city," Plato's illuminations on piety and the civic virtues in the Republic, St. Paul's call to "a common life worthy of the Gospel," St. Augustine's beatific vision of the City of God, or the gothic heights of medieval political theology, much of Western thought has found it necessary to think theologically about politics, and to think politically about theology. This series is founded in the hope that the renewal of such mutual illumination might make a genuine contribution to the peace of our cities.

FORTHCOMING VOLUMES:

David Deane
The Matter of the Spirit: How Soteriology Shapes the Moral Life

Adam Joyce
No More Pharoahs: Christianity, Racial Capitalism, and Socialism

Security after
CHRISTENDOM

Global Politics and Political Theology for Apocalyptic Times

JOHN HEATHERSHAW

CASCADE *Books* • Eugene, Oregon

SECURITY AFTER CHRISTENDOM
Global Politics and Political Theology for Apocalyptic Times

Theopolitical Visions series

Copyright © 2024 John Heathershaw. All rights reserved. Except for brief quotations in critical publications or reviews, no part of this book may be reproduced in any manner without prior written permission from the publisher. Write: Permissions, Wipf and Stock Publishers, 199 W. 8th Ave., Suite 3, Eugene, OR 97401.

Cascade Books
An Imprint of Wipf and Stock Publishers
199 W. 8th Ave., Suite 3
Eugene, OR 97401

www.wipfandstock.com

PAPERBACK ISBN: 978-1-5326-1533-7
HARDCOVER ISBN: 978-1-5326-1535-1
EBOOK ISBN: 978-1-5326-1534-4

Cataloguing-in-Publication data:

Names: Heathershaw, John [author].

Title: Security after Christendom : global politics and political theology for apocalyptic times / John Heathershaw.

Description: Eugene, OR: Cascade Books, 2024 | Series: Theopolitical Visions | Includes bibliographical references and index.

Identifiers: ISBN 978-1-5326-1533-7 (paperback) | ISBN 978-1-5326-1535-1 (hardcover) | ISBN 978-1-5326-1534-4 (ebook)

Subjects: LCSH: Political theology | Christianity and international relations | International relations | Religion and politics

Classification: BT83.59 H43 2024 (print) | BT83.59 (ebook)

Some sections of parts 1 and 2 appeared in John Heathershaw, "What Is Christendom to Us? Making Better Sense of Christianity in Global Politics," *International Studies Review*, Volume 25, Issue 4, December 2023, viad051. Some sections of the conclusion appeared in John Heathershaw "Theological Responses to the War against Ukraine: A Reply to Joshua Searle," *Anabaptism Today* 5.2 (2023), 56–66. Both articles were published under a Creative Commons CC BY license under which permission need not be sought.

For Liliya, Yuriy, Yelyzaveta, and Illia,
who know insecurity after Christendom

"Ruthlessly realistic analysis is not incompatible with hope, for hope is a theological not a political virtue."

—MARTIN WIGHT[1]

---

1. Martin Wight, "The Church, Russia and the West," *Ecumenical Review*, 1.1 (1949) 35.

Contents

Tables and Figures xi
Preface: A New Christian Realism? xv
Acknowledgments xix
List of Abbreviations xxiii

Introduction 1

PART ONE: *Christendom and Security*

1. Imagined Histories 31

2. Conflicting Geographies 54

3. Fading Theories 73

4. Retreating Ethics 94

PART TWO: *Global Politics after Christendom*

5. Security in a Secular Age 115

6. Insecurities of the Security State 136

7. Disorders of the Liberal International Order 160

8. Idolatries of Neo-Christendom 181

PART THREE: *A Theology of Security*

9. The Powers and the Apocalypse 203

10. Radical Inclusion 226

11. Nonviolent Protection 247

12. Abundant provision 273

Conclusion 295

Bibliography 309

Index 339

Tables and Figures

TABLES

Table 1: Centering and decentering imaginaries
of eastern and western Christendoms 70

Table 2: Imagined security communities in a secular age 133

Table 3: Christian and secular approaches to security 304

FIGURES

Figure 1: War in the very long run 252

Preface

A New Christian Realism?

How does faithful following of the person of Jesus Christ, the crucified and risen one, affect the form and substance of global politics? How does the concept of Christ's lordship shape the nature of global security today and in the future? What has been the role of the worldwide church, in partnership with the secular authorities, in both advancing security and causing insecurity? Is it possible for the church to articulate a Christocentric vision of the security of the world based on the belief that Christ possesses "all authority in heaven and on earth" (Matt 28:18)? These are the questions that animate this book. They are being asked in a historical context that is indisputably "after Christendom," in the sense that the partnership of church and government has been fatally and rightly undermined. Moreover, it is the premise of this work that to answer these questions we must move beyond the political imagination of Christendom—the idea of the church ministering to government and government securing the church—and construct a global political theology of post-Christendom.

These are not entirely new questions, but they are ones that remain without credible answers. They are increasingly urgent as we see that Christendom continues to cast a shadow over global security. In an address to a conference of Christian politicians at the Ecumenical Institute in 1948, commenting on the very first assembly of the World Council of Churches (WCC) and published in the first issue of the WCC's journal, the British scholar of International Relations (IR) and Christian realist Martin Wight called attention to the East-West conflict that was emerging in what became known as the Cold War. Wight commented:

> When we consider these two blocs or groupings or civilizations whose antagonisms determine world politics today, two things become apparent at the outset. It is an antagonism between two parts of what was once Christendom; and the conflict has reached its present dimensions *because Christendom, of which these were part, is dead.*[1]

For Wight, this conflict has its origins as a conflict within Christendom going back to at least the sixth century.[2] Seventy-five years after he spoke—with Russia and the West at loggerheads over Ukraine—Wight's words could be repeated in their entirety and remain apposite. However, as a Christian realist who dispenses with Christendom, Wight is left with merely a negative account of security—that is, of insecurity.

Christian realism is an inadequate account of security for two reasons. First, its realism is narrowly political—that is, it is devoid of sociological or theological realism but focused on the fundaments of the existing political order at a high level of generality—with a limited optic on what Wight called "the pattern of power."[3] It seeks to understand order in traditional geopolitical terms, principally via the concept of a balance of power: the idea of achieving parity of threat between two civilizational blocs or poles, such as those of the Cold War from the 1940s to the 1980s. However, the balance of power was and remains an extremely thin reading of how and why persons, communities, and our wider environment become secure or insecure. Amidst its "order" is extraordinary disorder and violence. Christian realists recognized the "instability" of the balance of power while Wight felt that a third world war with the Soviet Union was "inevitable."[4] But real insecurity lies beyond questions of great power politics. The balance of power says nothing about the Global South's exclusion from a more secure and prosperous world.[5] Realism says little about protection from armed conflict, which over the period of the Cold War came to be dominated by civil wars whose origins had little to do with great power blocs—although geopolitical divides often made them

---

1. Wight, "The Church, Russia and the West," 25, emphasis added.
2. Wight, "The Church, Russia and the West," 26n1.
3. Wight, "The Church, Russia and the West," 30.
4. Wight, "The Church, Russia and the West,"31.
5. Wight claims, in an ethnocentric statement which can only be sustained in abstract rhetoric, that "there is no nation and no part of the earth which lies beyond the range of the Communist organizer or the American businessman." Wight, "The Church, Russia and the West," 28.

worse. This political realism disregards question of provision, of the economy, and of the environment, as it considers these to be no more than tertiary questions of statecraft.

Second, Christian realism's Christ is remarkably contained; his lordship of history is put off till the end of the world. Thinkers such as Wight and Niebuhr felt that Christ's radical teaching lacked utility in a political world dominated by sin and violence. The Sermon on the Mount may as well be for another planet and the Christian ethic is a matter of personal salvation and conduct within the church before the second coming of Christ would deliver the radically new order in all its fullness. From this perspective, as Wight argued, "hope is a theological not a political virtue."[6] Christian realists drew a hard line between their political writing and their theology with the former being conventionally secular and the latter evangelically Christian. They attempted to square this circle by arguing that the best the church of Christ can do is limit the disorder of a fallen world, often by supporting warfare as a legitimate influence of statecraft. As the sociologist David Martin—who shared the premises of Christian realism—argued, "the cross will be carried into the realm of temporal power and will turn into a sword which defends established order."[7] The realism here is prominent. The loss of Christendom is lamented, and a new Christendom imagined.[8] But it is not clear where Christ appears, except magically at the end of history. What is missing is an account of security that proceeds, in Oliver O'Donovan's words, "from a Christology that has been displayed in narrative form as the Gospel."[9]

This book does not seek to evangelize the debate on war—for a recent and unsurpassed attempt to do so see Nick Megoran's *Warlike Christians in an Age of Violence*.[10] Nor does it provide an intellectual's political theology of post-Christendom—for such a genealogy I would refer to Kyle Gingerich-Hiebert's important *The Architectonics of Hope*.[11] Rather, this book sketches out the theoretical and practical terrain of a theology of security in a secular age. This question is wider than that of war and

6. Wight, "The Church, Russia and the West," 35.

7. Martin, *The Breaking of the Image*, 28.

8. Wight contemplates "spiritual beams which may or may not reach down to the future to fertilize a new Christendom ten centuries hence." Wight, "The Church, Russia and the West," 45.

9. O'Donovan, *The Desire of the Nations*, 133.

10. Cascade, 2017.

11. Cascade, 2017.

less intellectual than that of theological genealogies. In the debate about security the key terms are not war and peace between or in nations, but wider concerns of inclusion, protection, and provision on a global scale. Moreover, the debate cannot be confined to the realm of ideas but must pay heed to "real world" practices and outcomes. This world excludes based on power and wealth. Actual war rarely protects anyone, typically harms all sides, and provides only for those who lead states, sell weapons, and build militaries. Migration, climate change, poverty, and corruption offer numerous challenges of provision that nation states appear to exacerbate rather than attenuate. To live and act both faithfully and practically we need a new Christian realism, one that points hopefully to Christ's kingdom while being ruthlessly realistic about the world's kingdoms, the extent of their fall, and their eventual passing away. This book is the prologue to that project.

Acknowledgments

This book has been a labor of love and has thus taken many years to complete alongside my day job at the University of Exeter studying the conflict, security, and development of post-Soviet Eurasia through the immanent frame. This has led me to rely on more learned colleagues a great deal, many of whom have commented on draft chapters. We battled on together through the pandemic, seemingly constant bureaucratic "transformations," and all-too-frequent managerial intrusions into academic life. At Exeter, I could not have wished for a greater group of colleagues from which to learn as I prepared this book. I have been fortunate to be alongside the talented and hardworking Adrian Bailey, Bice Maiguashca, David Horrell, David Lewis, Farah Mihlar, Sarah Lucas, and Stephane Baele. Special thanks must be extended to Brandon Gallaher, Grace Davie, Gregorio Bettiza, Esther Reed, and Tim Gorringe, who made especially significant contributions that led to revisions on the first draft. Paul Cloke's encouragement was of special value in my early years as a lecturer at Exeter and his passing to glory was a great loss to his community, family, and church.

Beyond Exeter, I was nourished by the research and teaching of the Anabaptist-Mennonite Network of the UK at various points over the last fifteen years after moving back to Britain, including Andrew Francis, Brian Haymes, Fran Porter, Joshua Searle, Linda Wilson, Lloyd Pieterson, Simon Barrow, and Stuart Murray Williams. At Bristol Baptist College and Trinity College Bristol, I have benefitted from the insights of fellow students at MA and PhD levels and academic colleagues, including Helen Paynter, Jamie Davies, Peter Hatton, and especially the generosity of time and depth of insight of Steve Finamore. The students on Steve's Master's course on Revelation and those of the Centre for Anabaptist Studies at

Bristol Baptist College deserve a shout-out as it is on those studies from 2013–15 that the ideas for this book began to percolate.

In West Africa, I experienced the practice of the church amidst armed conflict and forced migration from Father Dekker, colleagues in the Anglican mission and UN, and many refugee and church friends. In Central Asia, I learnt what it was to be a Christian minority in the face of established and ethnically based Christian communities from Volodaya, Sasha, Barakatullo, and many more persons who will remain unnamed. In the United States, where this project began while I was a postdoc at the University of Notre Dame, I learnt from colleagues, including Gerald McKenny, whose doctoral-level course in political theologies was formative for me. Scott Appleby, David Cortright, and colleagues of various faiths at the Kroc Institute gave examples of how the sacred and secular were negotiated in traditions different to my own. Most especially, David Montgomery's friendship and hospitality, both intellectual and personal, has had a great impact on me. David also introduced me to the advice and acute intellect of his colleague Adam Seligman. Together, via Communities Engaging with Difference and Religion, we worked together on a British Council-funded dialogue exercise on Islam and secularism. Friends at Kern Road Mennonite Church modelled being an ecclesia after Christendom as my wife, baby daughter, and I were welcomed there as worshippers in 2006–7. The late Alan Kreider, whose *Journey towards Holiness* is the best discipleship text that places our security under God at the center, was also generous in introducing me to Mennonite theologies.

My thanks go to Stuart Murray Williams, who supported the book in its early stages, and the editorial staff at Wipf & Stock for their patience and support through this long process. The research and thought required to produce this book were supported by grants from the British Council, the Economic and Social Research Council, the British Academy, and the University of Exeter. Drafts of chapters and ideas from the book have been presented to the Anabaptist Studies group in the UK and to workshops at the University of Exeter, the Royal Institute of International Affairs (Chatham House), New College, University of Oxford, and the Faculty of Divinity, University of Cambridge. Along the way, I have benefitted from the invitations, insights, warmth, and comments of *inter alia* Adeeb Khalid, Courtney Kane, Cyril Hovorun, Daryl Ooi, David Nussbaum, James Walters, Jan van der Stoep, John-Harmen Valk, Joanildo Burity, Jodok Troy, Julia Costa Lopez, Kanat Kalmakiev, Kristina Stoeckl, Kristine Margvelashvili, Kseniia Trofymchuk, Luca Mavelli,

Lucian Leustean, Marianne Rosario, Mario Aguilar, Marko Veković, Morgan Liu, Moria Bar-Maoz, Marietta van der Tol, Oliver O'Donovan, Paul Lusk, Paul Weithman, Paul Woods, Petr Kratochvil, Roman Soloviy, Scott Thomas, Stacey Gutkowski, Tornike Metreveli, Vassillios Paipais, and Zoran Grozdanov. Finally, my great friend and colleague Nick Megoran read the manuscript in full and made suggestions big and small that have improved it immensely. It goes without saying that the argument is very much my own, reflecting my own biases, preferences, and background. In that sense, it is, like any study, for better or worse, a personal and parochial one.

John Heathershaw
Exeter, Summer 2022

List of Abbreviations

CPT	Christian Peacemaker Teams
EU	European Union
FoRB	Freedom of Religion and Belief
IPCC	Intergovernmental Panel on Climate Change of the United Nations
IR	International Relations
JWT	Just War Theory
NATO	North Atlantic Treaty Organization
UCP	Unarmed Civilian Protection
UN	United Nations
UNDP	UN Development Program
UNDPKO	UN Department of Peacekeeping Operations
WCC	World Council of Churches

Introduction

While people are saying "Peace and Security," destruction will come on them suddenly, as labor pains on a pregnant woman, and they will not escape.

1 THESSALONIANS 5:3

The word of God delivered by prophets is the main principle of Christian politics.

THOMAS HOBBES[1]

Since the mid-twentieth century war has been less frequent and less costly. Over the same period, the world has become wealthier with hundreds of millions having been raised out of poverty. Liberal internationalism marched forward in this time as decolonization produced many new democracies[2] and vast increases in the number of humanitarian organizations. New frontiers of inclusion—of class, sex, race, gender—have been breached over the last century. Reams of statistical data demonstrate these trends. And yet the United Nations reported in 2022 that "those benefiting from some of the highest levels of good health, wealth, and education outcomes are reporting even greater anxiety than 10 years ago."[3] So, why do many of us feel so insecure?

One reason may be that humanity is facing existential threats that were barely imaginable a century ago. Nuclear Armageddon remains a few clicks

---

1. Hobbes, *Leviathan*, "Christian Commonwealth," 32.
2. Until the early twenty-first century, when autocracy began to resurge. Freedom House, *Freedom in the World*.
3. United Nations Development Programme, "2022 Special Report on Human Security."

away and new military technologies such as lethal autonomous weapons systems (LAWS, ironically) offer the world's dictators the ability to kill at low cost and with impunity. One leading artificial intelligence expert claims chillingly that, for an image from science fiction grounded in reality, we may "think about the TV series *Black Mirror*, and specifically the robot bees from the episode *Hated in the Nation*. They aren't conscious. They don't hate people. They are precisely programmed by one person to hunt 387,036 specific humans, burrow into their brains, and kill them."[4]

Another answer concerns chronic and increasing insecurities. While the threats from new military technologies abound, complex ecological and economic challenges are in many ways more serious. Climate change is continuing apace with the distinct possibility that many regions of the world will become uninhabitable within the lifetimes of our children. And as diversity and inclusivity are celebrated in many states, new barriers come down against a vastly increased population of refugees and migrants. Even in the world's wealthiest and most secure country, insecurity is pervasive. From a total of seventeen polls conducted by Pew between 2002 and 2021, in thirteen the most popular description of the US's economic situation by Americans was "bad."[5] Such real and perceived insecurities generate demand for security. Once a niche term of spies and financial professionals, it has become the watchword for our times which is appended to almost any adjective—health, cyber, energy, and food to name but a few. At the same time, the attainment of such security seems an ever-distant prospect, even for the most privileged of our world.

It is the contention of this book that the security crisis we face is not merely a political problem of secular states and their temporal solutions. Government often declares "peace and security" (*pax et securitas*), the Roman imperial slogan and prophetic warning recalled by Paul in his first letter to the Thessalonians (5:3).[6] Security is a problem of *both* imperial practice *and* prophetic resistance—as the putative father of secular political realism, Thomas Hobbes, understood. It raises questions that are not just political but *eschatological* (of the purpose and end of the world), *ecclesiological* (of the place of the church in that purpose), and, most of all, *Christological* (of the centrality of Jesus Christ to that purpose). These questions

4. Russell, "The Future Role of AI in Warfare."

5. Pew Research, "Country's Economic Situation: United States."

6. Weima has made the argument for *pax et securitas* being a recognizable Roman imperial slogan at the time of the letter while White has claimed that, as *securitas* was not a common signifier in Roman political discourse until Nero, Paul's reference is more likely to prophetic warnings against security-seeking kings. Weima, "'Peace and Security'(1 Thess 5.3)"; White, "'Peace and Security'(1 Thessalonians 5.3)."

of how we understand the trajectory of the world, the place of the church in that trajectory, and the role of Christ in inaugurating and completing his work are integral to properly Christian approaches to security. But the grounds for studying security *after* Christendom are not merely theological but historical. The form that the questions and answers take is a specifically post-Christendom one. In the second half of the twentieth century, around 1,700 years of various forms of intimate partnership between church and state quite rapidly and apparently conclusively became unimaginable under the forces of secularization. There are around two-and-a-half billion Christians of one kind or another and the church is growing almost everywhere outside the West. The world is definitely not post-Christian. But those Christians who seek an accommodation between church and state are finding that changes in history have made this way of imagining their security increasingly untenable. Our crisis is one of security *after Christendom*.

It wasn't supposed to be like this. Following the "revised theory of modernization," advanced by the World Value Survey, "people's priorities shift from traditional to secular-rational values as their *sense of existential security* increases."[7] Further, the world's values, according to these secularization theorists, "shift from survival to self-expression values as their *sense of individual agency* increases."[8] Liberal secularism and its liberal international order were purported to be both the generative process and the final product of greater security. A great deal of data and analysis from the World Value Survey and many hundreds of other studies support this conclusion; it should prompt reflection among those of faith.[9] Where secularism is most established—from China to Denmark—people tend to feel more secure and, in some ways, to be more individualistic.[10] The Nordic countries, a number of which lay outside the main security alliance of Western states (NATO), set the standard for human wellbeing in our times and an exception. As the founder of the World Values Survey Ron Inglehart notes, something more complicated than the abandonment of faith is going on here. "Nordic people are not happy because they're less religious," he remarks, "but because their synthesis of advanced social policies and key elements of their Protestant heritage has made their societies relatively secure and egalitarian."[11] There are aspects of this claim we will question in this book but for now let us recognize this: security is a post-Christendom problem.

7. World Values Survey, "Findings and Insights."
8. World Values Survey, "Findings and Insights."
9. For a summary, see Inglehart, *Religion's Sudden Decline*, ch. 6.
10. Taylor, *A Secular Age*.
11. Inglehart, *Religion's Sudden Decline*, 143.

An Unwritten Chapter in the History of Religion

The philosopher John Gray, in his 2007 polemic *Black Mass*, argued that "modern politics is a chapter in the history of religion." The secular age, he contends, has been characterized by "the long dissolution of Christianity and the rise of modern political religion," while "the secular terror of modern times is a mutant version of the violence that has accompanied Christianity throughout its history."[12] Gray points to countless nineteenth- and twentieth-century Christian movements driven by millennial imaginaries both in the West and beyond. Although little known in the West, the insurgency of the Taiping Heavenly Army of mid-nineteenth-century China brought a conflict with over twenty million dead. Gray argues that the Jacobins, Nazis, and Soviets all absorbed the myth of redemptive violence that was fostered in Christendom and doubled-down by seeking an immediate and human-created conversion of society rather than placing salvation in God's hands.[13] "The political violence of the modern West," he plainly asserts, "can only be understood as an eschatological phenomenon."[14] Gray is correct. However, he is disinterested in exploring the theological questions of the apocalyptic that arise from his analysis.

Security after Christendom takes on this challenge. Secular academic analyses of security are most often askance in the face of militant religion and appalled by its apocalypticism. But given its foundations in Christendom, the rapidity with which the modern study of security was secularized, and thereby disregarded the question of eschatology, is indicative of the extent of the post-Christendom shift. In the US, this took place under the forces of behavioralism and rational choice theory in the American academy. In the UK, which was largely immune from these intellectual trends and whose field was also shaped by practicing Christians, "the way in which British International Relations (IR)[15] acquiesced in this secularization of the emerging discipline is remarkable."[16] By the end of the twentieth century, it was accepted that Christianity had been extinguished as a source of both

---

12. Gray, *Black Mass*, 1, 3.
13. Gray, *Black Mass*, 35–37.
14. Gray, *Black Mass*, 48.
15. In the academic field of International Relations, it is common to capitalise and to use the ugly acronym IR to distinguish the academic field from the subject matter, variously denoted as international relations, international politics, global politics, or world politics. I will generally use "global politics" to define the expansive subject matter as I understand it and "international politics" where the subject matter is defined more narrowly by the author in question as relations between states.
16. Jones, "Christian Realism," 372.

the objects and subjects of IR. Hedley Bull noted in his classic work *The Anarchical Society* that "the vestiges of Western Christendom came almost to disappear from the theory and practice of international politics."[17] Indeed, secularization accelerated after World War II but, crucially, secular society and secular academy emerged from Christendom rather than replacing it.

To speak of post-Christendom is therefore to imagine a world *after* that in which Christian thinkers and institutions shaped statecraft and ministered to government. To write of a political theology of global politics from a post-Christendom perspective is to disavow the prospect for equilibrium between cross and sword and to reconstruct the inherent tension between the two. Since the Christian realists of the mid-twentieth century, no political theorist or theologian has tackled the primary question of IR—security—from an explicitly Christian and biblical perspective in a research monograph. The attempts we have seen are add-ons to wider political theologies and are typically overtly revanchist, excessively normative, or both. On the revanchist side, the theologian John Milbank and the political theorist Adrian Pabst address international politics in the final two chapters of their co-authored polemic against liberalism. These authors seek to revive classical Christian realism even though the death of its formative historical conditions—those of Christendom—is a premise of their argument. While insightful, and consistent with much of the analysis in part 2 of this book, the authors differ from this work by retaining a geopolitical framing and thereby remaining state-centric despite their claim that in the international arena, "the social is really primary."[18] On the normative side, political theologies of post-Christendom typically adopt a pacifist stance that is averse to the idea of security. Most of these authors are focused on Western debates and cases; none, to my knowledge, offer a political theology of security. The closest that we have come to one in book-length form is perhaps Luke Bretherton's *Christianity and Contemporary Politics*, but this leaves the global to a final chapter focused on the positive value of security (provision for) rather than its negative value (protection from) and thereby lacks a unifying political theology of global politics.

It is my hope then that there is some novelty to this book. But novelty is not itself originality and may just as much indicate foolhardy ambition in the face of a puzzle that has been side-stepped by IR thinkers and theologians for good reason. I proceed in the hope that *Security after Christendom* will appeal to two groups. First, I would like it to be of interest to students and scholars of IR interested in both the intellectual history and contemporary

17. Bull, *The Anarchical Society*, 31.
18. Milbank and Pabst, *The Politics of Virtue*, 356.

perspectives on their field emerging from Western and Eastern traditions of what remains the world's largest faith group. Second, I hope it entices theologians interested in extending their analysis to the international in a way that engages the theoretical debates and evidence of that field. To both audiences, I wish to advance the cause of "theology after Christendom," and specifically theologico-political analysis, understood as a prophetic exercise that "should address the urgent issues in the public sphere" and "embody and inculcate humane virtues in society."[19]

Yet few books stand the test of time. By addressing the question of security "after Christendom" this book explores a particular but rather long historical moment diagnosed by many political theologians and social scientists of religion. Bishops in the declining Roman Empire, Franciscans in the twelfth century *Respublica Christianum*, and a whole host of confessants in the violence of the Reformation may have thought, for different reasons, that Christendom had ended. But as an imagined community it kept coming back. The post-Christendom moment appears as something like, and perhaps a successor to, the "Machiavellian moment" of the fifteenth to the eighteenth centuries where the conditions for republicanism and capitalism emerged.[20] In post-Christendom, these Machiavellian ideas have reached their nadir. Therefore, the question of "after Christendom" is not primarily one of historical periodicity, but of imagined community. It is a moment in which the idea of Christendom lost both its normative and descriptive value for thinkers and practitioners of all faiths and none.

Perhaps even fewer books stand the test of place. While history is a merciless exposer of the assumptions of the present, geography is an incessant reminder of how shackled we are within our own provinces. Important books on related questions are often profoundly ethno-centric. Taylor's *A Secular Age* is an extraordinarily insightful analysis but also a very Western story that pays little heed to the realities of the Global South and East despite their connections to the places at the center of his analysis via empire. Girard's eye-opening *Violence and the Sacred* only really makes sense within the intellectual framework of structural anthropology, opening Western intellectual eyes to the rituals of various "primitive societies." Biggar's stout *In Defence of War* is unintelligible without high-minded assumptions about liberal democracies; again, it draws on examples that are exclusively Western. The questions asked in this book would look different from a part of Christian-majority Africa where the Pentecostal church is growing and influential, or from Eastern Orthodox states where "symphony" between the

19. Searle, *Theology After Christendom*, 42.
20. Pocock, *The Machiavellian Moment*.

authorities has morphed into Christian civilizationism. A thinking priest of the Russian Orthodox church re-reconsidering "Russian World" theology and its impact on European security or a pastor and doctoral student from the new minority evangelical church in post-Soviet Kyrgyzstan wrestling with US-inspired theologies of "global Christianity," may wonder how a book such as this is relevant to them at all. For this book to come close to succeeding, it should help such persons navigate the extant Christendom imaginaries emerging from or being exported to their regions and identify their theologically errant and political inept character.

These questions of place and time complicate the attempt to bridge theology and IR. One response, common in the elite universities in which I have spent most of my career, is to write only in the immanent frame and jettison any questions of the transcendental. Despite Taylor's stature and influence, there are probably many more adherents to Talal Asad's rival and contingent account of the secular[21] and a greater number of contributors to the US Social Science Research Council's *Immanent Frame*, which despite being named after a chapter from Taylor's book do not accede to his wider Christological perspective. Girard is widely dismissed by anthropologists who abandoned structuralism decades ago and have little time for his epistemological imperialism and the transhistorical claim he makes for the Christ event. Biggar is sometimes vilified, for what is seen as his reactionary defense of an imperial Christian ethic of warfare: what, to my mind, is a defense of Christendom. In IR, Christian political theology is treated as an object of analysis rather than a subject partner in debates. It is difficult to tell stories about the world in International Relations outside of the "exclusive humanism" that Taylor narrates and critiques.

However, this book does draw explicitly on theologico-political analysis to sketch a new theoretical paradigm for the study of global politics and its premier concept of security. Theologians have established rich veins of scholarship in this area across various traditions, including recent work by figures as diverse as Pantelis Kalaitzidis,[22] William Cavanaugh,[23] James K. A. Smith,[24] and Daniel M. Bell Jr.[25] Although all touch on issues and secular accounts of global politics, none of this work explicitly addresses the subject matter as those trained in the field of IR would understand it. The best of this work does not restate orthodox debating positions in more

---

21. Asad, *Formations of the Secular*.
22. Kalaitzidis, *Orthodoxy and Political Theology*.
23. Cavanaugh, *Field Hospital*.
24. Smith, *Awaiting the King*.
25. Bell, *Divinations*.

resolute terms but recognizes that ecumenical boundary-breaking, rather than denominational camp-making, is necessary to reach a political theology of integrity. Some seek to reclaim Christendom while most are happy to see its demise. Contra the claims of theological "post-liberalism," to be a believer of any kind living in a secular world is not to express the certainties of a tradition where there are in fact few, nor to close conversations with those working exclusively in the secular realm.[26] My experience is that the immanent frame is both unavoidable and non-determining—and its sensible occupants are open to dialogue between faiths and secularities. To be a Christian academic, whether in theology or the social sciences, is to say: "The best sense I can make of my conflicting moral and spiritual experience is captured by a theological view of this kind."[27] That vocation is, with Taylor, "in my own experience, in prayer, in moments of fullness, in experiences of exile overcome, in what I seem to observe around me in other people's lives—lives of exceptional spiritual fullness, or lives of maximum self-enclosedness, lives of demonic, evil, etc.—this seems to be the picture which emerges."[28]

It is with these opening comments that we address the universal question of security: *How may we be included, protected, and provisioned to be human in a world of exclusions, violence, and scarcities?* And we keep Taylor's comments in mind as we restate this question in terms of the mission of the church: *How may we include, protect, and provision others to live faithful lives in a world that is both simultaneously fallen and redeemed?* A contemporary Christian approach to security must address both these questions simultaneously—both the question of the world and of the church. At the same time, it must recognize that the privileges previously accorded to churches to shape Western and Eurasian states—and via their empires to shape the world—are now being irretrievably eroded. This is no great loss. Although the dominion of Christendom has passed, its Christ was a diminished figure from the very outset. It is perhaps the enormity of the task of bringing Christ back to the center without excluding those that don't recognize his lordship that makes more sensible scholars demur. And yet this understandable modesty means we are left with the divide of (just) war versus (perfect) peace positions that have set the terms of the debate more-or-less constantly since the early church confronted the Roman Empire.

---

26. Milbank, *Theology and Social Theory*.
27. Taylor, *A Secular Age*.
28. Taylor, *A Secular Age*, 10.

(Post-)Christendom beyond the West

There is no way beyond this rather stale debate than by confronting the problem of security after Christendom. "The hold of the former Christendom on our imagination is intense, and in a sense, rightly so," argues the Charles Taylor in his definitive work *A Secular Age*.[29] In that sense it should not surprise us that there has been some pushback against the "after Christendom" agenda of John Howard Yoder, Douglas John Hall, and Stanley Hauerwas. Some in the Reformed tradition have even argued that "the fulfilment of the Great Commission therefore requires the establishment of a global Christendom."[30] The argument regarding the negative consequences of the Constantinian shift in history is far more nuanced than the recent polemic against Yoder's work by Peter Leithart[31]—an advocate of the "next Christendom" or "global Christendom"[32]—allows. Yoder's animus is neither against the sincerity of Constantine's faith nor that the shift may have reduced the violence of the empire. Rather he argues, according to one of his defenders, that the effect of Christendom is thus: "to deform the church's specific God-given identity by merging with worldly power structures and using top-down, coercive, worldly power to accomplish *what God has given his people to do without such power*."[33] Ultimately then, Yoder's claims about Constantine are not historical but *theological*.

Very different readings of early Christian history also emphasize the entwined political and theological processes of change. Allen Brent argues that the shift in the emphasis of the early church from an apocalyptic eschatology (of a coming final battle, in Mark and Revelation) to a realized eschatology (of a new kingdom of God formed in the church, in Luke-Acts) was crucial in this process.

> In place of the radical disjunction between the coming Kingdom of God and the pagan Roman Empire on its way to destruction arose, in a way generally characteristic of ultimately successful political movements, the view that the existing social

---

29. Taylor, *A Secular Age*, 734.
30. Federal Vision, "The Federal Vision on the 'Next' or 'Global' Christendom."
31. Leithart, *Defending Constantine*.
32. Leithart is an adherent to "The Federal Vision."
33. Nugent, "A Yoderian Rejoinder to Peter J. Leithart's *Defending Constantine*." The use of "his" and "he" here in this quote and throughout this book is not to take a stance on a gendered God but to indicate that this question is not of importance to this book and will therefore not be discussed. The use of "his" and "he" here in this quote and throughout this book is not to take a stance on a gendered God but to indicate that this question is not of importance to this book and will therefore not be discussed.

structures of the status quo could be transformed by the values of the movement that opposed it, rather than simply uproot and replace it.[34]

The playing out of this tension in political order has been seen in many different histories and geographies and has taken many different denominational and political forms. These range across Orthodox, Catholic, and Protestant creeds and conservative, liberal, and socialist ideologies. Regimes claiming Christian virtues have varied from anarchist communities, like the True Levellers in seventeenth-century England, to fascist dictatorships, such as that emerging in contemporary Russia during its war in Ukraine.

Therefore, to study Christendom and after is not to study one period of history followed by another. Christendom, as we will explore in part 1, is not a period of history but an imagined security community that has taken many different family resemblances across time and space. More precisely, it is:

A theologico-political imaginary of the partnership of church and government, with the church legitimizing government and government securing the church.

This definition comes with three qualifications.

First, it is a definition that seeks to capture the political ideas of Christendom as much as its theological rationale. It may be received skeptically by some theologians on those grounds. In particular, the notions of "partnership" (which includes everything from theocracy to informal relations), "legitimizing" (which also includes limited, constructive dissent and the production of ethics), and "securing" (which may either be sought or unwanted by the church) may be contested. Such challenges are reasonable as many of the churchmen of Christendom themselves would not deploy these terms. James K. A. Smith's sympathetic definition has different emphases to mine: "Christendom is a missional endeavor that labors in the hope that our political institutions can be bent, if ever so slightly, toward the coming Kingdom of love."[35] I do not object to that definition from Smith's Reformed persuasion nor do I think that it is inconsistent with my own.

A second qualification is that, although defined here in the singular, Christendom is necessarily *plural*. "Christendom" refers to a range of imagined relations between church and government that have taken different forms in different contexts in the past and, potentially, in the future. These extend from the *Imperium Christianum* of the Holy Roman Empire to the

---

34. Brent, *A Political History of Early Christianity*, 1.
35. Smith, *Awaiting the King*, 17.

established micro-Christendoms of constitutional monarchies and even formally secular republics like the United States. They may be found from the legitimizing ideas of Byzantine emperors to those of Christian statesmen in postcolonial Africa. In politico-theological terms the variety may include both Eastern Orthodox theocracies (and other forms of "centered Christendom") and Lutheran Two Kingdoms thought (and other forms of "decentered Christendom"). Such a definition may appear broad, but this breadth is necessary to account for the sheer variety of institutional and ecclesial forms that Christendom has taken. Christendom may also take non-state and non-territorial forms. Smith claims that the US civil rights movement is an example of the imagination of Christendom.[36]

Finally, the definition is explicitly not objectivist (Christendom as a fixed period of history) but subjectivist (Christendom as a narrative of history). Of course, social realities are always both objective and subjective; those things that are imagined take material and institutional forms. However, this shift to the subjectivist optic is important as it allows us to address the variety of forms, to discern how specific Christendoms rise and fall, and to trace how they are unimagined and reimagined. On the one hand, Christendom is unimagined where a given community possesses a Christian heritage but where contemporary public discourse generally accepts that the state operates according to principles of secularism and where the church is considered to be merely one societal voice among many. It is this change that has taken place across most of Western Europe over the last two or three generations; we are only just beginning to consider its consequences. On the other hand, Christendom may be reimagined in Europe where we see widespread support for Christian nationalism—even in places with low levels of church attendance. We have seen a wide variety of imaginaries of neo-Christendom too in Europe, from France's cultural Christendom of the National Rally to the undeniably theological and authoritarian "Russian World." To say that Europe is secular is a placeholder that conceals many forms of the unimagining and reimagining of Christendom.

Thus, the claim of any study "after Christendom" is not that all imaginaries and imagined communities of Christendom have died away. Political theologians in the Reformed tradition, such as Leithart and Smith, speak credibly about "redeeming" Christendom.[37] However, the contrary argument I shall make is rather that Christendom ideas and institutional forms have been in terminal decline over the modern era and that the secular age that emerged over the late-modern period is properly understood as an

---

36. Smith, *Awaiting the King*, 17.
37. Smith, *Awaiting the King*; Leithart, *Defending Constantine*.

advancement from rather than a negation of Christendom. In much work on this topic, this is an exclusively Western claim that is then, by sleight of hand, writ large for the world. This book seeks to shift away from such an account by interrogating and provincializing the Western experience, relativizing the normative claims of the Western advocates for both Christendom and post-Christendom, and drawing on examples and theological arguments from the Eurasian Christian world and more selectively the Global South. This is particularly important because, as Jehu Hanciles argues, "it is precisely those religious movements that refuse to adapt to secularism that are growing the fastest."[38] In moving "beyond Christendom," he notes, we must recognize the history-making power of migration and the immigrant church that had previously been overlooked in the focus on the missions of empires and states.[39]

I concur with Hanciles that our task is to imagine a world *beyond* Christendom rather than re-imagine Christendom as redeemed. I also agree that this requires more attention to Africa, Asia, and other former colonial regions. However, an element of humility is required here. While I spent a year working with the Anglican church in West Africa on refugee camps for Sierra Leone, a West African scholar such as Hanciles is far better positioned to consider security after Christendom in that region. In terms of the attempt to globalize political theology and IR this is little more than a modest step along a path trod by others, particularly those of the global East and South, including those operating without the privileges of the Western academy. It will take the *oikumene* and the worldwide and transnational *ecclesia* to build the study of global post-Christendom. This book suggests some possible ways forward by engaging more directly with the Eastern Orthodox experience and the Russian and Eurasian world, where I have greater expertise. It touches on examples from Africa too. However, rather than claim a global stance based on superficial examples from these regions I have tried to use them to shed light upon and, in some cases, provincialize the Western experience. It is not for this author to write a Eurasian or African account.

These caveats are necessary before we further clarify our scope. In studying "after Christendom," this book connotes three other afters that accompany the "after" of Christendom. Their correlation with the end of Christendom is so strong that they must be considered as intertwined processes with the emergence of the secular age. First, the study is necessarily *post-imperial*. In the latter half of the twentieth century, as Christendom

---

38. Hanciles, "Beyond Christendom," 93.
39. Hanciles, "Beyond Christendom," 109.

breathed its last gasps at the global level, the number of UN member states more than tripled, growing from fewer than sixty in the 1940s to greater than 180 in the 1990s.[40] This growth was largely due to the process of *de jure* decolonization from European states that once identified with Christendom, including both the former colonies of Western European states and those that emerged from the break-up of Eurasian empires (including the Ottoman and the Russian-Soviet empires). However, as we shall see below, empire still looms large in relations between the West, South, and East in the form of offshore tax havens, military bases, aid flows, and relationships of economic dependency, which characterize security after Christendom. As Milbank and Pabst rightly argue, "the international society of sovereign states was only ever a partial reality, heavily qualified by the injuring presence of imperial great powers and sociocultural ties across borders."[41]

Second, the study of post-Christendom necessarily grapples with the emergent *post-national* shift. It is no coincidence that those who defend Christendom also seek to minister to and nurture the nation-state.[42] National identities remain powerful, as demonstrated by the national independence movements of former colonies—and nation-states are still considered the primary actors in security relations. However, the point here is one of political economy. A less accessible term to denote this shift is post-Keynesian.[43] The British economist John Maynard Keynes is considered the main architect of the Bretton Woods agreement, which sought to re-establish national trading economies after World War II. Keynes and his contemporaries realized that for national economies to guarantee security of employment and the trading relations that might make war less likely, global finance must be restricted with capital controls in place and exchange rates fixed to the dollar. For a couple of decades these arrangements produced sustained growth across much of the developed world. However, by the early 1960s bankers were beginning to find workarounds for corporations and wealthy individuals who wanted their capital to be globally mobile and accessible. The markets for Eurobonds and Eurodollars and the creation of tax havens eventually made the system of exchange controls based on the US dollar untenable.[44] By 1971, facing rising inflation, President Nixon abandoned the system of capital controls, effectively destroyed Keynes's system, and

40. United Nations, "Growth in United Nations Membership."
41. Milbank and Pabst, *The Politics of Virtue*, 327.
42. Biggar, *Between Kin and Cosmopolis*.
43. This approach is associated with Austrian and Chicago School economists, including Friedrich Hayek and Milton Friedman. See King, *A History of Post Keynesian Economics since 1936*.
44. For an accessible history of this period, see Oliver Bullough, *Moneyland*.

accelerated the process of financial deregulation that characterizes our rules-free global market economy of today.[45] Most contemporary economists would argue that national economies are now so financially interdependent that they have ceased to be distinguishable from one another without the use of statistical tricks. Today, market-driven calculations about consequence and efficiency are far removed from those one would imagine according to the Judeo-Christian moral economy that was idealized under Christendom.

Third, and finally, to study post-Christendom is to study the *post-Western*. As the first half of part 1 of this book will show, Christendom was instantiated as much in the East as the West from its Roman and Byzantine beginnings. "For the entire period from 200 to 1000 [CE]," Brown argues, "Christianity remained predominantly a religion of Asia and of northern Africa."[46] However, in modern times, and especially in the English-speaking world, it has come to be associated with Catholic and Protestant forms of Western Christendom. In IR, the intellectual move beyond this obsession with the West to a properly global perspective is denoted as the post-Western. In the practical world of global politics, the center of economic power shifts from Western states to the East, to the growing Asian economies and especially to the rising global powers of China. But both in theory and practice, *post*-Western does not mean *non*-Western. What is required to understand the post-Western and post-Christendom world is the same as what is required to study the post-imperial and post-national worlds: a global perspective. Such a perspective is not merely concerned with global centers but with global flows—those patterns of trade, diplomacy, and cultural exchange that connect East to West and South to North. In terms of finance, Dubai, Hong Kong, and Singapore are becoming as important entrepôts as London, New York, and Paris. None of these are non-Western as Western empires, professionals, currencies, and jurisprudence are commonplace across them all.

The horizon is vast both in time and space. Any empirical study of security after Christendom faces formidable obstacles of data selection and analysis. As a social scientist, I ordinarily gather data from either fieldwork, including ethnographic observation and interviews, or desk-base study of legal and financial records. Some first-hand observation and primary textual sources are deployed here. However, the bulk of our sources are secondary, and the method is synthetic, exploring and analyzing the research of others across an array of fields, from antiquity to late-modern history, from New

45. Gray, "Floating the System."
46. Brown, *The Rise of Western Christendom*, xvi.

Testament studies to political theology, and across the social sciences from IR theory to fieldwork-based area studies. As a lone author, I have tried to be sensitive to my positionality as a privileged white male European while being global in scope. As appropriate, I draw personal examples and case studies from the regions in which I have lived, worked, and conducted research on security affairs, especially those of the former Soviet states, North America, and my home region of Europe.

Security as a post-Christendom problem

While security is a (post-)Christendom problem it is by no means clear that it is a Christian idea. There is neither a biblical concept of security nor any established church doctrine. Security is apparently a secular category that has produced a vast array of studies from a variety of perspectives. It is one of the "essentially contested concepts" of social science,[47] but with "common conceptual distinctions underlying various conceptions of security."[48] Whether it is objective or subjective, broad (including economic, societal, and environmental threats) or narrow (merely about political and military affairs), and negative (security from) or positive (security to) are some of the most important of these. The definition we take is both broad and well-established in security studies. According to Arnold Wolfers, security is, objectively, "the absence of threats to acquired values" and, subjectively, "the absence of fear that such values will be attacked."[49] The foremost of those values is life itself, both of a person and of a community.

By including the question of fear, the definition connotes further questions of community, of the other, and of politics that are essential to the actual experience of security. As such, security, or "the absence of fear," has three elements: (1) *inclusion* (who is to be secure); (2) *protection* (from threats to security), and (3) *provision* (to live life securely). These are the core question of security: *for whom? from what?* and *for what?* All theories of security must address all three questions or fall short. Political realists argue that it is the state that is made secure, primarily from the military threat of other states and secondarily to grow its wealth in the global economy. Liberals by contrast say that individuals and states are made secure by international law and organizations from the proliferation of war and to trade with one another. Marxists would say critically that it is the owners of capital that are made secure by their control of the state, which protects them from

---

47. Gallie, "Essentially Contested Concepts."
48. Baldwin, "The Concept of Security," 5.
49. Wolfers, "National Security as an Ambiguous Symbol," 485.

rebellions by the poor and ensures that they continue to receive the lion's share of global wealth. All theories effectively address all three questions but reach quite different answers.

In defining security in this way, it may seem as though we are allowing our subject matter to be defined by an anti-theological secular order, the charge made by Milbank against the social sciences.[50] Such dismissals are intellectually satisfying but appear to lack any conception of the inbreaking of "common grace"[51] into human reason and institutions—and thereby lose opportunities to draw on social science to develop practical Christian wisdom and political theology.[52] By contrast, Alan Kreider, drawing from the work on human needs of the psychologist Abraham Maslow, emphasizes that in the Hebrew scriptures, holiness was founded not on personal spirituality but on our collective reliance on God for provision and protection.[53] The tripartite definition offered above—of inclusion, protection, and provision—is consistent both with social science *and* Christian theology, in that it places the social order "within the context of Trinitarian action in creation, preservation, and redemption . . . in which God is at work in the world."[54] The parallel here between the three orders—creation, preservation [also known as providence], and redemption—and our three questions of security is worth noting. God the Father has created a world in which all are included, but insecurity is created by exclusions, be they national, racial, gender-based, etc. The work of the Spirit preserves and protects the world, but violent agents and structures constitute threats to security. Jesus Christ has redeemed the world and we are able to live securely in the knowledge that all is ultimately provided, although markets, concentrations of wealth, and patterns of over-consumption create scarcity. From this perspective, the capacity of the state to provide security to anyone other than itself is limited because it neither creates an inclusive community nor redeems those that are lost; it has a security role that is barely protective and merely provisional.

From a theological perspective, security is a global problem because of the fall of the created order, which has affected all the world. Consequently, security is also a (post-)Christendom problem in the sense that its study and practice have been deeply affected by how we have imagined our distance or closeness to God, and our relationship to the state, historically and

50. Milbank, *Theology and Social Theory*.

51. For a discussion of "common grace" and its relationship to "providence," see Smith, *Awaiting the King*, 122–24.

52. For example, Sykes, *Power and Christian Theology*; Ward, *The Politics of Discipleship*; Bell, *Divinations*.

53. Kreider, *Journey towards Holiness*, 45.

54. Wright, *Free Church, Free State*, 235.

politically. For realists in the study of IR, insecurity arises out of the enduring absence of world government. For liberals, in slightly different terms, it arises out of the temporal absence of laws, norms, and institutions. Either absence is concomitant with what IR theory calls the structure of anarchy where all states are like persons in the state of nature of political theory. Like the hunters in Rousseau's famous stag hunt, or the "war of all against all" in Hobbes' states of nature, they must each look after themselves and may therefore decide a rabbit for one will do rather than the stag that would provide a greater meal for everyone. Game theory models this as the prisoner's dilemma, where a lack of trust between multiple prisoners means they are each likely to confess and betray each other. This is because if they stay silent while one of the others confesses, they will go to prison for far longer. However, the net effect is that all prisoners receive a longer sentence. On matters of security, we assume similarly that avoiding the worst outcome typically triumphs over targeting the best and mutually advantageous outcome. This is the so-called "tragedy of the commons." Tragedies of the commons are most acute because the worse outcome is most likely death. Avoiding this at all costs means accepting suboptimal outcomes of extreme danger, such as arms racing or the condition of Mutual Assured Destruction (appropriately called MAD) rather than nuclear disarmament. Theorists of security call this the security dilemma, most famously illustrated in the Cuban missile crisis. In the dilemma, security is a public good, yet actors are unequal and unpredictable in their interpretations of and their responses to one another.[55] The dilemma is at least two-dimensional, raising two questions: (1) Are the actions of the other party a threat to me? and (2) How do I respond to defend myself but not antagonize the other?[56] Thus the dilemma leads to a further problem—the security paradox: "the vicious circle of security and power accumulation."[57]

It is here where the Christian problem with security becomes acute. Realists argued that without a common global government to mediate these interests and integrate them in a common position, the security dilemma is immutable. Rationalists and liberals contended that this was too bleak. As political scientist Robert Jervis showed, the security dilemma can be overcome in certain conditions where communication channels are established, and signaling is clear.[58] Others, including Anatol Rappoport, demonstrated that the outcome of the game-theoretic prisoners dilemma is more likely to

---

55. Herz, "Idealist Internationalism and the Security Dilemma."
56. Wheeler and Booth, *The Security Dilemma*.
57. Herz, "Idealist Internationalism and the Security Dilemma," 157.
58. Jervis, "Cooperation under the Security Dilemma."

be cooperative after it has been repeated many times.[59] Hedley Bull offered the hope that an international or anarchical society could emerge based on a secular positivist of norms, rules, and institutions that could be proven to limit conflict.[60] The constructivist Alexander Wendt similarly argued that global politics was more fungible than implied by the realists and "anarchy is what states make of it."[61] These notes of hope from within the cannon of IR were grounded in a "post-metaphysical turn" that precipitated "the decline of grand theory and the rise of secular positivism."[62] All concurred that God is dead and that theology had no role in theory. There was no providence here—much less an eschatology—but a theory-led discipline of IR where our understanding of global politics is determined by theoretical innovation and proliferation.[63] In the meantime, crises in the real world are repeated, and some learning does occur, but history itself is cyclical or indeterminate, and, in the nuclear age, the prospect of an apocalyptic war remains ever present.

What is ironic about this secular and positivist outcome is that it emerges out of Christendom rather than a blinding enlightenment moment or paradigm shift. Most of the terms of secular realism had already been formed by a specifically Christian realism represented by believers such as Reinhold Niebuhr, Herbert Butterfield, and Martin Wight that had set the dominant terms of our understanding of international security in the mid-twentieth century. Christian realists assumed that political authority was bestowed by a God who was the sovereign and provider of balances of powers and just wars in history. In the second half of part 1 of this book, we will explore this tradition alongside modern just war theory and how they both emerged from late-Christendom and declined in the secular age. I argue that these traditions did not merely decline because of disenchantment, desacralization, and the triumph of secular positivism over Christian virtue but also because they did not offer *political* visions of inclusion, provision, and protection that are normatively convincing and descriptively comprehensive. They cannot account for centrifugal and re-enchanting forces that shape contemporary global security in the form of the chaos of globalization and new religious movements in a secular age and therefore cannot theorize IR effectively or assess war ethically. The decline of Christendom has left us

59. Rapoport, Chammah, and Orwant, *Prisoner's Dilemma*.
60. Bull, *Anarchical Society*.
61. Wendt, "Anarchy Is What States Make of It."
62. Milbank and Pabst, *Politics of Virtue*, 358; see also Pabst, "The Secularism of Post-Secularity."
63. Dunne, Hansen, and Wight, "The End of International Relations Theory?"

not just with new threats but with the lack of a conceptual architecture to make sense of what is happening. Christian realism's vision was dependent on the existence of Christendom and its limited "hope" that some wars can be avoided relied on a culture of cooperation across border under a higher throne. With Christendom decaying, those attempting to revive Christian realism rely on a desperate plea to Europe "to recover its own interior identity and to engage externally in a commonwealth-creating global project," claiming "only the impossible may be remotely realistic."[64] Such oxymoronic rhetoric simply returns us to a Western perspective on global politics and denies the full extent of the challenge of engagement in a secular age.

Theology and International Relations in dialogue

To advance beyond this Eurocentric perspective and reactionary distancing from the secular we must reconsider the relationship between modern forms of religion and politics after Christendom. In the last few decades of the twentieth century, most social scientists assumed that religion in general, and the Christian faith in particular, was gradually vanishing under the forces of secular modernization. More recently, it began to be understood that Christianity is being transformed spiritually—from the traditional to the charismatic—and geographically—from the global North and West to the South and East. Thus, in the traditional regions of Christendom, religion is, after a few decades of disregard, once again both a factor to be considered and a problem to be solved. Sandal and James, for example, draw direct comparison between religion and "variables such as gender, race and ethnicity,"[65] implying that analyses might restore believers as objects much as they have come to include women and minorities.

There is a clear political purpose here in the attempt to restore religion to our gaze in modernist terms. The basic assumption of the "restorative narrative," Hurd argues in a more recent paper, is that "once religious moderates are understood, engaged and empowered, and religious fundamentalists identified, sidelined or reformed, the problems posed by religion will lessen and religious freedom will spread across the globe."[66] More recently, IR scholarship has begun to question this moderates-versus-extremists framing and developed a critical perspective on the secularist positing of the religious fundamentalist as the threat and religious freedom as the

---

64. Milbank and Pabst, *Politics of Virtue*, 374.
65. Sandal and James, "Religion and International Relations Theory," 10.
66. Hurd, "International Politics after Secularism," 944.

solution.⁶⁷ Gutkowski, for example, has shown how secularist assumptions have distorted British policy-makers' attempts to understand political Islam, both at home and in its counter-insurgency operations in Iraq.⁶⁸ For contemporary Western states like Britain, the apparent challenge to their secularism is made all the more acute by the emergence of growing religious minority communities of what are considered non-Western religions, particularly Islam, within their territories.

However, the point that Hurd's criticism makes is that we must study religion as integral to power rather than merely as an object or creature of power. In contexts where the church is or has been influential, Christianity is likely to continue to be a major source of ideas and activities in the security domain. She argues:

> Religion is not outside of power. It is often wielded most powerfully in complex formations by those in power, including states, market forces, and other global institutions. Rather than ask, "what is religion and how can it be brought in to help solve global problems?" the question becomes, what is accomplished in and through discourses of religion? What forms of authority are mobilized through particular discourses of religious toleration or religious freedom? What are their effects on the organization of social and political life in different contexts?⁶⁹

This incorporation of the religious into secular political authority extends to secular political discourse itself. Christendom ethics and institutions for governing authorities remain influential long after the majority of their citizens have ceased believing in Christ. The "immanent frame" is established but the filters of Christendom continue to shape what we see and don't see in Christian secular societies.⁷⁰

This immanent frame sits alongside "deprivatization," "desecularization," and the "postsecular."⁷¹ After decades of the neglect of religion in political science, in the 2000s much research took place in terms of the questions of Security Studies—particularly the role of fundamentalist religion in

---

67. Mavelli, "Security and Secularization in International Relations"; Gutkowski, "Misreading Islam in Iraq"; Bettiza, "How Do Religious Norms Diffuse?"

68. Gutkowski, "Misreading Islam in Iraq."

69. Hurd, "International Politics after Secularism," 953–54.

70. The Immanent Frame is the title of a project and blog supported by the US Social Science Research Council, inspired by the work of Charles Taylor. *Social Science Research Council*, "The Immanent Frame."

71. Casanova, *Public Religions in the Modern World*; Berger, "The Desecularization of the World"; Habermas, "Notes on a Post-Secular Society."

war, terrorism, and far-Right politics,[72] which was met by critical studies highlighting the myopia of the Western secular political gaze on Islam.[73] Fewer authors in IR have made this argument with respect to Christianity.[74] A smaller group of scholars in this "religious turn" has demonstrated the role of political theology, including the theological apocalyptic, in the intellectual history of IR[75] and as a constituent of modern political thinking.[76] A new and more systematic engagement with political theology has emerged in IR.[77] Among those few theologians they have engaged, William Cavanaugh notes that our very modern definition of religion emerges from how Westphalia and other European post-Reformation treaties are remembered as instantiating a clear distinction between religious and secular authority.[78] This distinction legitimized the rationalist denial of theology as a legitimate source of IR theory—a denial that would have been vehemently opposed by IR's founders. Kubálková's call[79] for the creation of international political theology has gone largely unheeded, perhaps rightly dismissed as seeking "to supplement mainstream approaches, not challenge their basic assumptions as derivative of the kind of secularity [Charles] Taylor describes, the modern social imaginary."[80] The few published attempts to derive concepts of IR from religious or non-secular sources have not come from the mainstreams of the two major monotheistic faiths of Christianity and Islam, but largely from other religions, especially Buddhism.[81]

72. Huntingdon, *The Clash of Civilizations*; Juergensmeyer, "Religion as a Cause of Terrorism."

73. Bilgin, "The Securityness of Secularism? The Case of Turkey"; Gutkowski, "Misreading Islam"; Hurd, *The Politics of Secularism in International Relations*; Mavelli, "Security and Secularization"; Petito and Hatzopoulos. *Religion in International Relations*; Thomas, *The Global Resurgence of Religion*.

74. Cf. Thomas, *The Global Resurgence of Religion*; Seiple and Hoover, *Religion and Security*.

75. Nicolas Guilhot, *The Invention of International Relations Theory*; Jones, "Christian Realism"; McQueen, *Political Realism in Apocalyptic Times*; Bain, *Political Theology of International Order*.

76. Fletcher, "The Political Theology of the Empire to Come"; Rengger, "The Exorcist?"; John Gray, "Apocalyptic Religion"; Paipais, "Necessary Fiction."

77. Kubálková, "Toward an International Political Theology"; Joustra, "The Religious Problem with Religious Freedom"; Troy, *Christian Approaches to International Affairs*; Gentry, "Feminist Christian Realism"; Paipais, "Introduction: Political Theologies of the International"; Bain, *Political Theology of International Order*.

78. Cavanaugh, *The Myth of Religious Violence*.

79. Kubálková, "Toward an International Political Theology."

80. Joustra, *The Religious Problem*, 136.

81. Acharya, "Global International Relations and Regional Worlds"; Behera, "Reimagining IR in India"; Ling, "Worlds beyond Westphalia"; Pasha, "Fractured Worlds";

There is thus a need for IR to re-engage Christian theology, and theology to re-engage IR. It is the primary purpose of this book to speak to theologians from an IR perspective about how this might be done. One way this is not done is by a division of labor where the ethics are advanced by theology while the analytics are provided by IR. As Yoder remarks,

> The fundamental problem is not how to express the Christian's analysis of political events, since the judgment of Christians who are well informed will often differ little in substance from the intelligent judgment of other social critics, but rather how to understand within a Christian framework by what right such a judgment may be formulated by Christians and addressed to social leaders.[82]

From the evangelical and rationalist perspective of this author, the issue is this: from a Christian theological perspective, how are we to understand by what right such judgment is necessarily conceived as *both* the revealed word of God *and* the careful accumulation of evidence and reason. To "retheologize" IR is no easy task that can be accomplished by appeals to renew the Western Christian empire.[83] It requires the germination of a universal and "secularizable" argument from a seed of political theology. But it must not stop there. A new Christian realism must also engage the church, calling it to develop a theological politics that is distinct from the safe ground of Christian secularism and the temptation of neo-Christendom. The challenges of this environment will be explored in part 2 of the book, which surveys the post-Christendom security landscape.

Contextualizing Christian internationalism

This work of dialogue with the social sciences allows us to sketch a political theology of an apocalyptic realism, a realism for the period after Christendom. An exercise such as this is necessarily theologically ecumenical, just as it must necessarily be open to IR. But in engaging political theology, I have been struck by the limits on ecumenism and the tendency of most scholars to stay within their silos. Why is Yoder dismissed as "voluntaristic" by O'Donovan even though they are "allies" who both value scripture while

---

Qin, "Why Is There No Chinese International Relations Theory?"; Shahi, "Introducing Sufism to International Relations Theory"; Shani, "Towards a Post-Western IR."

82. Yoder, *Christian Witness to the State*, 35.
83. Milbank and Pabst, *Politics of Virtue*, 374.

differing moderately in interpretation?[84] What problems arise from the generalized use of "Constantinianism" by Anabaptists?[85] Why, until recently, has Eastern Orthodox theology been largely ignored by all but a few intellectuals in the Roman Catholic and Protestant traditions?[86] These are the naïve questions of an outsider, but from an intellectual purist's perspective they beg answers. This book draws biblically from the powers debate in the New Testament and theologically *inter alia* from the Catholic René Girard, the Mennonite John Howard Yoder, the Episcopalian Michael Northcott, the Anglican Tim Gorringe, and the Orthodox Sergius Bulgakov to build a framework of new Christian realism. This pluralist and ecumenical approach identifies the explicit intertextualities between these sources. However, as a specialist in IR and the study of security, there is a certain naivete to the way I have done this, and I fully expect criticism of the third part of book for the not-fully-realized ambition of trying to combine these disparate sources into a coherent framework.

My own evangelical-biblical approach is that of the free church and is deeply sympathetic to the Anabaptist tradition.[87] I am a Baptist elder and an advisor or participant in a variety of evangelical and ecumenical projects of the church. Despite having attended a Mennonite church for a year while serving as a faculty fellow at Yoder's former academic home, the University of Notre Dame, and being part of the Anabaptist-Mennonite network in the UK, I am not of that tradition. Thus, this book does not emerge from Anabaptism nor sit easily within it. For example, I accept that "nonviolence" often has a coercive aspect and I accept the need for policing uses of force, which can be controversial in Anabaptist circles. At the same time, as Richard Bauckham argues, insofar as it is genuinely Christian, "internationalism will seek more than that balance of power which the self-interest of the powers requires."[88] What is lacking from the long-standing and long-stagnated debate of realism vs. liberalism is a failure to stand back critically and question the political and theological premises regarding security and politics on which this debate takes place. Has Christendom—and its notion of the church ministering to government—helped reveal these injustices, or is it the post-Christendom shift that has laid them bare? The argument of this book begins with the relatively uncontroversial claim that straightforward

---

84. O'Donovan, *The Desire of the Nations*, 223–24; Stanley Hauerwas and James Fodor, "Remaining Babylon: Oliver O'Donovan's Defense of Christendom," 31.

85. Haymes and Gingerich Hiebert, *God after Christendom?*, 2–5.

86. For an exception, see Williams, *Sergii Bulgakov*.

87. For an outline of such a position, see Wright, *Free Church*.

88. Bauckham, "In Place of a Conclusion," 215.

pro and contra Christendom premises are no longer tenable, if they ever were. The axiom that the most meaningful distinction between political actors is that of being inside/outside of Christianized empires or nation-states is increasingly absurd in a globalized world. The tragic Niebuhrian claim that moral *man* has no option other than to take sides in the wars of immoral society, or confine *him*self to irrelevance, is undermined by the fact that these wars are increasingly within states and over the regime, disproportionately at the cost of the lives of civilians, women and children included. And yet the liberal-pacifist position, that if enough people join the movement we can imagine ourselves out of the tragedy, fails to confront the reality that personal and structural sin is not confined just to a few but is a constant in a fallen world.

A critical Christian standpoint is, in Bauckham's words, "an exercise in the *contextualization* of Christian theology and Christian faith."[89] It is built on social scientific and historical evidence, but its argument is driven by theological reasoning. It combines secular political science and evangelical theology in a way that seeks to avoid the pitfalls of methodological atheism on the one hand and naïve foundationalism on the other.[90] Its message is *Christian* and ecclesiological, in that it outlines some of the pathways toward the ultimate destiny of humanity to be united with Christ in his kingdom as his church. In that sense, and in the sense that it recognizes this to be a traumatic process as indicated in the book of Revelation, it is an eschatological study in an *apocalyptic* time. It accepts the good/evil duel of the apocalypse as a necessary constituent of Christian political thought, but it does not seek the hour, the day, or any of the other detail of the end times. Finally, its account is also *realist*, in the sociological sense that it deals with the world at the granular level of *actual practice* rather than the traditional IR sense of assuming the primacy of the state and war in matters of security. It contrasts this practical approach to popular, intellectual, and official discourses that are either overly normative or based on such a high level of abstraction as to render them simulations rather than representations of reality.[91] It treats all these discourses as imaginaries and recognizes that some of these are highly influential on human action as forms of symbolic power, despite being patently false in terms of their factual claims about the nature of the "nation," the "state," or "security."

This approach can be defined as that of *new Christian realism* or *apocalyptic realism*. It argues that global politics is changing because of the

89. Bauckham, "In Place of a Conclusion," 213.
90. For example, Sykes, *Power and Christian Theology*.
91. Baudrillard, *Simulacra and Simulation*.

post-Christendom shift where the notion of a world of legitimate powers held to account by secular political ethics is manifestly untenable. This change in the place of religion in politics creates disorder but, counter-intuitively, is providential insofar as it allows new opportunities for inclusion, protection, and provision. It is concomitant with other important historical developments, both cultural and economic, with which the post-Christendom shift is entwined. Empire has bequeathed postcolonies connected to their former imperial centers via transnational kleptocratic ties. Nation-states, sovereignty, and democracy—all of which are key tenets of modern Christian realism and just war theory—are all feeling the forces of the accelerating globalization of people, cultures, values, goods, services, and most significantly finance capital. As nation-states are transformed and reassembled to further serve the power of capital, many Christian church leaders and a few theologians reassert Christendom arguments in increasingly desperate terms. Some idiosyncratically place their hope in "Cyrus" figures like Donald Trump—non-believer leaders who enact the will of God—as rescuers of their imagined Christian nations.[92] At the extremes, figures like Anders Breivik imagine themselves as "knights templar" of Christian crusaders against Islam. But it is not that warriors, emperors, and nations were once Christian, but no longer. It is that the fall of Christendom and the breaking through of the gospel message have revealed that the emperor is, and was always, wearing no clothes.

The argument here is that a better Christian realism is founded on sound interpretation of biblical texts, attends to their eschatological perspective, and is informed by a solid understanding of the historical and political contexts derived from the wider humanities and social sciences. My expertise is largely in the latter. I completed this book while on leave from my professorial responsibilities at the University of Exeter as a senior research fellow of the British Academy, where I spent most of my time on a project on the transnational economic and security relations between former Soviet regimes and the British financial and legal services industry. I have spent the last twenty years studying the globalized context of conflict, security, and development, largely in the Central Asian republics. One thing that I have found in that time is that there are few wars in which a Western banker or lawyer does not play a role in financing or defending the warring parties. Prior to my academic post, I worked as an aid worker with faith-based and secular organizations in West Africa and Central Asia, as a research analyst on the arms trade for both the UK's Ministry of Defence and the British NGO Saferworld, and as a consultant to various governments

---

92. Mitchell, "'I See Us in the Middle of Prophecy!'"

and international organizations, including the US, Germany, and the EU. Throughout this period, I have read much work by those from both the just war and pacifist traditions and been struck by how an analysis of security is lacking in both. Even Stassen's *Just Peacemaking* and its successors are concerned overwhelmingly with ethics and practices rather than politics and analysis.[93] The perhaps unrealistic hope of this book is that such traditions of thinking about war may be brought into a more productive conversation via a new Christian realism. Such realism accepts both the practically decentered nature of security and the Christ-centered nature of theology. It accepts the messy entanglement of the church in a violent world where relative judgments must be made about what constitutes nonviolent force and how it may be used to reduce violence.

A GUIDE TO THE READER

There are three narratives that are iterated across *Security after Christendom*. Each is present throughout, but each reaches its height at different points in the book. The first narrative is that of the relationship between Christendom and security. Part 1 deals with the history and modern artefacts of the Christendom idea. It establishes Christendom not as a fixed period but as an imagined security community that ebbs and flows over time largely due to theological and political dynamics within and beyond Christendom. The dialectics it presents between cross and sword, between sacralized centers and devout peripheries, did not originate in Christendom but were first institutionalized and imagined there in what the North African bishop St. Augustine denoted as "two cities." This narrative's nadir is reached across chapters 4 and 5 when we illustrate how just war theory simply cannot be sustained as the once-merged sword and cross return to their rightful state of divergence.

A second narrative of the book is that new dynamics have emerged in the wake of this divergence and of the secular age that has emerged after Christendom. Part 2 is focused on an investigation of the nature of security relations in the secular age. It shows that late-Christendom and related secular imaginaries have recurrently generated security communities where the state is the model security provider in a post-Christian secular mode. But this order is not stable. Rather than a decisive and irreversible shift to a secular and more secure age, we see ongoing tensions between the disenchanting and re-enchanting of politics, and between decentering and

---

93. Stassen, *Just Peacemaking*. See also Stassen, "Just Peacemaking as the New Paradigm," 137.

recentering on the state. The two vectors of the sword/cross dialectic—centered/decentered and disenchantment/re-enchantment—are shown to have intensified due to the concomitant and related forces of capitalism, individualism, and globalization in a secular age. The field of IR having largely disregarded theology for at least fifty years, has been neglectful of this historical process and is therefore blind to the significance of these changes for global politics and its disorders. This narrative peaks across chapters 6 and 7 as we debunk secular realist and liberal approaches to security—tragic and progressive respectively—which share the premise that the end of Christendom is, at most, a background condition rather than a destabilizing force.

The third narrative of the book is that a new Christian realism may be constructed that makes better sense of these tensions. *Part 3* picks up from the critique of Christendom and secular imaginaries and the tensions within and between them. Rather than considering these traumas as the mere context of inquiry, it brings theology back in to outline a post-Christendom account on the inescapable tension between the "two cities" and an original perspective on security in the secular age. Security has lacked theologico-political[94] analysis for more than half a century due not simply to the secularization of the social sciences but also to the withdrawal of theologians from questions of security. The interpretative key for this new account emerges with the Christo-centrism of Sergius Bulgakov and René Girard over chapters 9 and 10 of the book. While the Christendom dialectic produced the coming together of cross and sword, their decoupling exposes once again the Christian dialectic between love and law. This engine of history—which Augustine captured in the notion of heavenly and earthly cities—is found in the tension between Christ's nonviolent and eschatological witness of redemption on the cross and the violent and temporal demand of law and sword to solve security problems now. In Christ there is *both* theological *and* political hope. He *both* points to the ultimate and redemptive end of history *and* providentially inaugurates a truly global approach to security where law is precariously extended across national borders and the utility of the sword is blunted. This is witnessed to the world in terms of inclusion of and hospitality to migrants (chapter 10), unarmed civilian protection from violence and tyranny (11), and sharing in the face of scarcity and climate crisis (12).

---

94. I used this term to encompass theologically informed political analysis encompassing "political theology" (the speaking of theology to secular politics) and "theological politics" or "theopolitics" (the articulation of the church as *polis*) across both theology and social science. For a discussion of the shift to theological politics, see Bretherton, Luke, *Christianity and Contemporary Politics*, 16–18.

The book ends by summarizing its argument in light of the Russian war against Ukraine that began in 2022, a security crisis of neo-Christendom which brought insecurity to the world while the book was being completed. The conclusion points to the March 2022 Orthodox Declaration[95] in calling out the idolatry of the "Russian World" theology as an example of a post-Christendom security imaginary at work in the ecclesia. In the providence of history, the foundation and Lord are Christ, the secondary actor is his church, and the tertiary actors are the powers of the world, both providential and demonic. Political theologies of global politics such of those of twentieth-century Christian realism have failed where they have inverted this hierarchy and thereby not seen how the world has been turned upside down (Acts 17:6). In the Bulgakov's terms, a new Christian realism must reject human godhood [*chelovekobozhie*] and its false promise of order and instead be grounded in God-humanity [*bogochelovechestvo*] and the promise of the apocalypse. Hope, we conclude, is necessarily *both* a theological *and* a political virtue. This book is but one endeavor in the project of making that known.

---

95. Abatzidis et al., "A Declaration on the 'Russian World.'"

PART ONE

CHAPTER 1

Imagined Histories

Russians, Ukrainians, and Belarusians are all descendants of Ancient Rus, which was the largest state in Europe. Slavic and other tribes across the vast territory—from Ladoga, Novgorod, and Pskov to Kiev and Chernigov—were bound together by one language (which we now refer to as Old Russian), economic ties, the rule of the princes of the Rurik dynasty, and—after the baptism of Rus—the Orthodox faith. The spiritual choice made by St. Vladimir, who was both Prince of Novgorod and Grand Prince of Kiev, still largely determines our affinity today.

VLADIMIR PUTIN[1]

Not sedentary all: there are who roam, To scatter seeds of life on barbarous shores;
Or quit with zealous step their knee-worn floors, To seek the general mart of Christendom;
Whence they, like richly-laden merchants, come, To their beloved cells: or shall we say
That, like the Red-cross Knight, they urge their way, To lead in memorable triumph home.

WILLIAM WORDSWORTH[2]

---

1. Putin, *On the Historical Unity of Russians and Ukrainians.*
2. Wordsworth, *Ecclesiastical Sonnets.*

In July 2021, the president of the Russian Federation, Vladimir Vladimirovitch Putin, published an essay on history. It was by no means his first such essay but perhaps it was his most consequential. In November 2021, authors of the Carnegie Endowment argued that the essay, "amounted to no less than a historical, political, and security predicate for invading [Ukraine]—if and when that ever became necessary."³ A few months later, to the surprise of many, Russia invaded Ukraine and launched a horrifying war that was ongoing as this book went to press. Putin's essay was full of questionable facts and ideologically driven claims, but it was no work of fiction. Putin reached back to the ninth century to retell history. His was a narrative of Russia which was transnational and civilizational—a story of Russia as the guarantor of Christian faith and the Russian World (*russkii mir*) as the one true Christendom.

Putin's essay was not alone in adopting a Christendom worldview.⁴ Take just two examples. First, 81 percent of white American evangelicals voted for Donald Trump in 2016 in an apparent desire to see their Christian nation restored via command of the state and law: specifically, the appointment of conservative Supreme Court justices.⁵ President Trump also moved the US embassy to Jerusalem, against the advice of every serious expert in foreign affairs, largely to satisfy the Christian Zionism of many in his evangelical base. It may not be a stretch to say that Trump's act recalled, in a quite different context almost one thousand years before, the medieval papacy's declaration of a crusade to reclaim Jerusalem/Zion for the church. Second, and even more disturbingly, in his 800,000-word manifesto, the Norwegian terrorist Anders Breivik, who murdered seventy-seven people in 2011 in Oslo, mentions "Christian" (2,247 times), "Crusade" (263) and "Christendom" (119) throughout and describes himself as "Justiciar Knight Commander for Knights Templar Europe."⁶ Are Putin, Trump, and Breivik merely aberrations in a secular age? It is hard to answer affirmatively when two hundred years before them, the canonical English Romantic poet Williams Wordsworth imagined the mission of Christendom by invoking the language of barbarism, merchants, and knights.

As these examples show, all histories are not simply written but publicly and politically imagined. They are imagined in that a point of origin or objective truth is inaccessible to those who "see through a glass darkly"

3. Rumer and Weiss, "Ukraine: Putin's Unfinished Business."

4. Indeed, similar essays could easily have been written by the leaders of France, Germany, Spain, the United States, and several other states to justify their invasion of near or distant Christian peoples.

5. Stewart, "Eighty-One Percent of White Evangelicals."

6. Koch, "The New Crusaders," 1, 7.

(1 Cor 13:12). Multiple histories compete with other accounts of the same period. They must constantly be reimagined in order to survive as the lens through which an event or period is viewed. This is no less true of the history of what we call "Christendom," a family of different political forms over time in which the church has ministered to government and government has secured the church. Christendom animates debates in some quarters of political theology while in the study of politics it is widely neglected and relegated to being an artefact of history. But from almost all these perspectives, it is a singular and rather embarrassing period of the past—most often identified as the "Latin Christendom" of Europe's Middle Ages—during which the work of both church and state led to a great deal of violence in the name of Christ. As both a student of politics and theology, I sympathize with this normative perspective on Christendom and violence. However, I am extremely doubtful about the reading of history it offers and concur with Haymes and Gingerich-Hiebert's concerns about the efficacy of the Christendom versus post-Christendom divide as it currently stands.[7]

In this first chapter we elaborate our rough definition of Christendom from the introduction—that it is *a theologico-political imaginary of the partnership of church and government*. Conceived in such a way, Christendom is therefore the umbrella term for many and varied imagined communities that have been constructed in different ways over time rather than a single fixed period of history. It is the purpose of these first two chapters to explore some of this historical diversity before chapters 3–4 discuss its modern intellectual and geographical contexts. The oft-told international history of Latin Christendom is but *one* form of Christendom where church and government were imagined in union. Earlier forms involved the co-optation of the church of the East by various imperial formations, while later forms include the multiple "micro Christendoms" that emerged out of the magisterial Reformation. In short, our first failure regarding Christendom has been to see it as a historical singularity rather than *a plural phenomenon* which has ebbed, flowed, and taken many different contextual forms in Western Europe alone over at millennium and a half—and which continues to see many afterlives in our secular age.

One Christendom, two kingdoms

To consider how "Christendom" has been hitherto defined we must begin with historiography: that is, how history has been written according to a particular imagination of the relationship between church and state. To

---

7. Haymes and Gingerich Hiebert, *God after Christendom?*, 5.

most scholars of historical sociology, political science, and IR "Christendom" equates to Latin Christendom of the medieval period, formed in the crusades and codified by Pope Gregory, having its zenith in the eleventh to thirteenth centuries. Barry Buzan and George Lawson's recent and important book *The Global Transformation* denotes Christendom as a passing phase.

> The expansion of European international society required stark changes of identity, starting with "Christendom" in the emergence phase, then during the nineteenth century to "Western" in order to integrate the Americas and other European offshoots, and finally to the "standard of civilization" in the late-nineteenth century.[8]

Contra Buzan and Lawson, some significant voices have sought to emphasize the significance of religion over economic and non-religious forces. But despite this privileging of religion in their analysis, they continued to equate Christendom with *Latin Christendom*. This path is well-trodden. For example, Philips argues the Latin church was constitutive of international order in Christendom: a heterogeneous system of polities bound together by the centralized Roman church. By 1555 (The Peace of Augsberg), the order has broken down due to religious polarization, a process that would be completed by 1648 (Westphalia).[9] For Philpott, the Peace of Westphalia "elevated a form of polity whose authority was territorial and independent of ecclesiastical authority and sealed the decline of a united Christendom."[10]

In the study of theology, a similar trajectory is narrated both by those who attack and those who defend Christendom. Yoder's focus on "Constantinianism" equates it with the emergence, heights, and decline of Latin Christendom. By this reading, post-Christendom is a historical period brought on by the Reformation that is broadly equated with the secular age. In William Cavanaugh's account, for example, the sixteenth century is the fulcrum of history where the balance of power between church and state tips decisively to the latter and the Roman Catholic conceptions of "two swords" of the ecclesiastical and imperial authorities ended for good.

> Pre-sixteenth-century Christendom assumed, at least in theory, that the civil and ecclesiastical powers were different departments of the same body, with the ecclesiastical hierarchy of course at the head. The sixteenth century maintained

---

8. Buzan and Lawson, *The global Transformation*, 175.
9. Phillips, *War, Religion and Empire*.
10. Philpott, "Explaining the Political Ambivalence of Religion," 510.

the conception of a single body but inverted the relationship, setting the good prince to rule over the Church. The eventual elimination of the church from the public sphere was prepared by the dominance of the princes over the church in the sixteenth century.[11]

Those in the Reformed tradition may dispute the final sentence regarding the elimination of the church—and would take different positions on the theology and ethics of Christendom. Cavanaugh argues that Luther's doctrine of the two kingdoms relegates the church as an onlooker on questions of security and politics.[12] Defenders of Constantinianism, such as Leithart, argue that the critics dismiss the ministry of the church to the state in the ethics of politics and warfare, and therefore the possibility of public theology in this area.[13] However, what Catholic, Lutheran, and Reformed protagonists all agree on is the singular periodization and the distinction ("at least in theory") between the two kingdoms.

The grain of truth in this "Grand Narrative of European History"[14] means that it should not be dismissed in its entirety, and we will return to it in chapter 5. However, we must note from the outset of our study that the net effect is to make Christendom either present or absent from security affairs—indeed from the whole of history—rather than a social force that ebbs and flows and takes the different forms. This is true whether religion is taken seriously or not. On the one hand, both Philpott and Philips highlight the role of religious and theological change of the Reformation in the end of Christendom. Philips identifies the seeds of Christendom's demise from within the church. He emphasizes the shift from the medieval papal doctrine of two swords, where the church was supreme in both ecclesiastical and civil affairs but it "provisionally delegated" the latter to earthly rulers, to Luther's doctrine of two kingdoms, where the church was "as a purely spiritual community."[15] On the other hand, revisionist explanations focus on material and secular aspects.[16] For example, Benno Teschke argues that it was the economic and military organization of the crusades that "centralized, monarchized and militarized the Church" so that, already from the eleventh–twelfth century, "what used to be a center of faith turned into a

11. Cavanaugh, *Theopolitical Imagination*, 26.
12. Cavanaugh, *Theopolitical Imagination*, 24.
13. Leithart, *Defending Constantine*.
14. Brown, *Rise of Western Christendom*, 4.
15. Phillips, *War, Religion and Empire*, 88.
16. Teschke, "Theorizing the Westphalian System of States"; Osiander, "Sovereignty, International Relations, and the Westphalian Myth."

secularized church state (*kirchenstaat*) with a power-conscious foreign policy."[17] But both those who accept and those who dismiss religion as a factor, share a common perspective that Christendom was singular.

The Peace of Westphalia after Europe's Thirty Years War (1618–48) marks the end of Christendom to all these analysts. Although Philips accepts that post-1648 societies were somewhat more religiously observant than those of "Latin Christendom," these were subject to secular polities that placed political order over religious order. According to the logic of two kingdoms, government gradually began to dominate over the church. Europe shifted "from the heteronomous world of Latin Christendom to an Absolutist sovereign international order."[18] While Philips and Philpott emphasize the significance of theology as a causal factor, they work with an account of Christendom that is so narrow as to effectively relegate it to a historical artefact. The notion that the Reformation brought a radical and irreversible shift in the relations between church and state—while containing an element of truth—is in fact a reductive claim that occludes the variety of relations between what Augustine (354–430 CE) denoted as *civitas terrena* and *civitas dei* (earthly and heavenly cities). As we will unpack below, the dialectic between law and love, between earth and heaven, is present throughout history not merely as a metaphor but in the concrete practices of persons and institutions. Thus, these binaries—between cities, kingdoms, and swords—cannot simply be dismissed given the role they play in how we imagine state and church within the rubric of Christendom.

However, we must dwell for a few moments on what the one-two framing misses. Three points are made here. First, as is widely argued by Anabaptists, it is neglectful of the significance of the "Constantinian shift" for both church and empire. From the first to the third centuries the church lacked political power and eschewed violence, with most Christian leaders taking absolute pacifist positions against all participation of Christians in the Roman legion. "Between 100 and 313 no Christian writers," Driver claims, "approved of Christian participation in warfare. In fact, all those who wrote on the subject disapproved of the practice."[19] This apparently caused disquiet in Rome as the church grew exponentially in the second and third centuries. The Greek philosopher Celsus charged: "If all men were to do the same as you [Christians], there would be nothing to prevent [Caesar]

---

17. Teschke, "Theorizing the Westphalian System," 104.
18. Phillips, *War, Religion and Empire*, 82.
19. Driver, *How Christians Made Peace with War*, 14.

being left in utter solitude and desertion, and the forces of the empire would fall into the hands of the wildest and most unlawful barbarians."[20]

Many church historians would challenge this reading of a sudden Christendom shift. Brent suggests the process was more gradual and emerged within the church, as much as being imposed upon it by a Roman emperor's decree.[21] But this is not an either/or choice as developments in both kingdoms are intimately connected. The change was likely the combination of *both* iterations over at least two centuries *and* the sudden and political in the decisions of Constantine, as argued in more recent Mennonite work.[22] The net result was the same: the arrival of Christendom marked a dramatic transformation of Christian eschatology, away from the apocalypticism of Mark's Gospel and Revelation, and of political theology, from a church at the margins to a church of the center. But following the Edict of Milan's (313 CE) provision of (some) religious freedom, within little over a century Christendom was formed, with the emperor, according to the contemporary Eusebius, "directing, in imitation of God himself, the administration of the world's affairs."[23] Eastern and Western empires established Christianity as the official religion by 380 CE and all Roman soldiers were required to be Christian by 416 CE.

The Constantinian shift coincided with the fall of Rome. Perhaps Constantine and his successors were too late to reverse the damage done to martial Rome by the pacifying effect of Christian mission, as famously bemoaned by Edward Gibbon in his *Decline and Fall of the Roman Empire*. But for some scholars, theologians and historians, Christendom also brought the fall of the church, which never again saw the rate of growth it had experienced in the period prior to Constantine's edict. Leithart's defense of Constantine summarizes the charges against Christendom as "tyranny, anti-Semitism, hypocrisy, apostasy and heresy."[24] The conservative historian Tom Holland notes that "the Christ to whom Constantine and his successors compared themselves bore little resemblance to the Jesus who had died in excruciating blood-streaked agony on a rough-hewn cross."[25] When writers as different as Yoder, Wight, and Holland agree we must pay attention! Without the advent of Christendom, and the justificatory framework provided by the theology of Augustine, the Christian church's role of

20. Celsus, *True Discourse*.
21. Brent, *A Political History*.
22. Howard-Brook, *Empire Baptized*.
23. Holland, *Millennium*, 7.
24. Leithart, *Defending Constantine*, 9.
25. Holland, *Millennium*, 8.

international affairs would have remained, to Yoder's satisfaction (if not Wight or Holland's), marginal and dissenting.

Second, by defining Christendom as singularly Latin and medieval, IR scholars offer a Eurocentric view of international order across the Christianized world that denies the plurality of Christendom and the variety of its instantiations into international order. Christendom was already fractured and diverse well before Latin Christendom declined. Early Constantinian Christendom was divided between Eastern and Western empires from its outset. Eastern Christendom emerged and grew under Justinian's justification of a Christian Empire (sixth century); it subsequently fractured into differing Orthodox traditions that were bound up with the secular authorities in different parts of Eurasia. In the West, the Carolingian empire (ninth century) of the successors to the Frankish king Charlemagne, known at the time inter alia as *Imperium Christianum*, sought to recreate the Roman Empire, retaining its Christian identity.[26] Brown identifies various "New Christendoms" across Europe in the period 750–1000 CE in the east, in the west with Charlemagne, and in the north with the conversion of Scandinavia.[27] These Christendoms were fractured between kingdoms that were at war into the tenth century.

But this "pre-history" of Christendom is disregarded in the study of IR. In Philips, the Carolingian empire is mentioned in passing as background to the emergence of Latin Christendom, whose origins he finds exclusively in the crusades.[28] To Latham, focusing on the crusades, the church went "from junior partner in the Carolingian empire to an independent and divinely inspired agent of spiritual renewal within the Christian commonwealth," thereby creating Latin Christendom.[29] But while the Carolingian was a different type of Christendom, less consolidated and unified, it bore many of the hallmarks of other Christianized empires. It is not clear why these other, earlier Western and Eastern Christendoms should be discarded from our analysis of Christendom. They must not merely be seen as constituents of the pre-history of Latin Christendom. Closer attention to these periods from the perspective of the analysis of international order may improve our understanding of how such order is composed. For the sake of historical accuracy with respect the world before 1000 CE, it is necessary to provincialize

---

26. Folz, *The Concept of Empire in Western Europe*.
27. Brown, *Rise of Western Christendom*, 13–14.
28. Philips, *War, Religion and Empire*.
29. Latham, "Theorizing the Crusades," 229.

the Latin version. As Brown argues, "western Christendom was out on a limb. It was the Christianity of a peripheral zone."[30]

Third, the narrow definition of Christendom serves to over-emphasize the progressive decline of religion, politically with the Peace of Westphalia and intellectually and culturally with the Enlightenment. IR itself was a discipline founded by American and British thinkers in a counter-Enlightenment movement, as we will see in chapter 3. The leading figure of the "English School" of International Relations, Hedley Bull, in his discussion of "Christian international society" of the seventeenth to nineteenth centuries, postulated "a modern and secular equivalent of the kind of universal political organization that existed in Western Christendom in the Middle Ages."[31] Habsburg Spain, the Dutch Republic, the British Empire, and the United States have all institutionalized the church to varying degrees in their public policies and leaned on the clergy's moral justifications for their wars and imperial expansions. But none of these, to my knowledge, have been analyzed in terms of the category of Christendom.

Shades and afterlives of Christendom are also visible in more modern times. They continue today to suggest that Christendom as an imagined community lives on even if the secular West looks on it as a mere aberration. Colonial and postcolonial states in Latin America and Africa are some of those that have adopted integrative relations between church and state on the model imposed on them by empire. In the Eastern Orthodox world, the decline of established religion was both later and has been reversed in some contexts, as evident the Christian nationalism of the autocephalous churches and conservative movements as well as the civilizational claims of *Russkiy Mir*. Poland's Law and Justice (*Prawo i Sprawiedliwość*, PiS) and Hungary's Christian Democratic People's Party (*Kereszténydemokrata Néppárt*, KDNP) are among other movements that have framed their countries as Christian nations and deployed this moniker in their opposition to Western incursion into their sphere of interest. These fleeting examples serve to emphasize that the decline of *Imperium Christianum* did not mean the end of Christendom.

CHRISTENDOM AS IMAGINED COMMUNITY

This survival of Christendom beyond its Latin heights indicates its durability as an ideology of political community. In this sense, Christendom is analogous to any collective identity or institution, all of which need to be

---

30. Brown, *Rise of Western Christendom*, xvi.
31. Bull, *Anarchical Society*, 254.

invented and repeatedly imagined in order to exist. In his landmark study, the historian and political scientist Benedict Anderson argued that nations are invented by nationalists and nationalism; they are imagined communities in that, despite not knowing one another, "in the minds of each member [of a nation] lives the image of their communion."[32] Anderson, in his modernist conception, contrasts these nations to Christendom in their assertion of both national sovereignty (rather than God's sovereignty) and the limits of their borders. "The most messianic nationalists," he argues, "dream of a day when all members of the human race will join their nation in the way that it was possible, in certain epochs, for, say, Christians to dream of a wholly Christian planet."[33] This parallel between imagined Christendom and the imagined nation flows naturally from Anderson's Eurocentric rendering of "a stage of human history [the Reformation] when even the most devout adherents of any universal religion were inescapably confronted with the living pluralism of such religions." Therefore, the sovereign state arose as the institution to reflect the pluralization of Christendom where "nations dream of being free, and, if under God, directly so."[34]

Just as Christendom is a political community, it also takes a theological form particularly with respect to ideas of a people being elected as a "new Israel."[35] We might say that the relationship between its political and theological aspects is symbiotic. The fact of being imagined does not divorce Christendom from biblical origins, spiritual forces, and Christian eschatology. Nations—be they old or new Israel—are invented in the minds of their citizens, but this does not mean they are entirely voluntaristic or created "from scratch." Anderson and his fellow historians and sociologists, such as Anthony Smith and Ernest Gellner, debated their conditions of creation. Among these conditions were a common language, mass media, shared economy, and a sufficiently strong state to define and police borders. Just like nations—many of which are diasporic or lack their own territories and commanding political institutions—Christendom as a theological form is not entirely enclosed by its borders but can exist in subnational, national, international, transnational, or non-national forms across territories and states. Therefore, to speak of Christendom as "imagined" is not to deny its historical reality but to claim that it is made real in its imagining. As part

---

32. Anderson, *Imagined Communities*, 6.
33. Anderson, *Imagined Communities*, 7.
34. Anderson, *Imagined Communities*, 7.
35. Bader-Saye, *Church and Israel after Christendom*, 57–69.

of "the modern drama of peoplehood," Christendom, in terms deployed by Agamben and Givens, is "a biblical development."[36]

Givens' work is especially helpful in clarifying how a certain reading of scripture has emerged historically to justify an exclusivist Christian identity—a new Israel—against more radical and inclusivist readings of the church, especially of the Gospels.[37] Christendom has taken different regional forms whose borders are delimited by coming up against those of regions where a different Christian confession, other faith, or secular creed is ascendant. "The identity of Christendom was transnational," the historical sociologist Michael Mann argues, "based not on territory or locality as anyone could actually experience them but on something wider, something more abstract and transcendent."[38] In biblical thought, the citizenship of believers is in heaven (Phil 3:20). But this greater claim to transcendence by no means immunized the church from the politics of friends and enemies, of the borders of inclusion and exclusion. In that sense, the idea of Christendom provides the logic for many instances of what the IR scholar Emmanuel Adler calls "imagined (security) community"; that is, "cognitive regions" of International Relations. These communities "imagine sharing a common destiny and *identity*"; an identity against which they find enemies and for which they fight and die.[39] Christendom can take all kinds of spatial and territorial forms, from the local to the global. What each of these forms have in common—in distinction to Christ's commission of a universal and catholic church—is *exclusivity*.

With this interplay of transcendence and exclusivity, it should not surprise us that the most prominent form of Christendom since the Emperor Constantine has been an imperial one. It is a reasonable and often-repeated claim that, even if Christianity cannot be said to have caused Europe imperialism, its universalist claims and proselytizing zeal shaped empire according to the culture of Christendom. The decolonial approach, which has recently become appropriated from literary theory into both theology and the social sciences, frames the church as constitutive of imperial power. For Quijano, Christianity was central to the process by which the Iberian empires in Latin America "forced the colonized to learn the dominant culture in any way that would be useful to the reproduction of domination."[40] Such domination in empire, as in Christendom, was white and male. French,

---

36. Givens, *We the People*, 2.
37. Givens, *We the People*.
38. Mann, *The Sources of Social Power*, 380.
39. Adler, "Imagined (Security) Communities," 253.
40. Quijano, "Coloniality of Power," 541.

British, and American empires took similar theologized, racialized, and gendered forms. Mignolo observes that America was "not discovered" but "mapped, appropriated, and exploited under the banner of the Christian mission."[41] Thus, the "historical foundation of the colonial matrix (and hence of Western civilization) was theological."[42] At the same time, ideas of Christendom are deployed in Ukrainian resistance to Russian imperial action and by anti-colonial and postcolonial Zambian leaders against the British Empire, to take just two examples.

Why does Christendom arise both for and against empire, both in the Holy Roman Empire and in the republics and monarchies that arose in rebellion against it? Givens explains:

> As Christendom broke up in the colonialist scramble for dominance and Christian aristocracies sought antimonarchical bases of political order, Euro-American projects of peoplehood competed with one another to be *the new and true Israel*, and resistance movements in their colonies often mimicked them in opposition to colonial rule. Thus, the Christian supersessionism at work in Christendom leading up to modernity provided a key language, conceptuality, and optic for the imagination of modern peoplehood and the production of peoples.[43]

As an imagined, exclusive, and imperial concept of Christian community that has been transmogrified in modern empire, secular nationalisms, sectarian movements, and anticolonial movements, Christendom lurks in the background of all kinds of malign politics. As Givens argues, "such understandings of the people of God constitute what has been a most violent weapon in the shaping of the modern world, particularly the West."[44] Today, antisemitic, misogynistic, racist, nativist, Islamophobic, and Christian Zionist movements routinely deploy the language and symbols of Christendom. Examples of these are scattered throughout this book. Perhaps the most constant theme in Christendom's history is "antisemitism," which is most directly related to the supersessionist claim of the new and true Israel.[45] Most Christians—including this one—would decry such movements as apostasies and even as Satanic. However, it would be foolish to dismiss

---

41. Mignolo, *The Darker Side of Western Modernity*, 7.
42. Mignolo, *The Darker Side of Western Modernity*, 8.
43. Givens, *We the People*, 7.
44. Givens, *We the People*, 110.
45. Carroll, *Constantine's Sword*.

them as non-Christian in that their imaginations are explicitly those of Christendom.[46]

In sum, Christendom is *imagined* (which is not to say it lacks biblical roots and spiritual forms), *exclusive* (which is not to say it does not seek to integrate others in mission), and *imperial* (which is not to say that it cannot also bequeath anticolonial and postcolonial forms). When conceptualized in this way, Christendom is far broader than "Constantinianism." To make our definition practical we must also delimit Christendom according to its immanent features. First, Christendom requires the existence or prior existence of *a large and organized Christian population* which provides a common language via the Bible, theology, liturgy, and common modes of religious learning. These may be territorially concentrated or globally dispersed. Although the Christian population may be a minority (around 10 percent in the Roman Empire at the time of Constantine, for example), it is likely to be becoming or have been the most politically significant faith group in terms of organization and its location in and around centers of power. In today's China, with the population of Protestants and Catholics—two separate faiths, according to the Chinese Communist Party—rising to almost 10 percent, the party is making moves to politically recognize and control the faith rather than eradicate it, as previous Chinese governments had occasionally tried and failed to do. But it is not plausible to imaginatively make Christendom in China. Other ingredients are necessary.

Second, and in contrast to control over faith exercised by China or the Soviet Union, Christendom denotes a *set of formal or informal institutional arrangements between church and the political authorities that privilege the Christian religion above other faiths*. Today, these often cohere with the nation-state as the primary locus of political power in a given territory or territories. Such institutional relations may range from a theocracy, where a given Christian denomination is sovereign (as in the Vatican City or Athonite community today, the Armenian Kingdom of Cilicia of the eleventh to fourteenth centuries, or the Munster Anabaptists of 1534–35), to formal partnerships between church and state (as in Anglican Britain or Orthodox Russia), and even to informal partnerships between a leading political faction where influence is largely informal but may be no less potent (as in the United States between certain churches and politicians, or in many Christian-majority regions in the Global South).

---

46. Indeed, all Christian political imaginaries, including those of post-Christendom, implicate the Jews in substantive ways following the apostle Paul's olive tree metaphor (Rom 11). However, supersessionism remains an undeniable obstacle to Christian involvement the contemporary Middle East conflict, for example. Walters, *Loving Your Neighbour in an Age of Religious Conflict*.

Bearing a family resemblance, both formal and informal cases are species of the Christendom genus. A third species may be that which is non-territorial, diasporic, and global. In *The Kingdom of God Has No Borders*, Melani McAlister argues that American evangelicalism has acquired this spatial aspect through its world mission activities, which extend its imagined community beyond its concentration in the United States.[47] A similar argument is made, but in more sensational terms, in Elle Hardy's *Beyond Belief* where she argues that 600 million Pentecostals are "taking over the world."[48] Nor are Christendom and post-Christendom imaginaries necessarily mutually exclusive. American evangelicals—as well as lobbying for the relocation of the American Embassy in Israel—have pressed successfully for their government to promote Freedom of Religion and Belief (FoRB) overseas.[49] FoRB is a modern secular agenda, but one that clearly benefits Christian mission in general and the idea of a new global Christendom in particular.

Third, and consequent of the first two features, Christendom *indicates a discursive environment in which Christian political theology either directs or implicitly informs political ideologies, laws, policy, and public culture on questions of government, security, and international affairs.* Political theology is implicit within claims that are framed as either secular or primitively biblical. Where Christendom is imagined, political theology is at least immanent in these ideas rather than generated as an unintended by-product of them. For example, ideas of human rights have been secularized, marketized, and transformed, but they have their origins in part in Christian theology.[50] Similarly, the English Civil War leader Oliver Cromwell's Puritanism contained little more than a negative political theology against the papacy, but his "sense of dedication and destiny" was nevertheless politico-theological and centered on a Reformed conception of Christendom.[51]

With these three conditions we arrive back at an expanded definition. Christendom is *a theologico-political imaginary of the partnership of church and government, with the church legitimizing government and government securing the church.* This broader definition of Christendom as an imagined community enables us to do much more analytically. It allows us to explore how far variation in Christian populations, institutional arrangements with the church, and political theology affect the practice of politics in each

47. McAlister, *The Kingdom of God Has No Borders*.
48. Hardy, *Beyond Belief*.
49. Bettiza, *Finding Faith in Foreign Policy*.
50. Moyn, *Not Enough*.
51. George, "Puritanism as History and Historiography," 85.

time and space. It incorporates an important analytical distinction between Christendom and Christian. A given society may be post-Christian, in that the number of churchgoers and cultural influence of the faith are in decline, while its state remains in a Christendom mode. The UK, at least until very recently, appears to fit this mode as it has a dwindling Christian population and diverse religious context, but the state church had seen few of its privileges dismantled and remained influential in society. In other contexts, very rapid church growth has taken place in environments where the state has not been subject to Christendom and actively suppresses the Christian faith. China is the aforementioned example, but there are many more.

However, this broader definition also presents us with a new analytical problem. If there is a family resemblance between how church-state relations emerged in the time of Augustine and how they are still practiced in some states today, how do we explain variation? In this sweeping narrative of 1,700 plus years there are as many differences between these Christendom polities as there are similarities. How do we make sense of these differences? I argue for a distinction between *centered* and *decentered* forms of Christendom. The distinction is stylized for the purposes of the development of the argument. Christendom has been subject to centrifugal (centering) and centripetal (decentering) forces, both political and theological, which constitute competing imaginaries. In the remainder of this chapter, we explore how these imaginaries are themselves irreducibly both based in biblical and theological claims and in the conjecture of what is politically possible at the given time.

The Christendom dialectic

To understand Christendom's variety, we must grasp its dialectical relations between opposing forces that divide and merge at different moments. To get a sense of the dialectic we may look at how it appears in two quite different authors. The first is that found in the work of the historical sociologist Michael Mann,[52] where centered and decentered expressions of Christendom reflect broader political trends, centrifugal and centripetal. This is a methodologically atheist account but one that has some use in describing the varied forms of polity and economy, state, and empire, taken in the construction and eventual deconstruction of Christendom. The second is Augustine's dialectic between cities of earth and heaven, which is transposed into the distinctly Christendom dialectic between sword and cross deployed in the writings of the sociologist of religion David Martin and

---

52. Mann, *The Sources of Social Power*, vol. 1.

other Christian realists, including Martin Wight. The first dialectic is primarily material and the second is firstly spiritual. The challenge is to recognize the analogical relationship between the two dialectics on the grounds, according to a biblical Christian narrative, the material and the spiritual are always related. These two accounts are distinct but comparable and they both lead us to a dialectical understanding of internal processes of change within Christendom, which ultimately led to its demise. In this sense, the two dialectics both point toward the eschaton and a coming apocalypse (but that is for part 3).[53]

In both atheistic and Augustinian dialectics, centered forms of Christendom are ones where religious and political authority is integrated to the extent that the latter is sacralized, while decentered forms are where they are distinct but mutually constitutive in relationships of exchange. *Centered Christendom* is an imagined community of *imperium* centered on Constantinople, Rome, Moscow, Münster, or another center to the exclusion of the secular, other faiths, and dissenting Christians, with the messianic purpose of retaking Jerusalem or remaking it elsewhere. Centered, theocratic imaginaries of Christendom envision closeness between the bishops and the king, with the former consecrating the latter, or in the case of sacerdotal kingship, authority centered on a single person.[54] In the Calvinist model, a theocracy of magistrates and pastors is possible.[55] This approach affirms providential political power and adopts the supersessionist idea of the church as a new Israel.[56]

By contrast, *decentered Christendom* is an imagined community where government is constituted apart from the church, which receives special status and protection from the state but is primarily focused on its pastoral and missiological purposes. Most systems of national establishment or informal church-state relations are decentered, as in the classical Augustinian understanding and in Lutheran "two kingdoms" theology, where the legitimacy of the order relies on the distance between the two. This distinction is one of ideal types, which allows us to identify how different imaginaries of Christendom connote different security practices, how they come into conflict, and how their tensions are resolved. As Graham Ward argues, Christendom was divided from its outset, long before the Reformation. It

---

53. Mann's later work appears to nod in that direction. Mann, *The Dark Side of Democracy*.

54. Sykes, *Power and Christian Theology*, 36.

55. Sykes, *Power and Christian Theology*, 40.

56. Givens, *We the People*, 110. See also Bader-Saye, *Church and Israel after Christendom*, 57–69.

is best understood as "an ideology only partially realized and internally contested."[57]

From a Christian faith perspective, these kinds of shifts between centered and decentered imaginaries occur within history according to God's purpose of creating, redeeming, and renewing the covenant community of people freed from sin by Christ. In more general terms we may denote this process as *the Christendom dialectic*, or what Martin calls "the Christian dialectic."[58] In this most sweeping understanding of the dialectical, all social life, premodern and modern, secular and religious, democratic and autocratic, national and international, local and global, is the product of the tension between centering and decentering trends. In the secular social sciences, these are usually identified with the tensions between hierarchy and anarchy in any given closed social system. Hierarchy is visible in centrifugal forces that constitute centers of power and government, whereas anarchy is seen in centripetal forces from the margins that resist power and create new rules and constitutional orders. The distinction between hierarchy/anarchy is not that of order/disorder. One of paradigmatic debates of IR is to explain how (not whether) order occurs in the condition of anarchy, without a world government to order relations between states. Disorder is not essential to either centered or decentered Christendom but occurs when the centering and decentering forces are in conflict.

The medieval Christendom power dialectic was ideological, according to the schema of Mann in the first of his four-volume series *The Origins of Social Power*. In the imagined security community of Christendom, the church-state is *transcendent* yet it also empowers the "*immanent* morale"—that is, their sense of their place in history—of both the clerics of the church and the ruling lords of the state.[59] It is this contradiction between transcendence (the power of the cross) and immanence (the power of the sword) that generates the dialectic which produces centered and decentered forms of Christendom in practice. Importantly, both centering and decentering are processes not driven by logics of consequence, such as the lands or positions that may be gained via integration or de-integration with government, although these are the military, economic, and political functions of the Christendom dialectic. They are primarily ideological, taking a secularized theological form. Throughout most of their shared history, church and state have been "entwined in a dialectical process" between these two poles of

---

57. Ward, *The Politics of Discipleship*, 26.
58. David Martin, *On Secularization*, 3.
59. Mann, *The Sources of Social Power*, 377.

transcendent claims and immanent applications.[60] Mann's perspective is specific to Latin Christendom and is methodologically atheist (that is, it does not require God as actor or concept for it to make sense), but it describes a tension that may also be recognized from an evangelical point of view. We minister to the world but, as we do so, we risk being drawn into the world and losing the salt and light by which we minister.

In contrast to Mann, David Martin's Augustinian dialectic is applied not merely to the High Middle Ages but to the entire sweep of Christendom history. As something of a Christendom thinker himself, Martin frames violence as an enduring aspect of the social order, which is limited by Christian politics: "a continuous dialectic whereby the sword turns into the cross and the cross into the sword."[61] This dialectic provides a vivid explanation of how the church comes to legitimize government and receive security from it, even when it seeks to maintain an arm's length relationship. Equally, the church finds itself bearing the moral order of the established church. Martin contends:

> The cross will be carried into the realm of temporal power and will turn into a sword which defends established order. It will execute criminals and heretics in the name of God and the king. But temporal kingship will now be defended by reversed arms, that is by a sign of reversal an inversion. Every sign in the armory of temporal legitimacy will now carry the reverse implication.[62]

The cross may ascend but it will do so ambiguously, never overcoming, and in fact relying upon, the sword. But the sword will equally rely on the cross.

Such an order cannot be stable and will face evangelization movements acting against the collaboration of church and government. This dialectic plays out in history, according to Martin, in terms of waves, "successive Christianizations followed or accompanied by recoils."[63] This tension in Christendom is therefore a constant rather than one that has been resolved in one direction or another over time. Martin identifies "four Christianizations, each overlapping the others, and each creating massive wakes which are still with us." These are, in turn, two waves of Catholic Christianization to convert the monarchs and then the masses, and two waves of Protestant Christianization, one associated with the Reformation and a

---

60. Mann, "The Autonomous Power of the State," 206.
61. Martin, *The Breaking of the Image*, 28.
62. Martin, *The Breaking of the Image*, 28.
63. Martin, *On Secularization*, 3.

final nineteenth- and twentieth-century evangelical wave.[64] Martin's theistic account departs from Mann's atheism and is broadly compatible with recent sweeping histories of how the secular age and its sovereign individual emerged, not from an "enlightenment" outside of faith, but from conflicts between transcendence and immanence within Christendom's debates (see chapter 5).

In both Mann and Martin, the historical evidence to support the existence of such a dialectic is unavoidably selective. Any dialectical account risks oversimplifying messy historical reality in order to fit a structuralist logic. However, the notion of the Christendom dialectic is helpful for two reasons. First, it provides us with a different kind of temporality to that of the Constantinian rise, Latin heights, and modern fall of Christendom that is found among most of its apologists and critics alike. That account is inadequate in that, although it allows some room for providence, its eschatology is especially thin and potentially violent. If the church is in decline, surely the end is about to come with a martial Christ soon to lead his troops to earth to destroy the pagan governments that have sidelined the true church? Some in both Anabaptist and Calvinist camps, and others besides, have been attracted by this kind of timeline and its imagined apocalypse of the future. By contrast to such affirmation of violence, a dialectical account allows us to recognize a redemptive rhythm in history where decentering tendencies are doing work to limit violence and the excesses of political power in Christendom.

Second, the dialectic is valuable for allowing us to analyze the spatio-temporal variation of Christendom in systematic terms. We may break up the period and geography, which is otherwise presented as single Christendom from the fourth century to sometime in late modernity. Here, the centered/decentered distinction may be introduced, with centered Christendom more common in the first three waves of Christianization in Justinian's Eastern Roman Empire (sixth century), the crusades and high papacy (eleventh to thirteenth centuries), and the Protestant Reformation (sixteenth to seventeenth centuries). Decentered Christendom occurs in the recoil or wake of these three periods where challenges to the moral standing of the church and a loss of control by the secular authorities lead to the dispersal or even complete separation of church and state. It appears to be on the ascent in, for example, the Carolingian Empire (ninth to tenth centuries), the decline of medieval Christendom after the thirteenth century, and the Peace of Augsberg and English Anglicanism (sixteenth to nineteenth centuries).

64. Martin, *On Secularization*, 3–4.

In light of both these points, we must recognize the sustained dominance of decentered Christendom in the late-modern West that has given birth to our increasingly secular age. The absence of obvious manifestations of centered Christendom in Martin's fourth wave of Christianization is of most interest in debates about post-Christendom. This wave was "realized in the creation of evangelical and Pietist subcultures," whose highpoint "collapsed quite recently so we are immediately in its wake."[65] The failure to credibly imagine a new era of centered Christendom, where sword and cross are conjoined, in the present age suggests that something has shifted in the dialectic with the emergence of post-Christendom and the ascendance of the secular. While it is not impossible to imagine its return if revolutionary conditions allow, as graphically conceived in Margaret Atwood's militantly theistic Republic of Gillead of *The Handmaid's Tale*, centered Christendom is presently forsaken in all but a few zealous pockets of terrorists and insurgents. Even decentered imaginaries of Christendom are becoming less common, especially in the Western churches, as pluralization and globalization have continued apace, eroding the conditions for "micro-Christendoms" both within the church and without.

Yet the dialectical tension between heavenly and earthly city cannot simply end as the two go their separate ways. For Martin, this dialectic is essential to Christian accounts of history and cannot lapse. For Mann, and his followers in historical sociology, the dialectic in Christendom is a peculiarly Latin species of a wider genus: its oscillation is neither specific to any one period of history nor to the church-state dynamic, but is the "perpetual dialectic of movement between state and civil society."[66] The comparison of the two accounts allows us to see how the Augustinian dialectic has its echo across history in struggles between the state and civil society that are, at first glance, material and ideological but not spiritual. Typically, "if the state then loses control of its resources they diffuse into civil society, decentering and de-territorializing it."[67] The nineteenth and twentieth centuries saw successive waves[68] of decentering in the break-up of European empires and the decolonization in Latin America, Asia, Africa, and post-socialist Eurasia, in each case creating new states and democratic movements.

In the global North and West too, ours has hitherto been an era of decentering. Do these latest developments indicate the resolution of the dialectic in the favor of secular civil society which keeps the despotic power

---

65. Martin, *On Secularization*, 4.
66. Mann, "The Autonomous Power of the State," 195.
67. Mann, "The Autonomous Power of the State," 210.
68. Huntingdon, *The Clash of Civilizations*.

of the state in check? Mann is not so sanguine and reiterates that any process of decentering meets the reassertion of centering tendencies.

> Every dispute between the state elite and elements of civil society and every dispute among the latter which is routinely regulated through the state's institutions, tends to focus the relations and the struggles of civil society on to the territorial plane of the state, consolidating social interaction over that terrain, creating territorialized mechanisms for repressing or compromising the struggle, and breaking both smaller local and also wider transnational social relationships.[69]

Each region that has seen decolonization and democratization has also seen countervailing recentering trends back to authority, patriarchy, and territorial control. Recent theological calls to "reimagine" the "Christendom state" may seem fanciful.[70] However, we are now living through the consolidation of hierarchy in many Eurasian states where autocrats are rolling back democratization, often while rolling out their own imagined Christendom, as in Hungary, Poland, and Russia.[71] In the West, some similar centering tendencies are found in "strongmen" populist movements, including those of Brazilian president Jair Bolsonaro (2019–2023) and former US President Donald Trump (2017–2021), who instrumentally deploy moralizing language and "Christian nation" symbolism.[72] The journalist Gideon Rachman argues that Putin is the archetype for these patriarchs.[73] In the next chapter we will explore the security practices of Christendom, paying special attention to the conflict and cooperation between Eastern and Western forms.

From one Christendom to many Christendoms

Although this book concerns security *after* Christendom, it has been the purpose of this opening chapter to demonstrate that Christendom is not just history, either for the church or the world. The supersessionism of

---

69. Mann, "The Autonomous Power of the State," 207.
70. Nichols, *Christendom Awake*.
71. Even Mann himself entertained the notion in his 1984 article that the combination of despotic and infrastructural power in the Soviet Union may overcome the dialectic. However, the ascent of Mikhail Gorbachev to the Kremlin one year later set in motion decentering dynamics via civil society that were a surprise to most Western Sovietologists but much less so for Soviet dissenters and dissidents such as Alexander Solzhenitsyn. Mann, "The Autonomous Power of the State," 207.
72. Polimédio, "The Rise of the Brazilian Evangelicals."
73. Rachman, *The Age of the Strongman*.

Christendom remains visible in how many modern political elites sacralize their national communities. The Pauline call to respect the sword (Rom 13) and Christ's Gospel command to reimagine political life in terms of victory over strongmen (Mark 3:23–27)[74] have caused tension within Christian communities, and between them and the secular authorities, for two millennia. We will return to the biblical debate in chapter 9. For now, it suffices to say that few Christians would doubt that a relationship should exist between church and secular government; the debate is rather on the extent and means by which it is a cooperative relationship and those by which it is antagonistic. In any given time, relations will never be entirely cooperative; even at the height of Latin Christendom, where the conditions of Christendom were unequivocally met, there was plenty of both cooperation and antagonism. There is always dissent, but our emphasis here is on collaboration. "Christendom" is therefore not a distinct period of history but an imagined community of cooperative relations between church and state that has been realized approximately and in many diverse ways in practice. As an imagined community, far from being long gone, Christendom has its afterlives, and it is prone to revival. These include centered currents that tend toward theocracy and decentered flows where the church is, with civil society, subordinate to the secular state.

Our definition of Christendom as cooperative relations between church and government bears resemblance to Yoder's: "the identification of church and world in the mutual approval and support exchanged by Constantine and the bishops." Yoder's scathing critique remarks that "at best [Christendom] produces Puritanism, and at worst simple opportunism."[75] However, as other have noted, this critique is a dismissive and limited one, uncharacteristic of Yoder's otherwise careful analysis, and it does little to capture the variety and endurance of the ideas of Christendom.[76] The definition I offer is different to Yoder's in three key respects. First, Christendom becomes real insofar as it is an imagined community of the relationship between two kingdoms and cannot merely be dismissed as expediency and opportunism. Second, Christendom varies in its ecclesiologies, theologies, and politics according to its centered and decentered forms rather than the single Constantinianism identified by Yoder and most Anabaptists. Third, Christendom is a dialectical phenomenon that ebbs and flows in different places and times. Centered imagined communities are those that envision

---

74. Myers interpretation of Mark presents the Jesus movement as a radical political project that undermined the ideological basis of the Roman Empire without directly challenging it politically. Myers, *Binding the Strongman*.

75. Yoder, *Original Revolution*, 65.

76. Haymes and Gingerich-Hiebert, *God after Christendom?*, 3.

sacralized political authority; in modern conceptual language they are Christian nationalist, "ethnophyletist," or "caesaropapist" and are concomitant with security practices of exclusion, violence, and scarcity. Decentered imagined communities, in some contrast, merely seek an accommodation with government and thereby develop practices that are more inclusive, and tolerant of minorities, and open to trade and cooperation with others. The secular is, by implication, a radically decentered successor that emerged from Christendom itself. These claims will be elaborated in the coming chapters.

Despite these differences with Yoder's definition of "Constantinianism," and recent critiques of its simplistic dualism, there is much to admire in his and much earlier Anabaptists' critiques of Christendom. Foremost of these is their Christo-centrism. Early Anabaptists constantly quoted the words of Christ to correct the scriptural proof texts which were deployed instrumentally to justify their persecution. In sum, they asked Where is Christ in your Christendom? Their own answers pointed to the Gospel texts where Christ's relationship with the powers were not those of cooperation but either those of conflict or of withdrawal. For the most part, Anabaptists settled on retreat from engagement with government in the face of the assault on their communities in the name of Christendom. This tendency to violence in Christendom and its creation of Others is the subject of the next chapter where we consider the entwining of Christendom with Western imperial histories, highlight the Eurasian aspects of Christendom, and the variation in the forms and degrees of violence found in different imagined communities.

CHAPTER 2

Conflicting Geographies

He shall judge between the nations and shall decide disputes for many peoples; and they shall beat their swords into ploughshares, and their spears into pruning-hooks; nation shall not lift up sword against nation, neither shall they learn war anymore.

ISAIAH 2:4

Only nuclear weapons protect Russia from enslavement by the West.

VSEVOLOD CHAPLIN[1]

In 2019, Russia's nuclear forces announced a new tender. This sought "76 small icons with the image of Seraphim of Sarov with rhinestones, 45 folding icons with the image of the same saint, 70 folding icons with the image of Fyodor Ushakov, 66 panels of the Sarov desert of two types, 90 triptychs with icons and an image, and 188 packages with the emblem of the nuclear center."[2] It was not clear whether the icons and triptychs would adorn the weapons of mass destruction themselves or merely the barracks of those that operate them. This was one act in a series that have integrated the Russian Orthodox Church fully into the state's nuclear forces. These forces have their own cathedral, which blends military commemoration and orthodox

---

1. Chairman of the Synodal Department for the Cooperation of Church and Society of the Moscow Patriarchate from 2009 to December 2015, quoted in Gault, "Russia's Church Blesses Nuclear Weapons."

2. Kommersant, "The Nuclear Center in Sarov Will Buy Icons."

iconography, and their weapons are blessed by Orthodox priests. Mobile temples accompany intercontinental ballistic missiles and nuclear submarines have their own churches.[3]

Dmitry Adamsky denotes this state of affairs as *Russian Nuclear Orthodoxy*.[4] Such symphonia of weapons of mass destruction and religious conservatism is controversial within the church, which has seen various unsuccessful attempts by priests to challenge the policy.[5] But for others it is a core part of their job. Adamsky identifies what he calls "nuclear priests," which are "equivalent to Soviet-era political officers" and integrated into "the whole chain of command and join their flock on operational missions both on the ground and underwater."[6] Against the anti-nuclear stance of other denominations in Russia, the Orthodox Church confers legitimacy on the nuclear forces and "claims the role of one of the guarantors of Russian national security."[7] Parts of the now-autocephalous Ukrainian Orthodox Church have played a similar role, albeit in a defensive posture, blessing troops fighting Russian-backed separatists in the Donbas region.[8] Christendom imaginaries, far from being confined to the West, are recurrent features across space and time in Christian world. They may provide the rationale for opposition to the West and division within the non-West.

In the opening chapter we defined Christendom as an imagined community that varies between centered and decentered modes according to the dialectical tension between Christendom's cross and sword, between Augustine's heavenly and earthly cities. Any definition must by its very nature delimit the nature and form of that which it seeks to define. However, there is a risk inherent here: that the externalities against which Christendom is defined are hidden or neglected in our analysis. As Christendom is not just a religious community but a political one, its immanent form is produced with respect to its fears, its enemies, and its borders. All security communities define themselves in terms of their others. Sixteenth-century England with its new Anglican church defined itself against papal Europe. Eighteenth-century America and postcolonial Nigeria, with their secularism and presidentialism, defined themselves against monarchical Britain with its established church. Putin's authoritarian and Orthodox Russia distinguishes itself from the liberalism and licentiousness of the West. But in

3. Adamsky, *Russian Nuclear Orthodoxy*, 2.
4. Adamsky, *Russian Nuclear Orthodoxy*.
5. Gault, "Russia's Church Blesses Nuclear Weapons."
6. Adamsky, *Russian Nuclear Orthodoxy*, 2.
7. Adamsky, *Russian Nuclear Orthodoxy*, 3.
8. As depicted on the front cover of Megoran, *Warlike Christians*.

putting up barriers to their others, these (neo-)Christendom communities themselves become defined in terms of their opposition. Their externalities come to shape their internalities.

In this chapter we will explore how the external relations of Christendom have produced the two types of imagined community and their security practices. In the first half, we will look at how a centered Latin Christendom was entangled with Western empire and the nature and form of imperial violence, both to its own subjects and to its others. In the second, we will look at the decentered imagined communities that arose after the Reformation in the "micro-Christendoms" of Europe and the "Christian international society" of the seventeenth and eighteenth centuries. Our focus then is Western violence. But as we shine a light on it we find that it was neither uniformly violent nor exclusively Western. The purpose here is not to exonerate Western Christendom for its immense violence but to understand the variety of security practices that occur under Christendom and the fact that their geographical scope is not specifically Western, nor even Eurasian, but global.

The Imagined Security Communities of Centered Christendom

An imagined security community of Centered Christendom is one where the church has a "powerful interest" in "asserting ecclesiastical supremacy over [the secular] authorities."[9] Such an imagined community is an empire, state, city, or other polis, where church and government is envisioned as a formal theocracy or an informal harmony. Church law is written to have universal and exclusive domain over public morality. Moreover, the church directs government and foreign policy or government acts according to what it perceives to be the sacred and political interests of the church. Centered Christendom is most often associated with the Holy Roman Empire, the crusades, and the high papacy (eleventh to thirteenth centuries), beginning with the investiture crisis of 1076. Indeed, Latham argues plausibly that without the centering of Christendom on the papacy the crusades could not have begun.[10] However, earlier and later examples may be found from Justinian's Eastern Roman Empire (sixth century) and the Armenian Kingdom of Cilicia (eleventh to fourteenth centuries) in the East, to the Münster

---

9. Latham, "Theorizing the Crusades," 232.
10. Latham, "Theorizing the Crusades," 240.

Anabaptists (1534–35), Cromwell's English Protectorate (1653–59), and New England colonies (seventeenth and eighteenth centuries) in the West.

In the contemporary era, centered Christendom appears to be imagined by some in Orban's Hungary and Putin's Russia—states where a minority identify as Christian. But in Western Europe too this imaginary has purchase. In France, for example, despite its constitutional laïcité and being one of the most secularized countries in the world, Marine Le Pen, leader of the National Rally (*Rassemblement National*), has spoken of Putin as "Defender of the Christian heritage of European civilization" and received financial support from the Russian state.[11] In states with more Christians, by contrast, centered Christendom is less common. It has rarely characterized church-state relations in the postcolonial Global South, even in the eight states of sub-Saharan Africa where more than 90 percent are estimated to be Christian.[12] As these examples illustrate, this imagined community may be found across political geographies and Christian traditions, Catholic and Orthodox, Protestant and radical. But it is not an objective condition that arises when a Christian nationalist leader meets a majority Christian population. It is more a political construction than a religious condition.

The imaginary of centered Christendom has begotten a core of theopolitical concepts that are also not exclusively Western. The concept of *Imperium Christianum* or *Res Publica Christianum* of Latin Christendom are predated by ideas that crossed the Christian world as the Roman Empire began its decline. Augustine of Hippo (354–430) was from North Africa while the Emperor Justinian (537–65)—whose doctrine of *symphonia* restated Augustine's "two cities" theology—was an Eastern Roman emperor. According to symphonia, the priesthood and empire, "are regarded as closely interdependent, but, at least in theory, neither is subordinated to the other."[13] Yet, "in practice the two spheres were inseparable."[14] Similarly, secular law was considered a gift from God where law and morality fused. This practice of ecclesiastical and civil law as indivisible was first found in Justinian's reign, explicated by Aquinas, and returned to frequently in the Orthodox and Catholic traditions. The concept was invoked by Patriarch Kirill on his ascendance in 2009. In the presence of Russia's President Dmitry Medvedev, the patriarch noted that symphonia, while impossible to realize

---

11. UAWire, "France's Far-Right National Front asks Russia for €27 Million Loan."

12. These are Sao Tome and Principe, Congo DR, Cape Verde, Burundi, Angola, Lesotho, Rwanda, and Namibia. Center for the Study of Global Christianity, "Christianity in Africa."

13. Cross and Livingstone, *The Oxford Dictionary of the Christian Church*, 771.

14. Mann, *The Sources of Social Power*, 384.

in its original form today remains the "spirit" of church-state relations in that it "presupposes a harmonious combination of interests, the distribution of responsibility, and that the outline of the symphony is embodied in the canonical tradition of the Orthodox Church."[15]

Centered Christendom thereby bestows authority in ecclesiastical and secular authorities in so far as they are conjoined and act in unison. In *Imperium Christianum* authority was found in sacerdotal kingship derived from the political theology of the church. This principle set the king out as sacred, indeed Christ-like, and thereby above the people. "The sacral status of early medieval kingship," Rodney Bruce Hall notes, "was an important legitimating principle for a society that lacked a secular conception of the legitimacy of a social order or a political regime."[16] The implication of Hall's analysis is that such authority and legitimacy are unlikely when secular imaginaries compete with those of Christendom in plural societies. Where division emerged in the church, or it ceased to be the confession of the majority, centered Christendom begins to break down. "'Christ-centered kingship' left [the monarch] ensconced firmly on the throne," Hall continues, "but only so long as the Church continued to affirm him as sacred in his person."[17]

As the centering of Christendom was grounded in a theopolitical imagination, so it was driven by a security imperative. It is in this sense that Christendom may be understood as an imagined *security* community. In bestowing such personal authority in the king, centered Christendom invokes an eschatology of the millennium and the apocalypse whereby the king restrains the Antichrist and sits in Christ's place until his return. The king while sacral is also a temporal security provider. The historian Tom Holland notes that in the eighth century, before the crowning of Charlemagne as Holy Roman Emperor, the demand for the centering of Christendom came from popes who sat at the margins of empire and were vulnerable to attack by pagan forces. "From the pope's point of view," he notes, "[most alarming] was the failure of the emperor to fulfil his most sacred duty, and to offer to God's church the protection of sword and shield."[18]

As well as defense, *Imperium Christianum* engaged in offensive war in the name of both security and sanctity. From the time of the crusades, it became the role of the emperor to wage Holy War to reconquer territories for Christendom. In modern social science, there has been a lively debate

15. "Archpastors—participants of the Local Council attended a reception" [my translation].
16. Hall, "Moral Authority as a Power Resource," 601.
17. Hall, "Moral Authority," 601.
18. Holland, *Millennium*, 21.

on how far the crusades can be attributed to the theology of Christendom with a secularist interpretation attributing them instead to the international politics of alliance-building, order-making, or primitive accumulation.[19] More recent scholarship has effectively refuted those accounts, which deny the theology of the crusades, finding cause in the "crusaders' mentalité" and the discourse of "holy war."[20] In this holy war, Christian knights were *milites Christi, fideles Christi*, and *exercitus Dei* against the infidels and pagans.[21] By such account, "holy war" and the crusades themselves rested on a centered security community of Christendom where church and state were in lock step. While Cavanaugh and others have persuasively argued against the myth that religion—whether centered on political community or not—is more likely to cause violence, there is persuasive evidence from social scientists that institutionalized violence in the name of religion, like the crusades, lasts longer and is more brutal.[22]

The Security Practices of Centered Christendom

We may identify five distinct security practices or habits of this centered Christendom. Just as with any theory or practice of security, these relate to core questions of inclusion, protection, and provision. The examples given below compare the High Middle Ages in the West with the practices of the Russian Orthodox Church today. These vastly different contexts are not compared in order to suggest equivalence in their political orders—although both are similar in tending toward totalitarianism—but to show that centered imaginaries of church–government relations generate comparable security practices despite such differences in time and space.

First, under imaginaries of centered Christendom there is *little or no toleration of Christian dissenters*. For example, canon law was strict in universalizing papal decrees across Latin Christendom. Dissenting monastic orders were often brutally suppressed, as with the thirteenth-century papal strategy to promote the Dominican order and the inquisition. For the friar and inquisitor Moneta de Cremona, "God became incarnate on earth in Christ as a vehicle of violence and persecution"[23]—a claim he justified biblically in terms of Christ's gospel promise to bring a sword (Matt 10:34).

---

19. Fischer, "Feudal Europe, 800–1300."
20. Alkopher, "The Social (and Religious) Meanings That Constitute War."
21. Alkopher, "The Social (and Religious) Meanings," 723.
22. Cavanaugh, *The Myth of Religious Violence*; Horowitz, "Long Time Going."
23. Ames, *Righteous Persecution*.

More than the sword, however, what was most feared was exclusion in the form of excommunication under the principle of *extra ecclesiam nulla salus* (no salvation outside the church). This was not merely a matter of the basic survival of all under Christendom but also of the production of a security community with a trifunctional order of those that pray, that fight, and that labor. It was the church and canon law that legitimized this security community and made Christian dissent entirely illegitimate. As the historian of International Relations Julia Costa Lopez argues, "this process of Christianizing reason and redefining humanity was the enabling of the possibility of elimination."[24] The fate of dissenting priests against Russian nuclear orthodoxy today may be imprisonment and excommunication rather than elimination, but the principle of non-toleration remains.

Second, there is *the habitual othering of non-Christian minorities* (Jews and Muslims). For minorities within Christendom, this meant forced withdrawal and segregation to retreat into practices that may be forbidden, such as those of banking and finance. Beyond Christendom, this othering may be extraordinarily violent, both culturally and physically, and it is the security logic of this othering that is most striking. The historical sociologist John Hobson notes that emergent European Christendom was riven by rivalries—decentered, that is—prior to the High Middle Ages. "The only way to forge a single identity," he remarks, "was to construct an external 'other' against which a homogeneous 'self' could be constructed. That is, given that there was no single 'self,' it was easier to define the 'self' by that which it was not."[25] Costa Lopez shows that the approach to both Jews and Muslims was strict segregation intermitted with violence where the goal was to "regulate and minimize as much as possible all interaction." In canon law, during this period, Jews were banned from having Christian slaves, excluded from the professions, and shunned in public and private.[26] After the fall of the tenth-century Emirate of Sicily and the caliphate of Cordoba of the Umayyad period (1031 CE), Arab armies rarely posed a threat to the security of Western Europe as the technology of the time made transcontinental exercises in military power almost impossible, but they were routinely portrayed as a threat for centuries to come. In contemporary Russia, it is the Muslim minority and the Central Asian migrant that is the similarly demonized other, often found at the margins of economy and society.

Third, in centered Christendom *war is practiced as a joint act between church and government* where a theology of "holy war" produces

24. Lopez, "Beyond Eurocentrism and Orientalism," 467.
25. Hobson, *The Eastern Origins of Western Civilization*, 107.
26. Lopez, "Beyond Eurocentrism and Orientalism," 462–63.

the *causus belli*. Hall argues that "the transnational moral authority" of Christendom was used "to domesticate a troublesome and belligerent class of vassal-knights" and "to place the material power resource that this class constituted at the service of the Church and crown at the end of the 'feudal revolution.'"[27] Latham finds that without the ecclesiastical and theological ingredients of Latin Christendom it is "hard to image anything like the crusades occurring."[28] While Jesus Christ raised young men as his disciples to build the kingdom of heaven, the rulers of Christendom conscripted them to fight for their worldly kingdoms. The nuclear priests of Russia make similar calls in the modern era.

Fourth, holy war entailed *the territorial extension of Christendom through the conquest of pagan lands* (and sometimes elimination of pagans), most famously in the crusades. Foreign and security policy explicitly favor the extension of Christendom even to places where Christians are in minority. It did so in response to the superior power of pagan and Muslim armies, technically more advanced, invading from the East.[29] "Evangelization," Latham argues "was the fundamental motivation for all Church action; extending the bounds of Christendom, its very raison d'être."[30] In practice, of course, motives vary. Crusader-knights embarked for valor and penitence ("crusade-as-pilgrimage") rather than to settle and hold the East for Christendom as the papacy and political leaders hoped.[31] In his letter to the World Council of Churches in March 2022, Patriarch Kirill combined more secular arguments about NATO expansion with *causus belli* of the Ukrainian church's break with Moscow.[32]

Fifth, there was *very little or no trade with non-Christendom polities*, identified as main geopolitical enemies, in these times of centered Christendom. Given that inter-polity trade is a constant of civilization this is all the more surprising. But at the height of Latin Christendom, the papacy imagined it could forbid most trade beyond Christendom. For example, the late-twelfth-century canon *Ita quorundam* of the Third Lateran Council criminalized the export of goods to Saracens, "under threat of excommunication."[33] The Venetian fleet was allowed an exception to this

27. Hall, "Moral Authority," 591–92.
28. Latham, "Theorizing the Crusades," 240.
29. Hobson, *The Eastern Origins*, 106.
30. Latham, "Theorizing the Crusades," 230.
31. Hall, "Moral Authority," 606.
32. Patriarch Kirill, "Letter to the General Secretary of the World Council of Churches."
33. Lopez, "Beyond Eurocentrism," 468.

rule, demonstrating an element of pragmatism that survived the union of church and state. In general, however, centered Christendom produces polities that are violent toward and separate from other faiths. Cooperation beyond the boundaries of Christendom invariably proves impossible. Russia's Orthodox Christendom of 2022 faces similar confrontations with Western secular states.

Christendom Decentered

Such centered imaginaries are rarely found and—unfortunately for Patriarch Kirill and President Putin—often meet a violent end. Far more common, especially in secularized Western states, are decentered Christendom imaginaries. By contrast to the centered imaginary, in a decentered Christendom community the church is imagined as distinct from but either formally established or informally privileged in state. A decentered view insists that

> the search for a truer and more authoritative perspective than my own doesn't lead me to center society on a king or sacred assembly, or whatever, but allows for this lateral, horizontal view, which an unsituated observer might have—society as it might be laid out in a tableau without privileged nodal points.[34]

For the philosopher Charles Taylor this worldview is a modern social imaginary but one of which he sees glimpses in earlier periods when Christendom was unaccustomed to having a center. It is a worldview of Christendom in that the church remains the paramount source of social and political ethics for both society and a constructive force in security and foreign policy. St. Augustine's fifth-century articulation of "two cities," *civitas dei* and the *saeculum*, still stands as the intellectual marker of decentered Christendom. Its world is one without a center and their logic is one of distinction between church and government, not its unification. Ideas of "just war" originating in his thought continue to animate ethical debates in security studies.

These ideas of the decentered Christendom will be explored further in chapters 3 and 4. Here we consider their historical record in various examples of security community. For most of the early centuries of Western Christendom, up to and including the Carolingian empire of the ninth and tenth centuries, "the 'rational' strategy for the clergy had been to play the

---

34. Taylor, *A Secular Age*, 209.

role of junior partner in a political alliance with the monarchy."³⁵ From the thirteenth century, the Roman church was forced back into this position as early-modern polities emerged, acquired greater military power and began to compete among one another. As the dominant story of the sixteenth and seventeenth centuries tells us, it was the centripetal force of the creation of modern secular states that decentered Christendom. However, similar processes also took place in the East, prior to the Western Reformation. The Armenian theocratic state was overcome in the fourteenth century by the rise of the Ottomans. A Russia-dominated Eastern Orthodox international society began in the fifteenth century, well before the putative founding of Western Christian international society with the Peace of Westphalia in 1648. Eastern Christian international society lasted until the period of seismic change from 1905–17 when the establishment of the Russian Orthodox Church was first downgraded and then cancelled—lasting far longer than the decentered Christian international society of the West, which was ruptured by the revolution of 1789.

Decentering was also driven by Christendom's own dialectic where dissenters challenged the theological basis for alliance with the empire and centripetal forces were let loose. As Mann observes, from its emergence as a major faith,

> Itinerant preachers and mendicants . . . drew popular attention to the doctrinal and practical contradictions built right into the heart of Christianity: Although its officialdom encouraged submission to hierarchy, its shadow authority encouraged both confidence in human rationality and the judgment of all hierarchy by the apocalypse.³⁶

The Pauline dictum that "our citizenship is in heaven" (Phil 3:20) is emblematic of this tension as it captures the New Testament position that Christians must keep their distance from the worldly powers of the day— "not to contaminate themselves with the moral squalor of the pagan world," as Malcolm Muggeridge describes.³⁷

Under decentered Christendom in the modern era, citizenship is imagined as being both temporal and heavenly. That citizenship and the security establishment that stands behind it is national. Philpott has demonstrated that the Reformation created certain conditions for the emergence of nation states after the Thirty Years War and the Peace of Westphalia

---

35. Latham, "Theorizing the Crusades," 231.
36. Mann, *The Sources of Social Power*, 388.
37. Muggeridge, *The End of Christendom*, 36.

(1648). He argues that "the intrinsic content of Protestantism itself points to sovereignty."[38] Luther's *Doctrine of the Two Kingdoms and the Two Governments* revived Augustine's formulation and animated a series of transformations that finally dismantled the properties, temporal offices, and union of church and government in the Holy Roman Empire.[39] This was the political theology, with the backing of princes, that earlier reformist movements, such as the Lollards in England and Hussites in Bohemia, lacked.[40] The modern international political system of sovereign states emerged not merely due to the self-interest of elites but from "a new conception of humanity's relationship with God."[41] The role of distinctively Christian thought in the unravelling of *Imperium Christianum* speaks again to the Christendom dialectic identified by Mann.

And yet early modern Europe fell far short of what today we call post-Christendom. Christendom was pluralized rather than replaced, fractured rather than broken. Churches of different denominations became formally established or informally influential in polities like the early United States which were nominally secular, but which saw an evangelical incursion into politics from the 1960s. It should be no surprise then that the moral arguments through which imperial expansions took place echo Christendom in their language and zeal. European imperialism as late as the nineteenth and even early twentieth centuries was conceived as a "civilizing mission" against "Oriental despotism"; imperialism did not merely happen because the powerful could but because they *believed they should*.[42] The supremacy of Europe over the East was based on an imagined boundary that was discursively constructed under Christendom, according to supersessionist logics discussed in chapter 1.

These imaginaries of decentered Christendom have not been confined to the West. The diversity of polities and confessions was the norm of the Christian world through most of its existence, particularly in the East where today sixteen national churches sit under the Ecumenical Patriarchate in Constantinople. The Orthodox theologian Cyril Hovorun has identified a track of Orthodox political theology that is "more ecumenical and interested in the political ideas coming from the West."[43] He charts its beginning with the eighteenth-century Athonite monk Benjamin of Lesbos, who

38. Philpott, "The Religious Roots of Modern International Relations," 207.
39. Philpott, "The Religious Roots," 223.
40. Philpott, "The Religious Roots," 224.
41. Philpott, "The Religious Roots," 244.
42. Hobson and Sharman, "The Enduring Place of Hierarchy in World Politics," 87.
43. Hovorun, "Orthodox Political Theology," 1.

"used the concept of human rights and liberty to justify the struggle for Greek independence from the Ottoman Empire."[44] This continued in the nineteenth century with the ecumenicist theologian Vladimir Solovyov and in the twentieth with figures such as Fr. Sergey Bulgakov and Fr. Alexander Schmemann.[45] The dialectical nature of this decentering is clear in Hovarun's analysis, where Orthodox political theology evolves in the "dialectics of acceptance and rejection of Western ideas."[46] Theologians of a decentered persuasion were often reacting to centered Christendom views sometimes called caesaropapist, as represented in the imaginaries of Athanasios of Paros, the writings and novels of the Slavophile Fyodor Dostoevsky, and with the "neo-patristic synthesis" and Eurasianism of Fr. Georges Florovsky and others in the 1920s and 1930s.[47] The liberalism of the 1920s was met by support for dictatorship and fascism in the 1930s and was followed by a swing again the post-war period, mirroring the ferment in the Catholic church that led to Vatican II.[48]

THE SECURITY PRACTICES OF DECENTERED CHRISTENDOM

The security practices of decentered Christendom are those where church and governmental practices exist in parallel but not always in consort. These five practices are juxtaposed to those of centered Christendom. They are ideal type differences used for heuristic purposes to establish trends and fleshed out with examples. Some attempt has been made to provide and explain alternate examples so as to make the account less schematic. The work of Julia Costa Lopez has been especially important in identifying variety in the security practices of medieval Christendom polities before and during the ruptures and "wars of religion" of the sixteenth and seventeenth centuries.[49]

First, and unlike *Imperium Christianum*'s high period, decentered Christendom saw *some toleration of Christian dissenters*. In the West, after Augsburg (1555), princes would allow designated proportions of Christian minorities to practice their faith in the new territories and were not subject

---

44. Hovorun, "Orthodox Political Theology," 4–5.
45. Hovorun, "Orthodox Political Theology," 9, 14.
46. Hovorun, "Orthodox Political Theology," 5.
47. Hovorun, "Orthodox Political Theology," 8.
48. Hovorun, "Orthodox Political Theology," 9.
49. Lopez, "Political Authority in International Relations."

to forced conversion.[50] Religious wars occurred during the rupture of the Reformation when centered and decentered visions of Christendom came into direct conflict, theologically and militarily. But with power dispersed, schisms were more likely as different monastic orders and ecclesiastical denominations warred with one another—and the defeated were able to find refuge and sponsorship in exile. It was famously by this means that Protestants and radical reformers found haven in Europe and North America during and after the Reformation, further decentering Christendom. Within the Catholic church, rivalry appeared to increase between monastic orders countering the Reformation; for example, the rivalries between Dominicans and Jesuits in Poland-Lithuania from the sixteenth to the mid-seventeenth centuries related to conflicts between noble and clerical estates.[51] From the seventeenth century, laws on toleration began to emerge across Western Christendom while a hierarchy between national churches and the dissenters of the free church continues in some of the constitutional monarchies to this day.

Second, in decentered Christendom, *inter-faith relations and partnerships with non-Christian minorities (Jews, Muslims) may exist as laws on toleration emerge*. In decentered Christendom, Jews and Muslims were more often presented as object of mission rather than subjects of war. Similarly, the Fourth Council of Toledo of the seventh century forbade forced coercion, stating that it was a matter of free will and God's grace.[52] From the thirteenth century, Christendom had to accommodate Muslim minorities on the Iberian Peninsula and Sicily, referring to them in biblical terms as Saracens (*Saracenus/Sarracenus*) and Agarens (*Agarenus, Hagarenus*).[53] Costa Lopez demonstrates that in canon law Muslims were consistently presented as an other, but only inconsistently as a threat, arguing that it was not just theology that determined their treatment but the security dynamic that flowed from this basic act of othering. Jews were also tolerated in canon law to the extent that they were witnesses to the Christian truth and subordinate to Christians in society. "The Jew," she argues, "was a necessary Other within yet outside Christian society."[54] Cromwell passed limited laws of toleration of the Jews in his English protectorate for similar theological reasons—having a more benign supersessionism than that of High Middle

---

50. Philpott, "The Religious Roots," 212.
51. Stolarski, "Dominican-Jesuit Rivalry."
52. Lopez, "Beyond Eurocentrism," 464–65.
53. Lopez, "Beyond Eurocentrism," 457.
54. Lopez, "Beyond Eurocentrism," 456.

Ages—but stopped short of the demands for liberty and the toleration of heresy in the post-Christendom ideas of the Levellers and Baptists.[55]

Third, when Christendom is decentered institutionally and ideationally, we see *conditional rather than unconditional church support for war*. Unlike under either centered Christendom or periods of often violent transition (most prominently during the Reformation), religion was rarely if ever the *causus belli*. For example, as Christendom decentered, the emerging states reduced or ended their sponsorship in blood and treasure of the crusades, while the crusading lords themselves found their interests no longer coincided as they had when chivalry and pilgrimage, not conquest and pillage, were pre-eminent. Fischer argues:

> The crusaders not only carved up the newly won territories in the east into petty principalities but also continued to struggle against each other in Europe. And they ultimately failed to hold the east precisely because they could not square their particular interests with the universal idea that had inspired them.[56]

In fact, during periods where decentered imaginaries and forms of Christendom were preeminent, wars of aggression were formally prohibited according to *jus in bello* precepts. However, the incidence of armed conflict between Christendom polities may be high as the ordering principle shifts from hierarchical, under the church, to anarchical, between states. The rise of state sovereignty meant that "intervention" across boundaries was less common. Violence was increasingly dominated by governments and took place between them regardless of the stance of their respective churches.

Fourth, therefore, *wars within Christendom increased*. In the "Christian international society" of 1648–1789, ninety-two of the 141 years saw wars between Christian-majority states. These states were far more likely to go to war with one another than with the Ottomans or other Muslim-majority polities.[57] War was more likely in late-Christendom than in Qing-Confucian China, the modern Arab states system, or even the famously martial world of classical Greece.[58] "Despite a clear anti-war ethic and sense of shared community," Kelly notes, "Christendom (1648–1789) warred against itself relentlessly."[59] The distinction between centered and decentered Christendom explains this warlike outcome in terms of the

---

55. George, "Puritanism as History and Historiography."
56. Fischer, "Feudal Europe," 438.
57. Kelly, "A 'Confucian Long Peace' in Pre-Western East Asia?," 417–18.
58. Kelly, "A 'Confucian Long Peace,'" 420.
59. Kelly, "A 'Confucian Long Peace,'" 420.

theologico-political ordering principle where a decentered community is typically more internally conflictual than violently expansionist. At first glance, the recent confrontation between the civilization claims of Putin's Russia and the national claims of Ukraine and its autocephalous church appears to reflect this wider pattern.

A clearer example is perhaps Russia's debate over the Crimean War of the 1850s. A century and a half before Patriarch Kirill was advocating war for Orthodoxy in the same part of the world, the Crimea debate was characterized by a "crusading mood" and the perception of "a God-given opportunity to change Russia itself."[60] As a Christendom project, the Crimean War also attracted thousands of Greeks, Bulgarians, Serbs, and Romanians, who began to petition the Russian government to join the fight from 1853, with the Tsar responding by creating a special legion for Balkan volunteers. It was in the name of Christendom that the Greek government fomented rebellions on its borders with the Ottoman Empire. Britain and France joined the Ottomans against Orthodox Russia—although they both faced criticisms at home for supporting Islam against Christianity. The Anglican church in Britain assisted its government by othering Eastern Orthodoxy as an alien faith to the English state religion. In a sense, these Western policies continued "the centuries-long experience of Western crusades in the East," which, in Demacopoulos and Papanikolaou's terms, "likely marked a permanent turning point in Eastern attitudes towards the West."[61]

Fifth, while decentered Christendom sees conflicts increase internally, *it sees cooperation increase externally as extensive trade and geopolitical cooperation with non-Christendom polities becomes possible.* As Latin Christendom declined, and the power of the papacy decreased, it acquired interests in trade with non-Christendom polities for which it granted licenses and collected fees. Traders rebelled against the prohibition in trade decreed by the Third Lateran Council and, soon after, the Venetians successfully argued for an increasing number of exemptions.[62] Many more exceptions were granted, especially for the Iberian Peninsula with its extensive relations with North Africa. From the fourteenth century, "papal policy differentiated between several Muslim communities and, while still subordinated to the overall idea of the defense of Christendom, embraced the possibility that cooperation with some non-Christians may benefit the pursuit of those higher

---

60. Fairey, *The Great Powers and Orthodox Christendom*, 5, 3.
61. Demacopoulos and Papanikolaou, *Orthodox Constructions of the West*, 6.
62. Lopez, "Beyond Eurocentrism," 467.

objectives."[63] Those higher objectives were foremost those of conversion. As Jean and John Comaroff argue, the eighteenth- and nineteenth-century struggles to abolish slavery, led principally by nonconformists, were not themselves disavowals of the value of the power relationship between Britain and its colonies. "Once emancipated, his humanity established," they remark, "the savage would become a fit subject of Empire and Christendom."[64] Indeed, it was arguably the decline of centered Christendom in Europe that enabled its expansion to new frontiers where establishment and dissenting churches could each find their own space.[65]

So, the ancient and modern communities of Christendom were neither exclusively Western nor were they consistently crusading in their international politics. In decentered imperial Christendom imaginaries, the Christian community was imagined missiologically as "a universal civilization with no cultural barriers" as illustrated by the biblical place and person names that are replete across former European colonies.[66] The accounts of centered and decentered communities of Christendom given above demonstrate key differences in foreign and security policies across five issues (see table 1). But what they both share is a sense that as imagined security communities they became what they were in their relationships with their minorities within and their foreign others beyond. Their minorities were pagans, Jews, Muslims, and dissenting Christians—and to these they were variously tolerant and repressive over time. Their foreign others were successive Muslim caliphates that extended into the European continent in the Middle Ages. In the modern era, they found further non-Christian others at their own imperial frontiers of the Americas, the East, and South. These relations ebbed and flowed from conflict, particularly when Christendom was centered and mission expanded it frontiers, to cooperation, when Christendom was decentered and Christian princes warred with one another.

---

63. Lopez, "Beyond Eurocentrism," 469.
64. Comaroff and Comaroff, *Of Revelation and Revolution*, 88.
65. Comaroff and Comaroff, *Of Revelation and Revolution*, 78.
66. Comaroff and Comaroff, *Of Revelation and Revolution*, 216.

TABLE 1: CENTERING AND DECENTERING IMAGINARIES OF EASTERN AND WESTERN CHRISTENDOMS

	Centered Christendom Imaginary	Decentered Christendom Imaginaries
Definition	*Church and government are incorporated as formal or informal theocracy.* Church law has universal and exclusive domain over public morality; the church approves civil law and foreign policy.	*The secular state is sovereign but restrained by balance of power; Church is subordinate to and privileged by the state.* The church is the paramount source of social and political ethics; church is a constructive critic in law and foreign policy.
Associated security practices and patterns	CHURCH-STATE JOINT PRACTICES No toleration of Christian dissenters. Othering of non-Christian minorities (Jews, Muslims)—forced withdrawal and segregation. War as joint act between church and government, religion part of *causus belli*. Conquest of pagan lands (and sometimes elimination of pagans) authorized. Very little or no trade with non-Christendom polities, identified as main geopolitical enemies.	CHURCH AND STATE PRACTICES IN PARALLEL Some toleration of Christian dissenters. Inter-faith relations and partnerships with non-Christian minorities (Jews, Muslims) may exist—laws on toleration. Conditional church support for state's war, but religion not *causus belli*. Wars of aggression formally unauthorized but incidence of armed conflict is high. Extensive trade and geopolitical cooperation with non-Christendom polities possible.
Historical periods and places in ascendance	Justinian's Eastern Roman Empire (6th cent.) The crusades and high papacy (11–13th cent.) Armenian Kingdom of Cilicia (11–14th cent.) Munster Anabaptists (1534–35) New England colonies (17–18th cent.)	Constantinian Roman Empire (4th–5th cent.) Carolingian Empire (9–10th cent.) Lutheranism and Anglicanism (16th cent.–) "Christian international society" (1648–1789) Tsardom of Russia (17th cent. –1905)

WHERE IS CHRISTENDOM?

In this chapter I have argued that debates about the security communities (polities, international agreements, etc.) of Christendom often occlude its divergent geographies and security practices. Rather than being resolutely intolerant to others and its own dissenters, patterns of tolerance shifted partly because of centering or decentering imaginaries. Some Christendom imaginaries were more inclusive than others. Whereas under centered Christendom, religion could be a *causus belli* and the church was fully participative in wars and crusades, in decentered Christendom support was more conditional and fractured. This made "civil war" within Christendom more common. Finally, whereas centered Christendom saw itself as self-provisioning, decentered Christendom developed extensive trading and diplomatic relations with the non-Christendom world.

The most important geographical point here is that the emergence of the modern West—a regional security community that still exists today—took place in conditions that were imagined and practices as divergent from others, not just the colonized of the "uncivilized world" but the Eastern other of various instantiations of Orthodox Christendom. This was firstly a Eurasian process, an East-West conflict, that became global through the expansion of empire. Placing the Eastern church at the beginning of our analysis helps us expand our geopolitical gaze. The perfect union (*symphonia*) of church and state was imagined and institutionalized first in Constantinople more than two hundred years before Charlemagne. The more powerful and wealthy Eastern Christendom was the target of the Arab-Muslim armies, and it was those armies' failure to conquer Constantinople (718 CE) rather than the abortion of their foray into Tours and Poitiers that protected Western Christendom.[67] But even this "Eastern view" downplays the globality of Christendom. "The global transformation," Philipps argues, "was filtered through regionally distinct orders forged out of an earlier Eurasian transformation" where pacification took place under Confucian and Islamic orders, commerce grew along the many silk routes, and science flourished.[68] "Europe came to be known as 'Christendom,'" the decolonial historian John Hobson contends, "because its identity was imagined or invented as Catholic Christian in contradistinction to the Islamic Middle East."[69] Without these others beyond Eurasia—the intermittent warring enemies and trading partners—Christendom as we know could not have emerged.

---

67. Hobson, *The Eastern Origins*, 110.
68. Phillips, "The Global Transformation," 482.
69. Hobson, *The Eastern Origins*, 112.

The question of Christendom's *where* is as difficult to answer as its *when*. A global perspective is required. Christendom's past and present is arguably more Eastern than Western, and its future may be most prominent in the Global South. But this myth of the West's primacy has survived long after the decline of Western Christendom. It is not only the secular social scientists who have portrayed Christendom as Western. Yoder, Stanley Hauerwas, and other prominent "anti-Christendom" theologians are both overwhelmingly from the West and concerned exclusively with Christendom as a Western phenomenon. And in the mid-twentieth century, as Christendom began to recede, a group of theologians and scholars called Christian realists built the new field of IR based on assumptions formed in Western Christendom. They sought to theorize the security practices of the world dominated by the West in secularized terms. But, as Christian thinkers and theologians, the twilight of Christendom loomed large in their ideas.

CHAPTER 3

Fading Theories

[This earthly city] is spread throughout the world in the most diverse places, and, though united by a common nature, is for the most part divided against itself, and the strongest oppress the others, because all follow after their own interest and lusts, while what is longed for either suffices for none, or not for all, because it is not the true good.

ST. AUGUSTINE[1]

If we suppose the world to be ruled by God's providence, ... the entire community of the universe is governed by God's reason. And so the very plan of government, existing in God as ruler of the universe, is a law in the true sense. And since God did not conceive this plan in time but, as Proverbs 8[:23] says, eternally, we must call it an internal law.

THOMAS AQUINAS[2]

On May 13, 2005, I was awoken early by a loud knocking on the door of my accommodation in the Ferghana Valley of Uzbekistan. At the door was an Uzbek colleague from the American NGO Mercy Corps, with whom I was working as a consultant and evaluator of peacebuilding programs. "Quick," she told my colleague and me, "you must leave, there is fighting." Overnight, it transpired, a prison break had occurred in the neighboring city

---

1. Augustine, *De Civitate Dei*, Book XV, 4.
2. Aquinas, "*Summa Theologiae*," 417.

of Andijon and now the government was sending in troops to take back control. What was most evident, however, was not the facts of what happened—their precise details were and remain unclear—but the fear in the words and emotions of our colleague. Within three hours we would leave Ferghana, flying out of its airport while Uzbek troops and security services flew in. In Andijon, the authorities would storm the square where protests against the state were taking place leading to untold hundreds of deaths in what we become known as "the Andijon massacre." Calls for sanctions by the US and EU would lead to retaliatory actions by the Uzbek authorities against the American military base and Western companies.

However, of more interest to me at the time were my personal circumstances. Our Uzbek colleagues remained in the danger zone while we were safe in the head offices of Mercy Corps in the capital Tashkent. Because of the fear that the rebellion would spread, the security protocols of the NGO were enacted to demand the evacuation of expatriate staff to Istanbul, thousands of kilometers away. I lived in the neighboring country of Tajikistan with my wife and asked to be allowed to go back there instead. Reluctantly, the chief of party agreed but insisted that a Mercy Corps driver take me to the southern border and bring me back to Tashkent if it was closed. When we arrived at the border, it was indeed closed. However, after waiting for no more than twenty minutes, I spotted a Tajik government car approaching to cross. I spoke to the official, waved my UK passport, and he agreed to take me across the border from where I could travel on to my home and my wife.

What might easily sound like a story of dramatic escape is also something else: an illustration of privilege in the face of danger. The Uzbeks of Ferghana Valley could not leave their locked-down region and could not even cross the border to Tajikistan, even in normal circumstances (due to strained diplomatic relations between the two countries). My citizenship and status—my *inclusion* in political and professional communities—afforded to me mobility of which they could only dream. This was the mobility to intervene in the first place and leave at will. Some Andijon residents would eventually flee after massing on the eastern border with Kyrgyzstan; some would soon return, others would go on to Russia, and a very few would become refugees in the West. The highest profile exiles—journalists, opposition politicians, and clerics—would become targets of transnational repression, including rendition back to Tashkent and assassination attempts. Even in their supposed refuges, they lacked complete protection and lived a precarious life. The situation of their relatives back home was even worse as they were targeted as a form of reprisal.

This story is told to illustrate something of the intimate dynamics of contemporary security relations and the poverty of extant security theory.

When we think of security, we think firstly of security *from* threats (the realist emphasis on power) and secondly of security *to* live (the liberal emphasis on law). But there is a prior condition that is elemental to security: *the dynamics of inclusion/exclusion that generates boundaries of friend/enemy.* The field of IR has long recognized this boundary as being determined by nation-states and borders where government and citizenship creates security within a state from the dangers beyond the frontier. That is a simple version of the Hobbesian solution to the state of nature: the leviathan. But our vignette provides a more complex picture. In much of the world, non-citizens with passports of privilege and professional support are afforded mobility and safety while citizens are routinely targeted by their own governments, even far beyond their borders. While formally "included," Uzbek citizens are among the many who are formally excluded from the security provided to the country's elite and to foreign citizens.

The debate between power and law is thus inexcusably narrow. But what we now consider to be a debate between realism and liberalism has dominated Christian political theology since the onset of Christendom and the responsibility that arose to explain the relationship between church and world. On the one hand, Augustine preached a clear distinction between the "two cities," *civitas terrena* and *civitas dei*. Given the lust for glory of a fallen world, any given empire or earthly city (*civitas terrena*) is defined by power relations and the absence of a stable normative foundation for political community. Christian emperors, such as Augustine's contemporary Theodosius, may be preferable as the purpose of their power is to point to the majesty of God and enable the work of his heavenly city (*civitas dei*), but it is power not heaven that is the object of their politics. In such a world, Rowan Williams summarizes, "security is transitory, . . . since its common goals are not and cannot be those abiding values which answer to the truest human needs."[3] On the other hand, Aquinas deliberated that natural law binds the Christian commonwealth of a united church and state. Thomism's modern adherents explore the possibility of a "common good of universally human appeal, at once open and amenable to religious belief," while being "resistant, at least in principle, to cooption for intolerance and oppression."[4] Without faith, it is argued, the common good lacks substance. With faith, it lacks tolerance. Aquinas argues for the punishment of heretics and the promotion of church by state—both being commonplace in this

---

3. Williams, "Politics and the Soul," 737.
4. Keys, *Aquinas, Aristotle, and the Promise of the Common Good*, 5.

thirteenth-century world of Western Christendom—in order to achieve the common good over the divisiveness and lust for power emphasized by Augustine.[5]

This famous and long-standing debate in political theology is animated by two quite different accounts of security *against others*. For Augustinians, earthly security is always against others because the foundation of the common good under an omnipotent God cannot be attained and the world is essentially divided and prone to conflict. For Thomists, security for the commonwealth may be found in the approximation of this good in "natural law," but they nevertheless lack an explanation of how to deal with their others—those who do not accept the *Imperium Christianum*—other than by the institutionalization of natural law and/or violence. The possibility of security *with others* is something beyond either account; both agree that it can be found only within the church writ large. The state, in both Augustinian and Thomist accounts, always seeks security *against others*. As a scholar of International Relations, what I find most remarkable about this Christendom debate is how it set the terms for the founding of the field of IR. The dominant debate on the nature of international order was that between advocates of realism (the balance of power between nations) and liberalism, sometimes known as idealism (the rational regulation of global politics via laws and institutions). Christian realism came down on the side of power in arguing that it was only within states that law can govern human affairs. After the Second World War, the explicit Christian content was largely secularized, to the point that by the 1990s, when I studied at the university, it was barely mentioned and, when it was, it was merely as a curiosity. While we continued to study concepts and theories founded on the ontology and epistemology of Christendom, this foundation went unmentioned, and it was implicit that it had nothing to offer the secular quest for security—whether international, national, or human—which had come to dominate IR.

Our first two chapters have provided some analysis of the structural and dialectical patterns of the history of Christendom as imagined community. In the final two chapters of part 1, we consider Christendom's ideologies of security, both medieval and modern. In the next chapter, we look at just war theory, a body of thought that has sought to blend realism and liberalism, but which has more in common with the former, due, I argue, to its Christendom precepts. In this chapter, I will introduce how Christendom shaped theories of International Relations in the Anglo-American world. As a modern, Western, and English-language story, it is as Eurocentric as most of the histories of Christendom. Firstly, we chart the emergence of

---

5. Aquinas, *Summa Theologiae*, I–III. See also Keys, *Aquinas, Aristotle*, 226–39.

twentieth-century Christian realism, which, in its American and English schools, was seminal to the founding of IR. In particular, we consider Hans Morgenthau and his seminal work, *Politics among Nations* (1948, 1st ed.). Secondly, we look at O'Donovan's Christian realist-liberalist synthesis, especially in his *Desire of the Nations* (1996), which constitutes perhaps the most sophisticated attempt to reinvigorate our theological-political imaginary of Christendom.

Christian Realism and the "Balance of Power"

The imagined community of Western Christendom was integral to the development of the European system of states and empires from the seventeenth century. Inevitably, the main ideas and ideologies for understanding this new order emanated from the centers of power of the West. Building on the modern European cannon of the political and legal thought of scholars such as Thomas Hobbes, Immanuel Kant, and Hugo Grotius, the field was established in the early twentieth century by groups of elite British and American intellectuals and European émigré scholars to the United States to explain the international politics that had brought two world wars. This was the era of the decline of Europe and what was widely envisaged as attendant global disorder in an era of secular reason and technology, overshadowed by the specter of nuclear weapons.

Many of these scholars were convinced Christians as well as being American theologians (Reinhold Niebuhr, John Coleman Bennett), English historians (Arnold Toynbee, Herbert Butterfield, and Martin Wight), émigré jurists (Hans Morgenthau, who was Jewish, and Arnold Wolfers), and American diplomats (George Kennan and John Foster Dulles).[6] It hardly needs saying that they were all white men. Only recently has a feminist Christian realism gained attention.[7] Given their context, it is entirely unsurprising that late-Christendom provided the intellectual and historical lenses through which war and disorder would be explained. Key concepts emerging from these scholars were theologically grounded, with biblical referents. As such, modern IR—a field of the social sciences that is now extremely popular with students of all faiths and none—was founded as branch of Christian political theology. What follows is a brief introduction to the main contributions of these Christian realists, which continue to shape much of the debate of modern IR.

---

6. Many of them are covered in the excellent, Patterson, *The Christian Realists*.
7. Gentry, "Feminist Christian Realism."

The first great debate, upon which the field was formed, was that of the inter-war struggle between idealism and realism. The "idealism" that was the opponent for the emerging intellectual field of IR was as much theological and found in interwar Christian pacifism. The realism out of which IR emerged was that of "human nature realism" or "Christian realism." Against the idealists, Christian realists asserted that states lust for power (*animus dominandi*, borrowed from Augustine) and maximize their interests to seek advantage and, where possible, domination over others. At the same times these scholars—unlikely their largely agnostic or atheist neo-realist successors—argued both that objective laws of international security are founded on fallen and sinful human nature and that "universal moral principles" pertain to political action. In 1948, in the first edition of *Politics among Nations*, the foundational text of IR, which has been published in seven editions (two of them posthumous), Hans Morgenthau stated in his fourth of six famous principles of political realism (still taught to all students of IR) that "universal moral principles cannot be applied to the actions of states in their abstract universal formulation but . . . must be filtered through the concrete circumstances."[8] A German Jewish émigré to the United States who became professor of political science at the University of Chicago, the circumstances with which Morgenthau was occupied were those of European late-Christendom and Western post-Christendom.

Christendom did not merely provide the historical object of Morgenthau's analysis but a certain Judeo-Christian religiosity was germinal to his ideas about the tragic character of global politics.[9] Intellectual histories of IR have identified the influence of both neo-orthodox Protestant and conservative Catholic thought on the Anglo-American Christian realists who founded IR in the mid-twentieth century.[10] Reinhold Niebuhr was the most prominent neo-orthodox contributor to this debate and a thinker who spanned political theology and IR. His public commentary was a major influence on Morgenthau and other early IR scholars. In his 1941 essay "Why the Christian Church Is Not Pacifist" he charged Christian liberals and idealists of "heresy" and absolutism for their failure to recognize the reality of sin and its misapplication of the sermon on the mount in the political arena. "The ultimate principles of the Kingdom of God are never irrelevant to any problem of justice," he argued, "but that does not mean that they can be

---

8. Morgenthau, *Politics among Nations*, 10.

9. Valk, "Religiosity with/out Religion," 319.

10. Epp, "'Augustinian Moment'"; Jones, "Christian Realism"; Guilhot, *The Invention of International Relations Theory*.

made into simple alternatives for the present schemes of relative justice."[11] Niebuhr's political theology of relative justice is formed from his Augustinian understanding of relative power. In "Augustine's Political Realism" he argues for the existence of "natural order" guaranteed by a "dominant group" in any given time and space of the earthly city and contrasts this to the idealism of natural law theory, which finds "normative moral order amid the wide variety of historic forms or even among the most universal of these forms."[12] For Niebuhr, a stable natural order is conditional on "leavening the city of this world with the love of the city of God," something he naturally associates with Christendom and the church.[13] He leaves no room for a global government and provides no reason for stable political orders in non-Christendom regions. In that sense, in a secular and nuclear age, his work appears apocalyptic.[14]

The shadow of Christendom and the prospect of apocalypse are further apparent in a second progenitor of Christian realist thought. The conservative Catholic and German jurist Carl Schmitt (1888–1985) is a specter who haunts IR, given his theological conception of a secular field and his cozy association with National Socialism in the 1930s. Schmitt saw modern (European) international politics as a secularized artefact of Christendom where the political affairs of any given order are second-order effects of transcendent ordering principles. His emphasis on sovereignty and its friend/enemy distinction in his influential earlier work established his significance for the emerging field of IR.[15] But a further important contribution was his use of the *katechon*—a biblical metaphor, used in Paul's second letter to the Thessalonians, for the ordering force ("withholder," "restrainer," "delayer") that holds back the end of the world. He introduced this idea in the 1940s in his *Nomos of the Earth* (not published until 1950) as the "decisive historical concept" of the Christian empire of the Middle Ages: "the historical power to *restrain* the appearance of the antichrist and the end of the present eon."[16] In Schmitt's polemic, there is simply no other role that the empire and emperor can play than that of *katechon*; the Christian empire's existence is entirely dependent on successive emperors understanding and performance of this role.[17] Both individuals (Hegel) and institutions (the Catholic church) were

---

11. Niebuhr, "Why the Christian Church Is Not Pacifist," 111, 115.
12. Niebuhr, "Augustine's Political Realism," 129.
13. Niebuhr, "Augustine's Political Realism," 133.
14. McQueen, *Political Realism*.
15. Schmitt, *Political Theology*; Carl Schmitt, *The Concept of the Political*.
16. Schmitt, *The Nomos of the Earth*, 59–60.
17. Schmitt, *The Nomos*, 60–62.

included in his own list of potential katechons. The two world wars, from a Schmittian perspective, were all about establishing a new territorially based order and *katechon* from among the powers. The first failed in this regard while the second established the United States in this role.

Schmitt's influence is often downplayed. However, Gingerich-Hiebert argues that Schmitt set the terms of political theology, including for those like his contemporary Johann Baptist Metz, who reacted against his conclusion but accepted his claim about the "inherent violence" and "form of apocalyptic preservation" in an unredeemed world.[18] Similarly, Schmitt's work has had a clear influence on IR as a whole and particularly on the most important idea of Christian realism, and one that continues to be a core concepts of the field: *the balance of power*. A theological basis is no more than implied in Morgenthau's "balance of power" but its presence is clearly apparent to his modern interpreters.[19] It was his certainty of the force of God's providence in history that caused Morgenthau to describe the balance as a "general social principle." On the one hand, its instability is due to the "particular conditions" of a society of "sovereign nations." On the other hand, policies to maintain it are "not only inevitable but are an essential stabilizing factor in a society of sovereign nations."[20] The balance of power is not merely the result of the relative distribution of goods of the parties—as secular neo-realists now assert—but the "equilibrium" is a stabilizing force that itself acts.[21] A transcendent power, God's providence, lurks in the background here, but God's power is made immanent in what Morgenthau denotes, invoking Schmitt, as the "balancer" or the "holder" of the balance. The holder somehow sits atop the balance of power to "throw its weight at one time in this scale, at another time in the other scale, guided by only one consideration—the relative position of the scales."[22] Both Morgenthau and Schmitt identified the balancer (*katechon*) of the nineteenth century as Britain and in the twentieth it was the United States.[23]

Morgenthau also followed Schmitt in arguing that the restraining power was not the mere structural property of the balance but was also found in universal moral systems "from the bible to the ethics and constitutional arrangements of modern democracy," which in their "unifying and restraining element" function "to keep aspirations for power within socially

---

18. Gingerich-Hiebert, *The Architectonics*, 28.
19. Guilhot, *After the Enlightenment*, 92; see also Jones, "Christian Realism."
20. Morgenthau, *Politics among Nations*, 179.
21. Morgenthau, *Politics among Nations*, 181.
22. Morgenthau, *Politics among Nations*, 205.
23. Schmitt, *The Nomos*, 238, 259; Morgenthau, *Politics among Nations*, 204–8.

tolerable bounds."[24] Despite writing in the aftermath of the Second World War and in the dark shadow of Auschwitz, he was able to observe that "the civilization with which we are here of course mainly concerned—Western civilization—has been to a large extent successful in this endeavor."[25] The elitist Morgenthau attributed this success to the "monarchs and nobility of Christendom," whose decline, which he attributes to the late-nineteenth century, has become "painfully patent."[26] In dismissing most African states as "dictatorships," Morgenthau also laments the "disappearance of the colonial frontier." Having the outlet of imperial expansion for their *animus dominandi*, he supposes that the states of the Westphalian system were less wont to challenge the balance of power in Europe.[27] Conversely, the decline of the West has been commensurable with decolonization. "The moral and material decline of the West is an observable fact," he remarks. "What is not observable is the kind of order that could take place of the fading one created and maintained by the power of the West."[28] Despite revising his text in four new editions, from 1954 to 1978—the period in which African and much Asian decolonization took place—Morgenthau does not consider the non-Western world as part of the dynamics of a new global order. His vision is Western, Schmittian, tragic, and, due to its "top-down, state-centered perspective," lacking in an account of the moral responsibility of individuals and institutions for their participation in unjust orders.[29]

The British Committee and "Christian International Society"

Morgenthau's opposite number in the UK was Herbert Butterfield, the regius professor of modern history at Cambridge, who, like Morgenthau, received grants from the Rockefeller Foundation to establish a regular colloquium for the emerging field of IR in the post-war period. Butterfield was one of the founders of the British Committee of scholars—often known as the English School—in which Christian realism was predominant. Like Morgenthau, Butterfield identified the balance of power as a property of the system, in so far as the system was the modern European states system, in which responsible actions of "balancing" by smaller states may be crucial.

24. Morgenthau, *Politics among Nations*, 235.
25. Morgenthau, *Politics among Nations*, 239–39.
26. Morgenthau, *Politics among Nations*, 257–58.
27. Morgenthau, *Politics among Nations*, 258, 354.
28. Morgenthau, *Politics among Nations*, 363.
29. Klusmeyer, "Beyond Tragedy," 334.

In a dualism that connotes our distinction between decentered and centered Christendom, he observed "only two alternatives: either a distribution of power to produce equilibrium or surrender to a single universal empire like that of Rome."[30] Furthermore, Butterfield recognized that neither of these alternatives is "a thing bestowed by nature," but is "a matter of refined thought, careful contrivance and elaborate artifice."[31] Such "contrivances" and "artifices" must not be dismissed as they are precisely the forms of decentered Christendom that we saw in the preceding chapter.

While Butterfield's papers for the British Committee were shorn of specific reference to God and the church, his acclaimed post-war lectures, published as *Christianity and History* (1949), make clear that these contrivances and artifices are made fraught by sinful nature and the lust for power while being worked out by a God who is immanent in secular history. "Whether we are Christians or not, whether we believe in Divine Providence or not," he contends, "we are liable to serious technical errors if we do not regard ourselves as born into a providential order."[32] One such technical error, which both Butterfield and Morgenthau sought to correct, was the failure to see "wise and moderate statesmen" who had made "the path of self-interest coincide with the path of virtue."[33] The total wars of the twentieth century were, to Butterfield, instances of the pagan state claiming a universal jurisdiction that is in fact unattainable—a claim that Schmitt's former student Reinhardt Kosselleck associated with his teacher in his review of *Christianity and History*.[34]

Butterfield's co-convenor of the British Committee, Martin Wight, was, like Niebuhr, drawn to idealism (liberal pacifism) in the inter-war period. He registered as a conscientious objector during the Second World War before taking a Christian realist position in his post-1945 intellectual work. His detailed taxonomy of the meanings attributed to the balance of power in European diplomatic history is also indebted to the imaginary of Christendom. In (centered) Latin Christendom, the popes "created the system of balance of power as the security of their temporal power" whereas in (decentered) "Christian international society," from the sixteenth century monarch Elizabeth I to the nineteenth century prime minister Palmerston, Britain's rising power and territorial positioning gave it this role.[35] Wight

30. Butterfield, *Christianity and History*, 142–43.
31. Butterfield, *Christianity and History*, 147.
32. Butterfield, *Christianity and History*, 95–96.
33. Butterfield, *Conflict in the Twentieth Century*, 83.
34. Guilhot, *After the Enlightenment*, 112.
35. Wight, *Power Politics*, 162, 159–63.

concedes that "sometimes a balance has been held by barbarians outside the pale of international society," but he presents this as rare and precarious. He also saw it as "incompatible with the doctrines professed by the Afro-Asian states"—an apparent reference to the politics around the forming of the Cold War-era Non-Aligned Movement in 1961.[36] In his landmark essay "Why Is There No International Theory?" Wight considers how the balance of power may be a persistent attribute of international society without having been convincingly theorized in the modern era. His answer is that, the balance of power "has flourished with the flourishing of the modern state, and it has been seen as a means to that end."[37] Moreover, this merely reflected a wider "intellectual and moral poverty" caused by, "first, the intellectual prejudice imposed by the sovereign state, and secondly, the belief in progress."[38] For Wight, as with all Christian realists, the state's sovereignty was no more than provisional; "progress" was a matter of theology not politics.

A REALIST-LIBERAL SYNTHESIS?
OLIVER O'DONOVAN'S *THE DESIRE OF THE NATIONS*

As we see in the trajectories of Niebuhr and Wight, political liberalism looms large as a foil for political realism. Today it remains the primary interlocutor against which realist claims are made. It is Christian and secular liberals who have sought to retain the idea of the progressive accumulation of international order. David Davies was a Welsh nonconformist and Liberal Party MP who in 1919 established the first chair of international politics in the world at the University of Wales, Aberystwyth.[39] Like Niebuhr and Wight, the incumbents of Davies' chair followed the path from interwar Christian pacifism to a post-war secularized realism. In academic IR, the whole liberal paradigm with which Christian pacifism was associated declined after 1939 before a brief revival from the 1990s, especially in the literature on humanitarian intervention and the ideas of "human security" and "the responsibility to protect." Today, liberal internationalism is found in the secular rhetoric of international organizations, civil society, human rights movements, and politicians, largely in Western democracies. We will explore this "decentering" trend in chapter 7.

Of course, "liberalism" means something quite different in theology. Oliver O'Donovan was Regius Professor of Moral and Pastoral Theology

36. Wight *Power Politics*, 162.
37. Wight, "Why Is There No International Theory?," 39.
38. Wight, "Why Is There No International Theory?," 20.
39. Porter, "David Davies: A Hunter after Peace."

at Oxford from 1982–2006. His *Desire of the Nations* has great relevance for IR in its political analysis, which is, in Christopher Rowland's words, an "apology for a consciously theological, though much chastened, liberal polity."[40] So far, so Niebuhrian. However, his aims are grander and his work altogether more convincing than the nominal account of the state in most Christian realist work. O'Donovan, an evangelical Anglican, stands astride these positions in the sense of being theologically orthodox, politically realist, and classically liberal. He places the reign of God at the book's center to achieve an account of secular authority that is derivative of, not a replacement for, this reign and Christ's attendant Lordship. O'Donovan's is a salvation-history account where the gospel is fulfilled through Christendom and subsequent secular age, rather than this transition being understood as either restorative of the early church model or as decline to faithlessness and the apocalypse. This is also a structural and dialectical account. It is animated by the New Testament's "dialectic between law and communal determination on the one hand, and the Spirit and the endless expense of love on the other."[41] It is this dialectic of law/love—a cousin of Martin's sword/cross, and the Christendom dialectic proposed in chapter 1—that shapes salvation history. O'Donovan provides a sophisticated and convincing yet unfashionable argument that a whole basket of classical goods of liberalism—the modern constitutional state, democracy, the rule of law, and human freedom—were formed in the evolution of Christendom.

Rather than interrogate his hermeneutic—something done by numerous theologians—this analysis will explore his politico-theological arguments pertaining to the nature of law and communal determination as expressed in political authority, as it formed under Christendom. "The political act is a divinely authorized act," he remarks. In that sense,

> a political theology will seek to understand how and why God's rule confers authority upon such acts. It is not its goal to describe an ideal set of political institutions; for political institutions are anyway too fluid to assume an ideal form, since they are the work of Providence in the changing affairs of successive generations.[42]

The liberal state, we may conclude, was created as much by providence as by human design, and is a modern "Christendom state" in the words of Nichols, a sympathetic Roman Catholic interpreter of *Desire of the Nations*.[43]

---

40. Rowland, "Response to *Desire of the Nations*," 77.
41. Rowland, "Response to *Desire of the Nations*," 78.
42. O'Donovan, *Desire of the Nations*, 20.
43. Nichols, *Christendom Awake*, 75.

O'Donovan notes in classical Augustinian terms—and in keeping with what we have called decentered Christendom—that all political theology must speak to the two: *both* the society of the church *and* its rulers.[44] Those in the radical tradition, such as Hauerwas and Yoder, are targeted directly by O'Donovan for their exhortation of martyrdom and their failure to accept the two kingdoms. At the other end of the Christendom spectrum, those in the secular-nationalist tradition of "civil religion"—a modern form of what we have identified as centered Christendom—are not targeted by name but are accused of "introducing defensive actions into the church's armory."[45] They are in error because they assume the simple subservience of the former to the latter through law and institutions. This, of course, is a classical mainline Protestant critique but one pursued with erudition and elegance by O'Donovan.

O'Donovan defines Christendom as "the idea of a professedly Christian secular political order, and the history of that idea in practice."[46] He further denotes it as the political doctrine that is "characterized by a notion the government is responsible," in that it is temporary, provisional, and ultimately subordinate to the reign of Christ. To this idea and these doctrines, he assigns the symbolic start and end dates of 313 and 1791—between the Edict of Milan and the first amendment of the US Constitution.[47] Christendom may be an idea, but it was not a choice and cannot be unchosen. Rather, it was the inevitable product of the expansion of the church such that it could not be ignored by the rulers. Different instances of Christendom provided "equilibrium" between priest and ruler, but this tension remains throughout as only Christ can reconcile the two.[48] Therefore any other authority that claims this unity and finality—centered Christendom, in our terms, Constantinianism, in Yoder's—is identified by O'Donovan with the Antichrist. The Antichrist necessarily produces martyrs out of which the radical rejection of Christendom grows. This is again in line with a long Christian tradition right back to the Revelation of St. John through Pope Gelasius in the fifth century, long prior to the Reformers' critique of the papacy.[49]

Desire of the Nations offers a theological explanandum for the variety of forms and historical trajectories of Christendom, merely schematized in chapters 1 and 2 of this book, which is unsurpassed. It provides a necessarily

---

44. O'Donovan, *Desire of the Nations*, 193.
45. O'Donovan, *Desire of the Nations*, 218.
46. O'Donovan, *Desire of the Nations*, 195.
47. O'Donovan, *Desire of the Nations*, 19.5.
48. O'Donovan, *Desire of the Nations*, 203–4.
49. O'Donovan, *Desire of the Nations*, 214.

theological, indeed biblical, account of the liberal state and responsible government which is absent from most free-church narrative theology. But here its otherwise considerable agreements with the post-Christendom perspective is superseded by its desire for Christendom renewed.[50] To avoid the twin perils of the Antichrist and martyrdom, the challenge of Christendom is "one of mutual service between the two authorities [of priest and ruler], predicated on the difference and balance of their roles."[51] Mutual service between the two kingdoms does not necessarily require formal alliance, but O'Donovan's decentered Christendom avoids the Lutheran's neglect of the political on the one hand and the realist's neglect of theology on the other. The church must rest its security in Christ and leave its politics to the state.

> Its security is guaranteed by the ascended Christ and needs no further underwriting. Still less does the church need its declarations of Christ's judgment to become a matter for civil prosecution. The character of the church that "judges not" is impugned if secular authorities follow up its declarations with coercive actions of their own.[52]

As such, "the most truly Christian state understands itself most thoroughly as 'secular.'"[53] The quotation marks of "secular" indicate that O'Donovan's understanding here is the classical one of the *saeculum* being the realm of history (as opposed to eternity)—rather than the modern and disenchanted social order from which the sacred is considered expunged. Similarly, in language that evokes both Western exceptionalism and "powers theology," O'Donovan finds in modernity "*both* the triumph of Christ in liberal institutions and the coming of the Antichrist."[54]

The triumph occurs across several phases. In O'Donovan's New Testament dialectic, in each of the phases we see love restraining law.[55] First, there is the defeat of the notion of centered Christendom as world-empire by "plural secular order" and subsequently the emergence of international law between states depending on natural law (made manifest in international

---

50. For a thorough overview of Yoder and O'Donovan's agreements and differences, see Kroeker, *Messianic Political Theology*; see also Hauerwas and Fodor, "Remaining in Babylon."

51. O'Donovan, *Desire of the Nations*, 217.

52. O'Donovan, *Desire of the Nations*, 218.

53. O'Donovan, *Desire of the Nations*, 219.

54. O'Donovan, *Desire of the Nations*, 228.

55. These "phases" may be read in terms of the Christendom dialectic of centered/decentered which were narrated in chapters 1 and 2 although such terms are too schematic to do justice to the nuance of O'Donovan's analysis.

politics by the work of the Dutch jurist Hugo Grotius and in the treaty-making of seventeenth- and eighteenth-century "Christian international society"). Second, O'Donovan identifies the emergence of constitutional kingship by which "political authority begins to be perceived as office"; but contra liberal secular theory, this derives only secondarily from the Enlightenment's voluntarism and primarily from the "older theological principle" that "government is given from above." Third, there is, from the fourteenth century, the progressive emergence of the legal-constitutional order itself whereby kingly rights were not absolute, the rights of their subjects must be protected, and mechanisms for the removal of tyrants must be attained. In O'Donovan's terms, "the legal-constitutional conception is the essence of Christendom's legacy."[56] Christendom, in this "secular" or decentered conception, is a matter of the submission of the rulers to Christ in the form of laws and constitutions not submission of the church to the rulers.

Some problems from a post-Christendom perspective

Desire of the Nations provides a compelling argument from a two-kingdoms perspective. The fundamental eschatological problem with this stance from a post-Christendom perspective will be elaborated in part 3. But for now we may identify three features in O'Donovan's work that are especially important as they mirror the structural precepts found in the historiography of Christendom (chapters 1 and 2) and in the "Christian realist" and just war traditions (chapters 3 and 4). As criticisms of O'Donovan's work, these are somewhat unfair as they emanate from social science, not his field of theology, but not unwarranted. The points are made here to advance the dialogue between political theology and IR and move us further toward a new Christian realism.

First, O'Donovan's two kingdoms model of decentered Christendom is ontologically *statist*. As Kroeker argues, O'Donovan "too narrowly construes the political in terms of the secular state or judicial authority."[57] This may sound like an odd charge to make of an author whose conception of the state is a liberal one. On the one hand, he recognizes that the state is but one form of political rule and, to the extent to which it can be said to exist in antiquity and the Middle Ages, one that has changed its form dramatically in becoming the modern secular state with an excess of infrastructural power. On the other hand, he notes that "internationalism" has reasserted itself

---

56. O'Donovan, *Desire of the Nations*, 235–40.
57. Kroeker, *Messianic Political Theology*, 58.

and the state "has been in trouble ever since Christ rose from the dead."[58] However, he offers no political theology of sub-national, transnational, and non-national political authorities that other theologians have attempted;[59] he draws his examples exclusively from fully formed public institutions of nation-state and empire. As will be argued in this book, the powers and authorities of scripture, of history, and of modern global politics are found in both public authorities and private enterprises, both autonomous city-states and expansive empires, anticolonial movements and environmental activists, global celebrity superstars and self-styled "captains of industry," and much else besides. Moreover, states themselves are increasingly transnational, not exclusively national, something that remains hidden if one takes an exclusively territorial view of them. O'Donovan seems to fall into this trap via his Thomist reading of the emergence of constitutional law where "in appointing itself a head, society entered into a provision for political structure that God had decreed" and "had no political authority otherwise."[60] His interpretation of Romans 13 repeats this state-centrism where "government" is analyzed as national to the model of Israel.[61] O'Donovan has nothing to say about the radical decentering of the state that we will explore in chapter 7.

Second, O'Donovan repeats the error found across almost all English-language writing on Christendom: *Eurocentrism* or Western bias. Eastern Orthodoxy barely makes it into O'Donovan's analysis, with a few brief references to Byzantium, to Justinian, and to other Eastern emperors. Elsewhere, he points to the danger of cultural imperialism with respect to "societies outside the European sphere of influence, which do not have the historical experience of Christendom behind them."[62] But, as we have seen, Christendom has been a Eurasian not European phenomenon for most of its history while the Global South has experienced Christendom through its exposure to empires and mission by self-described Christian emperors. To simply exclude the East and the South from our analysis risks over-emphasizing the virtues of "secular" Christendom and overlooking theocratic elements that remain, for example, in the autocephalous Eastern Orthodox churches.[63]

58. O'Donovan, *Desire of the Nations*, 241.
59. Bretherton, *Christianity and Contemporary Politics*.
60. O'Donovan, *Desire of the Nations*, 237.
61. O'Donovan, *Desire of the Nations*, 147–49.
62. O'Donovan, *Desire of the Nations*, 230.
63. For example, the Cypriot branch of the Greek Orthodox church uses its influence in the state to teach a form of ethnophyletism, which has arguably exacerbated the politics of a divided society. By contrast, the Muslim-majority Turkish Republic of Northern Cyprus has a relatively "liberal" education policy. Loukaidis and Zembylas, "Greek-Cypriot Teachers' Perceptions of Religion."

Thirdly, in reading providence exclusively through Western Christendom, and as a consequence of his liberal and Eurocentric view of the state, O'Donovan understates the *problem of evil* and the extent to which all powers (including the liberal state) may be simultaneously responsible to one community and beastly to another. He remains silent on the wider processes of imperial expansion and control and their relation to Christian mission, decolonization, and the rapid acceleration and expansion of capitalism. While expanding franchises and rights at home, European legal-constitutional orders were dispossessing native peoples of lands, collaborating with indigenous leaders to enslave the poor and their ethnic rivals, and willfully bringing disease and taking more direct measures to eradicate entire ethnic groups. It is hard to see how a political theology that is so deeply attentive to the history of Christendom can ignore these processes, which were prosecuted by self-styled Christian nations on those beyond their borders. The desire for legal-constitutional order is, after all, not one that is limited to Christian peoples but is also felt by those nations dispossessed, enslaved, or wiped out by Christian nations.

Why consider O'Donovan here at the end of a chapter on Christian realism? *Desire of the Nations* is a work of theology and very different from the political writing of Niebuhr and the early IR scholarship of Morgenthau and colleagues. But what it shares with the Christian realists are the ideological bases of an imagined community—statism, Eurocentrism, and a relatively benign account of the history of Western Christendom. This creates a contradiction that one later reviewer summarized as "qualified Christian support for a political order that might represent the antichrist."[64] Should a Christian liberal make peace with modern secular liberalism (as theological liberals have) or should she seek a return to an explicitly theological liberalism that may only be possible under Christendom conditions? In answer to the charge that he sought to reinstate Christendom, O'Donovan answers,

> the important thing is not to be for Christendom or against it—what earthly point could there be in either of those postures, if Christendom is, as everybody seems to agree, not only dead, but quite decomposed?—but to have such a sympathetic understanding of it that we profit from its politico-theological gains and avoid repeating its politico-theological mistakes.[65]

In that sense, O'Donovan stands across both Christian liberal and realist thought that simply cannot see beyond Christendom, either theologically or political. This scholarship is valuable in the corrective it offers to

---

64. Cole, "Political Theology and Political Authority."
65. O'Donovan, "Response to Respondents: Behold, the Lamb!"

those traditions that caricature "Constantinianism" as nothing but heresy.[66] However, if our "sympathetic understanding" is such that it fails to wrestle with the frequent recurrence of imperial Antichrists in Christendom's history, how can we avoid repeating its politico-theological mistakes? Notwithstanding what Christendom may teach us about the past, as its imagined community and attendant ideologies are increasingly confined to history, its gains are increasingly ambivalent, and its mistakes point to a wider failure of interpretation. The post-Christendom challenge for both Christian liberals and realists is one of eschatology, the question of the ultimate purpose and destiny of humankind.

Security without Eschatology?

It was mid-twentieth-century Christian realism that began to write international theory—that is, theory of the limited state pursuing the national interest and the balance of power under conditions of divine providence. Later scholars of IR thoroughly ploughed over this with their positivist neo-realism. *Politics among Nations* was succeeded by canonical works of Kenneth Waltz,[67] and more recently John Mearsheimer.[68] These scholars shed realism of its assumption of sinful human nature, simply omitted its theodicy of God's providence in international order,[69] and secularized its concept of the national interest (*animus dominandi*) and balance of power (*katechon*) by making them endogenous properties of the system rather than produced by a transcendent God and held by the immanent *katechon*. These concepts continue to be the most influential paradigm of IR in the United States and globally. They have been passed on to generations of diplomats and leaders via programs of study and formal geopolitical discourse.

The most thoughtful of the later realists have been fully aware of the problems that arise when Morgenthau's thought is shed of its theological foundations. Indeed, Mearsheimer identifies a logical fallacy in Morgenthau's balance, asking, "if all states have a vital interest in taking advantage of each other [given their insatiable *animus dominandi*] whenever the opportunity presents itself, how can there be status quo powers in the

66. Kroeker, *Messianic Political Ethics*.
67. Waltz, *Theory of International Politics*.
68. Mearsheimer, *The Tragedy of Great Power Politics*.
69. It is by no means clear that all Christian realists would have opposed this secularization, although almost all of them had ceased publishing by the time the neo-realists displaced them. Wight quoted Kant critically to remark on "the slide-over to theodicy that seems to occur after a certain point with all international theory." Wight, "Why Is There No International Theory?," 33.

system?" Morgenthau, he quite accurately states, "has no explanation for this apparent contradiction."[70] As a political theologian, Morgenthau had no intention of providing explanation that would be acceptable to a positivist political scientist for the source of the balance. This is because the source was not endogenous to the political but found, Nicolas Guilhot argues, in the "eschatological fulfilment of human history that was beyond [the] reach [of the political]."[71] O'Donovan's theologically conservative but politically liberal *Desire of the Nations* is fully cognizant of these limits, as being those bestowed by Christendom, and seeks merely to reflect upon them rather than exceed them.

The Christendom context for this foundational thinking in the study of international security is clear. The concepts of the balance of power and Christian international society are "indexed to the concrete situation of a Eurocentric and Christian order" and they thereby assume "racialized and imperial land-partitions."[72] The intellectual historian Guilhot contends that the evisceration of theology from political thinking has far-reaching consequences for the state system, not just our ideas of it. "It is the theological background of Western Christendom," he notes "against which the state has developed as a principle of concrete territorial ordering that can provide legitimacy." In the apocalypse envisioned by Schmitt and Morgenthau, and we might add O'Donovan et al., "absolute secularization can only lead to the collapse of this principle," and thereby disorder and violence without restraint.[73]

Guilhot's analysis is powerful, but it is not without controversy. The theological reading of Christian realism has been questioned by those who interpret IR in entirely secular terms and note the Jewish émigré Morgenthau's distaste for Schmitt's collaboration the Nazi regime.[74] But the shadow of the German jurist is clear in Christian realism, as it is in political theology.[75] And there is little doubt that these founders built their theories exclusively on the historical experience and constitutive ideas of Christendom and Christian international society. Despite the variety of their religious commitments—from the agnostic Toynbee to the evangelical Niebuhr to

---

70. Mearsheimer, *The Tragedy*, 409n35.
71. Guilhot, *After the Enlightenment*, 114.
72. Guilhot, "American Katechon," 234.
73. Guilhot, "American Katechon," 243.
74. Williams, "Why Ideas Matter in International Relations," 645.
75. Gingerich-Hiebert, *Architectonics of Hope*.

the dissenting Butterfield—they all feared for the implications for national and international community as Christendom declined.[76]

However, there is a more serious problem with Guilhot's analysis: his confusion of the eschatological (the reading of history in terms of an ultimate divine purpose) and the apocalyptic (specific claims about the means and ends of times). From the perspective of eschatology, the problem of the Christian realists is not that their eschatology is apocalyptic but that their apocalypse is absent of eschatology. Realism as a paradigm was a twentieth-century response of Christian ethicists to the publication of Schweitzer's 1906 publication of *The Quest of the Historical Jesus*, which argued that Jesus had incorrectly predicted the end of the world and that his specifically Jewish eschatology was unacceptable to modern Christians. Christian ethics must therefore be non-eschatological and Christ's call for the radical transformation of politics could not therefore apply to the modern world.[77] John Howard Yoder denoted this as "peace without eschatology."

> The attitude that seeks peace without eschatology is that which would identify church and world, or fuse the two aeons in the present age, without the act of God whereby evil is removed from the scene. This means a confusion between the providential purpose of the state, that of achieving a "tolerable balance of egoisms" (an expression borrowed with gratitude from Reinhold Niebuhr) and the redemptive purpose of the church, the rejection of egoism in the commitment to discipleship. The confusion leads to the paganization of the church and the demonization of the state.[78]

This risk of confusion is the problem of Christendom, which we may redefine as *security* without eschatology, for peace in a biblical sense (*shalom, eirene*) is no more than an occasional moment in history, according to a Niebuhrian perspective.

What might the fact that Christ is the Lord of history and triumphant over evil mean for the end of Christendom and the emergence of secular international order? What might we expect the church to say to the state in these circumstances? Christian realism neither asked nor answered these questions, as it bracketed them as questions of personal salvation and redemption in contrast to the realist's questions of the world's affairs.[79]

76. For a survey of these Christian realists, see Patterson, *The Christian Realists*.
77. Carter, *The Politics of the Cross*, 144.
78. Yoder, "Peace without Eschatology?"
79. An exception to this may be the work of Herbert Butterfield whose free-church perspective is extolled by Yoder, "Peace without Eschatology?," 154–55, 158.

Niebuhr, Morgenthau, and colleagues continued a long modern history since at least the sixteenth-century Italian statesman Niccolo Machiavelli of "secularized apocalypticism"—an end brought about entirely by human action, be it of the gas chambers or nuclear weapons—in which "the Judeo-Christian apocalypse insinuated itself."[80] Christian ethics, in this context, are "pagan" in that they draw on non-biblical ancient and modern concepts—virtue, providence, prudence, etc.—to make sense of the world.[81] In order to avoid such error, according to the post-Christendom perspective advanced here, Christian ethics must address such non-biblical concepts—including security itself—as emergent from an underlying theology where God's sovereignty and Christ's Lordship are central.[82] Without such reasoning, what is left are anti-theologies: "intimations of sublimity beyond representation, so functioning to confirm negatively the questionable idea of an autonomous secular realm," as Milbank argues.[83] Perhaps the most prominent example of such secularized reasoning from pagan origins in the realm of security is found in what came to be known as just war theory.

---

80. McQueen, *Realism in Apocalyptic Times*, 148.
81. Brent, *A Political History*.
82. Gorringe, *God's Theatre*, 4–5.
83. Milbank, *Theology and Social Theory*, 3, 1.

CHAPTER 4

Retreating Ethics

Because they lead my people astray, saying "Peace," when there is no peace, and because, when a flimsy wall is built, they cover it with whitewash, therefore tell those who cover it with whitewash that it is going to fall. Rain will come on torrents, and I will send hailstones hurtling down, and violent winds will burst forth. When the wall collapses, will people not ask you, "Where is the whitewash you covered it with?"

EZEKIEL 13:10-12

It is life outside the Christian community which fails to be truly public, authentically political. The opposition is not between public and private, church and world, but between political virtue and political vice. At the end of the day, it is the secular order that will be shown to be "atomistic" in its foundations. *juris consensus.*

ROWAN WILLIAMS[1]

In the year 2000, Britain intervened militarily in Sierra Leone. It was the only one of Prime Minister Tony's Blair's four wars launched over four years from 1999–2003 that was deemed uncontroversial. NATO's war against Serbia over Kosovo (1999) lacked a UN Security Council resolution, due to the potential Russian veto. The post-9/11 war in Afghanistan (2001) was predictably protracted and unsuccessful in the face of the neo-Taliban

1. Williams, "The Politics of the Soul," 735.

insurgency and eventually ended in a calamitous withdrawal and humanitarian catastrophe. The US-led Iraq war descended even more rapidly into civil war and the eventual rise of Islamic State against a broadly pro-Western but corrupt and predatory government. Political and ethical arguments for the Afghan and especially Iraq wars concealed tragic blunders in the foreign policies of Western states and were the modern equivalents of Ezekiel's "whitewash."[2]

The Sierra Leone intervention was different. It took place at the request of the Sierra Leonean government to support the peacekeepers of the United Nations Assistance Mission in the country. After securing the airport and some early confrontations with the leading rebel group, the RUF, the mission was put in jeopardy when a patrol of British troops were taken hostage by a group called the West Side Boys. Three weeks' later, a special forces mission freed the hostages with no UK casualties. Most experts and observers agree that the effective insertion of force in support of a UNSC-sanctioned process tipped the balance in favor of the government and forced the RUF to sign a peace treaty and enter a disarmament, demobilization, and reintegration process. The UK withdrew its training and support mission in 2001 and peace has held in Sierra Leone, although the country remains poor and structurally violent.

Having worked in West Africa, under an inspirational Sierra Leonean pastor and mission chief on a UN refugee camp for Sierra Leoneans, I was relieved to see this mission take place and succeed in a relative sense. A former British colony, the country became independent in 1961 but quickly fell into military coups and a dictatorship after the system of balancing power between paramount chiefs broke down. A horrendous civil war, fueled by both elite predation (particularly over the diamond trade) and popular grievance, began in 1991. In late 1998, frustrated after seven years of warfare and with a lull in the fighting, around a dozen of the male refugees in our small camp, including my devout friend Samson, voluntarily repatriated themselves, against UN advice, by walking and motor transportation back to Freetown. In January 1999, the war returned with a heavy RUF attack on Freetown where up to 10,000 people were killed. I never heard from Samson and the other refugees again and so have no idea whether they survived the RUF and witnessed the arrival of the British troops a year later.

I give this example to illustrate the chaos and uncertainty surrounding war and the difficulty of making any assessment of its justice. Common sense tells us that the brutal civil war in Sierra Leone was unjust while the British intervention was just. In other words, African darkness finally succumbed

---

2. Porter, *Blunder*.

to European-inspired light. But such interpretations of just war won't do, not just because they are racist, but because they are incomplete and highly deceptive. They take the episodes of war out of their wider historical and international contexts and offer an atomistic analysis of fractured and divided world. It is hard to distinguish political virtue from political vice in such a world, as Williams notes.

In the 1990s, Britain had largely disregarded Sierra Leone, one its many former colonies that had been bequeathed a corrupt elite and weak state by Britain's rushed and somewhat reluctant decolonization of the late twentieth century. Ignoring any moral and political responsibilities in Africa, the UK focused its military on conflicts in Europe—both its own in Northern Ireland and in the former Yugoslavia—where violence was closer to home and its victims were white. In the 2000s, Tony Blair, emboldened by the success of Sierra Leone, went on to launch the disastrous campaigns of Afghanistan and Iraq, ostensibly to come to the aid of brown peoples in the East but in a manner that was driven by Western national and international security priorities. And the British army too can be brutal. Just one special forces squadron in Afghanistan allegedly executed fifty-four unarmed persons after capture during a single six-month tour in 2010–11, according to a four-year BBC investigation.[3]

Proponents of the idea of just war dismiss the suggestion that such murder is commonplace by all armies, including those of Western democracies. Nigel Biggar, the Oxford professor who succeeded Oliver O'Donovan, argues, "well-trained soldiers can discipline themselves to use only necessary force to compel the unjust enemy to stop fighting, and to avoid harming non-combatants whenever possible."[4] They do so, it is implied, as they have been formed in those parts of the world that have experienced Christendom and the secular professional ethics that emerge out of this history. It is this sense of civilizational superiority that appears to lie behind ideas of humanitarian intervention, a "force for good," and the rules-based international order are the focus of this chapter on war and just war. As Valerie Morkevičius argues, modern just war theory (JWT) has been influenced by liberal thought via the development of international law but is best understood as a form of realism in its Christian, Islamic, or Hindu heritages.[5] It is thus not essentially Christian but, in Michael Walzer's words, "just war theory began in the service of the powers."[6]

3. BBC *Panorama*, "SAS Death Squads Exposed: A British War Crime?"
4. Biggar, "This Christian Teaching Suggests It's Ethical."
5. Morkevičius, *Realist Ethics*.
6. Walzer, *Arguing about War*, 3.

This chapter will explore this realist and Christendom heritage of Christian JWT.[7] For the church (outside of the peace-church tradition), war is acceptable only when it is just. We will consider how the narrow concept of Christendom remains central to modern JWT, however secularized. This conception places limits on the "practical realism" of Biggar's *In Defence of War*, which we will explore in this chapter. It shall be argued that the distinctively Christian contribution of political theology to ethical thinking on war has almost ceased not merely because of secularization and globalization, but because of the normative and descriptive limits of Eurocentric Christendom—a security imaginary that is constrained by both its Western bias and its fixation with the state.

CHRISTIAN JUST WAR THEORY AS AN ARTEFACT OF DECENTERED CHRISTENDOM

If the balance of power is the governing or strategic principle of international order, according to Christian realists, then the operative principles for the use of armed force in this order are found in JWT. While both have Augustinian roots, just war has a much longer genealogy through classical philosophy, medieval jurisprudence, and modern international law. St. Augustine's just war thinking was a Christianization of Plato's pagan military ethics.[8] That is, its virtues were those that recognized the conditions of the fall and reversed the pre-Christendom tradition of Christian distance from the Roman army and its campaigns. With the Constantinian shift enabled and the demanded engagement by the church, Augustine argued against Cicero's contention that war may only be pursed for safety or honor, noting "the safety of the City of God is such that it can be retained, or rather acquired, by faith and with faith"; and yet he provided moral resources for emerging Christendom in portraying war as a necessity of natural order in the earthly city.[9] As such, the Christian JWT is entirely concomitant with the imagined security community of Christendom, especially in its decentered form.[10]

Nevertheless, the just war tradition was intended to have the purpose less of enabling and more of *limiting* war. In "Christian international society," the tradition sought to restrain war so that it was "fought only by those

7. This chapter has especially benefitted from the comments of Nick Megoran and his incisive recent critique of JWT. Megoran, *Warlike Christians*.

8. Syse, "The Platonic Roots of Just War Doctrine."

9. Augustine, *City of God*, XXI, 6; IV, 15.

10. Other traditions, particularly that of holy war, appear more prominent under centered Christendom imaginaries.

with proper authority, for a just cause and by just means."[11] The distinction between just cause (*ad bellum*), including the requirements of defensive action as a last resort, and just means (*in bello*), including the limited and discriminating use of force, was important in the emergence of the tradition. Hugo Grotius was the most important exponent of just war in internal law in the early modern period and it is the work of Grotius and others in this regard that are cited by O'Donovan as "the last and greatest of the legal accomplishments of Christendom."[12] Indeed, it is not an exaggeration to say that just war was the international legal partner to the international political institution of the balance of power and that together they are the two greatest creations of the international security imaginary of Christendom.

Just like Christendom, just war is considered to have been in perpetual decline since the Middle Ages. Thus, some Christian realists have been skeptical as to its relevance today. For Morgenthau, "with the ascendancy of the modern states system it was watered down to the vanishing point."[13] Bull, with his "international society" approach, demurs from this position, noting that just war remains a norm among most states; and yet the norm had been "overridden" by global political changes where civil war had become far more common than inter-state war.[14] The new debate was about the justice of intervening to prevent or end war and to protect civilians. As humanitarian intervention rose up the agenda in the 1980s, Bull was prescient in predicting that international society would struggle to find the "shared understanding of what justice entails, and no consensus on what level of human suffering would justify humanitarian intervention."[15]

The just war tradition has been applied to third-party interventions, the "responsibility to protect" (R2P), and terrorism in recent years. However, a shared understanding of when to prescribe and when to proscribe is conspicuous by its absence. JWT arguments were made both *for* and *against* the 2003 US-led military intervention in Iraq, for example, and began to lose credibility as the "last resort" and "reasonable chance of success" claims were exposed, respectively, by the failure to uncover an active Weapons of Mass Destruction program and the long-running insurgency, which continues to bight the country almost twenty years on.[16] As an artefact of Christendom, JWT is subject to the fraught process of rewriting doctrine in the

11. Bull, *Anarchical Society*, 34.
12. O'Donovan, *Desire of the Nations*, 236.
13. Morgenthau, *Politics among Nations*, 379.
14. Bull, *Anarchical Society*, 191–92.
15. Dunne, *Inventing International Society*, 153.
16. Fisher and Biggar, "Was Iraq an Unjust War?"; Peterson, "Did Iraq Ever Become a Just War?"

post-Christendom environment where secular modes of technology, rationality, and expedience make any exercise in applying criteria—although many just war advocates abhor this approach, it is a constant of contemporary governance—formulaic and a simulacrum of considered ethical reasoning.[17] As we shall discuss more extensively in subsequent chapters, it is a secularized logic of security that has overtaken this rewriting of political order.

Before that, it is important to understand the form of this debate. In particular, it is necessary to recognize that JWT has mutated from the "natural law" of Christendom to a secular legal positivism.[18] Furthermore, as "soft" international law, without either clear scope or means of enforcement, it necessarily raises the question of "whether the legal prescription of force is but a benevolent and elaborate duplicity conducted by states before other states, so that legal argument can be rallied to their cause no matter what the circumstances."[19] "International law," Kristios elaborates, is "best seen as a discursive exercise, in which states are able to make, address, and assess justifications and it is through this process that international law can develop and store its own 'self-knowledge.'"[20] In political terms, a "discursive exercise" is still better seen as a discursive struggle between factions in a plural international order. In this struggle and this order, differences are apparent both within and between JWT and Christian realist traditions.

Christian realist advocates for "secular" Christendom argue that it is necessary to authorise force under certain conditions and even to make it a duty to serve in the armed forces and use force for the maintenance of order. Niebuhr favored the Catholic just war tradition over the Lutheran one, despite his skepticism regarding natural law.[21] Passions are such, he argued, "that even the obvious case of aggression can be made to appear a necessity of defence."[22] The agonized position of Niebuhr is that "failure to employ discriminate and proportionate force, including lethal force, when required by demands of justice motivated by charity is blameworthy (or vicious) while the decision to fight in a just war is praiseworthy (or virtuous)."[23] Similarly, the Chicago professor and advocate of "Augustinian realism" Jean Bethke

---

17. For divergent perspectives, see Megoran, *Warlike Christians*, 100–104, and Reed, *Theology for International Law*, 26–30.
18. Elshtain, "The Just War Tradition and Natural Law."
19. Kritsiotis, "When States Use Armed Force," 49.
20. Kritsiotis, "When States Use Armed Force," 49.
21. Niebuhr, *The Nature and Destiny of Man*.
22. Niebuhr, *The Nature and Destiny of Man*, 283.
23. Pavlischek, "Reinhold Niebuhr, Christian Realism," 58.

Elshtain argued that without this tradition just war arguments merge with liberalism "and quickly degenerate into internationalist sentimentalism."[24] However, the just war tradition is broad and is inhabited both by those who tend toward *realpolitik* and those influenced by pacifism. On the one hand, Schmitt turns the doctrine on its head in arguing that the right to wage war (*jus ad bellum*) was essential to any legitimate international legal order.[25] On the other, Niebuhr's highly conditional acceptance of the tradition is criticized for his extant liberal theology with regard to war and the restrictions he would place on *jus ad bellum*.[26] The difference between the highly permissive Schmitt and highly restrictive Niebuhr seems to emanate from their respectively expansive and limited accounts of secular sovereignty—Schmitt's being consistent with the centered Christendom imaginary and Niebuhr's with one decentered to the secular age. As contemporaries, this distinction can only partly be attributed to their differences of context and may be seen as reflective of their differences of political theology within the broad Christian realist tradition.

Unsurprisingly, given his stated intent in *Desire of the Nations* to derive a political ethics, O'Donovan's just war reasoning is also derivative of his political theology of Christendom, which appears to be closer to Niebuhr's decentered tradition than Schmitt's. War is a social institution that is elemental to theologico-political order and cannot be objected outright, according to natural law. "The praxis of mortal combat is not destructive to human sociality as such," he contends, "it is simply a moment at which human sociality regroups and renews itself."[27] Further the supposed duality of the antagonists in war is superseded by the counter-praxis of salvation history, "that would overcome the confrontation of the two with the rule of one, revealing the unifying order of the kingdom of God."[28] O'Donovan rejects pacifism as an evangelical counter-praxis oppositional to the authorities (not being constitutive of them) that are ordained by God. Conversely, just war is constitutive of war and its putative outcome of peace. As a political act, rather, "armed conflict can and must be reconceived as an extraordinary extension of ordinary acts of judgment; it can and must be subject to the limits and disciplines of ordinary acts of judgment."[29] The peace implied

---

24. Elshtain, "The Third Annual Grotius Lecture," 11.
25. Schmitt, *Concept of the Political*.
26. Pavlischek, "Reinhold Niebuhr, Christian Realism."
27. Oliver O'Donovan, *The Just War Revisited*, 4–5.
28. O'Donovan, *The Just War*, 5.
29. O'Donovan, *The Just War*, 6.

here as the ultimate objective is that "among sovereign nations."[30] As such the purpose of the just war tradition is that of regulating international peace in general, not about assessing acts of war case-by-case. "History knows of no just wars," O'Donovan concludes, "as it knows of no just peoples."[31] Despite this, he contends that the struggle of making war "civil"—not in the sense of "civil war" but in contrast to uncivil—is a worthy one.

This brief summary of how O'Donovan defines and delimits just war is necessary to establish that it is derivative of his political theology and therefore reaffirms the premises of state-centrism, Eurocentrism, and the providence of the victor, which we identified in the preceding chapter. This is not a mere descriptive problem: that Europeans and states are no longer predominant. It is a normative and thoroughly politico-theological one: that the imagination of Christendom was and remains one of the domination of the powerful, which was a precursor to a violent secular world where the security of the few is the prime value and pursued with little limit or restraint.[32] We will explore this proposition further in subsequent chapters, but suffice to say at this stage that the claim being made by Christendom thinkers through the just war tradition is that with right authority and good judgment war will maintain order and advance justice. The most compelling recent statement of that case has been made by O'Donovan's successor at Oxford, Nigel Biggar. And it is one that reveals quite how exposed JWT has become in the "post-Christendom" context.

NIGEL BIGGAR'S *IN DEFENCE OF WAR*

In Defence of War has been portrayed as a once-in-a-generation book and compared to Paul Ramsey's landmark text, which revived the tradition almost fifty years before.[33] Like Ramsey, Biggar understands the state's use of force as a fact of the fallen world that must either be deployed by oneself or succumbed to when faced by others. As such, he argues that omission (not going to war) and commission (going to war) "are equally obliged to given an account of themselves."[34] His concern is "that just theory's moral prescriptions be realistic—and be realizable in practice."[35] *In Defence of War* therefore begins in resolutely realist terms with the slaying of the putative

30. O'Donovan, *The Just War*, 7.
31. O'Donovan, *The Just War*, 13.
32. O'Donovan, *The Just War*, 12.
33. Ramsey, *The Just War*.
34. Biggar, *In Defence of War*, 7.
35. Biggar, *In Defence of War*, 14.

opponents of this position, the theological pacifists. As both Stanley Hauerwas and John Howard Yoder consider the church to be a political actor, Biggar is correct to identify that the crucial question regarding their pacifism is "whether we regard God's peace—at least in part—a *present* reality."[36] If so, then it is not the omission of war but the commission of peace that must give an account of itself and how it is realistic and realizable in practice. Biggar, however, dismisses this possibility and is not interested in a serious investigation of peacemaking in practice, as he makes clear on his very first page.[37] This is, by his own account, a repetition of the error of the pacifists with respect to war. Biggar's interest is in cases of war: the military strategy and ethics of the Somme, Kosovo, and Iraq, discussed in the latter half of the book. However, it is here that Biggar departs from the realist tradition in favor of an idealism borne of Christendom. Theologically and morally, he contends, the matter at stake is "the right use of violence as an expression of love for the neighbor."[38] As it is the just cause, right authority, and prospects for success of this violence that he makes central to his argument, a brief consideration of the problems with how he treats these cases is essential to any discussion of his book.

In keeping with a certain methodologically averse tradition in the humanities, but in some contrast to the social scientific study of war, Biggar offers no scope conditions or case-selection criteria. But unlike his colleagues in moral theology, he is happy to make strong claims about cause and effect. What he lacks in method, he makes up for in the length and detail of his moral and legal reasoning. He picks important cases from those that stand up to the Western mind while neglecting contemporaneous examples (from the East and South, where similar or greater numbers were killed and where governments also claim to be acting morally) such as the Great War on the Russian front until 1917 or the second Congo War of 1998–2003. In both cases far more died than the contemporary Iraq War. The unstated selection criteria here appear to include the leading role by a Western state of (post-)Christendom and to exclude civil wars, despite the fact that since 1945 the vast majority of wars have been of this type rather than between states.[39]

Historical and methodological naivetes are suggested by Biggar's discussion of the cases. Kosovo (1999) is largely divorced from the Yugoslav wars that irrupted in 1991 even though the crisis with respect to the Kosovar Albanians was precipitated by the omission of Kosovo from the

36. Biggar, *In Defence of War*, 20.
37. Biggar, *In Defence of War*, 1.
38. Biggar, *In Defence of War*, 61.

39. This basic fact of armed conflict—completely disregarded by almost all just war writing—will be elaborated in the discussion of protection after Christendom in chapter 11.

1995 Dayton Peace Accords. The question Biggar asks is whether Western intervention can be done well, rather than a full assessment of a war in which Christians (including the Serbian Orthodox Church and state) stood on several sides. Statesmen Paddy Ashdown and Rory Stewart are called as witnesses for the realistic prospects of success in Kosovo and Iraq, while the voluminous academic literatures on both cases are ignored.[40] Realists in IR at the time and since have routinely dismissed the Iraq War as an exercise in "warlike idealism"; Britain's participation is characterized as blunder brought about by a collection of delusions, including those of the efficacy of "regime change," the distinct character of "rogue states," and the necessity of paying a "blood price" for the alliance with the United States.[41] However, Biggar argues that, in addition to having these reasonable prospects for success, for these wars to be just, "injustice must be the *basic* reason for the authority's reaction," rather than a "pretext."[42] Authority must be rightful but need not be legal, he avers; in that regard, Kosovo is the paradigmatic case deployed not just by Biggar but by Blair—who presided over four wars during his time in office. If these are the shallow criteria by which war is adjudged to be just, then Biggar is correct that the Iraq war may be plausibly cast as a good war.

Such a resolutely idealist defense of just war is something of a departure from other voices in the tradition. Unlike O'Donovan, Biggar is confident that history *does* know of just wars. Unlike Elshtain, he is quite happy to evaluate—according to the *ad bellum* and *in bello* criteria—specific armed interventions by post-Christendom Western states. Unlike both, he is prepared to label just war as "theory" not "tradition." Biggar is unnervingly countercultural in his defense of the proportionality of trench warfare of the Somme and the just cause of the Iraq War, and entirely conventional in confining his analysis to the recent armed conflicts of the West. *In Defence of War* is just what it says, a muscular defense of the justice of war by a thinker who clearly cleaves to the legacy of Christendom and finds value in thinking through the rationales and moral judgments inherent in military strategy. "Britain," he seems proud to claim, "has never entirely lost a sense of direct responsibility for global order"—a fact he supports by quoting a British strategist on the legacy of empire.[43]

Such normative statements in defense of war and empire have provoked ire for Biggar from political opponents. My concern is not to reprise

40. Biggar, *In Defence of War*, 235–37.
41. Porter, *Blunder*, 2–3.
42. Biggar, *In Defence of War*, 252, 322.
43. Biggar, *In Defence of War*, 12.

these normative debates but to uncover the weakness of the descriptive claims in which they are evidenced. As is typical of this genre, the analysis of just war is immune from attendance to the wider politics and security relations—and the before and after of any given armed conflict. For Biggar, the relevant period for the Great War is 1914–18, for Kosovo, 1999, and for Iraq, 2003. On the rare occasion he acknowledges the wider historical context, it is with respect to an earlier military confrontation where peacemongers or irresolute leaders blunted the providential power of war, as in the case of the US-led coalition not enacting regime change in Iraq in 1991.[44] But what is clear to any student of armed conflict since Clausewitz's *On War* is that war is always the continuation of *political* commerce by other means.[45] Therefore, any assessment of its justice is an assessment of the "political commerce" of which it is part. But in Biggar there is almost no discussion of this politics and no sustained political theology, the like of which O'Donovan provides.

The late St. Andrews professor Nick Rengger, in a book published in the same year as *In Defence of War*, does provide such a discussion. He notes, "the justification of force is intimately tied up with questions about what the character of political community might be said to be."[46] The point is not that force is a constant in human history—that much is obvious—but that the character of its use in, by, and for political community is "radically changing."[47] Rengger makes the crucial observation that in late-modern history, particularly since the end of Christendom, the nature of that political community has begun to change quite dramatically toward what he denotes, following Michael Oakeshott, a "teleocratic" form, which he takes to be a "foolish—and harmful—trajectory" to increasingly "uncivil" condition.[48] This is a state that appears like a modern economic enterprise rather than a cultural-religious association.[49] Rather than challenging increasingly uncivil authority, just warriors have been "complicit" in expanding rather than restraining the use of war for teleocratic ends.

Rengger argues that the advocates of JWT—who have been ignorant or disregarding of the uncivil condition—have effectively been a constitutive force for the purposive, crudely utilitarian state insofar as the modern and utilitarian just war thinking is consistent with such a state. What is emerging is a security state—which may appear in liberal or authoritarian, Eastern

44. Biggar, *In Defence of War*, 7.
45. Clausewitz, *On War*.
46. Rengger, *Just War and International Order*, xi.
47. Rengger, *Just War and International Order*, 6, 8.
48. Rengger, *Just War and International Order*, ix, xii.
49. Rengger, *Just War and International Order*, 33–34.

or Western guises—which has altogether more infrastructural and symbolic power at its disposal that the early modern states denoted in Charles Tilly's famous aphorism: "war made the state, and the state made war."[50] This security state declares the "supreme emergency" on an almost daily basis and insists the crisis can only be addressed via itself.[51] Governments like Blair's are able to go to war four distinct times in just a few years precisely because of the predominance of security—not diplomacy and certainly not ethical consideration—in their policy thinking. In partnering with this state, the just war tradition fails to question its political basis and whether a different world is emerging that is both more diverse and less in control of its own destiny. To Rengger, such critical questioning would be more faithful to the Augustinian tradition.

Therefore, inspired by Rengger's intervention, we can say that the general problem of just war—acute in Biggar but found widely in the tradition—is first and foremost one of *a flawed realism*. Force is not merely an instrumental act of a given moment but part of a series of recurrent and symbolic acts that generate systems of domination, and that meet resistance. As such, force is a matter of power and security. Biggar is not *anthropologically* realistic enough about the instinctual and emotive means by which decisions are made in the politics of armed conflict. He is not *morally* realistic enough about how far the condition of war normalizes and perpetuates political violence rather than brings peace. And finally, he lacks the *political* realism of Niebuhr, Butterfield, and Wight about the nature of the actually existing secular state. It was perhaps also Niebuhr's theology of responsibility that meant, despite his critique of pacifism, he never fully endorsed JWT.[52]

It is this realism and theological responsibility held by earlier Christian realists that we must retain as we proceed with our analysis. These virtues are embodied by Rowan Williams, in a famous sermon given in 2004, while leader of the church in which Biggar also serves as priest, to highlight the political manipulation of evidence with respect to Iraq and to question the loyalty that Christians owe to such a government.

> Credible claims on our political loyalty have something to do with a demonstrable attention to truth, even unwelcome truth. A government that habitually ignored expert advice, habitually pressed its interests abroad in ways that ignored manifest needs and priorities in the wider human and non-human

50. Tilly, "War Making and State Making as Organized Crime."
51. Rengger, *Just War and International Order*, 162–66.
52. Paipais, "Reinhold Niebuhr and the Christian Realist Pendulum."

environment, habitually repressed criticism or manipulated public media—such a regime would, to say the least, jeopardize its claim to obedience because it was refusing attention. Its policies and its rhetoric would not be designed to secure for its citizens an appropriate position in the world, a position that allowed the best kind of freedom because it did not deceive or encourage deception about the way the world is. It would be concerned finally about control and no more; and so would be a threat to its citizens and others.[53]

What Williams is saying here is that Western governments are increasingly a threat to their societies as well as others partly because they truncate the time and space in which political decisions are made. The argument here is neither consequentialist (although the longer-term outcomes of the Iraq War were barely considered by the invaders and are only briefly addressed by Biggar) nor deontological (although again it is not clear what rules of decision-making were applied). Rather, Williams' point refers to the fundamental lack of virtue by decision makers with respect to the war. In Oakeshott's uncharacteristically ugly term, they proceeded according to "teleocratic" principles. We call this "security without eschatology" and will return to explore it further in chapter 5.

Just war—a provincial perspective

Before we proceed to these questions of telos, we shall dwell for a moment on the fact that a thorough examination of war according to the principles of just war must not merely consider the event of war but the conditions of its time and place. Today's conditions in the world-leading military power and liberal state are those of the military-industrial complex. As US President Eisenhower outlined in his farewell radio address of January 1961, which brought the term into common usage,

> The conjunction of an immense military establishment and a large arms industry is new in the American experience. The total influence—economic, political, even spiritual—is felt in every city, every statehouse, every office of the federal government.... In the councils of government, we must guard against the acquisition of unwarranted influence, whether sought or unsought, by the military-industrial complex.[54]

---

53. Williams, "John Mere's Commemoration Sermon."
54. Eisenhower, "President's Farewell Address."

Eisenhower's warning was especially prescient regarding the military-industrial complex of the United States of the 1960s (which has grown immensely again in the last two decades). But we may also make it with regard to the genteel South-West of England—a largely rural region with a tradition of Methodism and the Brethren which hasn't seen major political violence for almost four centuries and where I have lived for the last fifteen years.

Shortly after I arrived in the region, in 2008, the city of Exeter briefly hit the national headlines after a troubled young man with learning disabilities and recently acquired jihadism tried to blow himself up in a local restaurant. The attack failed, but it was the reaction to the attack that exhibited its own symbolic violence in the anger expressed in below-the-line comments on the local news website and in the threats made against the university's Institute for Arab and Islamic Studies, which led to a police presence briefly being placed outside the building. The more general reaction was one of shock: "How could it happen to us?" How could we be a target in the war on terror? National newspapers repeated this line in cliché-ridden reports of how a region associated with holidays, beaches, and cream teas could suffer such a travesty. But what all these reactions shared was an utter failure to understand the relationship between the local and the global—and to grasp the simple fact that the South-West of England provides much technology, is most economically invested, and provides the greatest proportion of UK troops in wars such as Iraq and Afghanistan.

A first condition of British wars in which the South-West may be seen is *technological*. Wars are driven by technology and may be deemed just or unjust because of the precision of their weapons or the accuracy of the information they are able to generate. The concept of a Revolution in Military Affairs (RMA) captures this reality;[55] RMAs are rare, but most strategists argue that changes in information technology in recent years have made wars more networked, more distant, less reliant on human judgment, and more "doable." This new type of war is epitomized by the distant drone operations center or by autonomous vehicles operating according to artificial intelligence. But in the case of British counterinsurgency in Iraq and Afghanistan it was a more banal technology that made the difference. This took the form of advancement in anti-ballistic protection, fitted to Supacat armored

---

55. Defined by Andrew Marshall, director (1973–2015) of the US Department of Defense Office of Net Assessment, as "a major change in the nature of warfare brought about by the innovative application of new technologies which, combined with dramatic changes in military doctrine and operational and organizational concepts, fundamentally alters the character and conduct of military operations." Maloney and Robertson, "The Revolution in Military Affairs," 445.

vehicles by their manufacturer in Plymouth, a city forty miles from Exeter from where the jihadist Exeter bomber hailed. With significant numbers of, British troops dying in Afghanistan from 2006–9 due to the vulnerability of their vehicles to improvised explosive devices, these upgrades were deemed essential to make the continuation of the war politically acceptable.

A second condition of British wars in which the South-West plays an outsized role is *economic*. Companies like Supacat are required to arm both Britain's wars and those it sponsors overseas, such as Saudi Arabia's war in Yemen. Major British defense companies are based in the region, particularly in the South Gloucestershire district where they are woven with the state via the UK Ministry of Defence's Abbeywood site. The South-West region has the highest proportion of armed forces and civilian defense personnel in its workforce. It also has more than three times the national average of jobs directly dependent on defense expenditure. Corruption by major Western companies is commonplace in the defense world—the details of BAE "inducements" to the Saudi government remain unknown after the Blair government cancelled a Serious Fraud Office investigation in 2006, while Rolls Royce's faced a £671 million fine for bribery offences in 2017. The damage to the rule of law caused by the presence of this economy must also be part of any consideration of the justice of war.

A third condition of wars is *cultural*—they require a provincial outlook and way of life based on the idea of the benign self and the malign other. Such a culture is gendered, localized, and nationalized. As the feminist Cynthia Enloe argued in 1993, war is

> kept going by merely drawing on a type of civilian masculinity. . . . It requires drill sergeants . . . and men's willingness to earn their manhood credentials by soldiering: it also requires women to accept particular assumptions about mothering, marriage and unskilled work as well as policies, written and unwritten, to ensure certain sorts of sexual relations.[56]

The normative challenge to patriarchy in these remarks is less important to us than their descriptive basis. While all roles in the British army are now open to women, they remain just over 10 percent of armed forces personnel.[57] The army remains a male bastion. A disproportionate number of these men are from the South-West of England. Of the hundreds of military deaths from the wars in Afghanistan and Iraq over the 2001–14 period, there were a greater proportion (relative to the size of population) from the South-West than any other region.

56. Enloe, *The Morning After*, 253.
57. National Statistics, "UK Armed Forces Biannual Diversity Statistics."

Who dies in war and *how* are both crucial questions in any assessment of its conditions. In the UK, almost as many military deaths have occurred from suicide (310) as have lost their lives in combat (454) over this period of time.[58] Both these figures are tiny compared to around 250,000 civilians who have died in Afghanistan and Iraq from 2001–21, according to figures from Brown University.[59] Anand Gopal shows how the US invasion of Afghanistan went badly wrong because of reliance on the faulty intelligence of people who used the US army to settle their grudges, and reliance on drone warfare.[60] Such statistics indicate two types of "sacrifice" in armed conflict: the representative deaths of the overwhelmingly male soldiers fighting on behalf of a cause and a country; the barely represented deaths of the civilians, disproportionately women and children, who are the intentional or "unintentional" victims of state violence. The former deaths are marked with great ceremony, while governments will go out of their way not to acknowledge or even investigate the latter.[61]

According to the logic of national security, sustaining such a system of representative death is difficult unless the state can foster the ethos of national sacrifice in children. Recruitment to the army is sustained by an extensive system of cadet groups for eleven to sixteens, which are very common in the South-West and often serve as first steps for the region's young people to enter the army. Children can join the British army at sixteen, making the UK one of the few Western democracies to have child soldiers—one of only twenty countries in 2011 with the others including North Korea and Iran.[62] British child soldiers died in the Falklands (1982) and Iraq (1990–1) wars but can no longer serve in combat until they are eighteen. The reason why these young people—largely boys—serve and die in the armed forces are linked to masculinity and patriotism. The commemoration and ritual surrounding military deaths takes the form, according to Hutchinson, of the sacralization of the nation, giving a "quasi-religious" character to the relationship between warfare and the secular state.[63] This is most evident when the church itself gets involved in the sacralization of the nation—something we will discuss in future chapters.

58. *BBC News*, "Dorset Veteran's Wife Wants More Help for Veterans with PTSD."
59. Watson Institute of International Affairs, "Costs of War."
60. Gopal, *No Good Men among the Living*.
61. UK political and military leaders have consistently refused to investigate civilian deaths while the relevant chapter of the seven-year-long Iraq Inquiry refused to draw conclusions on the number of casualties. The Iraq Inquiry, "Section 17: Civilian Casualties."
62. Forceswatch, "Armed Forces Report Reveals MPs' Confusion."
63. Hutchinson, "Warfare and the Sacralization of Nations."

The end of just war theory?

There are good reasons to believe that JWT is losing ground in the most secularized and pacified societies after Christendom. Dombrowski argues it has been in a death spiral since 1945, given that we now have warfare where the intentional killing of innocents is commonplace and the unintentional killing of innocents is apparently unavoidable.[64] Recorded civilian casualties are far more common than they were in early modern, medieval, and ancient wars. What appears to be occurring in the West—the region that has produced modern Christian just war thinking—is an increasing disjuncture between a normalized security state and a pacified society. By contrast, the modern just war tradition assumes a state making the decision to go to war as an exception and a society connected to such war through military service and potential conscription, practices now unthinkable in many states where post-Christendom has taken hold.

One result of this is that war has become more contentious, although often this discord lies just beneath the surface. In the UK, a general level of support for the military is accompanied by increasing skepticism about war and warfare. This was illustrated by the so-called Wootton Bassett phenomenon of 2007–11, when a small town in South-West England, which was the first through which the returning and flag-draped bodies of British casualties traveled after arriving at the nearby air force base, saw the spectacle of hundreds or thousands of citizens lining the streets in respects, many of them traveling for hundreds of miles to do so. They came, all observers concurred, not to support the divisive war but to honor the noble warrior. As one academic analysis of the phenomenon concluded,

> The Wootton Bassett repatriations honored the dead without speeches, claims or slogans, allowing mourners, onlookers, and commentators to imbue them with their divergent meanings: personal grief, respect for the military, anger at government underfunding of the Forces, and opposition to or support of UK foreign policy.[65]

Dismissed as "grief tourism" by some, this caused unease from military officers unaccustomed to such public outpourings. When military death becomes personalized and politicized in this way it ceases to be a representative death and becomes a contentious one. As war has become

---

64. Dombrowski, "The Death of the Just War Theory."

65. Jenkings, at al., "Wootton Bassett and the Political Spaces of Remembrance," 360–61.

both disputed *and* industrialized to a greater degree, so the notion of just war is increasingly controversial.

We have closed part 1 with two decidedly Western chapters on Christian realism and just war and we have hinted at both the possibilities and limits of a political theological narrative of security grounded in the imagined community of Christendom. Neither Augustinian nor Thomist thought necessitates such a focus on the state as recognized by their most careful exponents. And yet the adaptation of their thought in late Christendom and the secular age has led inexorably, and perhaps unavoidably, to the assumption of state sovereignty. Neither Christian realists nor just war ethicists derive a complete political theology of sovereignty from Schmitt or any other source. But the practical questions of (post-)Christendom that they and other inheritors of either tradition face are *how* virtue and law are enacted for the world, if not via the sacralization of the state and sacrifice on its behalf, and *how* will the common good be put into practice amidst the divides instantiated by sovereignty and the chaotic pluralism present in world politics.

There are, of course, no easy answers to these questions. Rowan Williams reminds us that Augustine's answers are not to be found in institutions but "persons and processes."[66] A "wholly consistent programme" from *Civitas Dei* may be a chimera.[67] But modern warfare, Williams argues, cannot be a means to an end from a properly Augustinian perspective: "to defend the city of God" would be a "sign of unfaith, and abandonment of the church's integrity."[68] This reading of Augustine differs markedly from that of JWT. Christian pacifists would concur that to defend the earthly city militarily is a matter for the earthly rulers and not the church. They would further agree that the balance of power or just war are pagan ideas that have been superficially Christianized as we have sacralized the nation. As this chapter has argued, Christian JWT over-reaches beyond Christian realism in assuming rather than ascertaining the order-generating power of these increasingly disenchanted institutions of Christendom. In part 2, we will explore both the disorders and the hopes of this secular age before, in part 3, reconstructing a new post-Christendom approach to order and security that does not rest on the kingdoms and wars of this world but the persons and processes of the nonviolent kingdom of God.[69]

---

66. Williams, "Politics and the Soul," 734.
67. Williams, "Politics and the Soul," 734.
68. Williams, "Politics and the Soul," 745.
69. Weaver, *The Nonviolent God*.

PART TWO

CHAPTER 5

Security in a Secular Age

Have this mind among yourselves, which is yours in Christ Jesus, who, though he was in the form of God, did not count equality with God a thing to be grasped, but emptied himself, by taking the form of a servant, being born in the likeness of men. And being found in human form, he humbled himself by becoming obedient to the point of death, even death on a cross. Therefore, God has highly exalted him and bestowed on him the name that is above every name, so that at the name of Jesus every knee should bow, in heaven and on earth and under the earth, and every tongue confess that Jesus Christ is Lord, to the glory of God the Father.

PHILIPPIANS 2:5–11

But politics is defined by power, so faith in an alternative kingdom, once it is socially influential or established, is bound to end up colluding with the kingdoms of this world, that is, secularized. The power of the cross will be converted into the violence of the crusade.

DAVID MARTIN[1]

In 2005, I was working for the American aid agency Mercy Corps in the post-Soviet Central Asian republic of Tajikistan, which sits just north of Afghanistan. We were contracted to implement large-scale international

---

1. Martin, *On Secularizaton*, 186.

peacebuilding programs for the US Agency for International Development (USAID) largely involving infrastructure projects and community development in villages that had seen some of the worst fighting in the country's 1990s civil war. One day a Tajikistani member of staff shared that local people where he was working referred to Mercy Corps as "the Christians." My expatriate colleagues, all agnostic or atheist to my knowledge, expressed surprise and some concern that we were thought to be religious. "Well, you know," a Tajikistani colleague responded to them, "the logo of Mercy Corps is a cross and a dove, and the Russian translation of our name is *Korpus Miloserdiyie* [Body of Grace]."[2] This remark prompted a discussion about whether the organization should change its logo and name to rid itself of its Christian heritage.[3]

I reflected on this fleeting conversation years later when the organization was thrown into crisis. Mercy Corps, of course, like many humanitarian organizations in the West, has Christian origins, which it has since largely forsaken in a process of secularization. It was founded by Ellsworth Culver—an evangelical and son of missionaries—and fellow believer Dan O'Neill in the early 1980s in Portland, Oregon. Initially a project to help refugees from the genocide in Cambodia, it had gone on to become one of the largest humanitarian aid agencies in the US, working in around forty countries and with revenues of over a half billion dollars a year, much of it direct from the US government. In August 2005, just a few weeks after our conversation in the field office in Dushanbe, Culver died and in obituaries was lauded as one who "wanted justice done everywhere."[4] However, unbeknownst to the staff I worked among and the obituary-writers, Culver's past, contemporaneous with his founding of Mercy Corps, told a different story.

This was revealed much later in an investigation by the *Oregonian* newspaper, "No Mercy," in the wake of the #MeToo movement. In early 1990s, Ellsworth Culver's daughter, Tania Culver Humphrey, had come forward to Mercy Corps with allegations of terrible and systematic sexual abuse against her by her father when she was a child in the 1970s and 1980s. At the time of the abuse Culver was president of Mercy Corps and he remained senior vice-president when the allegations were dealt with by the organization in an internal review that recognized the organization's "dysfunction" without acknowledging the truthfulness of the allegations of

---

2. *Miloserdiyie* may be translated as "mercy," "charity," or "grace," but is the Russian word used for the translation of the New Testament Greek term *charis*.

3. Mercy Corps' logo was changed shortly afterward to remove the cross symbol.

4. Crombie, "No Mercy."

sexual abuse or reporting them to the police.⁵ Acknowledging that "a person who creates a dysfunctional family, will be a dysfunctional influence in an organization," Chairman Raymond Vath told Culver Humphrey in an April 1994 letter that Mercy Corps would take a "redemptive approach" while "attempting to give opportunity for growth to all involved in the organization, including your father." Culver Humphrey was assured that "your sacrifice will bring blessings to not only the staff but the recipients of our programs internationally."⁶ In 2018, when Culver Humphrey and her husband wrote to Mercy Corps to ask them to re-open the investigation, they were referred to the organization's lawyer who themselves declared that their files on the matter "no longer exist." However, after the publication of the *Oregonian*'s investigation in 2019, Mercy Corps, under new leadership, responded by hiring a law firm to conduct an independent investigation that reported, in May 2021, that up to eight members of staff may have been involved in Culver's abuse of multiple victims, including locals in Honduras and other overseas locations.⁷

It was not just Mercy Corps that failed Culver Humphrey but Christian leaders at the time and the social services and police who refused to proceed with a full investigation and prosecution when she came forward in the early 1990s as a young adult after having revealed her past of abuse at a church prayer meeting. But that Mercy Corps refusal of its responsibility to report sexual abuse was wrapped in the language of Christianity ("redemption" and "sacrifice"), while being sheltered by the immanent practices of secular law and bureaucracy, is harrowing. What emerges is a story that is both personal and bureaucratic, familial and institutional, global and local, Christian and secular, where both actual fault and potential redress lie across all of these domains. In these senses, it is a very post-Christendom story where a nominally Christian agency committed to fighting globally against human insecurity finds its privileges lost and purpose questioned.

Just like Mercy Corps' failure of governance and crisis of identity, places that were once solidly part of Christendom—with all its hidden violence and public virtue—have been wracked by the forces of disenchantment and decentering. Any attempt to provide an account of (in)security in these environments that fails to account for these forces of the secular age will fall short. Equally, a secularist account that sees this process as linear, final, and ending in the evisceration of religion from the public sphere is also wholly inadequate. When postmodern and post-Christendom states go to war, they

---

5. Crombie, "No Mercy."
6. Crombie, "No Mercy."
7. Crombie, "No Mercy."

still sacralize their nations with flags, insignia, and metaphysical statements, while engaging in the profane techniques of violence that have characterized armed conflicts for millennia. Sensible attempts to make sense of security after Christendom are those that are open to both disenchantment and re-enchantment of society, both decentering and recentering the church's relationship with the state.

Part 2 of this book tells this story in terms of these two pairs of countervailing trends: disenchantment (chapter 5) and re-enchantment (chapter 8); recentering (chapter 6) and decentering (chapter 7). We begin with disenchantment. While Christian realism and just war were dominant modes of interpreting security well into the twentieth century, by its latter decades they were losing followers and influence. This trend is not an isolated pathway of secularization, but the culmination of a centuries-long process of increasing disenchantment, desacralization, and differentiation narrated by Charles Taylor, Talal Assad, David Martin, and Elizabeth Shakman Hurd, amongst others. Its implications are profound for international security, and yet, as we saw in chapter 1, identifying a specific break with the past is both untenable and unhelpful. Rather, to understand how security has been disenchanted, is to identify, in a Weberian manner, the rise of secular space, ethics, and time over a "world of spirits, demons and moral forces which our ancestors lived in."[8] In that light, this chapter will make a statement of theory that elaborates Taylor's and Martin's thought for the study of global security. The "secular"—despite, from a theological perspective, the crusading and idolatrous excesses and claims to sovereignty of some militant secularists—is not a realm autonomous of Christ, but one founded on his act of "emptying" himself (Phil 2:7).

Secularization revised

We explore the secular age as a condition that arises dialectically along two vectors: first, the extreme decentering of the church away from political power *and* its recentering on the secular state; second, the disenchantment of societies as reflected in their relationship to the church *and* their re-enchantment as demonstrated in the emergence of new sacralizing movements. This is most visible in Western democracies over the last two centuries—and it is from those contexts that this debate has arisen—but is a much broader process that both has global causes and has spread out from its centers in the West to other regions. It has also faced resistance both within and, more significantly, beyond the West in places that have

---

8. Taylor, *A Secular Age*, 26.

remained enchanted or been re-enchanted by religious change or revival, and places where the church has retained or regained a centered relationship with state. Such resistances have been especially visible in the postcolonial Global South and post-Soviet Eurasia. In other words, in half the world the trend has been as much resistance to secularization as secularization itself.

Unfortunately, the debate on post-Christendom has been dominated by the English-speaking world over the last half century. Stanley Hauerwas, whose landmark *After Christendom?* includes an important question mark, acknowledges much of the debate here has not been over Christendom as such, but about the nature of the church's relationship to political authority.[9] All voices in this debate accept that the church is not entirely devoid of influence but that its position with respect to the secular authorities is decentered to a degree perhaps not seen since before Constantine. So, the question is what form decentering is taking and ought to take. Almost all post-Christendom thinkers agree on the church as *polis*, but debates arise over the form and content of its theological politics.[10] Should the church compromise with the secular in order to retake the center? Should it simply offer its products to the market in confidence that they are ultimately higher quality and more enticing? Should it keep its distance, building communities at the margins and refusing all attempts at co-optation?

Sitting in a secular university, and having worked in and with government, it is striking to me how these debates are mirrored in the *saeculum*. The emergence of a secular West has been proceeding apace since the mid-twentieth century. While politics may be theological to the church, religion has become decidedly non-theological for government. Our multi-faith societies work, according to government, to the extent that absolute truths and theological claims remain private or sequestered in faith communities, away from the public sphere. Otherwise, they are a threat to the imagined security communities of the secular. This is most visible in the treatment of Islam in militantly secular France,[11] but reflects a wider disenchantment of political imagination. Therefore, one of the great puzzles of the humanities and social sciences over the last fifty years has been that of explaining the causes and consequences of secularization, a process that was once widely believed to be an irreversible trend in Western societies since the nineteenth century. Various thinkers have attributed secularization to pluralization (the proliferation of confessions),[12] privatization (the triumph of the individual

9. Hauerwas, *After Christendom?*, 7.
10. Bretherton, *Christianity and Contemporary Politics*, 17.
11. Bowen, *Why the French Don't Like Headscarves*.
12. Berger, "The Desecularization of the World."

subject),[13] and modernization (including the triumph of science and the relegation of religious knowledge).[14] But these broad claims were fraught with uncertainty and caveat from the outset. In the 1960s, the American sociologist Peter Berger stated his secularization thesis, while his British counterpart and Anglican priest David Martin demanded that any general theory must account for considerable variation, even within the West.[15]

More recent research on the secularization thesis has shown both the spatial inconsistency and temporal indeterminacy of secularization. The second edition of Pippa Norris and Ronald Ingelhart's *Sacred and Secular* drew from the World Values Survey (WVS) to argue that "secularization is a tendency, not an iron law," but one that is strongly related to security. The authors argue that a greater degree of secularity is found when "people have a sense of existential security—that is, the feeling that survival is secure enough that it can be taken for granted."[16] This is a revised version of the secularization thesis, written almost fifty years since Berger's original statement, but one that remains contentious, especially in light of Berger's 1999 recantation of his earlier claim, his introduction of the term "desecularization," and his argument that it was secular Europe that was the exception.[17] By 2013, diehards like Steve Bruce felt compelled to launch empirical defenses of an "unfashionable theory."[18] In support of Bruce, the most recent data from WVS 2021 indicated a global decline in religiosity since 2007, particularly in the United States.[19] This appears to have been further exacerbated by the coronavirus pandemic.[20] The takeaway from this mixed picture is that "secularization" consists of countervailing and dialectically related trends.

In sum, there is a mountain of empirical evidence that points to a global trend of *disenchantment*, the quantitative decrease in professed belief (measurable in surveys such as WVS), and a qualitative shift in the practice of faith (that is, a weakening, according to an orthodox Christian perspective). Further, and in line with the histories synthesized in part 1, there is considerable evidence for *decentering*: the disassociation of church from state over several centuries. However, three caveats must be placed

13. Berger and Luckmann, *The Social Construction of Reality*.
14. Bruce, *Religion and Modernization*.
15. Martin, *On Secularizaton*.
16. Norris and Ronald Inglehart, *Sacred and Secular*, 4.
17. Berger, "The Desecularization of the World."
18. Bruce, *Secularization*.
19. Inglehart, *Religion's Sudden Decline*.
20. Benjamin Sledge, "The Decline of the American Church."

on these two trends. First, they are resisted in the form of re-enchantment and recentering. In Weberian terms, "the process of modern disenchantment is thus better understood as a dual vector of disenchantment and of re-enchantment in the form of rationalization."[21] Second, and consequently, while pointing to a general condition of a secular age, these trends belie clear historical distinctions between Christendom and post-Christendom imaginaries. Third, therefore, there are many different varieties of the secular age and its security communities. Secularism, Elizabeth Shakman Hurd argues, "is located on the spectrum of theological politics" and is "imagined and enacted within an unquestioned Christian framework."[22] It emerges out of Christendom, but "it is foisted upon countries outside of historical Christendom and its settler colonies."[23]

Charles Taylor's *The Secular Age*

These varieties of post-Christendom have emerged out of, rather than against, a secular age. In turn, the secular has emerged out of the decline of Christendom. As we have discussed, both were plural processes. These processes were not external to the church. Rather, the church fully participated in its own disenchantment. Here, the Catholic philosopher Charles Taylor's magisterial *The Secular Age* has made a field-defining intervention that provides an important waymarker for this book. This "secular" is defined by Taylor as a modern social imaginary that recasts and disenchants religion rather than merely expelling it. Taylor's secular imaginary—an objectified economy, the pre-political public, and an increasingly radical self-government—is one that emerges from the decentered Christendom imaginary we introduced in part 1. But it has gone further in much of the West and global elite culture, becoming thoroughly "immanentized" and "exclusively humanist" in Taylor's terms. It is in this sense, according to James K. A. Smith, who draws on Taylor, that the secular age is *both* a providential product of Christendom *and* the sign of a fallen world in need of redemption.[24]

---

21. Valk, "Poetics and Politics," 3.

22. Hurd distinguishes two varieties of state secularisms: *laïcité* (what we denoted as *post-Christian secularism*, which seeks to counter and deny its Christian parent), and *Judeo-Christian* (what we called *Christian secularism*, which seeks to nurture this heritage and retain a privileged position for Christianity). The term "Christian secularism" is more legitimate here given the link to Christendom and its history of anti-Semitism. Hurd, *The Politics of Secularism*, 237, 241.

23. Hurd, *The Politics of Secularism*, 237.

24. Smith, *Awaiting the King*, 17.

Taylor's interest is in what it means to be secular and how the secular—where "you can engage fully in politics without ever encountering God"[25]—came about. As Taylor asks, for the period from 1500 to 2000, "How did we move from a condition where, in Christendom, people lived naively within a theistic construal, to one in which we all shunt between two stances, in which everyone's construal shows up as such; and which, moreover, has become for many the major default option?"[26] This book concerns itself with the security dimension of that question. What does it mean to move from a Christian world in which the identification of threat and the use of force were deemed to be sanctioned by God to a global order where these matters become the preserve of largely godless governments, driven by ideas shorn of their theological aspect? "Our primary service to each other," according to Taylor, "has become the provision of collective security, to render our lives and property safe under law."[27] This reframing of the "after Christendom" question in terms of the secular age sets the boundaries for what this book seeks to investigate.

Taylor's question is helpful because it avoids the mistake of framing the secular as something entirely separate to Christendom. Rather than being replaced by the secular, the church survives and thrives, albeit at the margins away from the main currents of culture, economy, and politics. What both church and government face is a process of disenchantment—what Taylor, following Weber, calls a "subtraction story" of moving away from a world of God, spirits, and demons—and also the rise of new forms of "fullness," many of which are non-theistic, including (in postmodern times) "expressive individualism."[28] The political, cultural, and technological processes associated with secularization by sociologists are all discussed by Taylor, but he, unlike they, charts how disenchantment and individualism emerge *within* the church, not simply against it. Disenchantment makes the church *and* world more likely to seek immanent means to salvation *and* security—both values that were once found only in a transcendent God. Expressive individualism indicates that such security is felt and experienced in highly personal and subjective ways—whose security? is the question to ask, with security under God no longer a credible answer to give. What is required is "the ability to grasp society from a decentered view, which is no one's."[29]

25. Taylor, *A Secular Age*, 1.
26. Taylor, *A Secular Age*, 14.
27. Taylor, *A Secular Age*, 166.
28. Taylor, *A Secular Age*, 25–27.
29. Taylor, *A Secular Age*, 209.

Disenchantment and individualism, by Taylor's account, are genealogically tied to Western Christendom with its concerns for both liberty and security.[30] He explains:

> And so more than one vector in Western Christendom contributed to the cut between immanence and transcendence; not just the rage for order which was implicit in much of the more intense piety, and whose drive to disenchantment is clear; but also the need to make God more fully present in everyday life and all its contexts, which led people to invest these contexts with a new significance and a solidity.[31]

God is made more fully present in forms of such solidity, from self-help discipleship courses to Christian peacemaking in civil wars. To quote O'Donovan, these "features of a liberal society," from the personal devotional to the international interventionist, are both secular and draw on "the narrative structure of the church, which is itself a recapitulation of the Christ-event."[32] They indicate that it is difficult for Western individuals and governments to act collectively without the invocation of Christendom principles of sacrifice and church-like practices of service. These principles and practices suggest, in the terms of Graeme Smith, that contemporary secularism is "the latest expression of the Christian religion" and "Christian ethics shorn of its doctrine."[33] Just as peacemaking is a Christian secularized practice so too is the blessing of nuclear weapons. However, reading great works like Taylor, those of the secularization debate, and those of the history of Christendom, one is struck and troubled by how little both the non-West and the illiberal appear.[34] There is a need to read Taylor against the grain, to expose the intimate connections between the secular and Western post-Christendom, and to look beyond these limits to see what this vision obscures or omits completely. With Taylor, there are three tracks we may follow relating to space, ethics, and time.

---

30. Smith, *Awaiting the King*, 102–5.
31. Taylor, *A Secular Age*, 145.
32. O'Donovan, *Desire of the Nations*, 250.
33. Smith, *A Short History of Secularism*, 2.
34. Non-Western secularisms in Egypt, Pakistan, India, or Turkey are rarely considered. This point is made most acutely by Asad, *Formations of the Secular*.

THE SECULAR SECURITY STATE
AND THE WITHDRAWAL OF THE CHURCH

The first way in which the secular-age-as-post-Christendom argument must be specified is *spatial*. Taylor begins his book by questioning "*in* what this secularity consists," and identifies its first mode as being that of "common institutions and practices—most obviously, but not only, the state."[35] In Christendom, these common institutions, even those of politics and security, were intimately connected to those of the church. Under secularism, such institutions are increasingly divorced from churches, which themselves become part-privatized and relegated institutions, excluded from matters of politics and security. Secularization means that for many today a specific role for the church in legitimating state violence and the institution of the armed forces is considered controversial or even dangerous. Indeed, the "myth of religious violence" explicitly separates a transhistorical phenomenon called "religion" from the rest of society. According to Cavanaugh, the myth is "absolutely central to secular social orders."[36] The spatial question here is that of the extent to which institutions and practice may be "common"—that is, shared across society and centered on the state—if "religion" is excluded from public space, as it must be, according to the myth. Security in Christendom consisted in the cooperation or even cohabitation of government and church; in a secular age it consists in the state divorced from all religious institutions.

This entanglement between secularism and security, whilst longstanding, has recently returned to the attention of scholars working in International Relations.[37] IR scholars Luca Mavelli and Mike Williams[38] have shown how scholars in the field of security studies, according to a conventional view of the emergence of the modern European states, take it as axiomatic that political theology poses a threat to the state and that security thus requires secularization.[39] Following the geographer David Campbell,[40] Mavelli postulates that as the state supplanted the church as the source of political authority in early modern Europe so it externalized theopolitical

---

35. Taylor, *A Secular Age*, 1, emphasis added.
36. Cavanaugh, "Girard and the Myth of Religious Violence," 8.
37. Hurd, *The Politics of Secularism*; Bilgin, "The Securityness of Secularism?"; Gutkowski, "Secularism and the Politics of Risk"; Mavelli, "Security and Secularization in International Relations."
38. Williams, "Identity and the Politics of Security."
39. Mavelli, "Security and Secularization."
40. Campbell, *Writing Security*, 44–48.

views as threats to order.⁴¹ This was seminal to the discourse of danger, which is essential to the emergence of the modern, secular, Western state.⁴² However, just as there were variations in the security practices between centered and decentered Christendom, so there is variation in a secular age. The distinction between assertive and passive secularisms is helpful here as it helps us distinguish between those secularists who demonize religion and those states that seek to exclude it from the public sphere, on the one hand, and the majority of secular state forms, where religion remains a formal and informal source of ethics, on the other.⁴³ Assertive secularism is usually entangled with atheism while passive secularism is typically sympathetic to faith. Both agree, however, that faith itself is a principally a private matter and one whose contribution to politics must be limited to ensure the security of the state.

A privatized faith is one whose expressions are restricted to certain spaces rather than one that is dying out. As Taylor argues, "this emptying of religion from autonomous social spheres is, of course, compatible with the vast majority of people believing in God and practicing their religion vigorously."⁴⁴ The dominance of the secular public sphere does not mean the absolute exclusion of sacred spaces from security practice; rather, it means the incursion of secular institutions and agendas into sacred spaces. Luke Bretherton, from an Augustinian perspective, identifies three responses of the church to secularization: "letting the church be co-opted by the state, or situating itself in competition with other minority groups in society, or commodifying Christianity."⁴⁵ These options in the area of security might include the celebration of the armed forces in non-conformist churches (co-option), seeking a certain approach by the state to "freedom of religion and belief" that favors Christian mission (competition), and accepting conditional state funding of Christian international development charities (commodification). From a Christendom perspective, these are all forms of merger that apparently resolve the cross/sword dialectic. However, the churches that imagine post-Christendom are frequently places where modern security practices of war, nuclear deterrence, counterterrorism, and counter-migration measures are challenged. The secular age never goes uncontested.

41. Mavelli, "Security and Secularization," 184.
42. Campbell, *Writing Security*, 48.
43. Kuru, "Passive and Assertive Secularism."
44. Taylor, *A Secular Age*, 2.
45. Bretherton, *Christianity and Contemporary Politics*, 3.

The shift to the church as a venue for a secular and multi-faith debate on security according to an agenda set by political authorities is a problem that presents an opportunity. With subcontracting roles, charitable status, risk assessments, safeguarding rules, data protection, and financial reporting guidance, the state is in the church to a degree that was unimaginable before the growth of the secular bureaucracy after 1945. It is now the state that makes the church immanently secure, while the state increasingly disregards questions of transcendental security. However, the extent of this sequestering differs greatly from context to context given the plural forms the secular takes. As the *saeculum* lacks autonomy, it never accedes to the sovereignty it claims. Gallaher, drawing on Bonhoeffer, frames this as a "creative tension" between the sacred and the secular, between church and world. He imagines an Eastern Orthodox Christian theology of secularism deploying the notion of kenosis ("emptying," Phil 2:7). "The church," Gallaher argues, "itself founds, undergirds, and then, by kenotically withdrawing to remain present, sets free the world to be itself and develop independently in the secular space, which is then far from being 'neutral.'"[46] Such secular space is a *post-Christendom* space, a product of God's providential work in history. By contrast, forms of the secular that are *post-Christian*—which effectively deify some part of the world—are those that, via a programmatic or militant ideology, demand that faith and church remain in sequestered spaces.[47] The post-Christendom spaces of the church are potentially sure foundations from where the church may push back against the post-Christian excesses of the secular security state.

Public disagreement and the absence of consensus

Taylor's second mode of secularism relates to public belief in God and ethics derived from God. He describes secularization as "the falling off of religious belief and practice, in people turning away from God, and no longer going to church."[48] This is a shift from public expression of faith being compulsory to it becoming a matter of voluntary association. Therefore, not only are modern states confronted by religious plurality but they have developed various types of secular political forms to formally accommodate yet informally privatize religious faith. In Christian secular settings this includes the retention of national-religious language and iconography and in some cases established state churches, while at the same limiting or reducing religious

---

46. Gallaher, "A Secularism of the Royal Doors," 113.
47. Gallaher, "A Secularism of the Royal Doors," 116–17.
48. Taylor, *A Secular Age*, 2.

practices in states spaces, such as school prayers and the keeping of religious holidays. Exclusive humanism is the governing logic while Christian language remains in public discourse.

While the secularization theorists provide a great deal of data to suggest that disenchantment increases the feeling of security, our conception of security after Christendom suggests that the nature of security as a value has changed. It is no longer the transcendental sense of having security as a people under God, but the immanent sense of being included, provided for, and protected as a person. Being physically and emotionally "secure" is an ethical maxim for a secular world. It is therefore of little surprise that secularization has most advanced in Western Europe, which has seen an unprecedented period of peace since 1945. Whether this is the product of the protection offered by the United States in the Western alliance, as purported by realists, or the deep integration between states that has occurred under the European Union, as suggested by liberals and as designed by Robert Schuman and his fellow founders of the European Coal and Steel Community, is the paradigmatic debate in the study of European security.

But how exactly does this condition of security cause the secularization and the emergence of post-Christendom where just war and Christian realist ethics have become subordinate to the secular? What Martin denotes as "the subsumption of Christianity by secular nationalism," is one where, especially in his homeland of Britain, "secular nationalism generated a vernacular semi-Christianity" of remembrance services that sacralize the nation as they worship Christ. More informally, in the United States, the battle hymn of the republic specifically compares Christ's sacrifice on the cross to that of the troops on the battlefield.[49] Such practices with respect to the commemoration and valorization of warfare by secular states are examples of what Martin calls the "sub-text where that injunction [that the kingdom of God does not come by violence] is subtly reversed."[50] Such secular reversal takes places "where religion becomes virtually co-extensive with society and thus with the dynamics of power, violence, control, cohesion, and the marking out of boundaries."[51] In the case of Europe, argues Martin, with the political realists, this is a matter of the luxury of being "pacified for over half a century by living in the ambit of American power."[52]

In a Christian secular context, our desire for immanent security is such that the Christian realist recognition of the immorality of all societies,

---

49. Martin, *Reflections on Sociology and Theology*, 122–25.
50. Martin, *Reflections on Sociology and Theology*, 134.
51. Martin, *Reflections on Sociology and Theology*, 134.
52. Martin, *On Secularization*, 187.

and the inadequacy of all ethical codes, gets lost in the sense of one's own rightfulness and need for defense against the other. The desire for security causes the person to turn away from the uncertainty and insecurity of living between the city of God and that of the world, in favor of a secular ethic where the concerns of the world dominate public ethics, but in ways that are parasitic on the language and tradition of "the city of God." The reverse here is so subtle that many churches, yearning for a return to Christendom, participate in the performances of this secular ethic but with what secularist observers may rightly describe as an "ulterior motive." They adopt these secular and typically national forms while (re)inserting specifically religious content, often originating in Christendom, such as in the pursuit of the human right of freedom of religion and belief.[53] Conversely, secular organizations—from the army regiments to universities to aid agencies like Mercy Corps—continue to maintain Christian names and crosses on their emblems while vacating their constitutions of specifically religious content.

The sheer variety of what is possible in terms of "disagreement"—and the contradictions that arise—is remarkable. It is common to see self-proclaimed faith groups advancing agendas in secular terms and avowedly secular groups advancing theirs in religious terms. For all sides, such engagement comes with risks where global post-Christendom conditions are used to push for either post-Christian or neo-Christendom goals. The admiration of conservative American evangelicals for Russian Orthodoxy's brand of fundamentalism is a case in point. "In fact," Orthodox theologians Aristotle Papanikolaou and George Demacopoulos argue,

> Russia looks a lot like what American evangelicals hope for in the United States—a legally supported moral framework that centers around sexual ethics, including laws against "gay propaganda" and proposed laws that could restrict abortion as well as freedom of religious assembly (which ironically affect American evangelicals). In a sense, Putin his globalized the American culture wars, and one could argue that the new geopolitical East-West divide has been drawn on the basis of debates about what constitutes the secular.[54]

It is inadequate then to see fundamentalism as a largely Eastern problem whose solution is the largely Western secular. The two are dialectically related and cannot be geographically essentialized.

---

53. The Christian churches are by no means the only representatives of world religions to deploy human rights language for instrumental ends. Bielefeldt, "Misperceptions of Freedom of Religion."

54. Papanikolaou and Demacopoulus, *Fundamentalism or Tradition*, 8.

In sum, secular ethics (of security) are those of a common public form that conceals a diverse range of positions and doubts in an increasingly fractured society. Secular security ethics in Christian-majority places are performances that construct an imagined community and artifice of shared identity often against "fundamentalist" Christianity or the people of another faith. But from a theological perspective, the absence of shared values is also inherent to a secular society. This lacuna cannot be addressed by a post-Christian humanism that might, in the liberal imagination, lead to a commitment to human rights, international aid, open borders, or the responsibility to protect. This is because, as Martin puts it, "there remains an irreducible religious realm of transcendent possibilities that cannot be straightforwardly realized on the plane of politics."[55] The extreme differentiation we are seeing today is creating a qualitative shift toward the kinds of radical and fundamental disagreements over public ethics that characterize a post-Christian world. In the secular age, John Rawls' ideal of an *overlapping consensus* appears increasingly conspicuous by its absence.[56]

The Immanence of Time and Imminence of Threat

Taylor relates his third mode of secularism to "certain contemporary modes of postmodernism," which "want to make a point of stressing the irredeemable nature of division, lack of center, the perpetual absence of fullness."[57] The personalization of faith and the privatization of church—the "buffered self" of exclusive humanism rather than naïve public and collective religion—are evidence of how postmodernism and secularism are intertwined since the late-twentieth century. Like the secular age, which may be considered its parent, the postmodern condition is not only spatial ("the lack of center") and ethical-ideological ("the irredeemable nature of division") but also temporal ("the *perpetual* absence of fullness," emphasis added).[58] This theme of perpetual absence emanating from the preceding conditions will be returned to persistently in coming chapters. The time-horizon of secularism is not merely that of leaving behind public religion as a thing of the past, becoming post-Christian. Rather, secular time constitutes a paradox: that time is of both the immediate moment and the unimaginable vastness.

First, secular time is a matter of treating the temporal not as a dress rehearsal for the eternal but as the immediate and immanent reality. As Taylor

55. Martin, *Reflections on Sociology and Theology*, 135.
56. Asad, *Formations of the Secular*, 2–6.
57. Taylor, *A Secular Age*, 10.
58. Taylor, *A Secular Age*, 10.

puts it: "humans are no longer charter members of the cosmos but occupy merely a narrow band of recent time."[59] This is not given but has been made. "We have constructed an environment in which we live a uniform, univocal secular time, which we try to measure and control to get things done."[60] A disenchanted world is one where all tasks, especially those of security, are immanent and therefore at least potentially predictable and controllable. This is not merely a matter of technological advancement but of a cultural shift where time is no longer imagined in terms of eternity but within the realm of what is immanently possible. This extends to questions of national security and the development of military technology in the sense that the objective is not to restrain evil in preparation for the coming king (as it was for the Christian realists), but to balance it for the immanent realization of security. In theological terms, Jürgen Moltmann argued, in the context of weapons of mass destruction, that the lifespan of the future "is within human power and we must keep creating new respites for life."[61] In terms of security practice, the secular state is one that requires capacity for real-time intelligence and the immediate use of force. Its demand is for security *now*.

A second feature of secular time is what Taylor denotes as its "dark abyss." "We have moved," he writes, "from a world which is encompassed within certain bounds and static to one which is vast, feels infinite, and is amid an evolution spread over eons."[62] As everything is sped up, so at the same time everything must be controlled, planned, and sequenced. This doesn't happen merely because it technologically possible—it's not, in an absolute sense, as military technologies for seeing in real time are fallible, rely on flawed or partisan intelligence, and always lead to "unintentional" civilian casualties. It happens also because our secular security imaginaries desire it. In his fascinating *The Eye of War*, Antoine Bousquet argues that today's advanced warfare is characterized by a desire to see everything and know everything at once. "While total transparency of the battle space remains stubbornly elusive," Bousquet argues, "a convergence of perception and destruction has in effect been realized today."[63]

There is something almost theological in this convergence, recalling the capacity only previously imagined to be held by God acting from on high. Advancements in optical and informational technology from the late-twentieth century onward have made all kinds of killing not only technically

---

59. Taylor, *A Secular Age*, 327.
60. Taylor, *A Secular Age*, 59.
61. Moltmann, *Creating a Just Future*, vii.
62. Taylor, *A Secular Age*, 323.
63. Bousquet, *The Eye of War*, 2–3.

possible but plausibly autonomous of human control. The artificial intelligence (AI) of unmanned aerial vehicles makes warfare post-human, as evinced by the now-widespread use of drones in so-called "kill boxes" to the point that, according to the US military task force on drone policy, "basic categories such as 'battlefield,' 'combatant' and 'hostilities' no longer have clear or stable meaning."[64] Both space and time contract. In the disenchanted world, both vastness and immediacy come together to create a sense of helpless that is palpable: we are so small, and so responsible.

The response of the church to this contraction of time appears trapped between going with the flow and putting on the breaks. It is the mainline Protestants—both established and free churches—that are most likely to abandon liturgy and tradition and adapt to the immanence of time. By contrast, Taylor's response, with MacIntyre, has been to return to the constancy of the Catholic natural law tradition and neo-Aristotelianism. Similarly, in the Orthodox churches, recent political theology has been dominated by the so-called "neo-patristic synthesis" of the Russian Georges Florovsky, to the extent that it is "quite hard to find an Orthodox theological exploration of the positive nature of modernity."[65] With respect to security, neither of these extremes are viable response to imminence of threat.

There are surely choices other than the accelerator and break. For example, more sophisticated forms of JWT, such as Esther Reed's Augustinian one, adapt the tradition to new and "imminent" challenges from a "changing" security environment.[66] Reed outlines

> a continuum running from "ordinary" acts of illegality and aggression (requiring domestic or international policing, judicial procedures, judgment, and enforcement measures), through exercise of this right of self-defense by a nation-state, to "extraordinary" judgement and other actions in contexts where there might be a failure of "ordinary" means. This continuum of just defense and security is the basis for responsible innovation given AI-enabled grey zone and hybrid threats running from domestic criminality to international armed conflict, with attention paid to new (and old) questions of preparations for possible future conflict (*jus ante bellum*).[67]

---

64. Bousquet, *The Eye of War*, 5–6.
65. An exception in Orthodoxy with the work of Pantelis Kalaitzidis. Gallaher, "A Secularism of the Royal Doors," 135.
66. Reed, "Ecclesial Life and Political Practice."
67. Esther Reed, correspondence with the author.

The place of time in Reed's account of the adaptation of tradition to "new" challenges via a "continuum," "innovation" and "preparations for possible future conflict" is instructive. *Jus ante bellum* (right before war) is a third temporal category added to the *jus ad bellum* and *jus in bello* largely in response to the contemporary "responsibility to protect" agenda (see chapter 7).[68]

Notwithstanding the limitations identified in chapter 4, the JWT tradition in this form recognizes that imminent risks engender ethical responsibilities in advance of an event. This is true both for the state and for the church, to the extent that it wants to be a responsible actor in security affairs. Secular time demands that Christian reasoning responds to immediate threats in direct and practical ways. This is not so much a matter of theological preference as a condition of the age. At present, both the practices of the UN as Reed admits, and those of the post-Christendom peace church, as we must admit, are at best playing catch-up.[69] A new Christian realism is required to speak to the secularized world of security today. Such a realism is neither a defensive adaptation nor a simple reassertion of tradition. It must be a realism that derives its approach to security from a recognition of creative tension, an absence of consensus, and the imminence of threat. As we explore in the next chapter, twenty-first-century secular modes of realism are no more realistic enough about these challenges than the Christian realists of the twentieth century.

Some varieties of the secular

As we have discussed the three markers of security in the secular age, we have begun to probe variation in their imaginaries and communities. For conceptual clarity, it makes sense to identify the main types of imagined security community in the secular age. This can be represented for heuristic purposes on a simple 2 x 2 schematic with four ideal types that emerge from the four dialectically related forces recalled above (see table 2 below). This is an approximating exercise but a necessary one if we are to accommodate variation in "security after Christendom" while still seeking a general theory and theological interpretation of its form. The first three types will be interrogated over the next three chapters; each will be found inadequate on both

---

68. Brown and Bohm, "Introducing Jus ante Bellum."

69. Reed writes, "Allowing international law to play 'catch up' with US and UK routinized practices falls a long way short of Augustinian standards for politics east-of-Eden wherein the purpose of law is for the maintenance of order and hope of peace." Reed, "Ecclesial Life and Political Practice," 424.

normative and descriptive grounds. Most importantly, each will be found to be deeply unstable in their dialectical relations and thereby productive of insecurity.

Table 2: Imagined security communities in a secular age

Church-State Church-Society	Recentered	Decentered
Disenchanted	The Security State (chapter 6)	Liberal International Order (chapter 7)
Re-enchanted	Neo-Christendom (chapter 8)	Post-Christendom (part 3)

The first two ideal types are those where the disenchantment of society has been greatest, but even here theology is not entirely absent. The security state (chapter 6) is, as introduced above, the quintessential secular creation, emergent since at least Graeco-Roman times, which most clearly centers space, time, and ethics on itself. The liberal international order (chapter 7) arguably finds its origins in the late-Christendom "standard of civilization" debates in the imperial West of the nineteenth century,[70] however, it has arisen in its secular form since 1945 under American hegemony, economic interdependence, and security "co-binding" where states are tied to reciprocal agreements.[71] The intellectual imaginaries associated with these two security communities are political realism and liberalism, both of which, as we have seen, have strong Christian roots but which were thoroughly secularized as neo-realism and neoliberalism in the late-twentieth century. The second two ideal types are those where disenchantment has been weakest or where it has been faced with a process of revival or re-enchantment. *Neo-Christendom* (chapter 8) is a security community that is centered on the state or regime that it claims is defending the virtues of Christendom. Here, certain churches may partner in a Christian nationalist or civilizationist agenda, often against other denominations, faiths, and/or political ideologies. Vladimir Putin's Russia and its "Russian World" imaginary is the aforementioned approximation of this type,[72] and itself a reaction to Soviet-era

---

70. Phillips, "Saving Civilization from Empire."

71. Deudney and Ikenberry, "The Nature and Sources of Liberal International Order."

72. Stoeckl, "The Russian Orthodox Church's Conservative Crusade."

disenchantment and post-Soviet disorder.[73] By contrast, *Post-Christendom* (part 3) is found in a society where multiple denominations of the Christian faith and/or other faiths coexist. Here the patterns are most undetermined with the church sometimes engaging and sometimes withdrawing from the state, sometimes cooperating with other denominations, faiths, and/or political ideologies, and sometimes coming into conflict with them. Examples of this type are necessarily both global and local.

Toward post-Christendom

Simple schemata allow us to collect our thoughts, but categorizations of a given time or place as liberal international order or neo-Christendom are necessarily no more than crude approximations. In the real world, any given local movement, state institution, or transnational organization is likely to engage in an amalgam of practices and deploy a mixture of ideas that have their origins in various prior enchantments, disenchantments, imagined centers, and decentering imaginaries. Therefore, we need to probe further into processes of (dis)enchantment and (de)centering to grasp the conditions of security after Christendom and the challenges it presents to the church.

While each of Taylor's three modes of the secular are breaks from the traditions of Christendom, none of them are essentially antithetical to the Christian faith in its manifold and various expressions. The first, the secular security state, may be seen as one half of the Christendom dialectic and, where its executive decisions are limited by the checks and balances of a constitutional order, may not be excessively violent or idolatrous. The second, public disagreement, is plural, intermittent, and has commingled with religion at times to produce ideas like post-Christendom, the separation of church and state, and inter-faith dialogues. The third, the immanence of time, is arguably consistent with Christianity's own counter-Enlightenment thought and radical skepticism toward both dialectical materialism and crude progressivism; this much, at least, may be agreed by Nietzsche and his predecessor, the Christian existentialist Søren Kierkegaard. There is therefore encouragement to be found in disenchantment and its attendant security practices. Where once we imagined ourselves at the mercy of the world, we now see a great deal of the evil of that world to be constructed and therefore potentially deconstructed. The pacification of Europe's post-war and post-Christendom societies surely gives some grounds for hope.

---

73. Luehrmann, *Secularism Soviet Style*.

The challenge of post-Christendom is neither to row back to a time of eternal Christendom and the very public church nor to build uncritically upon the secular. Rather, as Christian generations past have done, the task may be construed as that of once more infusing the kingdom of the world with a witness to the kingdom of Christ. There are opportunities for this in the contemporary debate in the UN on so-called killer robots, as Reed observes. After the first recorded killing of a person by an autonomous UAV in Libya in 2020—that is, the first death in warfare chosen according to artificial intelligence—there was renewed urgency to agree a ban on the development and use of such weapons through the United Nations Convention on Certain Conventional Weapons. But the most-recent attempt to do so failed in December 2021 due to the familiar problem of the security dilemma, with states that claim to practice just war adjudging that if we don't develop these weapons others will. The US alone spent US$18 billion on autonomous weapons between 2016 and 2020.[74] The secular offers an opportunity to Christianity as, in David Martin's words, it "brings out the tensions between Christian virtues and the virtues of the citizen, between Christian martyrdom and republican heroism."[75] These tensions are our grounds for hope, the means to providence, and the reminder of redemption. It is these tensions we will highlight as we proceed to explorer each of the security communities of the secular age.

---

74. Dawes, "UN Fails to Agree on 'Killer Robot' Ban."
75. Martin, *On Secularization*, 188.

CHAPTER 6

Insecurities of the Security State

So, Samuel told all the words of the LORD to the people who were asking for a king from him. He said, "These will be the ways of the king who will reign over you: he will take your sons and appoint them to his chariots and to be his horsemen and to run before his chariots.... He will take the best of your fields and vineyards and olive orchards and give them to his servants. He will take the tenth of your grain and of your vineyards and give it to his officers and to his servants. He will take your male servants and female servants and the best of your young men and your donkeys, and put them to his work. He will take the tenth of your flocks, and you shall be his slaves. And in that day, you will cry out because of your king, whom you have chosen for yourselves, but the LORD will not answer you in that day."

1 SAMUEL 8:10-11, 14-18

But who guarantees us that this "strong state" which offers protection and security will not itself become the wolf and eat up its citizens, moving from the security State to "state security"? As history also shows, out of the security States have come the dictatorships which disregard and destroy people, to which we have given the names of the well-known animals of prey: the terrible "Leviathan," the state "Moloch"[1] and the "stasioctopus."[2] How do we

---

1. Moloch is a Hebrew name for a bull-headed idol, apparently referring to a Cannanite God mentioned in Leviticus (18:21; 20:2-5).
2. The octopus was a common metaphor for the East German secret police. Koehler, *Stasi*, 9.

then come to pluralistic freedom without chaos and to peaceful unity without dictatorship?

JÜRGEN MOLTMANN[3]

On the morning of December 8, 2021, the then British foreign secretary, Lis Truss, gave her maiden policy speech at the Royal Institute of International Affairs (Chatham House) in London. Entitled "Network of Liberty," she cast a vision for a future after Brexit, "an outward-looking, sovereign nation, we are rebuilding our muscle to fulfil the promise of Global Britain" which will "advance the frontiers of freedom."[4] In the manner of her hero, Margaret Thatcher, Truss framed the state as the defender of individuals over the collective, untrammeled free markets over regulation, and democracy over autocracy. Some in the audience that day were skeptical. They may have pointed to the fact that liberty may be used by individuals and corporations with power and wealth to exploit those who are weaker. The deregulation of markets under Thatcher made these things more likely. They could also have noted that democracy can be subverted to ensure wealthy donors and big business protect their private interests over the public good. One journalist in the audience asked Truss specifically about the UK's openness to kleptocrats—those that have earned their money through political connections in highly corrupt states—particularly in the former Soviet states: "Is the British Government doing enough, in terms of restricting the access of Russian finance to the City of London to launder its cash?" Truss's answer was the shortest of the dozen questions she faced overall: "We have very tough anti-money-laundering rules here and anti-corruption rules."[5]

Several hours later that day, in the very same room, my co-authors and I launched our Chatham House report, *The UK's Kleptocracy Problem*. The report showed that the UK's rules were not working. Clients with profiles indicating high risk of corruption were just as likely to be served by UK banks as those without such profiles.[6] Thousands of investor visas—around half the total from 2008 to 2015—had been given to wealthy businesspeople from kleptocracies.[7] Our report included an appendix with £2 billion worth of properties purchased in the UK by elite businesspeople, political

3. Moltmann, "Covenant or Leviathan?," 19.
4. Truss, "Building the Network of Liberty."
5. Chatham House, "Foreign Secretary Liz Truss."
6. Heathershaw et al., *The UK's Kleptocracy Problem*, 22–24.
7. Heathershaw et al., *The UK's Kleptocracy Problem*, 50–54.

elites, and their relatives from some of the most corrupt post-Soviet states, especially Azerbaijan, Kazakhstan, and Russia.[8] Measures promised by the David Cameron government in 2016 had failed or stalled with no "unexplained wealth orders" used and the promised public register of property ownership not yet introduced.[9] *The UK's Kleptocracy Problem* also explored the reputation management service offered by London lawyers and agents to facilitate philanthropy to charities and universities and donations to political parties. Several of the ruling Conservative party's largest donors—naturalized British citizens—made their money in the post-Soviet states with major questions over their sources of wealth and fealty to the regimes under which this money had been made.[10] We concluded that successive UK governments had weakened the efficiency and effectiveness of the rule of law and exposed Britain to security threats associated with hosting corrupt capital and rival kleptocratic factions in the UK.[11] In similar terms, Milbank and Pabst dismiss British contemporary foreign policy in this way: "an oligarchic cabal whose loyalties are more to an international moneyed elite has abandoned all semblance of an industrial strategy intimately linked to the United Kingdom's security at home and its ability to project power abroad."[12]

The link between kleptocracy—and the failure to counter it—and security were becoming evident. In Salisbury, in 2018, Russia used biological weapons to target Sergei Skripal, one of their former intelligence officers who had defected to Britain and was providing insights into Russian organized crime in Europe. The attack led to the death of the innocent bystander Dawn Sturgess. When the UK responded via expelling diplomats, the Russian Embassy responded by tweeting about the bond issuance for EN+, one of its major energy companies, on the London Stock Exchange three days after the Salisbury poisoning with the provocative question "business as usual?"[13] In the aftermath of the attack, the Foreign Affairs Committee and Intelligence and Security Committee of the House of Commons both

---

8. Heathershaw et al., *The UK's Kleptocracy Problem*, 27–33.

9. Heathershaw et al., *The UK's Kleptocracy Problem*, 34–43.

10. After the report's publication, Chatham House received pre-action letters from two of these donors who quibbled at the precise language we used to describe their involvement in criminal offences of money laundering and the paying of bribes. At the time of writing one of these actions remained open. They are both strategic lawsuits against public participation (SLAPP).

11. Heathershaw et al., *The UK's Kleptocracy Problem*, 46–47.

12. Milbank and Pabst, *Politics of Virtue*, 348.

13. Quoted in Foreign Affairs Committee of the House of Commons, *Moscow's Gold*.

issued separate reports arguing that the UK's security was harmed by its exposure to kleptocratic cash.[14] Despite these events and reports, the Boris Johnson government appeared unwilling to do anything about the problem. Its most high-profile measure, anti-corruption sanctions for individuals introduced by former foreign secretary Dominic Raab, was left unused by Raab's successor, Liz Truss, during her time as foreign secretary.[15] The UK's 2021 *Integrated Review of Foreign and Defence Policy* made no mention of kleptocracy and only a few passing mentions of "corruption," mainly with respect to the global anticorruption sanctions that would go unused under Truss.[16] The government's traditional view of statecraft—based on some amalgam of dominant realist and liberal approaches to diplomacy and defense relations between states—blinded it to the full nature of global politics and the character of the state.

The UK's blinkered perspective on foreign affairs was exposed when Russia invaded Ukraine in February 2022. The sanctions threatened in the weeks prior to the invasion were too late and apparently served as no serious deterrent to the Kremlin, which had grown used to moralizing rhetoric by the West, which continued to buy Russian commodities and host its corrupt elites and monies in their states.[17] This was "business as usual." That this hypocrisy and strategic incoherence was now laid bare caused Western governments to impose sanctions with an unexpected severity. In the UK, hosting many billions of dollars of Russian companies and assets, sanctions were initially delayed as the UK's Office for Sanctions Implementation was under-resourced and unprepared. A panicked surge in recruitment in March and April 2022 sought to double its size.[18] Legislation was rushed through parliament to remove the review process on sanctions, to finally introduce a register of the beneficial ownership of properties, and to make it easier for the government to freeze "unexplained wealth."[19] Well over a thousand sanctions designations against Russian and Belarusian individuals and

---

14. Foreign Affairs Committee, *Moscow's Gold*; Intelligence and Security Committee of Parliament, *Russia*.

15. Redress, "UK Anti-Corruption Sanctions."

16. HM Government, *Global Britain in a Competitive Age*.

17. This point was also made after the 2022 invasion of Ukraine by the Irish prime minister, Michael Martin. Kelso, "UK Response to Salisbury Poisonings 'Indulged' Russia."

18. As of March 2021, the OFSI had 37.8 staff, in comparison to an estimated 259 FTE staff members at the US Office of Foreign Assets Control. In March and April 2022, it advertised for thirty-three new staff, mainly at entry-grade level. Personal communication to author.

19. HM Government, Economic Crime Act 2022.

companies were eventually expedited. All of this merely demonstrated the outsized role that the UK—and "Londongrad" in particular—had played in Russia's kleptocracy.[20] This was not just about gas sales. Without the integration of the Russian kleptocracy into Western Europe, it is hard to imagine the Kremlin having the confidence that its invasion of Ukraine would go unchallenged. The surge of sanctions was too late.

There is little theoretical work in the study of security that addresses kleptocracy as a form of centering power with implications for who is included, protected, and provided. In the next two chapters, and in light of the problem of kleptocracy, we explore the main approaches that do exist: secular realism (focused on the centered state and national security) and liberalism (a decentered approach focusing on the liberal international order). In both these approaches, Christendom's cultural and scriptural referents continue to be drawn upon, but inconsistently and sometimes unwittingly. We will see over the remainder of part 2 how secular state power is effectively established through a continuous and precarious process of recentering the state. In this recentering we see some functionally similar security practices to those we saw in chapter 2: the division into geopolitical blocs as seen in the Cold War, limited trade and cooperation across those divides, and a tendency to cast the conflict in civilizational and zero-sum terms. However, this recentering is undermined by two inter-related problems: first, in the post-Christendom context it is increasingly difficult to generate consensus from a secular public regarding national struggles; second, the state in practice has been transformed to facilitate flows and concentrations of global capital to benefit elites, oligarchs, and kleptocrats. Therefore, the remainder of this chapter proceeds in three parts. It first outline realism after Christendom and reveals the omissions and inadequacies of the paradigm's account of security. Second, it introduces the concept of "securitization" to explain how states and other actors attempt to generate consensus over security threats. Finally, we consider the political economy of a state that kills, steals, and cures in order to get a fuller grasp of the nature of (in)security under the modern secular state.

Political Realism in a Secular Age

We will begin this exploration of secular security by considering how national security is constructed after the putative death of God. (Christian) realism had embarked from the premise that anarchy in international politics—not chaos, but the absence of world government—made survival of

20. Belton, *Putin's People*.

the state and national security their primary and unavoidable tasks. From this perspective, states could not easily withdraw from the imperative to arm themselves, use force and the threat of force, and form defensive alliances with other states. If they did so, they would be insecure and open to coercion and invasion. Or so the story goes. However, there were two main problems with this theory. The first was about the primacy of protection over provision: how threats emerge; how certain things become matters of security, while others do not. The second and prior problem concerned inclusion: who or what is a security actor. For realists, states are the agents of this order, seeking survival through means of self-help. Threats to this order are real and objective. According to this view, humans are prone to aggression and violence—something that Christian realists attributed to the fall, but secular neo-realists theorized as being the product of the absence of world government. Either way, national security and war are inevitable (and necessary) evils and are therefore, in the Clausewitzian dictum, the continuations of politics by other means. Power is the end of politics and the means of national security—and is therefore a good. Peace, as such, is a temporary and fragile condition; it is achieved by the balance of power. There is little point disturbing such a balance by provocative actions, such as challenging Russian kleptocratic wealth in London, as that wealth is considered by realists to be secondary and largely unrelated to national security.

We ended chapter 3 by touching upon the secularization of Christian realism at the end of the twentieth century in the work of Kenneth Waltz and John Mearsheimer. Rather than a distinct theory, realism (realpolitik) is a paradigm that has begotten a variety of debates and approaches. Waltz was a structural realist who in *Man, the State and War* (1959) critiqued the first and second images of international politics—that is, the emphasis on sin and human nature (the first image) and the character of the state (the second image), which had been central to the Christian realist's explanation for war and insecurity. In his *Theory of International Politics* (1979), Waltz focused on the third image: the anarchic structure of the international system. He used anarchy in the manner of the political theorist to denote not the presence of widespread violence but the absence of hierarchy. With no God at work in history and no world government there was nothing to constrain the power-seeking and security-maximizing actions of the state. In the most anarchical of circumstances—those without a balance of power—the security dilemma would necessitate that war between great powers was frequent and costly. However, although Waltz was rightly criticized for ignoring the tradition of anarchism and constitutionalism in political theory,[21] he did

---

21. Prichard, "What Can the Absence of Anarchism Tell Us."

recognize that bipolar systems with effective military balances could deter direct conflict between great powers for extended periods of time. Mutual Assured Destruction was therefore good for security.

While Waltz was a theorist of the Cold War, Mearsheimer provided a theory of the post-Cold War era in *The Tragedy of Great Power Politics* (2001). Whereas Greek tragedy was founded on the hubris of political leaders, for Mearsheimer this hubris was a structural necessity brought about by the absence of God and government in international affairs. To this point, Mearsheimer was in keeping with Waltz. However, while Waltz explained a bipolar system and thereby arrived at defensive realism where "states concentrate on maintaining the balance of power," Mearsheimer's focus was the "unipolar moment" where the United States acted offensively to secure its primacy at the end of the twentieth century.[22] No realist felt this could possibly last, not just because the rise of China was on the horizon, but because dominant powers never remain unchallenged, according to International Relations, for long. At least, this is what the history of Europe appeared to tell us from the Peloponnesian Wars of the Greeks to the brief moments of British imperial heights in the mid-nineteenth century and Nazi dominance over Europe in 1940.

Mearsheimer focused on the tendency in international politics to revert to multi-polar systems with several great powers competing with one another for the prize of hegemony.[23] It is these great powers that matter, he argued, with small states and unrecognized peoples cowering in their wake. Britain sought hegemony of the global seas to expand through empire, deploying slavery, embargoes, and famine in partnership with its local proxies and wiping out several people groups in the process. Germany sought hegemony over the European continent for the Reich via invasion and occupation, with more extreme but mort short-lived consequences. These are both examples of what Mearsheimer denotes as "offensive realism," where "the international system creates powerful incentives for states to look for opportunities to gain power at the expense of rivals, and to take advantage of those situations when the benefits outweigh the costs." As such, offensive realists "believe that status quo powers are rarely found in world politics."[24]

Like any credible theorist, Mearsheimer admits that "a few cases contradict the main claims of the theory, . . . although the better the theory, the fewer the anomalies."[25] However, the problem for realism in recent de-

22. Mearsheimer, *Tragedy*, 22.
23. Mearsheimer, *Tragedy*, 5.
24. Mearsheimer, *Tragedy*, 21.
25. Mearsheimer, *Tragedy*, 10.

cades is that such exceptions have proliferated. The US has arguably sought global economic hegemony—to make everyone do business in dollars on its terms—and in normative hegemony for its idea of the world, often at the expense of its military security. But there was also plenty of evidence that the US and its allies sought to expand what it called the liberal international order, as it understood it, in small states like Kosovo and Sierra Leone, often against its interests and the advice of realists inside and outside of government. Some regions (especially the European Union) were not anarchic but had deep levels of integration between states, which relied upon each other for strategically important goods. Other regions (including much of sub-Saharan Africa) also lacked strong states but in a way that led to armed conflict between militias and insurgents, not states.[26] Many former Soviet states managed to have good relations with Russia, China, and the USA without needing to bandwagon behind a particular one.[27] Several states, like Kazakhstan, gave up their nuclear weapons without the reasonable prospect of protection under the "nuclear umbrella" of any power and formed a "nuclear weapons free zone" in their regions.[28] Some sought to amend realism to account for these shifts. Mohammed Ayoob offered "subaltern realism" to explain the predominance of intrastate conflict.[29] Ruth Deyermond explained the coexistence of Russian, Chinese, and Western powers in Central Asia from 2001–13 as "matrioshka hegemony," using the metaphor of the Russian wooden doll.[30] Even after the US/NATO withdrawal from Afghanistan in 2014, Russia and China manage to coordinate and cooperate in their "common adjacent region" against the expectation of the realists.[31]

Effective answers to these questions required recognition that the state is not a unitary actor whose only attribute of true importance is its military power. Rather, states are complex and fractured institutions, parts of which pursue defense, other parts economic growth or societal stability, and still others moral causes. The more thoughtful realists had long accepted this reality but considered it a secondary or marginal concern. But by the end of the Cold War, issues such as terrorism and migration, which offered either little or no threat to national security (that is, to the state), rose to the top of the security agenda. Understanding why and how this happened is essential for us to explain and understand security. The question that security

26. Reno, *Warlord Politics*.
27. Cooley, *Great Games, Local Rules*.
28. Kassenova, *Atomic Steppe*.
29. Ayoob, "Inequality and Theorizing in International Relations."
30. Deyermond, "Matrioshka HJegemony?"
31. Cooley, Lewis, and Herd, "Russia and China in Central Asia."

scholars faced was, if security and insecurity are not generated purely by objective (and God-given) conditions that demand a strong sovereign and well-armed polity, and if the subjective security agenda is no longer consistent with the logic of national security, what explains both how something becomes a threat, and how the nation state remains at the center of international security policy and practice. In other words, how is security (re)centered on the state?

Realists have dismissed the 1990s with its "new interventionism" and a "unipolar moment" of American power as a "holiday from history."[32] However, during this time the world stopped behaving and thinking as realists had expected it to during the Cold War and it has not returned to the realist model of balances of power and the ever-present risk of armed conflict between countries. Inter-state war has been in perpetual decline since 1945 as political violence has transformed to be about the state and/or by non-state actors rather than between states. With the end of the Soviet Union, a new armed conflict between the US and a rising great power, particularly China, has thus far not occurred despite realists talk of a "Thucydides trap."[33] Mearsheimer advocated that a newly unified Germany, as the Great Power of a new Europe, should acquire nuclear weapons to guarantee its security[34]—but German chancellors from Helmut Kohl to Angela Merkel have not followed suit. Migration has risen as a major security threat, according to many European states, which have deployed their militaries, rewritten their laws, and built new border defenses against it.[35] None of this made sense from a realist perspective.

That these developments were unexpected was, according to critics, due to core intellectual deficiencies in realism, particular in its secular modes. First, the state-centrism of realists assumed and ascribed exclusive agency to the governments of great powers. At the very least, publics also matter. No post-Cold War German leader who wished to be re-elected would have proposed a nuclear weapons program.[36] Second, the assumption that threats were objective blinded the realists to how something like drugs or migration or kleptocracy can become a threat very quickly or how whole societies could be transformed to something like a total-war footing with respect to the novel coronavirus pandemic. Countervailing evidence

---

32. Krauthammer, "The Unipolar Moment Revisited," 6.

33. "The Thucydides Trap" refers to the classical Greek author's argument that the rise of Athens inevitably led to war with Sparta.

34. Mearsheimer, "Back to the Future."

35. Lazaridis, *Security, Insecurity and Migration in Europe*.

36. Brown, *Understanding International Relations*, 79.

was dismissed as subjective and therefore irrelevant. Third, secular realists, particularly of the structural kind, were excessively materialist, assuming that the size, technological capacity, and effective deployment of militaries was the key determinant of security. And yet, one critic observed, "500 British nuclear weapons are less threatening to the United States than 5 North Korean nuclear weapons."[37] This may seem obvious, but from the neo-realist perspective that dominated the study of IR in the late twentieth century—where shared histories and cultures are of minimal importance, all alliances are temporary, and states must remain functionally independent of one another—it was a puzzle to be explained.

Finally, and cumulatively, the arguments of realists were extraordinarily circular. Military affairs were the primary matters of security because the theory said so (despite the fact that the failure to control the 1919 influenza epidemic killed more people than the direct and indirect deaths from the Great War). War between great powers is assumed to be inevitable. Such "realism" dominated geopolitical thinking on both sides during the Cold War. Soviet leaders right up to Gorbachev thought war with the USA was unavoidable. Churchill laid plans to invade the Soviet Union after World War II while American nuclear planners debated first-strike plans for a nuclear war in the 1950s. Both East and West assumed war was inevitable. Realists like Mearsheimer told them this was because there was nothing to prevent dangerous and aggressive attempts to maximize military security. They pointed to Cold War "proxy wars" in places like Vietnam (with US support for South Vietnam) and Afghanistan (with the Soviet occupation after the invasion of 1979). There was some truth to these claims, but they told us little about how local and regional dynamics shaped these wars. In sum, realism was failing in each of its tasks: descriptively, it was providing a partial and inaccurate description of post-Cold War affairs; prescriptively, it was recommending nuclear armament and future wars for which (thankfully) policy-makers were not preparing; normatively, it assumed order amidst chaos and human suffering, which it disregarded as at most of secondary concern.

Realism was especially poor at dealing with aspects of empire and "civilization" that were hugely significant in an era of decolonization. In Christendom, "civilized" states, which were often also empires, were bound to a common space of Christendom; beyond these spaces, the gloves came off. However, in a secular age, security spaces are both more local and global; what we have is a patchwork of security practice in what the field of IR denotes as a multi-polar world. The US famously declared

---

37. Wendt, "Constructing International Politics," 73.

American-controlled territory in Guantanamo as legally non-American and therefore outside the reach of the constitution for the purpose of using legal torture in interrogation. The UK allows the tax havens of British Overseas Territories to launder money for organized criminals and corrupt politicians not as an exception to British banking but for the purpose of a set of services of financial secrecy and complexity offered by the city of London.[38] Guantanamo and offshore tax havens are political choices, but choices made possible by the post-imperial geography of global politics where Caribbean and other overseas possessions remain under the sovereignty of states such as the US and the UK. At the same time, the decline of the imperial structures of the Christendom world has been accompanied by a proliferation of new states, both recognized and unrecognized. The number of UN member states has roughly tripled since the organization's founding since 1945, with 193 recognized in 2021 and many more having no UN status. Global and regional organizations proliferate in this environment, and yet none of these, apart from the European Union, can claim to offer a common security space anything like Christendom.

In sum, realism's limits can be found in the superficiality of its explanation. Any meaningful theory of security must account not for its uniformity—states being forced to behave in the same way—but its *variety*—the state (and many other actors) differing widely on what is a considered a threat and which policies must be pursued. Arnold Wolfers argues, in the height of the Cold War,

> After all that has been said, little is left of the sweeping generalization that in actual practice, nations, guided by their national security interest, tend to pursue a uniform and therefore imitable policy of security. Instead, there are numerous reasons why they should differ widely in this respect, with some standing close to complete indifference to security or complete reliance on non-military means, others close to the pole of insistence on absolute security or of complete reliance on coercive power.[39]

There is simply no single foundation against which choices between indifference and absolute security may be assessed. Alexander Wendt, writing in the Cold War's aftermath, made this stark: "[international] anarchy is what states make of it."[40] And what they make of it is a matter not of divine instruction but of social construction. By failing to recognize this variety of security, realism was simply not real enough.

38. Bullough, *Moneyland*.
39. Wolfers, "National Security," 491–92.
40. Wendt, "Anarchy Is What States Make of It."

SECURITIZATION AND THE RETURN OF RATIONALISM

If national security is neither real (in the sense of objectively given) nor rational (in the sense of reflecting a shared vision of the common good), what produces and reproduces it? How are threats identified, provisions allocated, and protection offered? These are questions both of how something becomes a security matter and how elites generate consensus about these threats. To answer these questions, we may return to the thought of a Christian realist, the late-twentieth-century "English School" thinker Martin Wight. In his lectures of the 1950s, Wight argued that IR theory is formed of three traditions: realism, rationalism, and revolutionism.[41] For Wight, the revolutionists were those of Kantian globalism, but this category may be expanded to other structuralist and post-structuralist accounts of how global economy and culture undermine international order. Over the remainder of part 2, we will tap the Marxist tradition alongside the equally revolutionary currents of postmodernism, feminism, and postcolonialism that emerged in response to Marxism's historical materialism and structural determinism. First, we consider a branch of rationalist thought called constructivism, which with respect to the study of security developed the concept of securitization.

From the 1980s, scholars in Europe began to debate the process by which something became a matter of security. The Copenhagen School was the name attached to a group of scholars associated with the University of Copenhagen whose influence has been considerable in the study of security. Following the ideas of the Danish political scientist Ole Waever, the British IR scholar Barry Buzan, and colleagues in Copenhagen, this process has been denoted by the term *securitization*. A whole lexicon has developed as the concept has been applied so that we can say that migration has been *securitized* in Europe while Irish republicanism has been *desecuritized*. Securitization is not a theory of security itself but a descriptive concept that helps us better understand how competing recentering, decentering, and reenchanting actors do security differently and confront each other in a dialectical manner. It is social constructivist and denotes, "the [social] process by which something gets designated" as a matter of security.[42] The process entails something going from being a normal matter of law and politics to one where survival is at stake and exceptional and violent measures could be taken against identified threats. The Copenhagen School invoked the idea of security "speech act," following the performance theory of the British

41. Wight, *International Theory*.
42. Buzan, Wæver, and De Wilde, *Security*, 21.

linguistic theorist J. L. Austin and others as the grounds for its emphasis on discourse and the power of its words. When securitization takes place, a *securitizing actor* identifies a threat to the survival of a *referent object* in order to convince an *audience* and take *extraordinary measures*. These threat claims and measures typically require cooperation from *functional actors*, often in the face of opposition from *desecuritizing actors*. The purpose of this analysis was to take the mysterious and secret world of national security into the realm of normal political analysis where we may ask: What's at stake? Who wins? Who loses?

What is valuable about the concept of securitization is its ability to narrate change: old security threats ceasing, new security threats arising, and whole new actors entering the fray. It helps describe how certain "new" security challenges were securitized (e.g., terrorism) while others were barely securitized or securitized long after the evidence indicated that their objective threat is existential (e.g., climate change). Air travel is an illustrative example. In fifteen years from 2004 to 2019, the number of scheduled passengers boarded per year increased sevenfold from 650 million to more than 4.5 billion,[43] substantially increasing carbon dioxide emissions to over a billion tons in 2018.[44] Governments encouraged this growth by investing public funds to build new airports and offering subsidies to airlines to use smaller regional airports as an engine for economic development. Had climate change been securitized this would not have happened. What is all the more remarkable about this growth is that it took place at a time when air travel was securitized for the entirely different reason of counterterrorism. Passengers were forced to endure intrusive new checks on their persons and possessions while liberal democracies began to interdict at airports those it suspected of involvement in terrorism for interrogation and sometimes torture.

To distinguish between these different types of securitization, the Copenhagen school identified five sectors in which securitization takes place. The (1) political and (2) military sectors were the traditional domains of security while the (3) economic, (4) environmental, and (5) societal were novel to security theory.[45] Although poverty, natural disaster, and racism had been threatening survival since human civilization's beginnings, these threats never before had security theory that could explain how they may be securitized or, more commonly, how they were desecuritized by actors who stood to lose economically from these matters becoming security issues.

43. Statista, "Number of Scheduled Passengers Boarded."
44. Ritchie, "Climate Change and Flying."
45. Buzan et al., *Security*.

In certain cases, "threats" were securitized despite the economic costs to business of doing so due to their perceived threat to societal security. Some of the early work of securitization theorists was to highlight how migration, which benefitted European economies, had come to be portrayed as a security threat.[46] They identified this political shift almost twenty years before anti-immigrant populism spread across the continent and led the new nationalist governments in the 2010s, produced a security-based approach to the Syrian refugee crisis, and fueled Brexit in the UK.

The rationalist Copenhagen School appeared to correct the theoretical errors of the realists. First, they avoided state-centrism. The referent object in securitization were often states but they may also be private and societal groups, including those representing ethnic groups, other identity groups, a corporation, or a social movement, or even the planet and its ecosystem.[47] Even if the referent object was the state, the securitizing actor—a person or group with authority—may be a media outlet, business, or a celebrity acting on their behalf. Equally, states can and do securitize the media, corporations, and social media stars. Second, securitization theory recognized that objectivity was not given. What became a security matter was a product of relations of authority and performance by which those with power and influence denote a threat to their survival—it is thus a "self-referential practice"[48] and, in our terms, a recentering project. Third, securitization theorists recognized that "material facilitating conditions," such as wealth and military power, are often less important than cultural orders that frame how we think about security.[49] Ideas about religion and the state, such as those of *Russkiy Mir*, also shape security relations. These theoretical steps promised a sea change in security analysis. Sometimes, and unwisely, they over-estimated the symbolic aspect to the extent that they ignored material factors almost entirely. But the best of this work constructed genealogies of security to demonstrate how conventional wisdoms about who is an enemy and what was a threat come about. In some cases, a very public moment of embarrassment locked in discourse of enmity between groups. For example, consider how Cuba and Iran were securitized as threats by the US foreign policy establishment after their revolutions, which had led to the expulsions and dispossessions of Americans from their territories.[50] In other cases, enduring gendered or racial biases have meant that those with authority have

46. Huysmans, "The European Union and the Securitization of Migration."
47. Buzan et al., *Security*, 21–23.
48. Buzan et al., *Security*, 25.
49. Buzan et al., *Security*, 57.
50. Campbell, *Writing Security*.

for many decades not spoken out publicly and taken action—that is, make security speech acts—even though many women, children, and minorities in their societies were suffering harm.[51] Securitization is about actions and inactions.

It is of little surprise that in a Europe living through the postmodern zeitgeist, and in a security environment poorly explained by realism, securitization quickly replaced it as the dominant security theory taught in universities. Its ideas also coincided with new security policies, which paid more attention to non-state actors, soft power, and the symbolic aspects of security. Development, peacebuilding, counterterrorism, and climate change, among many others, all became security issues. In Europe, the threats were happening largely to someone else (development and peacebuilding), were overwhelmingly symbolic threats to authority rather than physical challenges to the state (terrorism), or they remained over the horizon (climate change). In securitizing these issues, policy-makers were no longer behaving as the realists expected. The realists could not explain how they had ignored or disregarded the issues that made most people insecure for so long.

Despite these advancements on realism, the rationalists' securitization theory was not without its defects. It lacked a normative or prescriptive perspective on security. It could not tell us what security was *for*. On the one hand, it seemed that desecuritization was the moral good, as "extraordinary measures" are by their nature beyond the law and of uncertain effectiveness.[52] In democracies, we assume that most policy questions are best addressed within the normal realms of law and politics. On the other hand, if certain possible "threats" to certain groups are hidden or silenced in the policy of states, there is perhaps value in securitizing them, such as in the invocation of "human security" or "women's security." To more radical thinkers, the relative silence of the Copenhagen School on questions of gender and race indicated its inherent conservatism, gender-blindness, and even racism.[53] Over time, the lens of securitization was broadened. Psychological and emotional processes of elites and publics becoming fearful were crucially important.[54] Images, videos, the built environment, and the organization of space all matter too. A more verbose but realistic definition of securitization emerged. According to Thierry Balzacq, securitization is:

51. Hansen, "Gender, Nation, Rape."
52. Hansen, "Reconstructing Desecuritisation."
53. McSweeney, *Security, Identity and Interests*; Hansen, "Gender, Nation, Rape"; Howell and Richter-Montpetit, "Is Securitization Theory Racist?"
54. Van Rythoven, "Learning to Feel, Learning to Fear?"

an articulated assemblage of *practices* whereby heuristic artefacts (metaphors, policy tools, image repertoires, analogies, stereotypes, emotions, etc.) are *contextually* mobilized by a *securitizing actor*, who works to prompt an *audience* to build a coherent network of implications (feelings, sensations, thoughts, and institutions) about the critical vulnerability of a *referent object*, that concurs with the securitizing actor's reasons for choices and actions, by investing the referent subject with such an aura of unprecedented threatening complexion that a *customized policy* must be undertaken immediately to block its development.[55]

Such securitization took place in many states of the global North to respond to COVID-19 as extraordinary limits were placed on freedom of movement through lockdowns, "zero-COVID" policies, and the long-term closures of borders to foreign travelers. However, we saw relatively few of these measures in the Global South. There is nothing essential or necessary to any given customized security policy; sometimes they are based on sound science (as in the COVID-19 case), and other times they are based on myth and conjecture. Stereotypes and emotions matter in all cases, however scientific is the basis for the policy.

As a descriptive concept, securitization broadened, deepened, and radicalized the traditional study of security while offering little hope itself for better provision and protection. The moral concern of the critics was rather that of inclusion. Security studies, reflecting changes across academia, increasingly focused on who was included and who excluded in security policies and practice. As Williams argued, the security process may still be circular as issues go full circle from the non-political to the political and to security level before the measures themselves become normalized and no longer subject to debate or much fear.[56] While there is an objective or external reality to war—the battlefield—security has no such basis. "The subject of security," one leading critic declared, "is the subject of security."[57] By this, he meant that if we know who gets to write security policy, we discover who is included, protected, and provided for in the name of security. National security claims to represent a shared vision of the common good, but it rarely achieves widespread acceptance of this common good by the members of the nation. National security, to paraphrase Robert Cox, is for some people and some purpose.[58] If well-educated white men in wealthy

55. Balzacq, "A Theory of Securitization," 3.
56. Williams, "Securitization as Political Theory."
57. Walker, "The Subject of Security," 78.
58. Cox, "Social Forces, States and World Orders," 128.

Western states are disproportionately influential in international security affairs, why should it surprise us that they are those who are most secure? The remainder of the chapter summarizes the consequences of a state that works for certain parts of the nation and not others.

The State That Kills, Steals, and Cures

While securitization opened up the possibility that other actors may replace the nation-state as the subject and object of security, for now most political imaginaries, both secular and theological, retain the state at the center. Therefore, we must consider how this recentering takes place in the aftermath of Christendom. How have the spatial and temporal grounds upon which national security is reproduced shifted? This is not merely about the designation of enemies (spatial othering), but about flight from a backward past (temporal othering). "Religion," as defined by the state, is the foremost spatial and temporal other of the secular state, as by excluding religion, state actors are able to deny and thereby rewrite the role of theology, religion, and violence in their own political order.[59] At the same time, this "other" is a constituent ingredient of the secular self. There is thus an inherent contradiction at the heart of secular security imaginaries.

Recalling our argument, the modern state arises not against the sacred and its wars of religion but out of theological debates around the violent state-making process that occurs along with the decentering of Christendom from the thirteenth century onward. At its point of origin, in the late Middle Ages, the secular state is distinctly "Judeo-Christian" (in Hurd's terms) or "confessional." It is, as Luca Mavelli summarizes, the product of "the process of centralization of sovereignty and territorial demarcation that, following the confessionalization thesis, appears to be itself involved in the production of violence and therefore in the production of insecurity."[60] It is here where we may extend Schmitt's familiar dictum that "all significant concepts of the modern theory of the state are secularized theological concepts."[61] Therefore, state-centric national security is negative and exclusive in the manner that the security practices of late-Christendom also tended—under assumptions of nominalism and voluntarism (see below)—toward boundary-making and fear-mongering.

This national security of post-Christendom is most visible when we recognize that the security the state collectively seeks is not just physical

---

59. Cavanaugh, *The Myth*.
60. Mavelli, "Security and Secularization," 183.
61. Schmitt, *Political Theology*, 36.

but *ontological* in the manner identified by David Campbell, Jennifer Mitzen, and others. "Security," according to this view, "is not just a category of political issues, nor even a basic function of the state, but an idea that is productive of the state."[62] In Charles Tilly's more materialist account, "war made the state and the state made war"; the state he argues is a "protection racket." But what it seeks to protect is not the lives of its human collective but its very identity as a corporate and national entity.[63] That identity is one that reflects the interests and values of its elite—largely capital-owners who, in the West at least, are disproportionately white and male. In the background, meanwhile, it is overwhelmingly poor, brown, and female labor that sustains the state at the street level. The idea of ontological security necessitates that a state collective identity is formed. This cannot simply be some instrumentally composed amalgam of elite interests but based on a friend/enemy distinction between trusted allies and long-standing enemies. Rather than merely being subject to the security dilemma, from which they are unable to escape, states require the conflictual relations of the security dilemma for their very existence.[64] The security dilemma is constitutive of the state. Similarly, tragedy is an accurate descriptor of political affairs not because of some metaphysical realities of anarchy and the security dilemma, but because it is both "constructed and inescapable."[65] Such a claim is not merely theoretical but theological. In the language of social science, we may say that the secular state "requires discourses of 'danger' to provide a new theology of truth about who and what 'we' are by highlighting who or what 'we' are not, and what 'we' have to fear."[66]

This discourse of danger "replicates the logic of Christendom's evangelism of fear," the period in the thirteenth to sixteenth centuries where a weakening *respublica christianium* sought to counter threats from without (the Ottomans) and within (radical sects) by whipping up fear of these others.[67] But how can we reconcile Christianity's putative universalism, which the secular state has lost, with Christendom's "evangelism of fear," which it has retained?[68] For Mavelli, it was the nominalism and voluntarism— "a world characterized by chaos and lacking an underlying unity"—that

---

62. Bourne, *Understanding Security*, 74.
63. Bourne, *Understanding Security*, 75.
64. Mitzen, "Ontological Security in World Politics," 341.
65. Paipais, "Necessary Fiction," 147.
66. Campbell, *National Deconstruction*, 48. See also Mavelli, "Security and Secularization," 183.
67. Campbell, *National Deconstruction*, 50.
68. Mavelli, "Security and Secularization," 184.

marks the beginning of disenchantment in the late-medieval period. This transformation within Christendom made our idea of the state. Nominalism and voluntarism supplanted a dominion that was once multinational, plural, and inclusive under decentered medieval Christendom with one that was national, singular, and exclusive under anarchy.[69] The putative solution of seeking a new center turns out to exacerbate the problem. It was the attempt to construct a political center by some Christendom leaders, and the backlash against this from within the empire itself, that undermined the idea of a universal Christian community.[70] In short, the apparent and precarious triumph of secular states over a world governed by Christian international law is a product of the Christendom dialectic outlined in chapter 1.

The empirical implications of this analysis are found in the fact that the rise and extraordinary expansion of the secular state have actually increased violence. This bears out the conclusion that "insecurity and fear become not only central, but *essential*, to the modern secular state-centric project."[71] What emerged in the twentieth century was a "security state" with an unprecedented amount of infrastructural power and a national budget to protect and provide for its population.[72] During the century, the general budgets of industrialized states grew around fivefold from around 10 percent of GDP at the start of the century to almost 50 percent by its end.[73] However, even within the state, the promised civil peace of the leviathan has not been borne out, even in liberal societies governed by the rule of law. The increase in state capacity and statist policies in the mid- to late-twentieth century saw a rise in homicide rates across the West.[74] The modern era has also bought the three deadliest wars: the First and Second World Wars and the Taiping rebellion. According to the logic of the state, national minorities become national security problems as they disturb the ontological security claims made by secular states and become subject to othering discourses of danger.[75] The secular age has seen an enormous rise in violence against national minorities and the emergence of the phenomenon of genocide.[76] The political scientist Rudolph Rummel spent his career cataloguing what he called democide—death by government. Rummel counted approximately

69. Mavelli, "Security and Secularization," 185.
70. Sykes, *Power and Christian Theology*.
71. Mavelli, "Security and Secularization," 188.
72. Mabee, "Security Studies and the Security State."
73. Higgs, "Government Growth."
74. Bourne, *Understanding Security*, 77.
75. Feldman, "Estranged States."
76. Rubinstein, "Genocide and Historical Debate," 36–38.

262 million deaths in the twentieth century and argued that the greater the power held by government, the greater the amount of killing.[77] Notwithstanding the limits of these headline figures, we can say that the modern secular age is the age of "death by state" to a far greater degree than any prior age.

Not only does the state kill at an unprecedented level, it is also a vehicle for theft at an enormous scale. The example given at the beginning of the chapter illustrates some more general truths than simply the facts of Western centers of power and their relationship to Eurasian kleptocracies.[78] First, the emergence of the secular state repeats the enduring problem of statehood about which the prophet Samuel warned the people of Israel when they demanded a king: that state formation provides the vehicle to control an economy and enrich an oligarchic elite. As Augustine asked in Book IV of *City of God*, "remove justice, then, and what are kingdoms but large gangs of robbers? And what are gangs of robbers but small kingdoms?"[79] Second, the process of globalization, and particularly the financial globalization that accelerated in the late-twentieth century following the deregulation and "offshoring" of US and UK governments, has globalized these kleptocracies, making them larger, more hidden, and less accountable leviathans—the kind of state against which Moltmann warns. These two processes are concomitant with the disenchantment explored in the previous chapter. In this light, "national security" is the ideology of state security policy but, in many states, this is merely cover for regime security: actions to safeguard and enrich a governing elite that took office due to its collaboration with the imperial power during empire and decolonization. The families and elite factions that run many of the world's states constitute such postcolonial regimes. Many of these can be classified as patrimonial regimes or kleptocracies. While these forms of rule are ancient, they are on the rise. Today, political economists identify a "global patrimonial wave"[80] or "rise of kleptocracy."[81]

Classically understood as "rule of thieves," *kleptocracy* has found a new generation of analysts in the last decade. The term has been popularized by

---

77. Rummel, *Death By Government*, ch. 4.

78. In British English, the first recorded usage is in the press in the early nineteenth century. In the UK parliament, 100 of 148 total usages of "kleptocrat" and "kleptocracy" since the record began in 1800 have occurred since 2017 and just under half (71) occurred from January to May 2022. See Hansard, *UK Parliament*.

79. Augustine, *City of God*, IV.5.

80. Hanson and Kopstein, "Understanding the Global Patrimonial Wave."

81. Walker and Aten, "The Rise of Kleptocracy."

Bullough,[82] Burgis,[83] and Chayes,[84] while it has also been widely deployed by civil society.[85] The UK's Financial Conduct Authority indirectly provides a definition in its guidelines on countries with a high risk of corruption as those with "a political economy dominated by a small number of people/entities with close links to the state."[86] A similar term is "grand corruption" (i.e. "the abuse of high-level power that benefits the few at the expense of the many, and causes serious and widespread harm to individuals and society"),[87] which may be used interchangeably with kleptocracy as both indicate the subversion of political office for personal enrichment and advantage. While no robust global indices of kleptocracy exist, it is likely that most people in the world live in countries where kleptocratic practices are commonplace. China and India demonstrate certain features of grand corruption and the UK too, as we have seen, is not entirely immune.

What is distinct about kleptocracy in the post-imperial era is the global form it takes. As has been demonstrated from data leaks, such as the Panama Papers (2016) and the Pandora Papers (2020/21), kleptocrats are not national but global citizens. Multi-millionaire heads of state are not confined to reside and educate their children in their country's impoverished state schools but acquire real estate, citizenship, and education overseas for their family members. These activities require that offshore bank accounts are acquired in dollars or Euros, kept secret, and used to make purchases; this requires bankers, company formation agents, and lawyers willing to provide these services. But moving money from "a political economy dominated by a small number of people" constitutes a form of suspicious financial activity and may be money laundering, according to both national and international laws. Those who do it without enhanced due diligence checks are either complicit or negligent. They are transnational enablers who launder money from a kleptocratic state to one supposedly bound by the rule of law. These activities are not unusual but part of a vast services industry that has grown under conditions of globalization.

These two gloomy conclusions about the recentered state must be tempered with a third. As much as it kills and steals it also cures. Rises in life

---

82. Bullough *Moneyland*.

83. Burgis, *Kleptopia*.

84. Chayes, *Thieves of State*.

85. Sibley and Judah, *Countering Global Kleptocracy*; Transparency International, "Who Is Opening the Gates for Kleptocrats?"

86. Financial Conduct Authority, "Finalised Guidance," 9.

87. Transparency International, "What Is Grand Corruption and How Can We Stop It?"

expectancy correlate strongly with increases in state capacity and wealth.[88] The Asian miracle of post-war economic growth took place under strong development states with industrial strategies for protected economies.[89] Similarly, post-war growth in Europe occurred under massively expanding and democratizing states that either nationalized or heavily regulated industries.[90] These instances of what became known as the developmental state demonstrated that state intervention in the economy—in the form of subsidies, industrial strategy, and import-substitution—is effective at achieving growth. In the twentieth century, that growth was the precursor to reduced poverty when combined with investment in education, health, and welfare. The developmental state model fell out of fashion in the late-twentieth century as it was disregarded in a new "Washington consensus" of pro-market reforms. Unsurprisingly, these policies coincided with a large reduction of annual economic growth and rises in inequality in many states.[91]

In the twenty-first century, the example par excellence of the secular state that kills, steals, and cures is the rising power of the People's Republic of China. It is perhaps the "perfect dictatorship"[92] and the quintessential case of the Leviathan, Moloch, or Stasioctopus that Moltmann feared. However, according to the World Bank, from 1990 to 2016, the number in absolute poverty in China fell from 750 million (about two-thirds of the population) to just 7.2 million (0.5 percent of the population).[93] Poverty-reduction on this scale is extraordinary and unprecedented. But this has occurred in the same state that killed millions in the Cultural Revolution and suppressed restive provinces and administrative regions with security campaigns in Tibet, Xinjiang, and Hong Kong. The price for being pulled out of poverty is that all Chinese, at home and abroad, have become subject to an increasingly effective and top-down system of state control under Xi Jinping with aspects of genocide toward the Uyghur minority.[94] Violence and development are two sides of the same coin in contemporary Xinjiang, as restive Uyghurs are surveilled and interned, while those that stay loyal to the communist parties have increased opportunities for education

---

88. Besley and Persson, "The Causes and Consequences of Development Clusters."
89. Stiglitz, "Some Lessons from the East Asian Miracle."
90. Dincecco, "The Rise of Effective States in Europe."
91. Caldentey, "The Concept and Evolution of the Developmental State."
92. Ringen, *The Perfect Dictatorship*.
93. Goodman, "Has China Lifted 100 Million People Out of Poverty?"
94. Smith Finley, "Why Scholars and Activists Increasingly Fear a Uyghur Genocide."

and business.⁹⁵ This is a system that demonstrates kleptocratic features but where "widespread corruption" takes place under relatively "uncoordinated networks of corrupt officials."⁹⁶

Leviathans of the Secular Age

For better or worse, the secular state is the security actor of our age, creating life and taking life, generating and capturing wealth. This chapter has charted the recentering of the secular state and highlighted, as Mavelli states, a "state-centric logic revolving around discourses of fear and the politics of the exception which makes us objects rather than subjects of security."⁹⁷ While the securitization process suggests the possibility of a greater variety of security actors, pre-existing authority claims and modes of thought are "relatively sedimented" in security affairs and tend to make the state both the subject of security and the entity to be defended. In this chapter we have offered an integrative account of the secular security state that is political (the maximization of power for the purpose of survival), economic (the extraction of resources for the purpose of elite wealth, sometimes to the extent of kleptocratic rule), and social (the manipulation of public discourse and culture to ensure the state remains hegemonic in security affairs). The secular realist account is overwhelmingly focused on the first of these processes but a fuller account necessarily attends to elite kleptocracy and the securitizing speech acts of authoritative actors.

What this fuller account shows is the ontological problematic that the secular security state faces. There is no security beyond that which is made immanent. For the elite, capital ownership and their cultural values are defended through the state. At the same time, as a corporate entity, the modern state has demonstrated greater capacity for poverty reduction (which may reduce the elite's wealth through taxation unless the state is used to protect elite concentrations of capital) and for killing (which may be turned on the elite if revolution occurs). Therefore, the existential questions for the state elite are just as great as for the state itself. The elite and the state are dependent on one another. Security continues to center on the state: both the right to kill and the requirement to protect, the right to national development and the provision of national welfare. The disenchanted and recentered state is by most secular accounts the dominant actor in security after Christendom, a Leviathan that demands fear and fealty. But against

---

95. Greitens et al., "Counterterrorism and Preventive Repression."
96. Wedeman, "Does China Fit the Model?"
97. Mavelli, "Security and Secularization," 193.

these forces of the state, we see others of decentering and of re-enchanting where the tensions that characterized Christendom continue to disrupt security affairs in a secular age. To grasp these processes, we need to deploy more revolutionary approaches to the study of security which expose the disorders of globalization and the post-secular resurgence of religion in international affairs. Together, they are forces working against the continuing power of the state and toward an environment that is more chaotic, indeed apocalyptic.

CHAPTER 7

Disorders of the Liberal International Order

But in those days, after that tribulation, the sun will be darkened, and the moon will not give its light, and the stars will be falling from heaven, and the powers in the heavens will be shaken.

MARK 13:24-25

It may be, indeed, that we will have to go through a thoroughly "uncivil condition," both internationally and perhaps also domestically, before we begin to see the pass to which our illusions have brought us. And this will take longer than it should, I suspect, because many of the illusions that bind us are hopeful ones, predicated on our desire to do good in the world with our (sadly equally illusory) belief that we are, and can be, masters of our fate.

NICK RENGGER[1]

In the year 2000, at the height of the UK Government's much-vaunted "ethical foreign policy," I made a curious career move. I transitioned from being a researcher at the international non-governmental organization Saferworld—part of a movement for human security that emerged out of the Campaign for Nuclear Disarmament (CND)—to being a research analyst at Britain's Ministry of Defence (MoD). While moving from an internship in the charity sector to the security of the civil service was not itself unusual, I had the slightly odd experience of producing the very research reports for

1. Rengger, *Just War and International Order*, xii–xiii.

government that I had been critically interrogating a few weeks before. At Saferworld, I had contributed to a forty-thousand-word audit of the UK Government's annual arms export control report.[2] In the MoD, I began to produce the statistics to which the critical report responded. I was quickly denoted as a "poacher turned gamekeeper" by one of my MoD colleagues who was glad that I was no longer writing the long and detailed reports that he had been required to read.

But there was a further irony to my move. Rather than moving from the margins to the center of power, in some respects I had done the reverse. The statistics on arms exports produced at the MoD were required to be published in detail under the terms of new national arms export control criteria and a regulatory regime that had been introduced by the New Labour government in 1997.[3] These very criteria were initially drafted by Saferworld staff and Labour party officials when the party was in opposition and was hitting the government hard over the Arms-to-Iraq scandal of 1980s (which had been brutally exposed by the 1996 Scott Report).[4] Saferworld worked with the special advisor to Labour's shadow foreign secretary, Robin Cook, to produce eight criteria pertaining, among other things, to ensuring no UK arms exports were used for internal repression and human rights abuses by the recipient state. These criteria were subsequently adopted by the European Union as part of the Consolidated EU and National Arms Export Licensing Criteria and later became UK law under the *Export Control Act 2002*.[5]

In this case, and many others, central government was not leading policy. Rather, a small group of elites, including an NGO with a couple of dozen staff, fed policy ideas for the bureaucracy to pick up. This was then adopted at EU level and continues to be adhered to by the UK, despite Brexit. The nation state was stuck between two other political forces "below" and "above": those of domestic society and supranational institutions. Indeed, as I discovered as a civil servant, the ability of MoD to respond coherently and effectively to policy change was often low. There was not even an agreed definition of arms export across government due to huge grey areas surrounding "dual-use" technologies with both civilian and military purposes. When MPs asked questions in parliament about the volume of exports, they

2. Isbister, *An Independent Audit*.
3. For a summary of this period, see Curtis, *The Good, the Bad and the Ugly*.
4. For a discussion, see Bogdanor, "The Scott Report."
5. These criteria remain in place today and caused controversy from 2015–17 over the allegation that the government had broken the law by issuing export licences for the shipping of UK arms to Saudi Arabia that were used to kill civilians in the war in Yemen. Stavrianakis, "Playing with Words while Yemen Burns."

would receive one of three different answers depending on to which department the question was sent. Typically, the answer would be three times higher if sent to MoD than if sent to the UK's foreign ministry. I was asked to convene a group to discuss these discrepancies between departments but hit an immediate brick wall. This lack of a single position is common in central government and appears to have increased in Westminster in recent years. But it is part of a more general trend. In this case, certain parts of government (what was then the Defence Export Services Organization and the Department for Trade and Industry) work closely with the arms industry and therefore had little interest in harmonizing with the ethical foreign policy being promoted by other parts of government. The imperative to blend private and public interests is what drives their work.

This personal story—which hopefully falls short of breaking the official secrets act to which I was bound—speaks to the decentered character of what became known in the late-twentieth century as the liberal international order. This reality is that states are the site of contestation between various private and public actors, both normative and commercial, across which power is dispersed. The export control criteria had been adopted under the influence of human security, including the moral imperative to reduce armed conflict and human rights abuses in places where there were no UK national interests at play. At the same time, they ultimately failed to prevent British arms being exported to be used against civilians in Yemen and many other countries partly because of the influence of the global defense trade and its powerful multinationals, which have far more material resources to deploy than does civil society. The British state, despite being seen as having one of the most capable bureaucracies, is increasingly fragmented, wrought by the logic of the market. It has arguably become a forum for struggle between networks of NGOs promoting global sets of rules on the one hand, and the forces of the private sector that oppose these rules on the other. A "managerial state" model has emerged over more than four decades.[6] The UK is an extreme case of a broader trend in the West. By the time of the Brexit and COVID-19 crises, the implication of the reliance on outsourcing led serious voices to raise questions of "state failure."[7] It is this abiding failure—in the terms of modern public policy managers—to "execute strategy," "resource change," and "deliver" anything close to actually-existing security that undermines all existing secular logics of security. The late Nick Rengger's warned of the "uncivil condition" that follows the breaking down of

---

6. Clarke and Newman, *The Managerial State*.
7. Chislett, "The UK and Brexit: A Failing State?"

an international order of just war and, we might add, Christendom. Such "tribulation" as St. Mark suggests appears to have an apocalyptic aspect.

This chapter explores the decentering of state and world in a secular and apocalyptic age through the attempt to build a liberal international order after the geopolitical moments of 1945 and 1989. It does so by distinguishing between different forces of decentering in the security environment and probing the putatively liberal claims of each. The securitizations of liberal actors are different to those of the national security state as they tend to objectify threats to individuals and minorities, to international laws, and to economic relations. First, we look at normative individualism and human security, the liberal claim to protect the rights and provide the needs of the poor through aid and intervention. Second, and in a similar manner we consider the odd amalgam of realism and liberalism in attempts to fix failed states. Third, we look at liberal hopes for international order and expose how imperial practices and artefacts continue to structure that order even after decolonization. Finally, we interrogate neoliberal globalization and the transnational forces that some still hope will build a standard of global governance for the world. In each case, we show how ideas of a liberal order are belied by the disorder of decentering forces. Recalling our argument from part 1, the chapter postulates that these forces emerge from, and are functionally similar to, the decentering that took place under Christendom in that they serve the dispersal of power away from a sovereign entity. As in decentered Christendom, features such as the toleration of minorities, partnerships across geopolitical divides, global and imperial economic relations, and the proliferation of violence are also visible. However, they are substantively different in that they are the forces of a disenchanted world where secular actors—from civil society to private businesses—predominate and the church is no longer a partner or even a secondary political actor to the state.

The promise of human security and the responsibility to protect

Arguably the leading policy alternative to realism and national security over the last thirty years has been human security. The concept of human security has been articulated in lock step with what was known as the "liberal peace" approach to international affairs and particularly third-party intervention in places of civil war and extreme insecurity. Its theory and policy of security places ontological and normative primacy in the individual. The process of secularization is deeply entwined with human security as it is that process that made the individual rights fomented in late-Christendom societies sovereign. Charles Taylor has defined this as "the coming of exclusive humanism."[8] Taylor, along with MacIntyre, labels the late-twentieth-century variant of this "expressive individualism" and points to its self-referencing and therapeutic form. The praxis of human security is arguably one outworking of this "exclusive humanism" identified by Taylor. It is impossible to imagine human security and liberal peace without the expression of individualism more broadly.

Human security was first defined by the United Nations in the early 1990s as an attempt to elevate human rights and human development up the policy agenda by "securitizing" them as threats that require extraordinary measures. Its intellectual origins however lie in broadly liberal peace-studies scholarship focused on the effects of armed conflict and poverty on individuals and communities, especially in what was then known as the developing world. For John Burton,[9] this was a matter of basic human needs. For Edward Azar,[10] the absence of such human needs was at the root of what he called protracted social conflict, where war and poverty combined. The UN Development Project (UNDP) in its *Human Development Report* (1994) defined human security as:

> First, safety from chronic threats such as hunger, disease, and repression. And second, it means protection from sudden and hurtful disruption in the patterns of daily life—whether in homes in jobs or in communities.[11]

This broad definition led to a policy and academic debate about the content and limits of human security. A narrow school argued for "freedom from fear": that is, personal, political, and community security for individuals and a reduction in civilian casualties from political violence.[12] A more influential broad school argued for "freedom from want": economic, environmental, health, and food security, noting that poverty kills far more than war.[13]

Not only did human security offer a massive expansion of the protection and provision aspects of security, it also implied a radical approach to inclusion—that political solidarities extend beyond borders. It was the

---

8. Taylor, *Secular Age*, 19.
9. Burton, *Human Needs Theory*.
10. Azar, "Protracted International Conflicts."
11. UNDP, *Human Development Report*, 23.
12. UNDP, *Human Development Report*, 30–34.
13. UNDP, *Human Development Report*, 25–29.

"international community" that sought to achieve human security for all persons. The UN produced a Human Development Index (HDI) and from 2005, a Human Security Report began to be published. The concept of human security has been influential in both objective-setting with its influence seen in the Millennium Development Goals and Sustainable Development Goals. Perhaps more significant, however, has been its influence on policy and practice as development agencies have increasing felt bound to frame their programs in terms of security to receive international recognition and funding from major state donors like USAID and the UK's DfID which dominate the development sector. The virtue of human security was something that apparently everyone could agree upon.

What was less clear was human security's viability in practical terms.[14] The policy influence of human security was matched only by its policy vagueness: "a concept that aspires to explain almost everything in reality explains nothing."[15] What drove its success was something other than effectiveness in its own rather uncertain terms. Already in the 1990s, Mark Duffield, an academic and former Oxfam aid worker, identified the merger of security and development. This process of merging, he argues, has had two phases. The first phase was the incorporating of the language of security by non-governmental actors into humanitarian discourse and the concomitant adoption of developmentalist language by militaries and defense ministries.

Rather than human security offering a rival program and institution of security—a kind of global social security—it merged conceptually with national security as states adapted it into their policy frameworks. The German Development Corporation, for example, and with reference to the UN Development Programme, conflated "guaranteeing human security" with "national security"—an approach that has also been adopted by the Organization for Security and Co-operation in Europe (OSCE).[16] The merging of security and development remains a powerful discourse. "Packaged so neatly," Chanaa notes, "it was easy to present, attracting not only attention, but also considerable material support."[17]

14. The subsequent paragraphs draw upon Heathershaw, "Unpacking the Liberal Peace."
15. Andrew Mack et al., *Human Security Report*.
16. Chanaa, *Security Sector Reform*, 27.
17. Chanaa, *Security Sector Reform*, 27.

Fixing failed states

If human security lacked coherence and conceptual precision, it at least indicated the emergence of a wider industry of global security composed of public, private, and third-sector bodies. Human security may have merged with national security, but it was often non-state or private sector actors that facilitated this merger. With 9/11, and the onset of the "global war on terror," a rather similar process occurred under the idea of state-building. Writing at the end of the 1990s, Duffield noted with far-sightedness that "the idea of underdevelopment as dangerous and destabilizing provides a justification for continued surveillance and engagement [in countries of the Global South]."[18] The claim that underdevelopment is dangerous—embodied in tropes such as "failed states," "uncivil society," and "extremism"—is replete through major policy texts put out by development and defense ministries alike. "Failed states," for example, serves as a justification for state-building interventions such as that in Afghanistan in both the US National Security Strategy of 2002 and the UK Department for International Development (DfID) White Paper of 2006.[19] Duffield is surely right to see in the merging of development and security "that liberal peace contains within it the emerging structures of liberal war."[20] Even in the less martial domains of health and migration, the invocation of "security"—that is, the process of securitization—effectively finds threats in the very bodies and movements of others. If disease and population flows create threat, then extraordinary measures are required against the individuals and communities that embody those threats.[21] This is a secular "biopolitics" of the post-Christendom era that makes "life and its properties" a matter of security.[22] The correlation of increasing aid budgets with increasingly securitized borders indicates, "a susceptibility within global liberal governance to normalize violence and accept high levels of instability as an enduring if unfortunate characteristic of certain regions."[23]

The truth of this normalization of violence is found in the fact that human insecurity is present in Western states too. But in these cases, it has nothing to do with state failure and, in some respects, is caused by state strength. Alice Goffman's study revealed the chronic insecurity of young

---

18. Duffield, *Global Governance and the New Wars*, 7.

19. United States of America, *National Security Strategy 2002*; Department for International Development, *Eliminating World Poverty*.

20. Duffield, *Global Governance*, 15.

21. Aradau, "Security and the Democratic Scene"; Elbe, "AIDS, Security, Biopolitics."

22. Dillon, "Underwriting Security," 311.

23. Duffield, *Global Governance and the New Wars*, 17.

black boys growing up in the Sixth Street district of Philadelphia as a result of a lack of basic needs in society, such as identity, (basic physical) security, recognition, creativity, control, belonging—which leads them to seek these things in gang membership and in prison.[24] Similarly, Sudhir Venkatesh has shown how, faced with chronic insecurity, street gangs in Chicago operate in a manner that can be compared to militias and insurgent groups in "failed states."[25] But they do so not because of the lack of state, but in armed conflict with the police force of the most powerful state in the world, yet a state that has failed to achieve equal rights to basic security for its citizens. Homicide, sometimes at the hands of the police but more often at the hands of one another, is by far the highest cause of death among young black men in the United States.[26] Infant mortality rates among black Americans are higher than in Costa Rica, Fiji, or Thailand. The Center for Disease Control in the United States reports that "white men with 16 or more years of schooling can expect to live an average of 14 years longer than black men with fewer than 12 years of education."[27]

Notwithstanding these problems in their own strong states, the fixing-failed-states agenda was a product of policy networks that over time became increasingly influential in Western governments. It was shaped by a few thousand individuals and a few dozen organizations of a very similar background and type. As a debate, it finds its origins, developments, and main critiques in cultural and intellectual debates of the West. Its protagonists, although often educated in the elite institutions of the West, are from all over the world. *Fixing Failed States*—the title of a book by future Afghan president Ashraf Ghani and the British development policy expert Clare Lockhardt—was a misnomer on three grounds.[28] These "states" were actually coalitions of networked warlords. They were not "failed," as the networks functioned very well for their members as a means of extracting capital and resources from the country. And they were not being "fixed" but merely fueled in their corruption with the supply of international aid.

The problem with the ideas of "human security" and "failed states" arises from their underlying assumptions about the progressive nature of

24. Goffman, *On the Run*.
25. Venkatesh, "The Social Organization of Street Gang Activity."
26. In 2014, the most common cause of deaths among black males (20–24 years) was homicide (48 percent). Among white males (20–24 years) it is injury (51 percent). In 2015, black men were more than five times more likely to be killed by the police than white men. Center for Disease Control, "Leading Causes of Death"; Swaine et al., "Young Black Men Killed by US Police at Highest Rate."
27. Center for Disease Control, "Leading Causes of Death."
28. Ghani and Lockhart, *Fixing Failed States*.

politics, if only law, institutions, and resources are deployed. These ideas are partially correct and convey important truths that have emerged as de-centering processes become more pronounced and the myth of the primacy of national security has begun to break down. But as ideas emerging from the centers of power in the global North, they fail to see the role of these states and economies in creating the very problems they seek to solve. It is at the margins where these myths are exposed, and the disordered and de-centered nature of contemporary security affairs are most starkly observed. These margins are both within the global North (e.g., the black populations of American inner cities) and South (e.g., Afghanistan). Rather than these margins constituting the periphery of security affairs, they may be best thought of as being the very places where the violence of the putatively liberal center is laid bare. Thus, containing or limiting violence in the name of "human security," "fixing failed states," or any other ethically grounded and military-backed security action on behalf of a third party is *prima facie* untenable based on the majority of the historical evidence. As the theologian Michael Budde argues, state actors "mostly don't give a damn about our ethics when the chips are down."[29]

The case of "responsibility to protect" (R2P)—the claim that state sovereignty is conditional upon the protection of human rights and, where this condition is not met, external actors have a responsibility to intervene—is perhaps the most acute example of where good intentions meets the imperial realities of power. We brushed by R2P in the discussion of the imminence of threat and *jus ante bellum* in chapter 5. Indeed, a great deal of work on R2P has been done by theologians seeking to explore it as a bridge between just policing (pacifist) and just war positions.[30] For the Thomistic and Roman Catholic thinker Braun, this is about "attaining right balance between armed force and nonviolence."[31] By contrast, the Mennonite scholar Schlabach suggests such a "grand compromise" is based on a misunderstanding and that the real need is for the "willingness to work in appropriate coalitions."[32] However, as Budde argues, there is a chasmic disconnect even between just war principles such as right intention and proportionality as they are taught in military ethics and the wider culture of the armed forces, which necessarily are institutions focused on requiring men and women to kill for the state, the pressures and extremes of the battlefield, and the

---

29. Budde, *Foolishness to Gentiles*, 66.
30. Schlabach, "Just Policing, Responsibility to Protect"; Braun, "Quo Vadis?"
31. Braun, "Quo Vadis?," 17.
32. Schlabach, "Just Policing," 73, 75.

shifting, often short-term, nature of political decision-making.[33] Budde facetiously suggests that military interventions in the name of R2P could only succeed if we return to the Christian military orders of Christendom. Perhaps the only way to make "R2P compatible with Christian just war principles, is to have soldiers deeply formed by Christian convictions and practices?"[34] With the end of Christendom, the idea of warfare conducted according to Christian ethics has become fanciful.

SECURITY AFTER EMPIRE

The gangland dynamics observed in American cities by Venkatesh and Goffman are fundamentally similar to those of warlordism in so-called failed states. Disorder here is instrumental and efficacious for elites. Patrick Chabol and Jean-Francois Daloz argued in their study of the African state that "the real business of politics is taking place where analysts are often not looking," as the political system is "re-shaped by local conditions to such a degree that it comes to be used for thoroughly different purposes."[35] The comparison between America and Africa here is suggestive. The political system of the United States provides security to those with capital, social and material; those of Africa do likewise. The differences of context are vast—and the proportion of those who feel secure in the US is far greater—but the fundamental logic that "international order" serves some over others is indisputable. As such, "dysfunctional" states may not be aberrations at all but typical of state- and empire-making processes, which require that power is deployed at the periphery—at borders, in ghettos, and in extracting commodities—but that capital is accumulated at the center.

There is nothing new about this process, which predates the secular age. The history of empire, particularly modern European empire, suggests that it was not that imperial powers were strong and that strength enabled their colonization of other places, but that it was their colonization that made them strong, wealthy, and powerful. In the sixteenth century, the GDP of the Mughal Empire, following its own imperial expansion across the Indian subcontinent and into Central Asia, was estimated to be around a quarter of global wealth, and exceeded that of the entirety of Europe.[36] For example, Britain was a weak state on the periphery of Europe in the fifteenth century but became a global power by the nineteenth century because of

33. Budde, *Foolishness to Gentiles*, 71–79.
34. Budde, *Foolishness to Gentiles*, 78.
35. Chabol and Daloz, *Africa Works*, 1, 10.
36. Maddison, *Development Centre Studies*, 259–61.

its imperial expansion, especially in India, which suffered an extraordinary relative decline. Importantly, this was not directed by the government in London but by decisions and actions taken in the field by the East India Company and other private actors, including annexation, treaty-making with local elites, slavery, and a form of indentured labor that succeeded slavery after its abolition in 1833.[37] How far military technology, naval power, the exploitation of coal in Britain, and the technological advancements of the industrial revolution also contributed to the rise of British power is a matter of debate among historians. However, these were not exclusively national achievements, and it is indisputable that Britain would not have been a Great Power without its colonies.

Nor is this imperialism geographically specific to the region of Christendom. The role of empire and colonization in the growth state power is not exclusively European and appears to be a universal phenomenon. This point is demonstrated in some of the empires of the non-West, particularly of East Asia.[38] Victoria Tin-Bor Hui shows that similar domestic and international processes of governance were occurring around the same time in early modern Europe and Qing-era China, such as the annexation of new territories, the emergence of territorially bound sovereign units, the development of bureaucracy and the concept of balance of power.[39] Andrew Philipps argues that the transformation of both Christendom and the Sinosphere were driven by a similar sets of domestic and external factors, including institutional decay, the emergence of anti-systemic ideologies, and increases in violence.[40] Alastair Johnson's study of Chinese military engagements with the Mongols during the Ming Dynasty suggests that they were not so different from European *realpolitik*, a finding corroborated by Ji-Young Lee's study of the Qing-era tribute system.[41]

Empire in a secular age takes a different form. For Hardt and Negri, whose *Empire* (2000)[42] is perhaps the most influential account across IR and theology, today's empires cannot sustain a center and lack the identifiable borders of empires past. They are decentered and deterritorializing with their flows of goods and people determined by the concentrations of capital

---

37. The Indian indenture system transported 3.5 million Indians to other parts of the British empire and continued from 1833–1920.

38. See also Owen, Heathershaw, and Savin, "How Postcolonial Is Post-Western IR?"

39. Tin-Bor Hui, *War and State Formation in Ancient China*.

40. Phillips, *War, Religion and Empire*.

41. Johnston, *Cultural Realism*; Lee, *China's Hegemony*.

42. Hardt and Negri, *Empire*.

and the margins of the poor.⁴³ An example from a US ally during the war on terror nicely illustrates the nature of security—inclusion, protection, and provision—under empire. From 2005 to 2010, the government of Kurmanbek Bakiyev in Kyrgyzstan set the country up as an offshore jurisdiction through which an amount of money flowed that was many times greater than the size of the country's economy.⁴⁴ Bakiyev's son Maxim, a Latvian investor, and a Russian-American financial professional dominated the country's banking sector and took their cut. Two former US senators sat on their bank's board. The United States—Kyrgyzstan's key ally at the time—looked the other way and provided lucrative subcontracting opportunities for the regime to refuel the air transit center, which was supplying the US/NATO mission in Afghanistan. By 2010, resentment against the exclusiveness of the Bakiyev regime and the failures of public services led to an uprising and subsequent ethnic violence in which hundreds were killed. Although Kyrgyzstan had become a dictatorship by 2009/10, its state had become the vehicle for a domestic and foreign elite to enrich themselves by moving money around the global economy. Business in such an environment is necessarily a matter of politics—and therefore of security.

Without limits, empire shapes all aspects of life—government, economy, culture, religion, and security. According to Hardt and Negri, war in such a place has become a generalized state requiring constant national "policing" by paramilitaries, private security companies, or international "peacekeepers."⁴⁵ The theologian Daniel Bell summarizes the nature of security in such an empire as follows:

> This is the war of smooth space; a war without end in the sense of war that is both continuous and devoid of any *telos*, whose goal rather is the removal of boundaries and ends that would obstruct or block the flow of capital. This is war for a generalized but nebulous and elusive condition called "security" that is fittingly captured in the concept of "preemption."⁴⁶

For Hardt and Negri, this world without telos is inevitable and cannot be contested. The only hope for resistance to the exercise of "war without end" is found in "the multitude." While Augustine's multitude was a people under God but with no earthly sovereign, in Hardt and Negri such a people "resides on the imperial surfaces where there is no God the Father and no

43. Hardt and Negri, *Empire*, 325.
44. This story is summarized from Cooley and Heathershaw, *Dictators without Borders*, 143–57.
45. Hardt and Negri, *Empire*, 353.
46. Bell, *Divinations*, 140.

transcendence." In place of this, "there is only immanent labor."⁴⁷ A lot of weight is placed here, and in work by the comparable post-Marxist thinker Giorgio Agamben, on the power of disenchantment to reveal a common and immanent democracy of the multitude.⁴⁸ And yet there is also faint support in Hardt and Negri for the decentered and deterritorializing power of capitalism and its destruction of the basis for local and therefore particular community.⁴⁹ Thus, as Bell rightly concludes, "this new democracy is entirely at the mercy of the whim of the indeterminate and therefore indifferent will of the singularity" and is therefore "utterly arbitrary."⁵⁰ Pluralism in these post-Marxist readings remains tragic.⁵¹

Globalization and security

As Hardt and Negri appear to understand in theory but not in practical implication, globalization does not necessitate global governance *above* the state but constitutes global forces that flow *through* states and affect all possibilities for human community beyond the most local of scales. Most of these forces are economic and are driven by the power of global capital flows. The nature of the state in global conditions of capitalism is fundamentally fragmented and decentered. Privateers have long been part of national military campaigns. Even the most powerful nation-states contract out security services to private military and security companies (PMSCs), which offer standard global products to their state clients but do so by subcontracting to consultants and local companies in their areas of operation.⁵² PMSCs are now major players in the overseas wars of great powers, including the US and Russia. Staffed by ex-soldiers and often led by former senior officials or politicians, they are considered a "safe pairs of hands." Russian PMSCs were instrumental in their intervention in eastern Ukraine in 2014, providing the Kremlin with deniability while also reducing their ability to control the behavior of their forces. In the US' wars in Afghanistan and Iraq, PMSCs were sometimes incorporated within American command structures. Again, there is nothing new about such privateers, but their globalization suggests

---

47. Hardt and Negri, *Empire*, 396.
48. Bell, *Divinations*, 155.
49. Hardt and Negri, *Empire*, 43, 47.
50. Bell, *Divinations*, 156–57; Bell's Augustinian vision, by contrast, has its foundation on "the circle of communion" and the "smooth space of fraternity" found in imitating the person of Christ. Bell, *Divinations*, 168.
51. Cavanaugh, *Migrations*, 61.
52. Abrahamsen and Williams, "Security beyond the State."

a qualitative shift in the nature of security. These private actors operate on a global scale to a degree that has rarely been seen even at the height of European maritime empires, competition between which made the two great wars of the twentieth century genuinely global in scope.

Given that great power military operations are far less centered than they first appear, it should not surprise us that non-traditional security affairs—such as those of health, migration, and the environment—are also extraordinarily decentered. Hameiri and Jones use the term "rescaling" to explain how both new global actors and local elites struggle over policy initiatives (and the profit-making opportunities they offer).[53] "The central state," they note, "shifted from a 'command and control' model based on direct intervention to secure economic, social, and political objectives to a 'regulatory' model, whereby central government merely sets broad targets and regulations for diverse public and private actors."[54] As a result, policy areas formerly administered by government have been displaced by diversity of actors, including domestic and multi-national corporations, charities and citizens groups, and semi-independent agencies.

Hameiri and Jones argue that states are rescaled and transformed in three specific ways. They are: (i) "*fragmented*, as formerly powerful central agencies disperse power and resources to multiple agencies—public and private—and retreat to a 'regulatory state' model"; (ii) "*decentralized*, as control over policy and resources is devolved to regions, provinces, and urban centers"; (iii) "*internationalized*, as formerly purely domestic agencies acquire an international role, and join, form, or promote different, rescaled forms of transnational governance and regulation."[55] It is not clear whether "command and control" was ever widely practiced in the civilian state in more than a few state socialist and social-democratic states in the twentieth century. Nevertheless, Hameiri and Jones are surely correct that three processes of state transformation are accentuated by globalization. Local elites engage in mock compliance with international rules where their interests are threatened (by increased regulation of their financial systems), shift the burden of compliance on to weaker groups (such as small-scale farmers), and create market advantage for the well-connected groups (such as big farming conglomerates).[56]

The fragmentation of the central state, the decentralization of power to cities, and the adoption of international standards is not confined to the

53. Hameiri and Jones, *Governing Borderless Threats*.
54. Hameiri and Jones, "Rising Powers and State Transformation," 80.
55. Hameiri, Jones, and Heathershaw, "Reframing the Rising Powers Debate," 1399.
56. Hameiri and Jones, *Governing Borderless Threats*, 209–16.

Global South. It also shapes security relations between great powers. As we have seen, while the UK has had a conflictual relationship with Russia, the city of London has had a cooperative relationship with its businessmen (or oligarchs), allowing them to launder money and providing them with investor visas.[57] This brought political violence to the UK. The likely motive for both the killing of Alexander Litvinenko in 2006 and the attempted assassination of Sergei Skripal in 2018 was that both had continued to brief European intelligence services on links between the Russian state and organized crime. Similarly, the deaths of Boris Berezovsky and several of his associates occurred in the context of transnational struggles between Berezovsky and oligarchs linked to the Russian state.[58] The UK and other Western democracies are also vulnerable to cooperation between its own elites and post-Soviet kleptocrats. As major studies have shown, Putin's Russia was built as a kleptocracy that demands the loyalty of its globalized oligarchs and extends its power overseas through transnational networks and intermediaries, including political donations to nationalist opposition and governing party figures.

Even the most centralized great powers are subject to these processes of fragmentation, decentralization, and internationalization via elite networks. In the case of China, as Beijing implemented policies of fiscal decentralization and deregulation to facilitate global economic integration, subnational agencies, institutions, and companies in the public and private sectors have increasingly developed their own foreign policies, which sometimes get ahead of central government's priorities.[59] The consequence of this shift in statehood, they claim, leads indirectly to its promotion elsewhere: "as China's economy expands beyond its borders, so does the 'governance frontier' of its state apparatuses."[60] Sometimes the activities of China's private companies and state-owned enterprises get ahead of Beijing's policy as in Chinese companies' commercial exploitation of the disputed South China Sea and more and more white elephant projects of the Belt and Road Initiative. The multi-billion dollar Hambantota Port project in Sri Lanka was not economically viable from the outset in 2007, was mired in corruption and debt, and was one factor behind the economic crisis that brought down the government in Colombo in 2022. Rather than being led by Beijing, it

57. Russians received over 20 percent of all investor visas given between 2008 and 2014, the so-called "blind faith" period when no checks occurred. Heathershaw et al., *The UK's Kleptocracy Problem*, 15.

58. Coroners have recorded unlawful killings or open verdicts in many of these cases, but no perpetrators have yet been convicted in any of them.

59. Hameiri and Jones, "Rising Powers and State Transformation."

60. Hameiri and Jones, "Rising Powers and State Transformation," 89.

was corrupt Sri Lankan elites and the Chinese state-owned enterprises that persuaded the Chinese government to provide finance to an ill-fated project that overwhelmingly benefitted the contractors.[61]

To a great extent, contemporary globalization is merely a return to longer-term imperial patterns where companies and company-states were autonomous actors. As Philipps and Sharman recall, the Dutch East India Companies and the Hudson's Bay Company made their own foreign policy without regard to that of their home government, "as they exercised corporate sovereignty over vast territories and millions of subjects."[62] Christendom imaginaries and secular realist thought have tended to ignore these dynamics. As Philipps and Sharman argue,

> what we now take to be the normal way of exercising political authority, through the sovereign state, was comparatively rare in most regions outside Europe until quite recently. The great significance of this point is that international politics has long been a game played by a diverse range of actors, not just sovereign states, especially outside Europe.[63]

This historical and contemporary reality not just demands that we pay more attention to non-state actors but that we rethink our centered understanding of the state.

Decentering the state, demythologizing security

These findings about great states and empires mirror a wider truth about all political order: that there is always a distinction between centered discourses and decentered practices. With respect to the state, the sociologist Philip Abrams classically portrayed this as the irreconcilable distinction between a centered-state idea and a practically decentered-state system. In a famous passage he argued that

> we are only making difficulties for ourselves in supposing that we have also to study the state—an entity, agent, function or relation—over and above the state-system and the state-idea. The state comes into being as a structuration within political practice; it starts its life as an implicit construct; it is then reified—as the *res publica*, the public reification, no less—and acquires an overt symbolic identity progressively divorced from practice as

---

61. Jones and Hameiri, *Debunking the Myth of "Debt-Trap Diplomacy."*
62. Phillips and Sharman, *Outsourcing Empire*, 1.
63. Phillips and Sharman, *Outsourcing Empire*, 2.

an illusory account of practice. The ideological function is extended to a point where conservatives and radicals alike believe that their practice is not directed at each other but at the state: the world of illusion prevails.[64]

As Mitchell notes, the gaping chasm between discourse and practice is not a problem that can possibly be overcome but rather a "clue to the nature of the phenomenon" and a condition of its very possibility."[65] Ideal-type secular states are not human communities but abstract concepts. Bevir and Rhodes denote this situation as the "stateless state," where the state is "the contingent product of diverse actions and political struggles informed by the beliefs of agents rooted in traditions."[66]

The state that has command and control is a myth in the anthropological sense of an idea that is divorced from everyday practice but nevertheless limits how we think and act toward the state. Beyond the basic fact that the state is mythologically centered and practically decentered—which applies as much to China as Congo—the contradictions are most apparent to states that have been through civil war or chronic insecurity: "informal" states that possess functions of government without international recognition;[67] "quasi-states" that enjoy international recognition without the functions of government;[68] "shadow" states based on paramilitary networks of organized crime that exist for rent-seeking and resource-extraction purposes;[69] "improvised" states that marshal international material and symbolic resources for themselves without enjoying independence of action.[70] Such modifiers suggest not aberrations but merely some of the more extreme variations of actually-existing states and national securities that bear little resemblances to the ideologies disseminated by their leaders. Such states engage in security governance rather than commanding government and are "more reliant on varied private and voluntary sector actors to devise, manage, and deliver policies and services."[71]

Perhaps the best account of the relationship between decentering practices and recentering imaginaries is found in the work of the political anthropologist James C. Scott on state-formation in rural Southeast Asia

64. Abrams, "Notes on the Difficulty of Studying the State," 82.
65. Mitchell, "Society, Economy and the State Effect," 78.
66. Bevir and Rhodes, *The State as Cultural Practice*, 20.
67. Isachenko, *The Making of Informal States*.
68. Jackson, *Quasi-States*.
69. Reno, *Warlord Politics*.
70. Jeffrey, *The Improvised State*.
71. Bevir, "Decentring Security Governance," 227.

and other imperial and colonial contexts. For Scott, "public transcripts" of conformity and unity—such as those of state power and national security—offer "an indifferent guide to the opinion of subordinates."[72] Thus, he introduces the idea of a "hidden transcript" that is "beyond direct observation by powerholders."[73] A hidden, alternative reality—"an extensive offstage social existence"—is sustained by what Scott calls "the infrapolitics of subordinate groups."[74] His *Seeing Like a State* highlights how attempts to impose "high-modernist" ideologies—from Soviet collectivism to Brazilian city-planning—onto various societies rely on "cunning" and "practical knowledge" that he denotes with the Greek term *mētis*—a quality attributed to the wily Odysseus in the Trojan wars.[75] *Mētis*, in Scott's usage, is synonymous with "common sense, experience, a knack," and is best observed at the local level, in craftsmanship and schemes of corruption, in attempts to maintain virtue and attempts to exploit it. The dialectical relationship between decentering and recentering is clear here. On the one hand, those at the margins use the cover of the "state" to legitimize their diverse practices. On the other hand, those at the center need those with *mētis* so as not to preside over a "failed state."

Scott's work is of particular value because it explains how states and empires achieve their objectives while delivering pay-offs and by-products via networks of local collaborators. It thus places agency both in the center and in the periphery and therefore in the relationship between the two. Philips argues in a manner consistent with Scott's *mētis*, that "European colonialism was the product of extensive collaboration with local intermediaries."[76] It was therefore changed and adapted by the cunning and know-how of native elites in the process. "Indigenous material, institutional, and normative resources," Philips notes, "provided the raw materials out of which colonial hierarchies were constructed."[77] *Mētis* works both for and against these imperial and security practices. High modernism is always parasitic upon *mētis*, without which imperial and state projects are ineffective. However, *mētis* is not merely for the empire, as it protects self-consciousness and reappropriates resources from empire for personal and familial use.[78] It is in this way that decentered security relations work not just for the appearance

72. Scott, *Domination*, 3.
73. Scott, *Domination*, 4.
74. Scott, *Domination*, 21.
75. Scott, *Seeing Like a State*, 6, 313.
76. Phillips, "Global IR," 64.
77. Phillips, "Global IR," 64.
78. Scott, *Seeing Like a State*, 340.

of central control but potentially for the protection and provision of the margins.

Returning to our case from Central Asia, some further findings provide a vivid example of how demythologizing security exposes possibilities for inclusion and protection that are not possible under states or empires. In 2010, ethnic violence broke out between Kyrgyz and Uzbeks in southern Kyrgyzstan in an environment of insecurity caused by a popular coup against the central government in the north of the country several weeks before. As discussed earlier in the chapter, this uprising was precipitated by the government's corruption, which was facilitated by an "offshore" banking sector and among the contractors supplying the huge American air transit center. According to what they declared was the principle of "national security," the Kyrgyz political elite portrayed this as a rebellion by Uzbeks against the state and therefore a "civil war." In reality, fighting between youths in the city of Osh in response to rumors on the streets had rapidly got out of hand and spread across the region, fueled by Kyrgyz state actors who took part in the fighting and provided weapons to Kyrgyz youths. Far more Uzbeks died than Kyrgyz, their neighborhoods were razed, and after eight days of violence Uzbeks fled the country as migrants to Russia and neighboring states.

However, when our research team looked in more detail at what happened we found that there were many towns and villages to which the violence didn't spread. Research showed that these were places where Uzbek business and community leaders and Kyrgyz elites maintained close ties and were able to work together to prevent the arming and spread of weapons and violence in their areas. For example, one ethnic Uzbek Kyrgyzstani researcher, Alisher Khamidov, observed firsthand how this worked in his hometown of Aravan, Kyrgyzstan. Both horizontal (between ethnic groups) and vertical ties (to the state) were important. Islam provided a common identity while the links between the local Kyrgyz and the police were vital to ensure that the state did not intervene and exacerbate the security dilemma.[79] State actors subsequently took credit for the ending of violence while the international Organization for Security and Cooperation in Europe tried to intervene with a community-policing initiative, which was blocked by the national government. In reality, neither city nor national government nor international organizations were able to bring about the reduction of violence. It was local leaders whose participation was vital and who were thus able to protect their communities from the worst of the fighting. It was civilians and informal leaders who were better able to provide protection

---

79. Khamidov, Megoran, and Heathershaw, "Bottom-Up Peacekeeping in Southern Kyrgyzstan."

than the state itself. Unlike Hardt and Negri's multitude,[80] their identity is not based on their immanent universality but on working together in their locality and their shared Muslim faith. This is a theme we will return to in part 3.

ON PIETY AND PURCHASING POWER

This chapter has covered a great deal of ground, presenting various evidence and arguments about the decentered nature of security under conditions of globalization. Together, these suggest that the dominant policy imaginaries of realism, on the one hand, and liberalism, on the other, offer no more than deceptive headlines of the actual experience of being secure or insecure. Yes, states launch (and win) wars, assassinate terrorists, deploy peacekeepers, and disperse extraordinary amounts of aid in the name of human security. However, the on-the-ground realities (the *mētis*) of these policies are far from how they are planned in capitals, reported in official documents, or envisioned in UN. The UN Security Council sessions, in the words of one International Relations scholar, simulates world order in its absence.[81] National security, according to secular realists, means that we can speak credible about an "American-led" order since 1945, not a "liberal" one.[82] In this order, according to Patrick Porter, "coups, carpets bombings, blockades and 'black sites' were not separate lapses, but were part of the coercive ways of world-ordering."[83] This order advantaged some parts of the world, but even in its center, the United States, it faced rebellion amidst a perception of worsening economic and societal insecurity. Human security, according to the HSR, has increased globally, but the poor face enormous barriers to their basic freedoms in the form of the "global patrimonial wave," an absence of rule of law, and other transnational structures of economic and cultural violence. The error of the liberal international order "is to suppose that American power and its liberalism was not only good, but *essentially* good."[84]

In a world more real than that described by political realists, many citizens are more likely to be threatened by the domestic elites of the state and their security services than a foreign state and its military. The concept of human security describes part of this reality, but it fails to provide

80. Hardt and Negri, *Multitude*.
81. Debrix, *Re-envisioning Peacekeeping*.
82. Porter, *False Promise*, 4.
83. Porter, *False Promise*, 6.
84. Porter, *False Promise*, 7.

explanation as to why human insecurity is distributed across the planet, in both Global South and Global North. Conversely, casual observers express surprise that there are many billionaires in a very poor country such as Nigeria. These people didn't become billionaires despite the poverty of their citizens; their citizens became poor because of the elite's wealth. In a process that is now routine in the global economy, the wealth of the country was channeled through the state into offshore accounts from where it can be accessed by the country's elite. This is the broader logic to the global economy, identified by Milbank and Pabst, where

> neoliberal market and bureaucratic oligarchy impose an economistic mediation between a massive spectacular authority and the mere appearance of individual choice, while policing any aberrantly real choices with an ever increased police surveillance.[85]

Here the dialectic of Michael Mann between the recentering of chapter 6, driven by the political-military elite, and the decentering here, driven by the political-economic elite, is apparent.

Where does post-Christendom fit in all this? The IR theorist Hedley Bull labels such a world as the one described over the preceding two chapters as neo-medievalism, "a secular reincarnation of the system of overlapping or segmented authority that characterized mediaeval Christendom."[86] Indeed, the decentering processes outlined here are not functionally different from those of decentered Christendom where the church was a major economic actor and source of moral authority distinct from the state. Both piety and purchasing power have always driven centripetal forces. These forces and their dialectical relations with central state power that characterized Christendom continue in the secular age and are now found on a global scale. As a matter of their very existence as sovereign subjects, secular states are bound to assert control and act as if they can protect and provide for their citizens. Yet this ideological claim is met by the reality of the distribution of power not just between states but to elites within states and among them at a global scale. Not only do they often generate violence and insecurity, but the security dynamics also enable how far their citizens feel protected and provided for, and they are determined more by capital movements and legal instruments at a global scale than by national security strategies. *The state is both ideologically centered on secular government and practically decentered to local actors and elite networks.* It is little wonder that such a disenchanted world meets resistance in the form of movements and process of re-enchantment, both religious and secular.

85. Milbank and Pabst, *Politics of Virtue*, 336.
86. Bull, *Anarchical Society*, 244.

CHAPTER 8

Idolatries of Neo-Christendom[1]

And Jesus began to say to them, "See that no one leads you astray. Many will come in my name, saying, 'I am he!' and they will lead many astray. And when you hear of wars and rumors of wars, do not be alarmed. This must take place, but the end is not yet. For nation will rise against nation, and kingdom against kingdom. There will be earthquakes in various places; there will be famines. These are but the beginning of the birth pains.

MARK 13:5–8

It is because we have wanted to distance ourselves from religion that it is now returning with such force and in a retrograde, violent form. The rationalism that you mention was thus not real distancing, but a dike that is in the process of giving way.

RENÉ GIRARD[2]

On 6 December 2017, President Trump announced his intention for the United States to move its embassy in Israel and recognize Jerusalem as its capital. "This morning a lot of foreign policy professionals in Washington are left scratching their heads," the BBC's North America editor opined, noting the political and security risks of the move in terms of the Middle East

---

1. This chapter draws on John Heathershaw, "What Is Christendom to Us?," paper under review.
2. René Girard, *Battling to the End*, 119.

conflict and US relations with Arab allies.³ Notwithstanding such reasoning, the Palestinian backlash has been successfully repressed by the Israeli security apparatus and the US and Israel signed the Abraham accords in 2020 with the United Arab Emirates and several other Arab states, further normalizing their relations with Israel. However, the impulse behind the recognition of Jerusalem was that it was a central objective of Christian Zionism, an influential movement among US conservative evangelicals. This fundamentalist Christian community, having laid to one side their misgivings about Trump's defects of morality, had swung decisively behind him in the swing states of the 2016 presidential election. This much was obvious. What was less noticed was the fact that the key states that swung for Trump in 2016—Michigan, Pennsylvania, and Wisconsin—were some of those with the highest rates of military sacrifice from the wars in Afghanistan and Iraq.⁴ Making America great again was both a religious and a geopolitical project. In a certain sense, it was a project of neo-Christendom.

The significance of Jerusalem to this influential minority is its putative status as Zion, the capital of the Jewish state that is imagined to later become the center of Christ's thousand-year rule on earth. It may not be a stretch to say that Trump's act recalled, in a very different context almost a thousand years before, the medieval papacy's declaration of a crusade to reclaim Jerusalem/Zion for the church. In terms of securitization, these speech acts connote very different referent objects of security than those constructed by secular realpolitik and the liberal international order. In theologico-political terms, the rationale for both acts is the same: to reclaim Christendom, however much violence and disorder this causes. To a certain kind of apocalyptic worldview, such insecurity is to be expected. But one doesn't need to be a premillennial dispensationalist Christian Zionist to notice religious disturbances in international security. Demagogic figures such as Trump and Putin do not merely arise out of domestic cultural shift but out of disillusion with the liberal international order, long-standing threat perceptions, and delusions of "leadership" and martial virtue.⁵ As the grander illusion of the centered secular state breaks down, and the promise of a rules-based order merely generates more insecurity, faith in rationalism also recedes. We live in an age when secular elites propose to decelerate the very processes—be they militarization, climate change, or financial capitalism—that have concentrated and accelerated in the secular age. Their rationalism is unsatisfying and, in Girard's terms, the "dike" they have

3. BBC, *Today* program.
4. Porter, *False Promise*, 137.
5. Porter, *False Promise*, 128–31.

constructed between the religious and the secular "is in the process of giving way." In such circumstances, it is natural, to nod to the apocalyptic, to "wars and rumors of wars" (Mark 13:6).

However, in pointing to the apocalyptic, theologians risk falling into a reactionary politics. John Milbank and his co-author Adrian Pabst are caught in this trap in the opening of their *Politics of Virtue* where they lament the "tacit, secret alliance" between economic and sociocultural liberals.[6] John Perry denotes this as "Grandpa Simpson mode." Perry refers to the eponymous grandpa of *The Simpsons*, who is "endlessly afraid of the strange world outside his care home, nostalgic for a past that never existed, and complains about everything getting worse, especially young people" and deploys the term directly to denote the stance taken by the post-liberals Milbank and Pabst.[7] Perry's argument is that the liberalism the authors lament does not prevent the virtuous lives that they seek. Moreover:

> We ought not be quietist in the face on ongoing injustice, such as in Guantanamo Bay, Syria, Sudan, and Bangladesh. And yes, Fortune 500 executives are still paid too much. But things nowadays are not that bad. Considering alternatives and how things used to be, things are pretty good.[8]

No doubt, Perry would point to the economic growth that has taken place to pull hundreds of millions (mainly in China) out of poverty and create a burgeoning "middle class" in many poor countries. But what Perry fails to acknowledge are the security implications of the "inequality between the very rich and the many" that he identifies.[9] It is these tensions between elites—political and professional, kleptocratic and neoliberal—and the poor that characterize the new era of conflict. Moreover, given that the social and political effect of Christianity was to fatally undermine the "assumption of natural inequality" in the imperial Christendom world through its proposition of the "moral equality of humans,"[10] this renewed awareness of inequality today and the loss of faith in the state is surely of far greater significance than acknowledged by Perry. There are a lot of Grandpa Simpsons out there. It is this inequality, and a yearning for an imagined past governed by Christian values, that is perhaps the primary cause of the re-enchantment of the world today.

---

6. Milbank and Pabst, *The Politics of Virtue*.
7. Perry, "Grandpa Milbank."
8. Perry, "Grandpa Milbank."
9. Perry, "Grandpa Milbank."
10. Siedentop, *Inventing the Individual*, 51, 65.

The theologians who have grasped the significance of this re-enchantment in their political theology are those, like Barth and Bonhoeffer, Johann Baptist Metz and Dorthee Sölle, who worked in the shadow of Auschwitz. Sölle, as the only woman and theological feminist among German political theologians, perhaps offers most help with her conception of a patriarchal "authoritarian religion."[11] Sölle notes:

> Authoritarian religion reveals an infantile need for consolation that expresses itself aesthetically and in the history of piety as sentimentality; it is matched however by a compulsive need for order, fear of confusion and chaos, and the desire for comprehensibility and dominance. It is precisely its rigidity that outlasts the other moments of a dying religion.[12]

In part 3 we will advance from this critique via a political theology of security—a new Christian realism—that seeks to consider the apocalyptic Christologically, and thereby avoids dropping into Grandpa Simpson mode. However, before embarking on this political theology, we will set the postsecular political scene via an analysis of the re-enchanting of the secular world. While the prerequisites of Christendom may be ebbing away, it remains a seductive imaginary across much of the Christianized world, including the Global South and East. These neo-Christendoms are dangerous and appear to exacerbate the very national insecurity they claim to address, often taking sectarian or militant form and arising from those communities and social groups that have been the most marginalized by the combined forces of the secular state and globalization.

Global Christianity and the Resurgence of Religion

As part 1 argued, Christendom has long been a global and plural phenomenon that was dispersed via empire to the colonies of Eurasian empires. But Eastern Orthodoxy is rarely considered in the English-speaking literature and is often divorced from its historical contexts. Our inattention to the histories and theologies of Eastern Orthodoxy is made acute today by the return of the Russian Orthodox church (ROC) to the center of political power in Russia, and the apparent increase in the influence of the church under its Patriarch Kirill. Even before Kirill's ascent, the ROC had successfully lobbied for the dubiously named Law on Freedom of Conscience and Religious Organizations (1997), a post-Soviet statute that limited proselytism and the

---

11. For an accessible introduction to her work, see Francis, *Dorothee Sölle*.
12. Sölle, "Fatherhood, Power, and Barbarism," 329.

rights of the non-state Christian churches in order to protect the ROC's privileged national Christendom.[13] Under Kirill, church-state relations have become more clearly evocative of Christendom, with the patriarch "increasing coordination in the policies of the Russian Ministry of Foreign Affairs and the ROC's outreach to its parishes outside Russian borders" and advocating the role of "the Orthodox Church in ensuring a patriotic education infused with reverential memory for Russia's past glories."[14] The ROC was also an enthusiastic support of Russia's hybrid wars in Ukraine from 2014 and 2022, purportedly in defense of ethnic Russians and "orthodox Christendom." Christian critics of Kirill within Russia have accused him of advancing the political interests of the state and the role of the church in those interests, rather than the core religious activities of the church.[15] Similarly many state churches across the contemporary Orthodoxy are rightly charged with "conflating nationalism with ecclesiology."[16] It is the imaginary of neo-Christendom from which these ideas and practices of the ROC have emerged.

While neo-Christendom affects the East, so it is increasingly found in the South. In the nineteenth century, as with Orthodox Christendom and the Ottoman Empire, the Western churches also became entangled with further-flung parts through processes of imperial expansion. Agensky argues that "reframing religion as part of a global, relational, and political field eschews Eurocentric tropes that characterize the West as self-sustaining and autonomous."[17] Western Christianity continues to be transformed by its colonial encounter and today many denominations are more populated in the Global South than in the North.[18] Missionaries that began to travel across empires from the late-eighteenth century set off processes that they could not control, which have led to indigenous churches that they may no longer recognize. Major developments in Christianity, such as the "prosperity gospel" (which began in the United States and has been popular among new evangelical churches across the world) and "liberation theology" (a pro-poor movement originating in Latin America), were missionary engagements for and against political conservatism. Some of the strongest voices for government according to Christian principles emerge from Catholic churches in

---

13. Papkova and Gorenburg, "The Russian Orthodox Church," 4.
14. Papkova and Gorenburg, "The Russian Orthodox Church," 5–6.
15. Druzenko, "Geopolitics from the Patriarch."
16. Marsh and Payne, "Religion, Culture, and Conflict," 808.
17. Agensky, "Recognizing Religion," 748.
18. Jenkins, *The Next Christendom*; McAlister, *The Kingdom of God Has No Borders*, 8.

the Global South, which have greater influence on their governments than the historic churches of the West. As Philpott argues, following disestablishment in the early twentieth century, "most Latin American churches then adopted a 'neo-Christendom' stance by which they sought informal but close ties with the state" and fostered "close ties to military rulers."[19] Even liberation theology, has been portrayed both as a critique of those churches that imagined a new Christendom via the strong government offered by the *generalissimo*[20] and a mode of "neo-Constantinianism" for its extant faith in the state.[21]

The increasing power of the Global South in Christianity is such that, according to Jenkins, if we want to visualize a "typical" contemporary Christian, we should think of a woman living in a village in Nigeria or in a Brazilian favela.[22] Christians in the global North are already in a minority of the global population and are estimated to constitute just 26 percent of those expected to self-identify as believers by 2050.[23] In the top five "Christian countries," following the US, places two to five are taken by Brazil, Mexico, Russia, and the Philippines, each of which have more than 70 percent of their population as confessing Christians.[24] Just as significantly, migratory patterns point to Christian populations in northern states that are far more global in terms of their link to diaspora. This has obvious political consequences. For example, the struggles within the Anglican Communion over issues such as female priests and gay marriage have not just reflected theological differences between conservatives and liberals but *geographical differences* between northerners seeking to adapt to a multi-faith society and southerners who feel they have the growth and influence to actively resist these forces.

These relationships are perhaps best understood not as narrowly international, between competing national churches, but transnational, taking place across global networks driven by theology and confessional allegiance. It is this global context that, Melani McAlister argues, has shaped the emergence in recent decades of politically conservative evangelical Christianity in the US.[25] In turn, this provides the backdrop for the emer-

---

19. Philpott, "Explaining the Political," 511, 512.
20. Ferrarotti, "Toward the End of Constantinian Christendom."
21. Schipani, *Freedom and Discipleship*.
22. Jenkins, *The Next Christendom*, 2.
23. Pew, "The Future of World Religions," 60.
24. Pew, "The Future of World Religions," 61.
25. McAlister, *The Kingdom of God Has No Borders*.

gence of freedom of religion and belief as a key tenet of US foreign policy.[26] In *The Next Christendom: The Coming of Global Christianity* Jenkins argues that population growth and migratory patterns combined with conservative biblical interpretation and theology may mean a more activist and political role for the church in the South and indicate the coming of "a new Christendom, which for better or worse may play a critical role in world affairs."[27] These churches, we can assume, are not likely to "bring their message more into accord with (Western) secular orthodoxies."[28] More likely, they might form an axis of South-South transnational cooperation between churches for a new Christendom characterized by "intensified rivalry [with Islam], by struggles for converts, by competing attempts to enforce moral codes by means of secular law" and the danger of fanaticism "that could well provoke horrific wars and confrontations."[29] Twenty years after Jenkins wrote, the Russian invasion of Ukraine offers glimpses of his fears. However, it is a "civil war" between "Christian nations" with the bogeyman of Islam nowhere in sight.

Neo-Christendom and the clash of civilizations

Jenkins' intervention, though speculative, is a reminder that a great deal is at stake in our analysis of security after Christendom. As Christendom is reimagined in the Global South it may generate no less armed conflict and ethnic violence than the previous instantiations of Christendom in the North. This is not a matter of a "clash of civilizations" over religious difference but transnational struggles within and across these putative civilizations, where American evangelicals partner institutionally or vicariously with Latin American conservative Catholics, Nigerian Pentecostals, and/or Russian Orthodox believers.[30] In this sense, perhaps the failure to examine contemporary Christendom is as much about a reluctance to engage with theology as it is with a historical short-sightedness and Eurocentrism. Furthermore, as one senior colleague noted privately, Christendom is simply too toxic for most intellectuals in secular universities to engage without serious questions being asked about their politics and ethics. I recognize these concerns but I feel that the return of imaginaries of Christendom is far too significant to be ignored.

26. Bettiza, *Finding Faith*.
27. Jenkins, *The Next Christendom*, 4.
28. Jenkins, *The Next Christendom*, 9.
29. Jenkins, *The Next Christendom*, 13.
30. McAlister, *The Kingdom of God Has No Borders*.

Neo-Christendom is perhaps most associated with the US and the rise of politically conservative Protestant Christianity; but other Christian confessions also propagate neo-Christendom ideas, such as those of the more conservative interpretations of the Catholic theologian Jacques Maritain's influential *Man and the State* (1952). There are also progressive defences of the endurance of the old order. Oliver O'Donovan's *The Desire of the Nations*, which we reviewed in chapter 3, is perhaps the most sophisticated recent articulation of a Western liberal-democratic conception of Christendom. Public intellectuals fighting culture wars in Western states may also be said to be broadly adherent to this approach, but once again a variety of imaginaries are observable. Samuel Huntington in *The Clash of Civilizations* denoted Western civilization as that which "used to refer to what used to be called Western Christendom."[31] Long before Huntingdon's seminal text, American conservative evangelicals were already fostering a nostalgia for Christendom. In this sense, civilizations in general, and neo-Christendom in particular, do not exist objectively but are given life and revived in political discourse and practice. Part of this politics is, in Jocelyn Cesari's framing, "a continuous struggle between actors to define the boundaries of the 'secular' and the 'religious.'"[32]

In parts of the Global South, and specifically what evangelicals used to denote according the geographical trope of the 10/40 window,[33] these neo-Christendom imaginaries against the Muslim other are strong, although they have often been propagated by a movement centered in the United States.[34] "The persecuted Christians movement positions Christians as simultaneously victims and warriors," McAllister argues, and provided "the logic through which some evangelicals envisioned a global conflict with Islam."[35] Here, it is "Christendom" through which some Christians imagine Christian unity for believers and conflict with Islam. Multiple African leaders have declared themselves to be Christian presidents of Christian states, including Fredrik Chiluba of Zambia, who superficially invoked the theology of the Lordship of Christ.[36] Such imagined communities cannot be easily dismissed as reactionary. Chiluba's predecessor and the country's founding president, Kenneth Kaunda, had offered a more syncretic imaginary that

---

31. O'Donovan, *Desire of the Nations*, 46.
32. Cesari, "Civilization as Disciplinization."
33. The parts of Africa, the Middle East, and Asia that lie between the 10 and 40 degrees above the equator and which are the home to many Muslim-majority states.
34. McAlister, *The Kingdom of God Has No Borders*, 144–58.
35. McAlister, *The Kingdom of God Has No Borders*, 174, 289.
36. Gifford, "Chiluba's Christian Nation."

he called "Zambian humanism"; as an anti-colonial leader he read Gandhi and combined socialism and pan-Africanism with Christianity. The chant "God in heaven—on earth, Kaunda!" was a rally cry of the 1960s and 70s.[37] While subsequent evidence of corruption often generates cynicism toward such neo-Christendom imaginaries, and African critiques,[38] Phiri plausibly argues that they also galvanize evangelicals to become far more involved in politics—at least in the form of witnesses and martyrs.[39]

It is perhaps in Russia and Eurasia where neo-Christendom theological imaginaries of foreign policy are at their present zenith. In Russia, as we have seen, Christendom theological imaginaries and Orthodox symbolism are now routinely deployed in discourses of Russia's role in the world and, despite formal secularism, the ROC under Patriarch Kirill takes part in political campaigns for closer cooperation with the state.[40] The notion of Moscow as a "third Rome" and Russia as being the Schmittian *katechon*, the restrainer and holder of the balance, are now influential in Russian foreign policy and appear to be invoked in both Vladimir Putin's and Sergei Lavrov's foreign policy speeches, particularly with regard to Russia's intervention in Syria.[41] According to this *Russkiy Mir* worldview, Russia's role as the balance-holder in Christendom is both a civilizational and a global one.

Variations of neo-Christendom that take a national form are especially found in southeastern Europe, including in states with national Orthodox churches (Ukraine since 2019, Greece) and Catholic churches (Hungary, Poland). As these examples suggest, national neo-Christendom imaginaries sometimes combine and sometimes conflict with one another and with civilizational imaginaries like *Russkiy Mir*. Another example is that of Serbian Orthodox and Croatian Catholic national imaginaries. The Croatian Catholic church in Yugoslavia organized *1,300 years of Christianity among Croats* (1975–84) to press for Croat national independence—which would eventually be realized by warfare in the early 1990s. According to one of its organizers, Živko Kustić, "the Church has consciously acted, convinced that serving national self-determination is indivisible with her call to serve human dignity.... Therefore, we have spoken about infusion of Christianity in the Croatian national being."[42] In his book, *Hrvatska: mit ili misterij* [Croa-

---

37. Kaunda, *The Nation That Fears God Prospers*, 152.
38. Sanneh, *Whose Religion Is Christianity?*; Kaunda, *The Nation That Fears God Prospers*.
39. Phiri, "President Frederick J. T. Chiluba of Zambia."
40. Stoeckl, "The Russian Orthodox Church."
41. Lewis, *Russia's New Authoritarianism*, 200–207.
42. Quoted in Grozdanov, "Christian Identity Between Nation and the Christ."

tia: Myth or Mystery], Kustić tells us that "we are not talking about nation as the community of citizens, but as a community that shares same cultural heritage. Therefore, we are not talking about demos, but about ethnos."[43] Such imaginaries feed and are fed by a long history of Croat religious nationalism and even fascism. These examples from Europe and Eurasia suggest an ethnic rather than civic form of national neo-Christendom.

Other imaginaries for a new Christendom blend civic and ethnic flavors and are found both inside and outside the church. With "civilizationalist" logic, but shorn of theology, the influential British conservative writer Douglas Murray refers to himself as a "Christian atheist" but is enthusiastically quoted by a UK evangelical Christian media group saying that "you cannot take Christianity out of the West and have anything that's recognizably the West."[44] In continental Europe, politicians and public intellectuals engage in Islamophobia to defend an imagined Judeo-Christian heritage.[45] For instance, Orbán argued in a 2015 speech to his Fidesz party faithful that the refugee crisis "offers the chance for the national Christian ideology to regain supremacy not only in Hungary but in the whole of Europe."[46] Further on the extreme Right, in European national "defense leagues" and the counter-jihad movement, crusader imagery and Christendom imaginaries are deployed ubiquitously.[47]

In what sense is Christian nationalism *Christian*?

It is easy for many Christians to dismiss these Christian nationalist movements as aberrations—misguided souls who have put their politics above their faith. This is both easy and incorrect. There are far too many Christians and churches that have been beguiled by nationalism through history to reasonably dismiss them as non-Christian. Moreover, there is a sense in which "Christian" is a self-designation. If churches and para-church Christian movements are advancing nationalism or some other form of civilizationism in the name of Christianity, deploying biblical proof texts and church doctrine, how can one deny their Christianity? The real question is not whether they are Christian but what causes their idolatry. Is it something internal to the Christian tradition that has led them to worship the nation alongside God? Alternatively, are there external factors that make

---

43. Grozdanov, "Christian Identity," 5.
44. Brahm, "Douglas Murray Cherishes Christianity."
45. Marranci, "Multiculturalism, Islam, and the Clash of Civilizations Theory."
46. Quoted in Lendvai, *Orbán*, 201.
47. Koch, "The New Crusaders."

them unwitting pawns of wider processes of culture and politics? As is often the case, the evidence from social scientists is mixed.

There is certainly a great deal of evidence that factors *external* to the church are driving Christian nationalism. In Serbia, in a manner invoking patterns of late-Christendom, nationalism blends with Christianity, 84 percent identifying as members of the Serbian Orthodox Church.[48] However, according to recent research by Marko Veković of the University of Belgrade, Serbs rarely attend church but relate to it in terms of "belonging without attending." Thus, support for the nationalists is not based in religiosity of the people, "but rather . . . it is a product of a long-standing history of close Church-State relations."[49] In extremely secular Sweden, a similar pattern is found, with a strong increase between 2014 and 2020 of support "for fostering a society with Christian values in Sweden" alongside a further decline in church attendance.[50] This rise in support, argues Magnus Hagevi, "cannot be explained by increased religiosity or espousal of church-based values among the Swedish population" but may be attributed to "changes related to increased support for a culturally homogeneous society and for conservative ideology."[51] And this is a particular problem of neo-Christendom in a secular age that is more acute than in Christian nationalisms of generations past. "While religious practitioners may perceive Christian values as infinite and universal," Hagevi notes, "secular individuals may take their lead from politicians who instead consider Christian values to be exclusive and nationalistic."[52]

However, other research demonstrates that there are ways in which theology and ecclesiology matter. For example, Emma Rosenberg explains positive references to Jews and pro-Israel narratives by white supremacist groups with a prior history of anti-Semitism in theological terms.[53] "The trope of the Jew becomes de-racialized," she argues, in order to appeal to the theology of the millennium found among many dispensationalist evangelical groups.[54] Rosenberg notes this millennial tune cuts both ways. Antisemitism is not erased from the programs of these groups and the theology that informs pro-Israel narratives also predicts the apocalyptic end of the Jewish people. Denominational differences also matter in explaining Christian

48. Veković, "Belonging without Attending?"
49. Veković, "Belonging without Attending?," 1, 6.
50. Hagevi, "Are Christian Values Religious or Political?"
51. Hagevi, "Are Christian Values Religious or Political?," 8–9.
52. Hagevi, "Are Christian Values Religious or Political?," 9.
53. Rosenberg, "Taking the 'Race' Out of Master Race."
54. Rosenberg, "Taking the 'Race' Out of Master Race," 4.

nationalism. Recent research on attitudes to the EU suggests that the historical affinity of Western European Catholics, based on the role of Catholic Christian democrats in its creation in the post-war era, is bowing under the pressure of theologies of national Christendom that have emerged in places like Poland and Hungary. Rosita Garskaite finds that Catholic Euro-skepticism is emerging in Lithuania.[55] In the UK, a majority of Catholics opposed Brexit, but this may be largely due to the presence of many EU immigrants in Britain's Catholic community.[56] By contrast, British-born Catholics and the laity of the established Anglican church supported the UK's departure from the EU in such a volume that without their votes Brexit would not have taken place. Most Christians from free church backgrounds opposed Brexit.[57] These kinds of differences on denominational lines suggest that both church history and ecclesiology of national establishment matter.

It seems reasonable to conclude that Christian nationalism is Christian insofar that it takes a neo-Christendom form, culturally and politically, theologically and ecclesiologically. It is precisely the kind of "natural theology" that the Swiss theologian Karl Barth warned against both in the Barmen declaration and his academic writing. The Croatian theologian Zoran Grozdanov contrasts the natural theology of Christian nations in the writing of John Paul II with Barth's hope that we are "originally and finally free" from nations, since they don't belong to "God's immutable orders."[58] Tim Gorringe summarizes Barth's perspective as follows: "the important thing is to deny the state the pathos, the seriousness, and the importance of the divine."[59] While Christian nationalism is Christian, theological (in a natural sense), and even (selectively) biblical, it is neither evangelical nor Christ-centered. Effective opposition to both Christian nationalism and secular realism must demonstrate an understanding of the political conditions that give rise to re-enchantment *and* offer its adherents hope that good news is found not in the nation but in the kingdom of Jesus Christ.

Post-Christendom alternatives?

Before this chapter ends and the reconstruction process begins, it is necessary to recognize quite how fractured the "re-enchanted" and recognizably "post-secular" world is in the twenty-first century. This is even true

55. Garškaitė, "Threats and Safeguards."
56. Kolpinskaya and Fox, "Praying on Brexit?"
57. Kolpinskaya and Fox, "Praying on Brexit?"
58. Quoted in Grozdanov, "Christian Identity," 4.
59. Gorringe, *Karl Barth*, 45–46.

Idolatries of Neo-Christendom 193

of some of its putatively homogenous blocs. White evangelicals—so often dismissed as apologists for white Christian nationalism—are fractured globally and politically. For example, Tearfund, an evangelical development charity based in the UK, engages in what McAllister denotes as "enchanted internationalism" and "victim identification,"[60] but often against the nostalgic agendas of conservative governments. One of the charity's bloggers argued in the context of Black Lives Matter that "anthems such as Rule, Britannia only remain in the British cultural sphere because we haven't been through a proper period of repentance for our historic role in slavery and colonialism."[61] Tearfund has also produced a "toolkit" that asks white British Christians to "acknowledge your privilege."[62] Still, these rumblings among white evangelicals are modest compared to the long history of anti-colonial and explicitly Christian resistance to which they respond. These "externalities" of the Christendom experience are important touchstones for any attempt to construct post-Christendom imaginaries in the West.

Many Christian theologians and activists from the Global South have long wrestled critically with the violence, racism, and empire of Christendom. Some of these thinkers appear unwilling to jettison its underlying theologies. The Nigerian evangelical theologian Samuel Waje Kunhiyop reasserts the Lutheran "two kingdoms" theology, where "Christian values permeate the nation," while pressing a peace witness in the manner of Yoder and the post-Christendom position.[63] However, there is a long history of decolonial practice in the African church. The leading African theologian Lamin Sanneh has had influence across the African church in his narrative of "the transition from 'Christendom' to world Christianity" and his argument against a "global Christianity," which "means a contemporary extension of Western Christendom—the religious idioms of Euro-America spreading triumphantly through other continents in a kind spiritual neo-colonialism."[64] Jehu Hanciles agrees that what characterizes the vitality of African Christianity is opposition to the conservative and imperial tactics of mission under Christendom in favor of a charismatic and properly global movement where all countries both receive and send missionaries.[65] What is distinct in much of this work is how the assertion of African resistance to

---

60. McAllister, *The Kingdom of God Has No Borders*, 9–13.
61. Tearfund, "How to Be a Good Ally."
62. Tearfund, "How to Be a Good Ally."
63. Kunhiyop, *African Christian Ethics*, 106.
64. Sanneh, "Whose Religion Is Christianity?," 281; see also Ranger, "Evangelical Christianity and Democracy in Africa," 113.
65. Hanciles, "Beyond Christendom," 109.

Western Christendom is often scripturally orthodox and averse to secularism. This recalls the Comaroffs' remark about how the first South African native church breakaways from Western mission in the nineteenth century were marked by "the way they applied the idiom of revelation to their own historical conditions; they had an unerring knack of using biblical rhetoric against the evangelists."[66]

The fact that African post-Christendoms are often locally syncretic—drawing on non-Christian registers of discourse particular to place (as Western Christianity does too!)—*and* scriptural puts it at odds with the secular post-Christendom thought of the neoliberal and post-Marxist kind we considered in chapter 7, which is both universalist and anti-foundationalist. The Ugandan Catholic theologian Emmanuel Katongole argues that contemporary African Christianity cannot survive without the bedrocks of local community and biblical revelation. "With the collapse of the Christian empire (Christendom)," he remarks, "the church always finds herself on alien ground totally surrounded by postmodern culture with no place that she could properly call her own." "Resistance and hope," he contends, is found in "the ability to free the bible from the liberal and individualistic notions of salvation so that we allow its full potential as the story of a pilgrim community."[67] That Africans have been brought into Western secular modernity in a manner that is deeply violent, and how such violence must be resisted through emancipatory practices of lament rather than reproduced through rebellious acts of violence, is central to Katongole's thought.[68]

The Eurasian context is different to the African one, more accurately described as postimperial than postcolonial insofar as many of the churches emerge out of imperial Orthodox instantiations of Christendom. That said, there are similarities in some of the ideas and practices that emerge. In Russia, there is a "small liberal opposition" within the ROC against calls for a new Christendom on broadly two-kingdoms grounds.[69] Ukrainian churches—prior to the break from the Moscow Patriarchate—participated widely in the Maidan protests of 2013, with the head of the Ukrainian Orthodox Church, Patriarch Filaret, observing, "when snipers shot at people at Maidan, the church stopped praying for the government and then the government fled."[70] Ukrainian theologian and former rector of Donetsk

---

66. Comaroff and Comaroff, *Of Revelation and Revolution*, 97.

67. Katongole, "Postmodern Illusions and the Challenges of African Theology," 521, 523.

68. Kantongole, *The Sacrifice of Africa*.

69. Stoeckl, "The Russian Orthodox Church," 274.

70. Searle and Cherenkov, *A Future and a Hope*, 65.

University, Mykhailo Cherenkov, and his co-author Joshua Searle make an argument for nonviolent resistance by the post-Soviet church to the Eastern Christendom imaginaries promoted by the ROC.[71] There is some evidence of this resistance emerging in a critique within Orthodoxy against ethnophyletism in general, not simply its particular imperial versions articulated from Russia against Ukraine. "The role of the church, her politics broadly speaking," the Orthodox Gallaher argues, "is to witness to the [becoming] kingdom [of Christ], to a new transformed way of life."[72]

Vladimir Solovyov (1853–1900), Sergius Bulgakov (1877–1944), and other Eastern Orthodox theologians sketched out something of a theological vision of a universal post-Christendom in terms of "sophiology," which can be understood as something like the mystical and ecclesiological development of temporal wisdom from Christocentric origins. For Solovyov, in Rowan Williams' interpretation, the purpose is to provide a vision of "what the world is meant to be, a reconciled whole centered upon humanity restored to mutual communion and communion with God."[73] His successor and interpreter, Sergius Bulgakov, was, in *The Unfading Light* (1917), able to extol "the positive dimension of 'secularization'" in the fact that it has overcome the "pseudo-theocracy" of the "Christian state."[74] In distinctly realist terms, Bulgakov recognized it is possible to "maintain loyalty to an unfavorable political order" and cautioned that the business of the church is the, "religious triumph over the 'political,' the *transfiguration* authority, which is also its manifestation in *New Testament* terms."[75] Regarding the latter, he felt that "only speculative hopes are possible."[76] This kingdom of God is spiritual and "near to us"[77] in the manner that Leo Tolstoy proclaims in *The Kingdom of God Is within Us*, his rebuke of the imperial Russian Orthodox church from which the great novelist was excommunicated. But the kingdom is also of this world, according to Bulgakov, in the inaugurated sense of "what was accomplished beforehand through government can now be realized through society—not from above, but from below—and the old coercive theocracy must give way to freedom."[78]

---

71. Searle and Cherenkov, *A Future and a Hope*.
72. Gallaher, "Eschatological Anarchism," 144.
73. Williams, *Sergii Bulgakov*, 115.
74. Bulgakov, "The Unfading Light," 159.
75. Bulgakov, "The Unfading Light," 160.
76. Bulgakov, "The Unfading Light," 160.
77. Bulgakov, *The Sophiology of Death*, 13.
78. Bulgakov, *The Sophiology of Death*, 23.

The biblical and eschatological working out of a theology of security from below will be explored in the next chapter in terms of Bulgakov's work on the New Testament. Some contemporary Eastern Orthodox scholars, most especially Pantelis Kalaitzidis, are working more systematically toward a political theology of this ilk in reaction to both the ethno-phyletism they identify among Orthodox conservatives and the paradigmatic and authoritarian political theology of Schmitt.[79] Kalaitzidis attributes that failure of Orthodoxy to develop a political theology "in the liberating sense of the term" to its experience of empires, those empire's legitimating theologies, and the imbrication of the church with post-imperial nationalisms.[80] Political theology of the progressive kind has been identified as the work of "the West" and/or "the Left," and therefore to be resisted in Orthodox circles. However, Kalaitzidis' political theology is not founded on a Western literature—although it comes to conclusions not dissimilar from post-Christendom theologians in the West.[81] "While Christianity is," he remarks, "historical, it nevertheless is oriented towards reality—the Kingdom of God—that is meta-historical but that, however, has already begun to affect and illuminate the historical present, in as much as the *eschaton* is constantly, albeit paradoxically, breaking into history."[82] Kalitzidis' work is, in this sense, a postimperial and Orthodox partner to the postcolonial and Catholic work of Katongole. Both point to eschatology and ecclesiology as the basis for political theology after Christendom.

Toward a new Christian realism

There is value, even necessity, in deploying theologies from the East and South as signposts for a new Christian realism in the analysis of international security. It is precisely these voices and histories that were ignored in Christendom theologies. Yet just as African and Orthodox theologies have legitimately arisen from within their own milieus so post-Christendom political theologies in the West must derive from their own resources as well as reaching out ecumenically to those of others. In our context this also means that any attempt to construct this approach must bridge theology and the secularized field of IR. This is especially so given the prophetic role of Christian political thought to speak to its (post)secular societies. Secularism is

79. For a summary of Kalaitzidis' thought, see Gallaher, "Eschatological Anarchism."
80. Kalaitzidis, "Toward and Orthodox Political Theology," 152–54.
81. His most systematic and comprehensive work is found in Kalaitzidis, *Orthodoxy and Political Theology*.
82. Kalaitzidis, "Toward and Orthodox Political Theology," 164.

not so triumphant that it can deny its heritage and limits. Elizabeth Shaman Hurd has perhaps stated this most directly:

> Judeo-Christian secularists, then, rely upon a "common ground" that is slipping away beneath their feet. What will replace it? How might scholars of International Relations equip themselves to recognize and to realize modified ideals of public life that do not fall prey to the limitations of either laicist or Judeo-Christian secularism? Are the options limited to either an embrace of secular reason or recourse to religious faith? To engage these questions productively may require a new perspective on the sacred, the secular and the political.[83]

Answers to these questions are inevitably multiple and competing. And in any such "new perspective" there is a risk of reinventing the wheel. What Hurd appears to be calling for here is a new Christian realism for a post-secular world that overcomes the limitations of the mid-twentieth century generation while retaining their commitment to speak to both theology and IR. The practical political imaginaries of neo-Christendom and their capacity for violence indicate an urgent need to develop not only theological correctives but politically realistic alternatives. Post-Christendom imagines the church as a prophet or witness, apart from and often critical of the state. At the intersection of political theology and IR, feminist and postcolonial critiques of Christian realism question the assumption of state sovereignty in the work of Niebuhr and others—a sovereignty claim that is integral to the Christendom imaginary—and charge this work with simply not being realistic enough about the dispersal of power.[84] These resources, and others of European and Eurasian provenance, will be explored in part 3 to reconstruct a new Christian realism.

It might be sensible to begin the quest for new Christian realism at the fringes of the old. Reinhold Niebuhr's warnings against the apostasy and folly of speaking of nations as Christian are certainly relevant in the face of the re-enchantment of politics.[85] However, Niebuhr's two-kingdoms thinking offers us little if the analysis of part 2 is correct. Other realists were more sanguine about the theological and political limits of these Christendom imaginaries. In "The Church, Russia and the West," Martin Wight offered perhaps the most explicit attempt to consider the implications of the Augustinian dialectic for international security in post-Christendom. "The two

---

83. Hurd, "The Political Authority of Secularism in International Relations," 252.

84. Alexander, "Christian Realism and the State as Idol"; Gentry, "Feminist Christian Realism."

85. Diggins, *Why Niebuhr Now?*

cities [of Augustine] are always mixed up in this world," he argued, "but there is a rhythm in their interaction, and sometimes it is their coincidence and sometimes their divergence that is more apparent."[86] Wight understood that the greatest divergence since Augustine was now facing the West, but unlike other Christian realists his vision was not confined to the temporal need for a balance of power to hold back the end times. Wight was always more apocalyptic than his Christian realist contemporaries who settled comfortably into a largely secular analysis of international order after 1945. He criticized Toynbee for his non-eschatological reading of the incarnation in history and complained about Niebuhr and Butterfield's neglect of New Testament scriptures, particularly those related to "the historical role of the church as the instrument of the Kingdom, the bearer of sacred history."[87] Wight's own sermons and theological writings were almost unique among scholars of International Relations in embracing the apocalyptic passages of the Gospels and even Revelation in a trenchant critique of historical Christianity. In his sermon "God in History," Wight argued that Christ directs us "that we should work a great deal in darkness in the place of Dragons and covered with the shadow of death."[88]

In recent years, a new generation has begun to pick up the challenge of writing an apocalyptic realism for our times. Wight's interpreter Daniel Young summarizes this challenge as follows:

> In post-Christendom, the era of Leviathan, the church no longer had a privileged place. It had to metaphorically retreat to the catacombs. The church would have to shift its emphasis from that of Romans 13, where St. Paul emphasizes government's role in administering justice, to that of Revelation 13.[89]

Wight himself did not carry this shift from Romans to Revelation from his theological work into his international theory. For Alison McQueen, the Judeo-Christian apocalypse is a political theodicy.[90] In this reading the Judeo-Christian apocalypse seems the very antonym of secular realism, and incommensurable as theory. However, for the literary theorist Rebecca Oh, "attending to apocalypse as a historical event makes it available to realism and therefore knowable as something other than the end of the world."[91] In a

86. Wight, "The Church, Russia and the West," 33.
87. Quoted in Young, "Martin Wight," 118.
88. Quoted in Young, "Martin Wight," 118.
89. Young, "Martin Wight," 118–19.
90. McQueen, *Political Realism*, 26–27.
91. Oh, "Apocalyptic Realism," 3.

similar manner, the close social scientific study of the traumatic ruptures of migration, the catastrophe of climate change, and the scale of state violence is rationally apocalyptic. It is in these terms that a new Christian realism is necessarily *apocalyptic realism*.

Over the course of part 2 of this book we have conducted a mapping of contemporary secular and sacred approaches to security theory in terms of the dialectical forces of re/decentering and dis/reenchanting. This sets the scene for us to trace, in part 3, a political theology of security in post-Christendom that re-emerges, rather than breaks from, the order of Christendom. The interplay of the sacred and the secular in the public theology of Christian realists like Wight has long been considered a "problem" by secular analysts. As Hall notes, this consideration reflects their own secular partialities as much as Wight's Christian ones.[92] There is no reason why either Christian faith or feminism or the decolonial or any other theological or ideological persuasion should be an impediment to serious scholarship if we accept that all scholarship takes place within and between narratives that persuade by presenting evidence that is commensurable across narratives. In a similar vein, secular social science—including in its postmodern modes—is not an impediment to that re-emergence of political theology but a helping hand as it reminds us that the exclusive and negative security claims of Christendom are not essential truths but constructs of a fallen world. These constructs point through a glass darkly to the order of powers and authorities as biblically idealized in Romans 13 and demonized in Revelation 13. It is to these theological referents that we now turn to construct, from first principles, a new Christian realism for these apocalyptic times.

---

92. Hall, *The International Thought of Martin Wight*, 22.

PART THREE

CHAPTER 9

The Powers and the Apocalypse

Then the end will come, when he hands over the kingdom to God the Father after he has destroyed all dominion, authority, and power. For he must reign until he has put all enemies under his feet.

1 CORINTHIANS 15:24–25

For the powers are defeated, according to both John and Paul, by their exposure.

TIMOTHY GORRINGE[1]

Forty years prior to President Trump's moving of the American embassy to Jerusalem, the United States was gripped by a particular vision of the Holy Land. Hal Lindsay's *The Late Great Planet Earth*[2] was the best-selling book of the 1970s, spawning a film of the same name (1978) narrated by Orson Welles. Lindsay's tome and the subsequent film were works of premillennial dispensationalist reading of the Apocalypse of St. John, the last book of the Bible. It is perhaps the most significant cultural work in the making of the Christian Right as a political force in the United States—a country where the evangelical church had leaned to the political Left until the mid-twentieth century.[3]

---

1. Gorringe, *Redeeming Time*, 153.
2. Lindsay, *The Late Great Planet Earth*.
3. Womack, "The Rise and Fall of Liberal Evangelicalism in the United States."

In the film, Lindsay states that our present is a "countdown to the end of history as we know it." Welles, as narrator, says that "70 percent of the prophecies written in the Bible have already been fulfilled," so "if the visions of the disciple John are truly prophetic, the remaining events are expected to be fulfilled in our lifetime."[4] As envisaged in Revelation, Lindsay identified the world as being in a state of Babylonian decadence, moral depravity, and delusion at the hands of Satan and the demonic powers of the universe. However, the comeback has begun. The birth of the state of Israel in 1948 and Jerusalem's return to Israeli hands in the Six-Day War of 1967 were Old Testament prophecies already fulfilled and evidence of God inaugurating the end times. The crisis of 1973 and dependency on Middle East oil were seen as further evidence that Jerusalem would become the point of conflict and "burdensome stone" (Zech 12:3) that would provoke Armageddon: the final battle to restore the temple at the site of al-Aqsa, destroy humanity, and bring forth the second coming of Christ.[5]

From this perspective, rather than resolve conflict in the Middle East, or mediate between faith groups, it is therefore the duty of the government of the United States and Christian political movements to shine a light on this conflict and take part on the right side, even if that requires torture and terror. As both theologians and social scientists have noted, these apocalyptic visions have been constitutive of US security policy under presidents influenced by the Christian Right. Ronald Regan justified his arming of the Contras—a right-wing rebel group that can reasonably be described as "terrorist" by the US government's own definition—against the socialist government of Nicaragua with reference to Isaiah 6, "a light unto the nations."[6] Following the terrorist attacks of September 11, George W. Bush invoked the apocalyptic metaphor of "an angel riding the whirlwind," deployed in a letter to Thomas Jefferson, to call for prayer for America to defeat al-Qaeda—a struggle that led to war, occupation, the use of torture by American agents, and eventual defeat in Afghanistan (2001–21).[7]

But what does all this have to do with Christendom? Apocalyptic visions are formative of many of the modern neo-Christendom imaginaries of security with which we ended part 2. In his book on the Bush presidency's apocalyptic geopolitics, Michael Northcott notes,

> Like so many of the emperors and monarchs of what came to be known as Christendom, [George W.] Bush and his speech

4. Dambeck, "The Late Great Planet Earth (1978) Part 4."
5. Dambeck, "The Late Great Planet Earth (1978) Part 4."
6. Ó Tuathail and Agnew, "Geopolitics and Discourse," 196–97.
7. Megoran, *Warlike Christians*, 30–31.

writers use distortion of Christian apocalyptic, combined with American Civil religion, to legitimate and sacralize imperial violence.[8]

In the preceding chapters, we have seen that Christendom has recurrently generated imagined security communities where the state is the model security provider. Over several hundred years, this community morphed into a secular order of great power politics and positive international law wherein Christendom's artefacts, such as the "balance of power" and "just war," continued to govern security thinking and ethical deliberation, both practical and intellectual. The social sciences have reflected this insofar as, according to E. H. Carr, the "study of International Relations in English-speaking countries is simply a study of the best way to run the world from positions of strength."[9]

However, the further secularization of the regions of Christendom and the intense globalization of world politics over the last half century have generated forces that have made these presumptions of Christian virtues and political strength increasingly implausible and made many in the West and beyond question their privileges. Our concepts of authority and democracy are in flux, while political tensions and security divides seem to have intensified in the secular age. According to the theologian Daniel Bell, the Western world is "awash in fear," driven by imaginaries of security both liberal and conservative, both secular and religious.[10] In some quarters of the church, they are salved with myths of a Christian nation and crude literalist readings of scripture that are conservative and defensive.[11]

These fears and the existential questions they involve cannot simply be dismissed but are unpacked and recast in our post-Christendom imaginaries. The task of reframing security after Christendom is necessarily eschatological and the apocalyptic. But these terms are shrouded in mystery for most social scientists. While the eschaton indicates the general and ultimatum purpose of history, the apocalyptic refers to the form of the final battle between good and evil. Ched Myers identifies six characteristics of the Christian apocalyptic in which present events are interpreted through scriptural referents as signifying the coming of a final battle where a select elite hear the revelation and suffer at the hands of evil. The dramatic duel and inevitable conflict are repeated over and over, moving us on to the eventual

---

8. Northcott, *An Angel Directs the Storm*, 12.

9. Quoted in Barkawi and Laffey, "The Postcolonial Moment in Security Studies," 349.

10. Bell, *Divinations*, 1.

11. Boyd, *The Myth of a Christian Nation*, 12; Yoder, *The Politics of Jesus*, 201–2.

final showdown.[12] Importantly, to Myers and other post-Christendom thinkers, the apocalyptic is not conservative and defensive but radical and hopeful. In these imaginaries, it is the nonviolent church (not the violent state) that is the agent of security. As Gorringe indicates, the mere exposure of the powers undermines their authority and leads to their ultimate defeat.

In part 3, this book develops a political theology of security that is both eschatological and apocalyptic. In this chapter we begin this process by looking at the biblical concept of "the powers" as forces in the fading "kingdom of the world," drawing out two explicitly post-Christendom approaches: the liberal eschatology of the Walter Wink (1935–2012), where the powers may be redeemed, and the apocalyptic imaginary of Sergius Bulgakov (1871–1944), where they become beastly and are ultimately defeated. These two approaches are then assessed in a comparison of the legitimate and illegitimate power in Romans 13 and Revelation 13 respectively. Rather than leaving the apocalypse to the fantasists of neo-Christendom, the chapter shows how the book of Revelation provides a hopeful future history of security after Christendom. In the next three chapters we build on this biblical basis to elaborate a theology of security across the three dimensions of inclusion, protection, and provision.

The powers and history—
two post-Christendom approaches

Many Christendom imaginaries of the past and all the neo-Christendom ones of the present are secularized apocalypses without a clear sense of the eschaton. By contrast, according to post-Christendom imaginaries, the old aeon of these kingdoms is dying away: the now-but-not-yet captured biblically by Paul in 1 Corinthians 15 and in Revelation. Central to this story of the end of the earth are assessments of the language of "the dragon" and "beasts" that must be tackled in any Christian political theology of security. However, in order to avoid over-determining the implications of such imagery it is important to analyze it within a theological frame and compare

12. First, the apocalyptic finds a historical key in the present crisis, which explains how we got here and where we're going. Second, there is a "radical apocalyptic dualism" between the "before" and "after" of the crisis. Third, there is a "combat myth" between church and world, where ultimate conflict is unavoidable. Fourth, in the apocalyptic there is an aspect of "secret revelation" that may be invisible to the most learned but grasped by a simple peasant. Fifth, the suffering of the just is required to bring down the old order and inaugurate the new. Sixth and finally, in narratives of the apocalypse we see recapitulation: the dramatic duel and inevitable conflict are repeated over and over, moving us on to the eventual final showdown. Myers, *Binding the Strongman*, 101–3.

it to that of the apostle Paul's language of "powers and principalities." The route to a post-Christendom alternative to Christendom political imaginaries may be found in the biblical concept of "the powers." But this raises questions about their fall and whether they can be redeemed or must be defeated.

In *The Politics of Jesus*, John Howard Yoder claimed that "the Pauline cosmology of the powers represents an alternative to the dominant ('Thomist') vision of 'natural law' as a more biblical way to relate Christ and creation."[13] However, Yoder made little move in that direction as he and other adherents, largely from free church perspectives, have overwhelmingly focused on the tendency toward Antichrist in the powers, rather than their order-keeping or providential functions.[14] On the one hand, what Barth called the "Lordless Powers"—those regimes and structures that preside over genocide, war, and economic and environmental pillage—often seek to co-opt or resist the mission of the church. On the other hand, those same powers are also effective vehicles for ending genocide, reducing war between states, and agreeing binding reductions in carbon emissions. This is a puzzle that theology has barely addressed since Niebuhr's Christian realist account.

In tandem with this theological lacuna, the powers remains an alien concept for the social sciences. In IR we have "superpowers" and "great powers," "middle powers," and "rising powers," as concepts to denote some of the world's strongest states. In biblical interpretation the concept is different and broader. The powers refer to *the spiritual forces that are unobservable and unverifiable, but which lie behind every human institution, corporate agent, network, or structure*. To many social scientists this is unsatisfying, but that may simply be because we social scientists ought to be humbler about the volume of activity we may positively identify. According to Barth, the powers are *the* social forces of the world.

> [The powers] are the hidden wire pillars in man's great and small enterprises, movements, achievements, and revolutions. They are not just the potencies but the real factors and agents of human progress, regress, and stagnation in politics, economics, scholarship, technology, and art, and also of the evolutions and reputations in all the personal life of the individual. It is not really people who do things, whether leaders or the masses.

---

13. Yoder, *Politics of Jesus*, 159.

14. Although others in this tradition have applied the powers to political questions with recognition for their potential for both order and disorder. Megoran, "Go Anywhere I Damn Well Please?"

Through mankind's fault things are invisibly done without an above man.[15]

While for IR theory, anarchy is what *states* make it,[16] from this Barthian theological perspective, anarchy is what *the powers* make it. For Tim Gorringe, Barth is addressing the same puzzle as did his contemporary, the Italian political theorist Antonio Gramsci. This is the question of hegemony or "the way in which we lose our freedom in the face of societal forces."[17]

To build theory in this area, our task is both theological and political. It must consider how the powers are conceived in the New Testament and how they may shape the immanent frame of international politics. We compare the readings of the powers of the liberal Protestant Walter Wink and the dissenting Eastern Orthodox Sergius Bulgakov. The choice of these two is based on the fact that they both specifically address the powers—their role in history and security—in explicitly post-Christendom terms. However, they do so from very different traditions and arrive at quite different answers. Wink's focus is the "powers and principalities" of the Pauline scriptures while Bulgakov's is the dragon and the beasts of Revelation. The two theologians indicate the range of post-Christendom eschatological choices from Wink's progressive redemption of the powers via law, civil society, and the growth of human rights to Bulgakov's apocalyptic vision of the millennial place of the church after the powers fall. Both avoid identifying dispensational ages in history as is characteristic of some neo-Christendom imaginaries, particularly in the United States.

Walter Wink's three-volume study of the powers is perhaps the most influential attempt to draw together social scientific theory and biblical interpretation to address this question from a broadly post-Christendom perspective. Wink accepts the social constructivism upon which securitization theory is based and draws on modern social science to push his critical account further. He defines powers as "institutions, social systems, and political structures"; and notes they provide us with "the means for developing a Christian social ethic from the language of the New Testament."[18] What appears to be an idealist account of the powers is in fact grounded in the most extensive historical-critical exegesis of their appearance across the New Testament found in the literature.

"Powers and principalities" (*archai kai exousiai*) are "the inner and outer aspects of any given manifestation of power," which are "only encountered

15. Quoted in Gorringe, *Karl Barth*, 2.
16. Wendt, "Anarchy."
17. Gorringe, *Karl Barth*, 2.
18. Wink, *Unmasking the Powers*, 5.

as archonalized in some form."[19] *Archē* and *archon* remain the common linguistic marker of organization of power in its survival in the English "anarchy," "hierarchy," "polyarchy" (democracy), etc., and their corporate entities.[20] *Exousia* is equally deployed to refer primarily to temporal forms of authority—"the legitimations, sanctions, and permissions that undergird the everyday exercise of power"—across the New Testament.[21] Paul's use of it in spiritual terms in certain passages of his letters (e.g., Rom 8:38–39) is unusual and, according to Wink, indicates a "peculiarly Christian" linkage of temporal and spiritual authority.[22] In fusing social scientific and theological analysis, powers theology arguably provides a biblical hermeneutic to account for the cyclical history of imperial conquest, expansion, and decline. However, this political-theological reading raises a long-standing question of how the irredeemable beasts of Revelation 13 may be compared to the seemingly anointed authorities of Romans 13,[23] and opens up conundrums of the problem of evil, the relationship between church and state, and the mission of the church.

For Sergius Bulgakov, these conundrums are visibly present throughout history. They point both to history's ultimate purpose (the eschaton) and divisive forms that the end times will take (the apocalyptic). The book of Revelation provides a "history of the world, set out in symbols and images";[24] it is therefore not merely descriptive but normative, inspiring political imaginaries, both conservative and radical. Bulgakov drew clear parallels between the beasts and the powers, referring to the Pauline "powers and principalities" multiple times in his discussion of Revelation 13. "The beast [Rev 13:1] obviously refers to the state," he argues, "and not simply in the sense of the governmental organization of law and order assisting humankind along its way [Rom 13:1], but of totalitarian state authority with its intention to become the only determinate and exhaustive principle in human life."[25]

Bulgakov identifies the beastly state with the Constantinian era "Christian state" that led to Orthodoxy's peace with autocracy.[26] Revelation, he

---

19. Wink, *Unmasking the Powers*, 3.
20. Wink, *Unmasking the Powers*, 13–15.
21. Wink, *Unmasking the Powers*, 16–17.
22. Wink, *Unmasking the Powers*, 16–17.
23. This was also a question for twentieth-century Christian realists. Wight, "The Church, Russia and the West," 35.
24. Bulgakov, *The Apocalypse of St. John*, 9.
25. Bulgakov, *The Apocalypse of St. John*, 93.
26. Bulgakov, *The Apocalypse of St. John*, 97–98.

argues, "gives form to history not as a needle of the so-called Constantinian era, but as a tragedy, inexhaustible and terrible, of the struggle with Christ of forces that are anti-Christian or simply Pagan and elemental."[27] As a Russian theologian and exile, he was particularly interested in the parallels between the socialist movements and Revelation's imaginary. According to Bulgakov, "socialist visions of a revolution followed by a Kingdom of freedom had to be understood as a secular version of Jewish and Christian apocalyptic visions which refer to the ultimate revelation of the Kingdom of God."[28] There is therefore a great deal in common between the liberal Wink and Orthodox Bulgakov in their interpretation of collective agents in global affairs—what Wink denotes as "the powers." However, while for Bulgakov, the collective agents become *demonic* and will be *defeated*, for Wink, the powers are *created* and may therefore be *redeemed*. To assess these two views biblically we must delve deeper into the tensions between the two key scriptural referents: the ideal-type authorities of Romans 13 and the beasts of Revelation 13.

Paul's legitimate "powers" in Romans 13

From various traditions of apocalyptic thought, several authors draw direct comparisons between Revelation's beasts and Paul's powers.[29] "John's vision," Spilsbury notes in relating the dragon to the spiritual forces of evil denoted in Ephesians (6:12), "confirms with stark clarity the grim truth declared by the apostle Paul."[30] However, prior to the work of Wink, this was by no means a widely held view, perhaps due to the apocalyptic dualism between the Christian and the other that it appears to engender.[31] Berkhoff, in the covenant tradition, offers a contrasting interpretation: "the Powers, instead of being ideological centers, are what God meant them to be: helps, instruments, giving shape and direction to the genuine life of man as child and of God and as neighbor."[32] Carr goes further and argues that "the concept of mighty forces which are hostile to man, from which he sought relief,

---

27. Bulgakov, *The Apocalypse of St. John*, 98.
28. Bulgakov, *The Apocalypse of St. John*, viii.
29. McAlpine uses these categories as two of four major positions on the powers. The others being the Reformed and "Third Wave" perspectives. McAlpine, *Facing the Powers*.
30. Spillsbury, *The Throne, the Lamb and the Dragon*, 89.
31. Caird, *The Revelation of St. John*, 16.
32. Quoted in McAlpine, *Facing the Powers*, 13.

was not prevalent in the thought of the first century AD" and nor can it be found in a close reading of Paul's letters.[33]

The early verses of Romans 13 are perhaps the reference to "powers and principalities" that is most obviously at odds with the notion of the dragon and beasts. Wink notes the clear reference to temporal-human institutions and actors (vv. 1–3) in this passage, and their rightful authority to wield the sword (v. 4) and raise taxes (v. 6). The countervailing case for them being angelic powers is therefore "weak."[34] However, it is this either/or bifurcation that is itself problematic, given that Paul apparently concurs with "the broader Greco-Roman conception of spiritual forces behind all earthly institutions," as is apparent in other key Pauline texts. In one of his letters (1 Cor 2:6–8), and in the Gospels (e.g., Luke 23:34), the rulers are presented as either not knowing or not understanding what they are doing, suggesting a false consciousness or "ideologically induced blindness," something commonly found among statesmen and scapegoaters.[35] This too is the context of Romans (13:1–7), which is preceded in chapter 12, in Yoder Neufeld's words, by an exhortation to "an energy-filled, eschatologically oriented radicalism" by the church and immediately succeeded by an assertion of the triumph of love over law (13:8–10) and a warning about the coming apocalypse (13:11–14).[36] Verses 1–7 of Romans 13 are thereby a caveat about the limited and providential role of government in the present aeon in a longer discourse about the redemptive mission of Christ and his bride, the church.

This evident tension creates a problem of interpretation regarding how 13:1–7 fits into the overall narrative. Barth's reading of the passage is that to "be in subjection" (Rom 13:1) effectively denies two stances: *both* that of the revolutionary *and* of the political conservative.[37] A fair reading of this section must conclude, Finamore argues, "the civil authorities manifest the wrath when they act in accordance with the purposes for which God instituted them . . ."; thus, "while wrath may be eschatological, or even primarily eschatological, it is not without its manifestations in history."[38] The question here is neither whether spiritual forces are at play in worldly government nor whether such governments necessarily use violence—as the text clearly affirms both these claims—but how Christians should respond to that

---

33. Carr, *Angels and Principalities*, 43.
34. Carr, *Angels and Principalities*, 45–46.
35. Wink, *Engaging the Powers*, 44–45; Girard, *The Scapegoat*, 111.
36. Neufeld, *Jesus and the Subversion of Violence*, 114.
37. Cullman, *The State in the New Testament*, 55–60.
38. Finamore, "Wright, Wrong and Wrath," 54.

worldly government whose sovereignty may only be ordained or withdrawn by God.[39] If wrath is a necessary task of the state, what does this mean for the Christian? Barth argues that the Christian must "withdraw" from the terms set by the "powers and principalities," and, by extension, look to Christ and the church for *the* means of forming and sustaining human community.[40] This is an argument for *ecclesia* providing an authentic political community apart from political power and the temptation of Christendom. As we have seen in part 2, the secular age is simultaneously one that is more conducive and more hostile to such apartness and authenticity. This exhortation to ecclesia as a response to the powers is a recurrent theme in Paul's treatment of them.[41] In this sense, putting on the armor of God is not to wage personal spiritual and cultural warfare against a secular society (Eph 6:11) but against "poverty, militarism, sexism, and all other forms of 'domination,'" both inside and outside the church.[42]

However, at least three problems arise from his account of the powers that cannot be ignored. Firstly, Wink's lack of precision in his definition of the powers as spiritual-political persons creates ontological confusion. He claims that this enables him to "unmask a nation's apostasy more ruthlessly, discern its vocation more perceptively, and love it, despite is evils, more faithfully."[43] Yoder Neufeld notes that "Wink is reaching for what New Testament writers would have taken as a given, namely that an either/or distinction between spiritual and material, social and political is inconceivable." As such, "we must try to put together what they could not have conceived as coming apart."[44] There is quite a tradition of doing just this by attributing personhood to the powers. For Beasley-Murray, similarly, powers and principalities may become beasts, "given the simple recognition that a minister can, like Judas, apostatize and become the instrument of the devil."[45] This anthropomorphic reading of political institutions is an ontological position that is more thoroughly developed by many social constructivists and critical realists in the social sciences but remains problematic.[46] N. G. Wright

39. Finamore, "Wright, Wrong and Wrath," 47.
40. Barth, *Epistle to the Romans*, 481–84.
41. Neufeld, *Jesus and the Subversion of Violence*, 144.
42. Neufeld, *Jesus and the Subversion of Violence*, 144, 147.
43. Wink, *Engaging the Powers*, 99.
44. Neufeld, *Jesus and the Subversion of Violence*, 145.
45. Beasley-Murray, *The Book of Revelation*, 212.
46. In modern theory of International Relations, Wendt and Wight are prominent supporters of the claim that states have collective agency to the point of personhood. See Wendt, *Social Theory of International Relations*; Wight, *Agents and Structures in International Relations*.

notes that the spiritual and political aspects of the powers are "symbiotic" but cautions against the "territorial spirits" approach, that Wink adopts, for its mythologizing effect.[47] Perhaps the "false spirits" of the powers, as imitators of the kingdom of heaven, are best thought of as ghosts, shadowing war and empire, haunting international politics, but ultimately coming and going as spiritual realities, knowing their time has gone?

A second criticism of Wink is found in Milbank's concern that the powers are grounded in a social scientist's ontology of violence. In particular, Milbank claims that in Girard—whose work is germinal to that of Wink—only the worldly, violent, and potentially beastly city is visible. An underlying and inaugurated order of the church-state is deliberately obscured by Girard's structural account of religious ritual.[48] For Milbank, Girard's is a fatalistic, non-theological account of temporal political authority "clearly rooted in modern, liberal culture," bereft of a Christology that would provide the resources of witness to the powers and the redemption that Wink seeks.[49] However, this criticism appears inaccurate. Girard does present a theological distinction between orderly and disorderly forms and grounds it not in a set of anti-theological liberal commitments but in a biblically based decentering that Milbank simply cannot accept. "When the false transcendence is envisaged in its fundamental unity," Girard notes, "the gospels call it the devil or Satan, but when it is envisaged in its multiplicity then the mention is always of demons or demonic forces."[50] He illustrates this with the story of the exorcism of the demons of Gerasa (Mark 5:1–17). When Jesus asks the demon (singular) its names, it answers: "My name is legion, for we are many" (Mark 5:9). Demons appear in "multiple and fragmented form," reflecting a "mimetic disorder," with the mob of the Gerasenes who bind the man and expel Jesus, mimicking the violence of the demons themselves who cause the man to self-harm. Both the mob and the demons are "legion," a clear reference to the dispersed military power of the Roman occupier, suggesting something not so much transcendent and enduring as structural and passing.[51]

A third, and related, criticism is Wink's unclear distinction between good and evil powers. His use of social constructivism, alike securitization, does not provide us with criteria for determining just or legitimate exercises in state sovereignty and uses of violence. Milbank is at least correct that

47. Wright, *A Theology of the Dark Side*, 146–47.
48. Milbank, *Theology and Social Theory*, 396–98.
49. Milbank, *Theology and Social Theory*, 397.
50. Girard, *The Scapegoat*, 166.
51. Girard, *The Scapegoat*, 173.

modern social sciences (explicitly) lack foundations against which moral judgment about legitimacy may be made.[52] For these things, we must begin in biblical studies and theology. Here Milbank's criticism stands up in that Wink does not develop a theologically grounded concept of legitimacy—if such a thing is possible—and ultimately falls back on his personifying of the powers. "The Powers," he remarks, "are no less the good creations of a good God than we are, and they are no more fallen than we."[53] However, the repentant person accepts God's grace, confesses their sin, and worships Jesus as Lord, ideally within a community of believers. On that basis their salvation is secure. But what of nations? By what means are they saved? How do they confess sin? We saw in part 1 that Christendom—even to its most enthusiastic advocates—is not the means for the redemption of nations. Equally, in part 2 we saw those secular states recentered on the nation and a national elite tend to idolatrously sacralize themselves. We need an alternative interpretative key to unlock how these powers may be demystified and exposed. Girard's theory of the emergence of corporate and institutional violence shall be explore in the next chapter. Before that, we must explore the biblical foundations—moving from the letters of Paul and the little apocalypse of Mark to the great apocalypse of Revelation.

The demonic beasts of Revelation 12–13

As an apocalyptic and prophetic text, as well as a letter to seven specified churches, the interpretation of Revelation (*Apokalypsis*) appears to be characterized by cacophony and chaos. Both the date and authorship of the book remain disputed. But this is merely the beginning of disagreements that lead to a variety of perspectives, from the credible to the outlandish. These include: academic historical-critical readings of the book as merely reflecting disputes within Judaism in the Second Temple period;[54] idealist and political readings of it as protest literature against all tyranny from ancient Rome to apartheid South Africa;[55] and, popular futurist readings of the Christian nation of the United States being called upon to defeat satanic monsters

---

52. Milbank, *Theology and Social Theory*, 278. The paradigmatic works on legitimacy recognize it as an inter-subjective phenomenon grounded in beliefs, institutions, and modes of consent produced mimetically according to logics of inclusion/exclusion. The problem that the concept has never overcome is that of "happy slaves," i.e. the majority of people under almost all unjust systems of rule, who do consent to the system. Beetham, *The Legitimation of Power*; Herzog, *Happy Slaves*.

53. Wink, *Unmasking the Powers*, 98.

54. Barker, *The Revelation of Jesus Christ*.

55. Boesak, *Comfort and Protest*, 96.

such as the pagan polities of both the Soviet Union and European Economic Community.[56] The sheer variety of these examples suggests the absence of widely accepted exegesis upon which contemporary demonic powers may be identified and, perhaps, the folly of such direct analogies.

However, as *the* work of Christian prophecy of the New Testament it is entirely to be expected that Revelation would be used in this way by believers seeking to make sense of their presence and future. According to Sergius Bulgakov, Revelation is "a kind of fifth gospel."[57] It is Judaistic in form and style but in content it is "a Christian philosophy of history, that philosophy bordering upon eschatology and crossing over into it." In Revelation, he goes on,

> we see unfurled the destiny of the Christian Church in the world, from one specific point of view—the struggle of Christianity with anti-Christianity. . . . Yet this destiny is not regarded in the light of earthly, human history alone, but the heavenly powers take part in it, so that we end up with an exposition of the Christian Church which is exhaustive in depth and power, a true "apocalypse."[58]

As such, Revelation is "a book *about the end* of earthly history, and everything to be accomplished in that."[59] These "external, actual events" include "wars and upheavals, social political, and cosmic, apostasy, the appearance of the Antichrist, but also [events] like the 'resurrection from the dead,' the conversion of Israel, the first resurrection and the thousand-year reign of Christ on earth."[60]

After outlining the predicament of church and world—and the redeeming power of Christ for both—across chapters 1–11, Revelation introduces the final battle. The imagery of the dragon and its beasts is introduced in chapters 12 and 13 and referred back to in the later chapters before the final victory over evil and the creation of the New Jerusalem. The "great red dragon" of chapter 12 denotes the forces of evil and replaces the simple use of Satan or the devil in the preceding chapters (Rev 12:9; 20:2). Understanding the purpose of this use of mythology is essential to understanding Revelation as a whole and the dragon and beasts language in particular. Spilsbury suggests that it "invites us to suspend our experience of the world

---

56. Lindsay, *The Late Great Planet Earth*.
57. Bulgakov, *Apocalypse*, 10.
58. Bulgakov, *Apocalypse*, 7.
59. Bulgakov, *Apocalypse*, 10.
60. Bulgakov, *Apocalypse*, 296.

around us," in order to "transport us to another reality."[61] This terminology is unfortunate as it suggests that there is something unreal or at least parallel to the meaning of the imagery. Caird has a much better grasp of the "powerful imaginative symbols of Revelation" through which "John rewrites the old pagan myth deliberately to contradict its current political application."[62] As such, John subverts the pagan symbols to emphasize the actual nature of evil, not simply for stylistic purposes. An unholy Trinity is introduced of the dragon and the first and second monsters, which, as many commentators have observed, offers a grotesque parody of the Father, Son, and the Holy Ghost.[63] As Satan is the great deceiver, so his deceptive images and claims are refuted in Revelation's narrative of the ultimate failure of these terrifying creatures.

The political references in the ancient myths deployed by John would have been clear to the Christians of Asia Minor, both in their spiritual and temporal-political instantiations. Chapters 12 and 13 are replete with images of Rome, with the seven heads of the beast from the seas seen as the seven hills of the imperial center (Rev 13:1; 17:9), while the seven kings (17:9-11) are typically understood as referring to seven Roman emperors, although there is great difficulty in picking out seven names.[64] One specific emperor, Nero Caesar, appears to be referred to at least twice: the head that "appears to have a fatal wound" that has healed (13:3, a reference to the *Nero Redivivus* myth following his apparent suicide); and, in the mark of the beast (13:18, see below). Finally, the ten horns of the scarlet beast (17:12) are claimed to "symbolize Roman client kings, possibly the same kings who commit fornication with the whore,"[65] denoting the economic, spiritual, and political entanglements of the local authorities with Rome and the devil. Elsewhere in the text it is suggested that none can participate in the Roman merchant economy without worshipping the beast (Rev 12:17).

The identification of both Babylon and Rome with the beast raises an obvious question about whether empire, in general, must be thought of as satanic. Three features of the text suggest that it is a decisively anti-imperial apocalypse.

First, in Revelation, Rome, as the servant of the dragon, is merely the latest manifestations of a string of empires in ancient Near Eastern history.

---

61. Spillsbury, *The Throne*, 32–33.
62. Caird, *The Revelation of St. John*, 148.
63. Caird, *The Revelation of St. John*, 156; Beasley-Murray, *The Book of Revelation*, 210.
64. Woodman, *The Book of Revelation*, 164, 166–67.
65. Woodman, *The Book of Revelation*, 168.

Here, the Babylonian empire is the master signifier. "Babylon" appears six times in Revelation (14:8; 16:9; 17:5; 18:2, 10, 21), with "the great city" and the "great whore" being frequently deployed to point to its opulence, idolatry, and aggrandizement of military, political, and economic power. Two books of the Hebrew scriptures provide reference points for the framing of Babylon. The first of these is Daniel's account of Nebuchadnezzar's empire.[66] John draws specifically on the book of Daniel (7:1–8) in his four beasts from the sea, representing four great empires. The second is Exodus' Egyptian empire (the first of Daniel's four beasts). The Exodus parallel reoccurs in multiple places in the text, including: the pursuit of the woman by the dragon (Rev 12:13) and Pharaoh's pursuit of the Israelites (Exod 14:8); being borne on eagle's wings to the safety of the desert (Rev 12:14; Exod 19:4), and the river of water that the woman and the Israelites escape (Rev 12:15–16; Exod. 14:29–30).[67] As such, pre-Constantinian Rome is not short of analogies in history.[68] At the same time, it is easy for interpreters to find post-Constantinian analogues on their times. For Bulgakov, it was "the Caesarism (Führerism) of our days, be it the Russian or Germanic type."[69] Teaching and writing in exile in the wartime Paris of the early 1940s, he makes explicit references to Nazism and Bolshevism.[70]

Second, the imagery of Revelation establishes an inextricable link between empire's earthly politics and the spiritual life of heaven. Understanding this relationship has caused commentators some difficulty. Woodman notes that, in Revelation, "the forces of the evil one are *either* depicted as satanic beings, *or* as earthly power structures."[71] In fact, the main images of Revelation invoke *both* a spiritual *and* a political truth at almost every juncture. As Woodman's own analysis testifies, "John portrays the dragon [Satan] investing power in the political and military might of Rome."[72] For Beasley-Murray, the prophet Daniel "gave John the precedent of depicting world powers as embodiments of the spirit of the chaos-monster."[73] Image after image in Revelation signifies both spiritual and political content. Idolatrous devotion is offered *both* to pagan gods and the emperor cult *and to* the political economy of empire (Rev 12:17). The beasts of the sea and earth are

---

66. Woodman, *The Book of Revelation*, 160–61.
67. See Caird, *The Revelation of St. John*, 158.
68. Finamore, *God, Order and Chaos*, 152.
69. Bulgakov, *The Apocalypse of St. John*, 96.
70. Bulgakov, *The Apocalypse of St. John*, 104–5.
71. Woodman, *The Book of Revelation*, 148, emphasis added.
72. Woodman, *The Book of Revelation*, 150.
73. Beasley-Murray, *The Book of Revelation*, 212.

both servants of the dragon [the devil] and enforce, in Bauckham's words, "a system of totalitarian control of economic life."[74] Rome is both beast and harlot (Rev 17:2, 4–5; see also Isa 23:15–18), whose "economic exploitation and the corrupting influence of her state religion go hand in hand."[75] For Bulgakov, the church's struggle with the dragon/Rome demands "fidelity and steadfastness,"[76] much like that of the people of an occupied country.

A third and final remark regarding the meaning of empire in the text relates to the subversion of the violent mythologies of ancient pagan empires—and, by extension, from a post-Christendom perspective, the militantly secular state-empires of the modern era. Caird notes the clear reference in Rev 12:3 to the Leviathan or Lotan (Tiamat) of the Canaanite creation story;[77] imagery that was used in ancient and modern times to indicate the recourse to violence to impose order.[78] But such recentering—necessarily plural, never singular—is multiple, chaotic, and ultimately self-defeating. Wink's interpretation of Revelation recalls that in pagan mythology Tiamat—the seven-headed monster of chaos—was slain by Marduk, god of order, and the universe was made from her corpse. However, he sees this reference to Tiamat as a specific point by the author to undermine the substantive claim to legitimacy of the Roman Empire based on its power to assert order between and within nations. Rather than the overcoming of chaos by order, John, according to Wink, subverts the myth to suggest that order and chaos are locked in a dialectic.[79] The means required to defeat the dragon and beasts ensures another "dragon" (Rev 17:15–17), and the unholy trinity resurges before their final defeat. "In itself," Bulgakov argues, the struggle of the faithful with the dragon and beasts "defines the content of history."[80] The ultimate victory of Christ is assured, but the ebb and flow toward this end is a matter of the fidelity of the church in the faces of many waves of disorder, each of which is framed as the bringing of order. It is vital that the church withholds allegiance to these demonic attempts to take back control.

The possible parallel here with the secular dialectics outlined in part 2 requires comment. Each time power is decentered, and the myth of the state

---

74. Bauckham, *The Theology of the Book of Revelation*, 155.

75. Bauckham, *The Bible in Politics*, 89, 91. See also Yabro-Collins, *Crisis and Catharsis*, 121–22.

76. Bulgakov, *The Apocalypse of St. John*, 92.

77. Caird, *The Revelation of St. John*, 150.

78. Consider that Thomas Hobbes' famous sixteenth-century treatise on political authority is titled *Leviathan*.

79. Wink, *Engaging the Powers*, 89–95.

80. Bulgakov, *The Apocalypse of St. John*, 92.

exposed, a countervailing force seeks to recenter it for its own domination; each time power is disenchanted, a new Leviathan seeks re-enchantment. "Now evil is represented," Wink goes on, "not as the threat of anarchy, but as the system of order that institutionalizes violence as the foundation of International Relations."[81] This interpretation has the virtue of being not only a fair reading of the dragon and beasts of Revelation but also a summary of an international system whose balances of power and imperial configurations of rule are only ever temporary. As we discussed in chapter 8, power here is sovereigntist but also fractured, "decentered and territorializing."[82] As Howard-Brook and Gwyther note, the Revelation of John is "not only about the Rome of his day, but also more broadly about how empire gains and keeps its subjects."[83] Today such satanic qualities are increasingly manifest in the exploitative global economy and imperial military adventures by all states, including liberal-democracies, with important implications for the mission of contemporary church. Most importantly, and as we have seen across the earlier chapters of this book, the struggle of the faithful and the dialectic of Christendom take place as much within as beyond the church.

This final remark indicates that it is the *recentering* of empire and church that is a mark of Revelation's beasts. It is this claim that puts the idea of legitimate powers in question. Unlike every example of Paul's "powers and principalities," the imperial dragon and its beasts are satanic, irredeemable, and ultimately defeated (Rev 17:14; ch. 18). Alike the powers, however, the empire-church of Christendom and its neo-Christendom imitators make sovereigntist claims based on the ability to impose order—an ability that appears to be legitimized in some of the Pauline texts. Therein lay the key question in their reconciliation with Revelation and a challenge for any political reading of the New Testament. How can the imposition of order, normative and political, be the basis for temporal power and authority? Can the powers, as Wink suggests, be redeemed or, as Bulgakov insists, must they be defeated?

Discerning the powers after Christendom

The comparison of these two passages is made for it provides a biblical-theological assessment of two post-Christendom political imaginaries: Wink's redemptive and Bulgakov's apocalyptic. Both Wink and Bulgakov agree that (neo-)Christendom polities, while aspiring to the legitimate

81. Wink, *Engaging the Powers*, 90.
82. Bell, *Divinations*, 154.
83. Howard-Brook and Gwyther, *Unveiling Empire*, 216.

powers and principalities of Romans 13, end up engaging in demonic imperial practices, as imagined in the dragons and beasts of Revelation 13. According to both these post-Christendom imaginaries, the dragon and beasts of Revelation *are* related to Paul's powers and principalities as both are instruments of security before, during, and after Christendom and before the full realization of the *eschaton*. Both these images correctly denote corporate spiritual-political entities with capacity for evil; where in the former case this is fully realized, in the latter it remains a latent trait.

This challenge of distinguishing between the two is an enduring one for theologians who have sought to understand the relationship between the illegitimate empire of Revelation 13 and the limited, legitimate authorities of Romans 13. The recognition that powers are, like dragons and beasts, always both spiritual and political, provides a particular optic on this problem. It allows Caird, for example, to reconcile the two texts rather neatly:[84]

> In the war between God and Satan, between good and evil, the state is one of the defenses established by God to contain the powers of evil within bounds, part of the order which God the Creator has established in the midst of chaos (cf. Rom. 13:1–7). But when men worship the state, according to it the absolute loyalty and obedience that are due not to Caesar but to God, then the state goes over to the Enemy.[85]

Stringfellow makes a comparable claim in his attempt to reconcile the two texts. "If Romans may be said to designate legitimate political authority," he remarks, "Revelation may be said to describe illegitimate political authority."[86] Cullman follows in this vein. In Revelation 13, he notes, the state becomes the beast because the powers of Romans 13 "have emancipated themselves; or rather they believe they have done so (for in reality they have already been conquered); and have thus become thoroughly satanic."[87] The conclusion to be drawn here may be that the limited (post-Christian) secular state is that denoted by Romans 13, while imagined (neo-Christendom) empires are those of Revelation 13. The liberal Wink would accept this interpretation, but others aver from such a distinction between the legitimate

---

84. See also Boesak, *Comfort and Protest*, 96: "They are in tension not in conflict with each other. Revelation 13 is in the bible because Romans 13 is in the bible."

85. Caird, *The Revelation of St. John*, 164.

86. Stringfellow, *Conscience and Obedience*, 39. Alike Caird, for Stringfellow, illegitimacy is understood as blasphemy, which itself is described as "the repudiation and defamation of the Lordship of Christ in common history by the ruling powers and political principalities." Stringfellow, *Conscience and Obedience*, 70. See also Beasley-Murray, *The Book of Revelation*, 211.

87. Cullman, *The State in the New Testament*, 73.

state and the blasphemous empire. Based on his assessment that the only point of tension between the Christians and the Roman Empire was the cult of the emperor, Cullman then finds problematically that Rome was a satanic power up *until* Constantine.[88] But this defense of Christendom is indefensible when one recognizes that the sovereignty claims of the empire are as much part of its blasphemy as is the religious cult. "In the Christian empire and its successors," Bauckham correctly notes, "the beast constantly reappeared in ever new Christian disguises."[89] The state with a Christian majority is just as likely to do this as a state without.

This problem is acute from a post-Christendom perspective. What may distinguish Wink's notion of the redemption of powers from Bulgakov's one of their defeat is Wink's optimism regarding the liberal state, which Bulgakov lacks. Unsurprisingly, it is the exiled Russian scholar Sergius Bulgakov, rather than the tenured American academic Wink, who offers the better explanation for how progressive orders become sovereigntist. Bulgakov draws a theology of the state from across New Testament powers theology and scriptures, including those studied by Wink. It is worth quoting one passage from Bulgakov at length:

> In other New Testament writings, such as those of the apostle Paul and the apostle Peter (Rom 13:1–7; Titus 3:1; 1 Tim 2:12 [sic]; 1 Pet 2:13–17), there is sought and found a certain acquiescence with the state, its recognition as the legal order of things, *the security of the external world*. The state here serves humanity as a means, not an end, subordinate to the higher norms of morality. In that sense, it can be said: "there is no power but of God" (Rom 13:1). This acknowledgement of the divine value of law refers to all power, i.e. not just Christian, but also pagan, in that it serves its own juridical aim, but is also limited by it. In those cases, where we are dealing with *a Christian state, so far as such a thing ever existed or can exist*, or rather a state of Christians, new frontiers and goals arise for it, *namely to serve Christian morality*. But such service *presupposes the existence of a certain spiritual equilibrium*, in which the state does not transgress the bounds of its juridical goals. But that condition always remains unattainable, and the state turns into a beast, when it transgresses those bounds. Then, at first, it forsakes the human principle of life and becomes animal, feral, losing its higher spiritual goals, and then *circumstances turn it into something demonic*, satanic,

---

88. Cullman, *The State in the New Testament*, 79.
89. Bauckham, *The Theology of the Book of Revelation*, 151–52.

anti-Christian, and it is thereby enlisted in outright combat with Christ and his church.⁹⁰

From the perspective of our analysis, there are four points here that are especially noteworthy. First, Bulgakov identifies powers with "the security of the external world" and the state. Second, as Christianity became the majority in certain states, they sought that their state would "serve Christian morality." Third, such a Christendom imaginary was a mistake because it "presupposes the existence of a certain spiritual equilibrium"—something impossible until the eschaton is reached. Fourth, such imaginaries create— we may say *socially construct*—states that are beastly and demonic. This last point raises the prospect that we may be able to discern the beastly "Christian nation" from the legitimate secular democracy by means of interpreting its social construction in post-Christendom terms.

However, we must proceed with care, attentive to the extant tensions and many pitfalls found in such exegesis. The full extent of the demonic is found in the imperial ambition of the state, which extends its sovereignty to control of the economy, culture, and spirituality. Failing to attain the more limited goals of maintaining order and redistributing resources, government doubles down. In light of the imperial political economy identified with beastly Babylon, the search to identify an actually existing modern example of legitimate authority becomes even more hopeless than that of finding a fully Christlike person. It is not simply a matter of "governmental power exceeding its proper bounds,"⁹¹ but about the very nature of nationalism and imperialism, and the very function of the economic and military power of nations and empires. Recent theological and biblical studies, informed by post-colonialism and critical political economy from the social sciences, have been attentive to the link between a theology of the powers and the extant conditions of empire. Facing empire, Yabro-Collins notes, "John and his book were socially radical in a variety of ways."⁹² Wealth and the ties of commerce are themselves identified as corrupting influences alongside idolatry, blasphemy, and the military campaigns of the empire.⁹³

How then do we reconcile these two accounts? While it is true that Paul recognizes that limited temporal authorities are ordained by God to bring order and justice, the powers' capacity for sin and the service of evil is ever-present in the apostle's account. Corporate and political entities are instituted as servants of God but fall short of this task. Their sin causes them

90. Bulgakov, *The Apocalypse of St. John*, 97, emphasis added.
91. Cullman, *The State in the New Testament*, 73.
92. Yabro-Collins, *Crisis and Catharsis*, 111.
93. Yabro-Collins, *Crisis and Catharsis*, 122–33.

not to serve God but to imitate and thus usurp him, blasphemously claiming the sovereignty that rightfully belongs to God. While persons may be redeemed, the powers are creatures of this aeon, subject to the Christendom dialectic between being legitimately disenchanted and decentered but also demonically re-enchanted and recentered. The question is then not so much of redemption or defeat but of witnessing to the powers with a post-Christendom imagination of their limits, in keeping with their very narrow mandate in Romans 13. In recent years, powerful critiques of empire have been developed from close readings of John's Revelation and Paul's letter to the Colossians calling for withdrawal from global economic and security structures.[94] Much like the original letters, the first addressees of these calls to action are local churches themselves.[95]

The implication of this analysis of the powers requires further unpacking over the remainder of part 3. However, as a provisional conclusion, we may say that powers that are not dialectically produced in relationship to prophetic resistance are those that become illegitimate and even demonic. When Israel called for a kingdom, they were not denied, but were prophetically warned about the economic exploitation and militarism of monarchs (1 Sam 8:10–18). The law thus restricted both wealth (Lev 25:35–43) and warfare (Deut 20). It is better here to denote legitimate governing practices than legitimate authorities. Legitimate practices are those who upheld these laws of *inclusion* of aliens, *protection* of life, and *provision* of life, as it is these that are the definition of security and that are foundational of legitimate kingdoms. There are precious few examples of such practices in Christendom but arguably more emerging under the post-Christendom imaginaries of the secular age. Such visions are those of *difference* and *distance* between church and world, not those of similarity and closeness. They are even more global and more hopeful than the Hebrew prophets as they preach a more inclusive and peaceable kingdom not the decline of a national power and exile of a people.

Powers as Suzerains

This chapter has sought to compare two post-Christendom accounts of the powers of the world. In arguing for the compatibility of Revelation's language of dragon and beasts with Paul's powers and principalities, it posited that both provide images for the spiritual-political institutions of states and

---

94. Howard-Brook and Gwyther, *Unveiling Empire*; Walsh and Keesmat, *Colossians Remixed*.

95. Berkhof, *Christ and the Powers*, 41–42; Yoder, *Politics of Jesus*, 147–49.

empires. The powers were designed as legitimate institutions in the service of God, but, in practice, they often claim sovereignty and become idolatrous, blasphemous, and therefore satanic. From this perspective, the structural conditions of global politics, which shape the actions of great powers, are themselves no more than secondary or tertiary responses of the work of Christ in history. Moreover, the powers' relationship to the Lord of History is clearly subordinate; perhaps they are no more than suzerains to his kingship. Suzerains can also be kings too, of course, but their kingship and their sovereignty are limited under the emperor. They are obliged and responsible to the true King. The imperial metaphor of suzerainty seems to capture the nature of the delegated and provisional authority held by the powers—an authority that is being passed on to the church in post-Christendom. As pre-exilic Israel was suzerain under the Hittites, Egyptians, and Assyrians (the powers of their day), so now roles are reversed. The new Israel (the church) sits on the throne with the King, while the powers are defeated, divided, and passing away. The church now shares in the triumph over the powers, disarming and exposing them (Col 2:13–15).

Suzerains—political and ecclesial—are not ontologically independent of the Lord and may have their authority removed by the king at any time. Insofar as they exceed those rightful limits and seek to aggrandize power—economic, political, military, and religious-ideological—beyond that which is necessary for the maintenance of order, they will providentially meet their end, as all empires, states, corporations, tribes, social movements, clergies, denominations, and sectarian movements eventually do. On the one hand, inspired by a crude account of Pauline political theology, the Christendom church has historically been too ready to defer to the "legitimate authorities." On the other hand, fearing the beasts of Revelation, (neo-)Christendom ideologues may arm themselves and form revolutionary millenarian movements. In arguing with and beyond Wink, via Bulgakov, this chapter has outlined a post-Christendom interpretation that the powers are not so much defeated or redeemed but, rather, *exposed*. Rather than being either allies or enemies, the powers are no more than *temporal institutions that are fading away*. The challenge from this perspective is not to witness to the suzerains and provide ethics for their security policy and practice, but *to recognize their passing, to disarm and expose them, and work toward the coming kingdom that is not of this world*.

This book's task in this challenge is limited: to work toward a political theology of security after Christendom that does not sacrifice fidelity for relevance, and yet does not retreat to sanctimony but humbly engages in conversation with the world regarding legitimate forms of security. Such a line is a very fine one to walk and many doubt whether it exists at all. Daniel Bell notes, in apocalyptic terms:

> War has become a generalized state, global and interminable, . . . a war without end in the sense of war that is both continuous and devoid of any telos, whose goal rather is the removal of boundaries and ends that would obstruct or block the flow of capital. This is war for a generalized but nebulous and elusive condition called "security."[96]

Security, according to this view, is nihilistically apocalyptic: the rationale for, "war as distraction, obstructing the potential emergence of alternatives to the current order of things."[97] Powers and suzerains demand security, but isn't this a distraction to the coming of the kingdom? The answer to this question is that just as the powers are fading away so is their security too. The obstruction presented by "security" is imagined as much as it is real. It is therefore incumbent upon us to rethink its three key components—inclusion, protection, and provision—in post-Christendom terms.

---

96. Bell, *Divinations*, 140.
97. Bell, *Divinations*, 140.

CHAPTER 10

Radical Inclusion

From this equality of ability ariseth equality of hope in the attaining of our ends. And therefore *if any two men desire the same thing, which nevertheless they cannot both enjoy, they become enemies*; and in the way to their end (which is principally their own conservation, and sometimes their delectation only) endeavor to destroy or subdue one another.

THOMAS HOBBES[1]

The Judeo-Christian revelation exposes what myths always tend to silence. Those who speak of "peace and security" are now their heirs: despite everything, they continue believing in myths and do not want to see their own violence.

RENÉ GIRARD[2]

In the autumn of 2021, the universities of St. Andrews and Kent in the UK were the latest in a series of British institutions to introduce compulsory training in Equality, Diversity, and Inclusion (EDI). At St. Andrews, students were required to agree with statements such as "Acknowledging your personal guilt is a useful start point in overcoming unconscious bias." When asked, "Does equality mean treating everyone the same?" students who said yes were told, "That's not right, in fact equality may mean treating people

1. Hobbes, *Leviathan*, XIII.3.
2. Girard, *Battling to the End*, 118.

differently and in a way that is appropriate to their needs so that they have fair outcomes and equal opportunity."[3] Meanwhile at Kent, the EDI course included education on the infamous topics of the contemporary culture wars of micro-aggression, preferred pronouns, and "white privilege." Students were told that one such example of white privilege is: "I can swear, or dress in second-hand clothes, without having people attribute these choices to the bad morals, the poverty or the illiteracy of my race."[4]

The conservative press burns with fury at such examples of apparent compulsion to a new normative code in "woke" universities and this code's ascription of guilt to those of privilege. There are many more examples of apparent left-wing illiberalism in the faculty and the increasing demands of the so-called "snowflake" generation. More tellingly, both St. Andrews and Kent universities claimed to be bowing to student demand—and thereby admitting their prioritization of the logic of the market over the value of education. The critics were right that in failing to defend freedom of thought and speech on campus, the universities were compelling their students to take a certain position on the nature of inclusion and the form that EDI policies should take. These cases evoked many others across the post-Christendom West at the time, from where activists and conservatives compete to claim victimhood. Is the feminist and lesbian professor of philosophy who left her university after a "witch hunt" the victim or is the transgender person who says they are made unsafe by her writing?[5] Is a "Maoist cultural revolution taking place in our centers of learning," as one of my colleagues claimed, or is it reasonable for academics teaching on empire to consider adding non-white authors to their reading list?[6] Such example of "culture wars" present themselves daily across Western secularizing societies after Christendom.

None of the above should surprise us from a post-Christendom perspective. First, we would note the sub-Christian content of the St. Andrews course in particular and the EDI movement in general. In siding with the downtrodden, their militant activists vaguely mimic Christ's ministry. In requiring the admission of sin without the possibility of mercy, they miss at least half of Christian truth. It was what one might expect from post-Christendom secularity: a "black mass" of rehashed original sin without common grace, as noticed by observers from Friedrich Nietzsche to John Gray. The white-majority churches of post-Christendom who unequivocally recoil

---

3. Woolcock, "St Andrews University Sets Bias Test for Entry."
4. Tobin, "Students at University of Kent Must Take 'White Privilege' Course."
5. Hayes, "Kathleen Stock."
6. Turner, "Russell Group University Accused of Soviet-Style Censorship."

from the notion of "white privilege," distance themselves from Black Lives Matter, or are quick to dismiss such EDI initiatives, mirror the errors of the militant activists. They notice the absence of mercy in these movements but fail to fully acknowledge the existence of sinful structures of racial injustice in their own societies.

Second, there is nothing new about the identification of privilege according to class or race on campus, a realization that increases as Christendom disappears in the rear-view mirror. In CP Snow's *The Affair* (1960), written sixty years before these most recent campus debates, Cambridge college master Crawford declares that "all over the world people were no longer prepared to see others enjoying privilege because of the color of their skin, or spoke in a different tone, or were born into [privileged] families." If the knighted, English conservative, and atheist professor Snow could identify racial and other modes of privilege, why is it so difficult for some of us today? And if it's not the "woke" zeitgeist that has led them to recognize privilege and demand inclusion, what is it?

The Catholic cultural theorist René Girard offers an answer: the radical moment of the triumph of the cross, which *both* atones for the sin of every individual *and* reveals and defeats the logics of inequality, hierarchy, and scapegoating, that characterize our social structures. That this revelation has been slow to mature is a matter, according to Girard, of "sacrificial Christianity" of the kind that dominated in Christendom. There are theological and political aspects to this alliance of violence and the sacred. It has taken so long to free the down-trodden and demand inclusion, *both* because the church has cleaved to archaic theology *and* because politically it has defended privilege and exclusion by its alliance with state authorities and empires. Atheists and humanists, from Snow to "snowflakes," are inspired by one half of the Christian message: the acknowledgment of sin. They are merely following the cultural logic of the post-Christendom West. As Christendom declined, and as the secular age emerged, so tackling privilege and demanding inclusion became core demands for both those with faith and those without. But the *guilt* that has struck secular European societies is sacrificial and even tyrannical,[7] if grace and redemption are absent.

What this example illustrates is that inclusion is a post-Christendom issue in the sense that the boundaries that once applied between the faithful and unfaithful have (rightly) been broken down by a desire to include those who were scapegoated or marginalized by "sacrificial Christianity." But how is it a matter of security? As we discussed in the introduction, security is not just about protection and provision. A prior question is that of *inclusion*.

---

7. Bruckner, *The Tyranny of Guilt*.

Who gets to identify threats and who gets to take extraordinary measures against them? And who tends to be identified as either the enemy or the victim? These two questions are often two sides of the same coin. When the policy elite of a minority of wealthy states tend to identify threats and act, they do so on behalf of those *they* have identified as victims and against those *they* have identified as threats. Any progress to a more secure world is one where that basic inequality is eroded and where those who are presently victims/enemies, demand, via democratic means, that *their* victims and *their* threats are addressed. Thus, before we begin to talk about questions of protection and provision, we must talk about inclusion.

These are the grounds on which the boundaries of inclusion/exclusion are matters of security. These boundaries are not fixed but constructed, imagined in discourse, and instantiated in discursive practice. Like any boundaries, they may also be breached, and, if breached repeatedly and routinely, the political entity that they demarcate loses is identity and integrity and begins to break down. In part 2 we saw the political and economic processes that have led to this transformation and crisis of the state, caught between recentering around national myths and decentering according to both the powers of capital and liberal normative agendas. In chapter 9, we explored the biblical and theological basis for the passing and ultimate defeat of the powers. In this chapter we will develop a post-Christendom approach to the question of inclusion through a study of the politics of migration and the theologically inflected thought of René Girard.

Girard embarks from Hobbes' observation regarding the "equality of hope" that leads people to desire the same things. They both argue that the reason for insecurity is not difference but this sameness—that is, the competition of all over the same—what Girard and others have called "mimetic desire." This sets an ontological trap for states in a secular age as they seek to set the bounds of inclusion and exclusion, producing and reproducing founding myths that are without foundation. However, Girard differs from the fatalistic Hobbes in that he provides an account of these myths breaking down, what Steve Finamore calls "truth as the engine of the eschatological process."[8] The chapter will explain Girard's theory of the place of sacrifice in establishing such myths in the ancient world and how contemporary secular conditions of *indifférenciation* (undifferentiation) have led to the breaking down of structural orders of hierarchy and difference, making violence arguably more disorderly and more global than it was under Christendom. As Dietrich Bonhoeffer understood,[9] Luther's idea of a settled compromise

---

8. Finamore and Heathershaw, "Mimesis, Market and Mission," 13.
9. Bonhoeffer, *The Cost of Discipleship*.

of "two kingdoms" becomes increasingly fraught, and an age where the church, mosque, or temple is more often pitted against the world is coming rapidly and perilously into view.

THE ILLUSION OF INCLUSION

Why is inclusion—the question of who is inside and who is outside of any social group or political community—such a fraught issue today? We have come to consider national and many other boundaries of identity as somehow natural and immutable. But, in fact, all such difference is socially constructed and may therefore be deconstructed. The problem for humankind, from an orthodox Christian perspective, is that both construction and deconstruction take place under conditions of the fall and are therefore subject to personal and institutional sinfulness. This creates a precarity and inevitable inadequacy to all human solutions to problems of equality, diversity, and inclusion. EDI is, in this sense, no mere modern concern but is visible in all myths of origin, not least that of the Hebrew scriptures.

The tower of Babel in the Torah, the story of humanity's attempt to build a platform to the heavens, where "the whole earth had one language and the same words" (Gen 11:1), is one of many origin myths. While traditionally read as a story of pride-and-punishment of humans seeking to challenge Yahweh, Hiebert convincingly argues that "it describes the origins of the world's cultures through a narrative world in which people desire uniformity and God desires diversity."[10] Rather than being naturally different, the story suggests that we may just as much be naturally the same. This creates a dialectical struggle similar to that we have seen between the centering and decentering forces of Christendom. For Anderson, the story is "a conflict of centripetal and centrifugal forces."[11] For Hiebert, the story, "embraces, as it were, both cultural solidarity and cultural difference in this open way, acknowledging their reality—and, in my opinion, their value." It was Yahweh's intention that humans would be diverse, apparently for reasons positive (the innate value of diversity) and negative (the potential violence of empire or highly centralized and large-scale polities expanding boundlessly). But it is also clear from the biblical narrative that human beings are to be reconciled to one another to become one in Christ Jesus (Gal 3:28). This is radical Christian inclusion challenging both familiar and secular modes of association. As Valk notes, "salvation religion shatters kinship ties by devaluing blood and marital ties in favor of ties to fellow members

10. Hiebert, "The Tower of Babel," 56–57.
11. Anderson, *From Creation to New Creation*, 165–78.

of the religious community."[12] According to an apocalyptic realist reading of Babel, unity is coming and is foreshadowed in the church; in the world of the meantime social differentiation keeps us all from tearing each other apart.

Social scientists have tended to view difference as the cause rather than the solution of inter-group violence. There is an obvious risk of tautology here. According to Freud, violent conflict, whether it is between persons or polities, is the "narcissism of minor difference."[13] Politically, what this term captures is the contrived and somewhat arbitrary differences between groups that then form opposing interests in seeking basic human needs that they in fact share. This conundrum is even more acute in the modern era of states where their hard borders of inclusion/exclusion are the very basis of the security dilemma. The leaders of states find it hard to agree to share a common pool of resources, not because of an objective condition of scarcity (as this is rarely the case), but because the boundaries of their community have created their own national identities in the global free market—and therefore their own national interests and fear of scarcity. As Jennifer Mitzen argues, security is ontological in that it relates to who "we" are and who "they" are in the world.[14] Similarly, Cavanaugh argues, "the nation state itself becomes a kind of religion."[15]

Alongside this process of creating the self through national identity and other forms of group construction there is a concomitant process of creating others. Such othering is often culturally, economically, and physically violent. Girard calls this the scapegoat mechanism, how certain marginalized persons and groups are deemed to be *rightfully* disadvantaged and *justly* punished. Scapegoating is a universal social phenomenon that occurs from the quotidian to the geopolitical levels. Christendom scapegoated its others: Jews, Muslims, and Christian dissenters. Empire and the postcolonial condition have developed new modes of inclusion/exclusion; not merely those of East/West and South/North, but also that the subaltern elites of empire are now those who have cashed in their new-found sovereignties to create kleptocracies and stash their newfound wealth in former imperial centers such as London and Paris. These kleptocrats, oligarchs, and elites are included in the secure world through diplomatic passports, residency visas, real estate purchases, elite education, and acts of reputation

---

12. Valk, "Poetics and Politics," 6.
13. Freud, *Civilization and Its Discontents*.
14. Mitzen, "Ontological Security."
15. Cavanaugh, *Migrations*, 49.

laundering, while most of their own citizens and also the majority of the citizens of wealthy countries are effectively excluded.

It is the challenge of international theory to scale up these theories of groupness to the global level. One way of doing this is in the literature on the inclusion or exclusion of states in the international community. Irredentist and unrecognized states, like Transdniestria Moldovan Republic or the Turkish Republic of Northern Cyprus, which have broken away from a larger state or empire, place enormous emphasis on gaining de facto recognition for their sovereignty via international sporting fixtures and cultural festivals.[16] Gulf monarchies such as those of the Emirates and post-Soviet republics such as Kazakhstan are the political vehicles of a group of families or elite factions that engage in extensive campaigns of national branding to make their states and nations out of the ashes of empire.[17] However, inclusion is not merely a task for former colonies. Status-seeking is widespread across global politics,[18] and is especially pronounced in states like Iran, which have long been excluded from the West and Western-led institutions.[19] In all these cases, inclusion/exclusion is not a binary condition but is socially constructed in shades and varieties. It is also politically contingent. While humans are reproduced biologically and "naturally," political entities are continued or discontinued according to the vagaries of power.

These vagaries of power in global politics have often been civilizational. Civilizations are not objective entities, neither of religion (Christendom vs. Islam) nor of culture, as Samuel Huntingdon's mistakenly supposed in *The Clash of Civilizations*.[20] However, civilizational politics are made very real in its subjective deployment by political entrepreneurs. "Civilizations" are typically invoked by very wealthy elites as part of their political projects. In the post-Christendom context, from Viktor Orban's Christian Europe to Vladimir Putin's dreams of restoring the grandeur of Greater Russia, to Donald Trump's and Jair Bolsonaro's supporters warning of the threat to the Christian world, all have little evidential basis but make subjective claims about who should be "in" and who should be "out."[21] Typically, their out-

16. Isachenko, *The Making of Informal States*.
17. Koch, "The New Crusaders."
18. MacDonald and Parent, "The Status of Status in World Politics."
19. Ozyakar, "A Constructivist Interpretation of Status-seeking Cultural Diplomacy."

20. Huntingdon famously identified seven or eight civilizations as actor-groups in global politics: Sinic, Japanese, Hindu, Islamic, Orthodox, Western, Latin American, and "African (possibly)" with the latter questioned curiously due to its "tribal identities"—although ethnic and sub-ethnic identities are common globally. Huntington, *The Clash of Civilizations*, 45–47.

21. Haynes, "Donald Trump, 'Judeo-Christian Values,' and the 'Clash of Civilizations.'"

siders are non-white and sometimes non-Christian. Elsewhere, Nahrendra Modi's Hindu nationalism, Recep Tayip Erdogan's Turkish Eurasianism, and Xi Jinping's articulation of a Chinese civilization do the same for India's religious minorities, secular Turks, and the Uyghurs and liberal Hong Kongers respectively. While Huntingdon's theory is facile and reductive, it has value as a description of an inter-subjective process rather than as an objective reality. Civilizations are deployed discursively to create borders between "us" and "them," thereby protecting the self and threatening the other.[22]

However, according to others, with the growth of global travel and information technology we appear to be living in the era of a new Babel. Why is neo-Christendom and the civilizational rhetoric of other secular and religious groups increasingly seductive at a time when processes of globalization appear to be breaking down the barriers between civilizations? Rather than this being a matter of civilizational politics occurring *despite* globalization, many scholars of International Relations argue that it is occurring *because* of it. As ontological security—our sense of identity—is threatened, religious nationalism is a potent political response.[23] Bettiza and co-authors argue that this creates an "ontological trap" where the liberal international ordering "requires societies, polities, and states globally not only to adopt certain liberal social, political, and economic policies and institutions, but also to be socialized in and acquire particular liberal identities." However, "if actors do not yield to the constitutive power of liberalism, they become the object of stigma and lower status recognition for falling below certain modern liberal 'standards of civilization.'"[24] Such an ontological trap may also describe the battle to claim victimhood and the controversies over inclusivity that are now found on a global scale.

Security is therefore first and foremost a matter of inclusion/exclusion, as anyone who has traversed from a privileged environment to an urban slum in one of the poorest countries in the world—or vice-versa—can testify. In a world of states and "civilizations," the boundaries of inclusion/exclusion are reproduced to the benefit of some and the detriment of others. This descriptive fact leads to the normative debates of theologians and philosophers, as evinced in the question of William Cavanaugh and colleagues.

> What kind of vision is required to see those who die invisibly and quietly, not in spectacular explosions but in silent deprivations

---

22. Coker, *The Rise of the Civilizational State*; Acharya, "The Myth of the 'Civilization State.'"

23. Kinnvall, "Globalization and Religious Nationalism."

24. Bettiza, Bolton, Dalacoura, and Lewis, "Civilizationism as Counter-Hegemonic Ideology."

of the basic necessities of life? Politics is defined not only by the concerns of those within the Beltway but also by the daily, material concerns that threaten to disintegrate both individual bodies and communal bodies of people.[25]

While such questions are telling, they are also insufficient. What political theology needs is not merely a standard against which secular and ecclesial practice may be critiqued, but a theory of why certain persons and groups come to be excluded, and others included.

The migrant as the scapegoat of the state

These whys and wherefores are most visible in the patterns of and debates over migration, an integral but often overlooked matter of security. Of course, migration is far more than a security issue and it has been credibly argued that it was a more important force in the spread of Christianity than European empires.[26] Indeed, migration has only been analyzed as a security issue for around thirty years.[27] This shift created a problem for the traditions of realism and liberalism as neither paradigm could explain why governments would treat migrants as threats and use expensive and onerous methods against them when there were no objective grounds to consider migrants as threats akin to enemy states or insurgent groups.[28] Indeed, reams of research have shown that labor migration is mutually beneficial in the vast majority of cases with recipient states acquiring cheap but often skilled labor and the migrants themselves able to achieve livelihoods unthinkable in their home states.[29] Remittances from migration are widely understood to be the most significant factor in international development contributing far more to poverty-reduction than either aid or trade. According to the OECD, at US$436 billion in 2014, they amount to more than three times the flow of overseas aid.[30] A more economically efficient mode of poverty reduction (in the narrow sense of the increase in GDP) would be to open the borders to migrants from the Global South.

By the estimates of the International Organization for Migration (IOM) the number of migrants—persons living in a country different to

---

25. Cavanaugh et al., *Contemporary Political Theology*, xxiv.
26. Hanciles, *Migration and the Making of Global Christianity*.
27. Weiner, "Security, Stability, and International Migration."
28. Adamson, "Crossing Borders."
29. Nyberg-Sørensen, Van Hear, and Engberg-Pedersen, "The Migration–Development Nexus."
30. Khodour, "Is Migration Good for Development? Wrong Question!"

that in which they were born—has almost doubled in thirty years to approximately 281 million in 2020.[31] Although that figure is just 3.6 percent of the global population, the overall figures conceal concentrations where it is not unusual for wealthier countries to have 10–20 percent of their population as migrants.[32] Poorer and conflict-prone states, as well as small island nations and land-locked countries, are huge sending states proportionate to their size. According to World Bank data, in 2020, the top five most remittance-dependent nations were Tonga, the Kyrgyz Republic, Tajikistan, Lebanon, and Samoa, each having more than 25 percent of their GDP from money sent home by migrants.[33] Of all migrants, around one-third (89.3 million), according to the UN High Commissioner for Refugees, were forcibly displaced, with this figure more than doubling in ten years (from 38.5 million in 2011).[34] Contrary to the myth that most refugees find their way to rich countries, 83 percent are in low- and middle-income countries and 72 percent are hosted in neighboring countries.[35]

Policy research on migration is generally divided between two conceptual perspectives.[36] First, there is the broadly realist "strategic approach" that focuses on migrants as potential terrorists—especially after attacks like those of September 11, which were committed by migrants—and worries about the capacity of states to govern migration (largely consistent with the state security model of the recentered states reviewed in chapter 6). Second, there is the liberal "human security" approach (introduced in chapter 7), which focuses on the wellbeing and security of the migrants themselves. In 2014–15 in Europe a crisis arose that was labeled a "migration crisis" by some, and a "hospitality crisis" by others. The human security threat to migrants themselves is clear. Between 2014 and the Spring of 2022, the IOM recorded almost 50,000 deaths of migrants in transit, of which around half occurred in the Mediterranean Sea.[37] Faced with such loss of life, one might hope that safe routes would be established for migrants that would reduce the demand for people smuggling on small boats. However, after a brief experiment in Germany and some European countries with an "open-door" policy, nationalist movements demanded strong border controls and new deals with Turkey and north African states to prevent migrant crossings and

31. International Organization for Migration [IOM], *World Migration Report 2020*.
32. IOM, *World Migration Report 2020*.
33. World Bank, "Personal Remittances Received."
34. UNHCR, "Figures at a Glance."
35. UNHCR, "Figures at a Glance."
36. Huysmans and Squire, "Migration and Security."
37. Missing Migrants Project, "Deaths during Migration."

hold them in detention camps, which vastly reduced the number of asylum applications.[38] After a Brexit vote driven partly by fears of "uncontrolled" migration, the UK paid France to take similar measures and by 2022 had agreed a deal to send migrants and refugees to Rwanda for processing. This was framed as a "migration and development partnership," beneficial to the government of Rwanda, which would be paid large sums to receive migrants, if not for the migrants themselves.[39]

The othering of migrants in the discourse of European states has been well documented and is one of the exemplary cases of securitization: the social construction of threat. But how does this relate to Christendom? Research on religion and security identifies state religions—be they secularized Christianity, Islam, or Hinduism—as one of the sources of the "racialization" of migration where states tend to be more open to migrants who are perceived as being kin of the majority ethnic group of their state.[40] In Western and Eurasian states where Christendom imaginaries remain, this means that anti-immigrant attitudes correspond closely with anti-Islamic views and a cultural Christianity. One recent study finds that this is especially true in central and Eastern European states, where political leaders "use anti-Muslim rhetoric to deflect potential discontent from poor governance and economic misery to gain support on the basis of 'imagined' ethno-religious community with Muslims used as scapegoats."[41] At the same time, it is often church and parachurch charities who are at the forefront of offering humanitarian assistance to migrants, including those from other religious backgrounds.[42] The ecumenical Sanctuary Movement, which began in the United States in 1980s to protect Central American refugees, often from dictatorships supported by the United States, from deportation by the US authorities has spread around the world and is one example of such resistance. The distinction between those who accept or refuse the right of the state to include/exclude may not be a matter of religious affiliation, but a matter of political and theological imagination.

---

38. DW, "Two Years Since Germany Opened Its Borders to Refugees."
39. Gower and Butchard, *UK-Rwanda Migration and Economic Development Partnership*.
40. Shani, *Religion, Identity and Human Security*.
41. Gusciute, Mühlau, and Layte, "All Welcome Here?"
42. Mavelli and Wilson, *The Refugee Crisis and Religion*, 3–4.

René Girard and the scapegoat mechanism

Of course, scapegoating and the dynamics of exclusion did not begin with Christendom. The Franco-American literary critic, cultural theorist, and Roman Catholic René Girard (1923–2015) offers a decisive interpretation as to why the borders of inclusion/exclusion are inescapable in social and political life, be it national or global. Girard argues that the inherent violence that is visible in all culture and religion may only be overcome in Christ. He contends that the desires of all persons are generated relationally through imitation—the process of mimesis—and maintains that recently neurological research has confirmed this scientifically.[43] The theory of mimesis states that we become rivals as we seek to copy each other and thereby come to compete over the same objects and goods. We are in conflict therefore not because we are different—even the narcissism of minor differences—but because we are the same. Faced with this basic equality, and the conditions of anarchy, desire, and apparent scarcity, human communities create borders between insiders and outsiders. They contrive violent rituals of othering outsiders to limit the potential for violent competition and to maintain order.

Girard's work since *Deceit, Desire, and the Novel* (1961) and especially *Violence and the Sacred* (1972) has explored sacrifice and the scapegoat mechanism as forms of such ritual which transpose violence into both sacred and secular forms. He argues that religion—and the institutions of sacrifice and the scapegoat they established—were the ancient and original solution for the existential threat of "unleashed violence."[44] In *The Scapegoat* (1982) he argues that historically all communities identify outsiders, within and without, who are to blame for disease, economic collapse, and war—Jews in Christendom Europe, the colonial subjects of Empire, sexual or racial minorities throughout history—and whom shall be sacrificed, literally or figuratively, for the good of the whole. Scapegoats, according to Girard, have an ordering effect: "they unite in opposition to themselves those who were organized in opposition to each other."[45] In modern secular societies, the judicial system has supplanted religion in this regard but has taken on many of its features and, as many cases shows, even in democracies it too is not immune to scapegoating. Such a system, "can only exist in conjunction with a firmly established political power."[46] Moreover, whether ancient or

---

43. Girard, *Battling to the End*.
44. Girard, *Violence and the Sacred*, 20.
45. Girard, *The Scapegoat*.
46. Girard, *Violence and the Sacred*, 25.

modern, "the procedures that keep men's violence in bounds have one thing in common: they are no strangers to the ways of violence."[47] The migration system is a great example of this with thousands of avoidable deaths of asylum seekers each year.

However, according to Girard, the cross and the resurrection change all this. Its exposure of scapegoating and, more broadly, the arbitrariness of all systems of violence, is the beginning of the process of their destruction. Girard argues that Christ himself provides the primal model of forgiveness and nonviolence in the face of cultures of scapegoating and violence. In Christ, God took on human flesh and bore witness to the fundamental equality of persons; on the cross, he became the ultimate and final "sacrifice" and thereby destroyed the institution of sacrifice. The scapegoat triumphed over the sacrificial system and exposed the arbitrariness and ineffectiveness of the scapegoat mechanism where a primal victim is chosen to represent the guilty. The scapegoat mechanism is thus defeated, but this has apocalyptic implications. Finamore summaries Girard's argument:

> The story told by the killers necessarily misrepresents what happened. In truth the primal victim is arbitrary. Once this becomes apparent, and the gospel renders this awareness unforgettable, there is no founding signifier to give stability to the rest. Little by little the whole edifice collapses from within. The possibility of meaning is lost. So, the gospel is an apocalypse in both senses. It is a revelation or unveiling of a truth that had been hidden, and it is something that has the capacity to bring the end of the world as humans understand it.[48]

As such, "every human culture exposed to the gospel is dying."[49] Cavanaugh makes a very similar argument in his *Being Consumed* with respect to his radical reading of the Eucharist, but strangely ignores Girard.[50]

The literature and culture of the Christian-majority world have followed in the wake of the gospel to gradually expose the inescapability of mimetic desire and the arbitrariness of scapegoating; these cultures therefore increasingly tear down barriers to inclusion and speak in favor of the victim. But they have done so very slowly as they have resisted the truth of the message and reverted to sacrificial systems that normalize violence. Girard argues that such sacrificial systems are not sustainable in a secular age, which is forcing the true message of Christ to emerge, sometimes against

---

47. Girard, *Violence and the Sacred*, 25.
48. Finamore, "Wright, Wrong and Wrath," 63.
49. Finamore, "Wright, Wrong and Wrath," 63.
50. Cavanaugh, *Being Consumed*, 94.

the opposition of the church. Girard's insights are particularly acute in this era, accelerating from the mid-twentieth century, in which national modes of Christendom (which he calls "sacrificial Christianity") have been challenged anew by both non-sacrificial expressions of Christianity and militant secularisms. Girard's charge, as Charles Taylor observes in his discussion of Girard's thesis, is that such "Christian counter-violence" is not borne out by the church's long relationship with government. The "purification of scapegoats" as demonstrated in the "long, violent history of Christian anti-Semitism" is not merely a "secularized variant" of the cross. It is a recurrent story of the church and, from Girard's idealist perspective, "a straight betrayal of the gospel."[51] "We are in a place between the full revelation of the scapegoat and the totally mythical," Girard argues. "In history, we are always between gospel and myth."[52] Where the church disregards the gospel and speaks for the victor—as many established or mainline congregations have done since the onset of Christendom—it engages in pagan practice: the reassertion of sacrifice and the notion that representative death in war is somehow sacred. From our perspective, these are neo-Christendom practices that do not limit war but idolize it. From Girard's perspective, "violence can no longer be checked" by such means and "the apocalypse has begun."[53]

The general relevance of Girard's work for thinking about security after Christendom ought to be immediately obvious, but accepting its value means accepting its premises. Girard's insights are founded on structuralist claims that were common in the French intellectual milieu in which he was educated. The foremost of these insights is that pre-modern societies, which lacked sophisticated economies and judicial systems, acquired violent religion to maintain order amid competing human desires. Dissenting against the poststructuralist fashion of his day, "Girard concluded that systems of differentiation take their beginning from the scapegoat mechanism and so do refer, albeit in a distorted way, to a reality beyond themselves."[54] In this reality, as all structures of sacrifice and scapegoats break down, chaos and violence are likely to proliferate as desire is undifferentiated and unquenched. In keeping with this argument, Girard claims that modern war emerges from mimetic rivalry and the sacrificial logic. It is therefore immune to the balance of power and the moral reasoning of JWT.[55]

---

51. Taylor, *Secular Age*, 709.
52. Quoted in Hamerton-Kelly, *Violent Origins*, 145.
53. Girard, *Battling to the End*, 210.
54. Finamore, "A Kinder, Gentler Apocalypse?," 198.
55. Girard, *Battling to the End*, 54–57.

Today—due, Girard argues, to the gradual breaking into the world of the gospel, which has destabilized orders of states and churches—forces of globalization, secularity, and postmodernity are eroding structures of differentiation between nations, classes, races, and faiths. Revisionist states assert their right to all possible economic opportunities and military technologies. Colonial people rightly demand recognition, representation, and even reparations. Girard's biographer, Cynthia Haven, summarizes this relevance in a manner that may chime with the concerns of Christian realists in International Relations.

> Individuals and groups even compete for the cachet of being a victim in the Oppression Olympics, as the power-holders play defense. Wars continue, but end with no clear resolutions. International rivalries still escalate toward uncertain ends. The stakes are higher than ever today: we teeter on the nuclear brink.[56]

However, although working extensively and suggestively with biblical texts, and giving occasional nods to security, especially in his final book *Battling to the End* (2010) in which he engages the Prussian military strategist Carl von Clausewitz's famous dictum that war is the continuation of politics by other means, Girard is neither a specialist in theology or IR. His work therefore needs interpreting through these traditions to bring him into dialogue with both.

SECURITY AND *INDIFFÉRENCIATION*

Girard's account of the gospel's entirely nonviolent overcoming of scapegoating appears to demonstrate a certain theological idealism in his thought, given, as we have seen in chapter 9, the powers are imagined in scripture (esp Rom 13:1–7) to rightly use force. However, the distinction between the providential role of the powers of the world and the redemptive role of the church of God is crucial to make sense of Girard's claim that a nonviolent God is one who works good from the violence of others but whose own work is always nonviolent. This distinction is mirrored in an ambivalence in Girard's thinking on mimetic crisis: he both welcomes the breaking in of justice and fears its attendant disorder. Providence is weakened, while redemption remains incomplete. This fundamental realist-idealist tension in Girard's thought, far from being evidence of error, is present in great theologians from Augustine to Niebuhr[57] and mimics the "two cities" dia-

---

56. Haven, *Evolution of Desire*, 4.
57. McQueen, *Political Realism*.

lectic that has been central to our narrative. As we have seen, throughout Christendom, the church recurrently centered itself on government in the name of providence, only to meet resistance from the faithful in the name of the gospel of redemption. This tension between providential realists and gospel idealists, between nature and grace, is manifest in any attempt to explore Girard's thought on security after Christendom with respect to the primary question of inclusion and the secondary questions of protection and provision.

First, on inclusion, Girard's insights affirm *both* the radical inclusivity of all persons in Christ *and* the escalating dynamics of social conflict generated by such inclusivity. In *Things Hidden Since the Foundation of the World*, Girard presents this predicament in a manner that recalls and reframes the basic security dilemma as understood since at least Thomas Hobbes:

> People [idealists and pacifists, let's say] imagine that to escape from violence it is sufficient to give up any kind of violent *initiative*, but since no one in fact thinks of himself as taking this initiative—since all violence has a mimetic character and derives or can be thought to derive from a first violence that is always perceived as originating with the opponent—this act of renunciation is no more than a sham, and cannot bring about any change at all.[58]

For Girard, the life, ministry, and death of Christ unveiled the arbitrariness of the scapegoating of others and undermined any cultural system of difference of "them" and "us," of elite and subordinate. To be Christian, according to his reading of the Gospels and the cross, is to escape from this arbitrariness and follow a God who is wholly nonviolent. In post-Christendom we see a system of thought emerging from the decline of Christendom that recognizes this arbitrariness, takes it as a starting point, and tries to work out a new nonviolent order in its wake. For Girard and followers, this new order must be based on the receipt of grace and the necessity of forgiveness.

Second, following from the above, limits of inclusion beget limits of protection. For Girard a world without nonviolence and forgiveness is a world that requires the continued work of the protectors and the balancers. However, the powers are *both* fatally undermined by the deconstruction of the scapegoat mechanism *and* remain indispensable to the maintenance of order in a system that is yet to transcend the sacrificial logic. In *I See Satan Fall like Lightning* he argues,

---

58. Girard, *Things Hidden*, 190.

The powers are never strangers to Satan, it's true, but we cannot condemn them blindly. Moreover, in a world that is alien to the kingdom of God, they are indispensable to the maintenance of order, which explains the attitude of the Church toward them.[59]

The powers' ability to limit violence through the police, the courts, and the armed forces rests on a transcendent claim to sovereignty. However, as Girard argued in his earlier *Violence and the Sacred*, "as soon as the essential quality of transcendence—religious, humanistic, or whatever—is lost, there are no longer any terms by which to define the legitimate form of violence and to recognize it among the multitude of illicit forms."[60] "A world with no absolute values," he argued, is one of "unlimited violence."[61] The modicum of protection (order) offered by polities—from tribal confederations to states and empires—is conditional upon their legitimacy, which itself rests on a claim to rightful authority. But what if this rightful authority is both substantial (based on the reduction of violence) and procedural (based on laws to that end)? We need some guidance as to the capabilities and limits of the rule of law and that is lacking in Girard. Yoder, Northcott, and Gorringe offer more help, and we will turn to them in our final two chapters.

Third, in that the protection offered by the powers is partial and fragmentary, so is their provision. Girard *both* sees liberation in the breaking down of distinctions between social groups *and* worries that such *indifférenciation* generates scarcity of desirous objects. It is sameness and imitation that generates all social conflict, from ethnic violence to culture wars. Rather than autonomous or "rational choices" of individuals leading to a security dilemma, threatened and actual violence arises out of the imitation of one another. Rather than the mutual recognition of one another and all victims, we see competitive processes of identifying worthy victims and stigmatizing new scapegoats, sometimes via initiatives in the name of equality and inclusivity. Yet, despite the occasional act of vigilante violence and urban riot, in complex modern societies it rarely leads to violence. Why?

In Christendom, a broader system of scapegoating through increasingly complex legal systems and economies, both religious and secular, created hierarchical (including feudal) systems of provision. In the secular age, we rely on the anarchy of liberalism and the market. In the rich world, these are considered the most effective means to security—to inclusion, protection, and provision—that history has ever known. However, in Girardian terms they have created a complex culture and economy to both create

---

59. Girard, *I See Satan Fall*, 98.
60. Girard, *Violence and the Sacred*, 26.
61. Girard, *Violence and the Sacred*, 26.

mimetic desire for certain objects via marketing and advertising and purport to satisfy it via the sale of fetishized commodities and "unique" experiences. Such systems are arguably the modern equivalents of the ancient customs analyzed in *Violence and the Sacred*, which prevent cycles of vengeance by channeling its desire into new cultural forms.[62] "The aim," Girard argues, "is to achieve a radically new type of violence, truly decisive and self-contained, a form of violence that will put an end once and for all to violence itself."[63] Such violence is indirect. The market has systematized vast inequalities of provision in the modern world but has also normalized them to the point they rarely generate political confrontation and physical violence. Its success at creating apparently pacified societies conceals a hidden darkness of mental health crisis in the rich world and systematic exclusion of the poor. Violence does not end, it merely becomes cultural and structural. There can never be enough of the status objects we all desire, even for all members of a relatively advantaged group. The market responds to this problem by the mass production of highly desired goods (more merchandise, more awards and recognition), but scarcity remains commonplace in a consumer society constrained by what the natural environment and popular culture can sustain. Scarcity and ecological limits on the one hand and cultural fads and inequities of provision on the other are problems that combine. It is these that demonstrate the limits of liberalism and the need for an apocalyptic-realist alternative.

Many readers, especially those new to Girard, may find this analysis to be overwrought and dismissive of the genius of the market and the value of its pacifying effects. There are further problems too. First, Girard's structuralism is unorthodox or even idiosyncratic, running against the post-structuralist current of social science since the 1960s. It is thus deterministic and leads him to discount countervailing processes, like those of pacification in Europe. Second, Girard's own method is not one that addresses this concern at all but simply seeks out these transhistorical structures within historically situated texts. Notwithstanding the canonical status of his proof texts (Greek myth, the Bible, Shakespeare, etc.) in Western literature and variety of his examples from anthropology, such structuralism exposes Girard to legitimate charges of ethnocentrism. Third, but by no means finally, there is a specific theological problem in his understanding of the nonviolent atonement. As we acknowledged above, his claims about the entirely nonviolent nature of God departs from biblical basis of most traditions.[64]

62. Finamore, "Hope."
63. Girard, *Violence and the Sacred*, 26.
64. Here Girard is likely to side with those Anabaptists who favor a kaleidoscopic

Beyond "inclusion" and dualism?

Girard's analysis is totalizing and, as with all such structuralist theory, herein lies it strengths and weaknesses. *Battling to the End* is especially apocalyptic in that Girard identifies intensified competition and conflict; this cycle can only be broken via repentance and mutual forgiveness before the final judgment. But penitence is in short supply, Girard asserts, and "unquestionably, we are accelerating swiftly towards the destruction of the world."[65] The space of the individual to exercise "choice" or at least a degree of control over their life—always a myth of neoliberalism—remains small, as the borders and dangers against migrants demonstrate. Barth's warnings from a century ago of the powers supplanting human agency appear to be even more prescient today. The lines of inclusion/exclusion are drawn according to the logics of states, which faces legitimacy questions due to their services of elites over their citizenries. The articulation of security threats to the state or to civilization from migrants and other outsiders are both the means by which "order" is created and themselves the mechanisms of exclusion.

In Girard's account, only the gospel, with its victory of the scapegoat, provides a mechanism for *truly global inclusion*. This has remained hidden since the Christ-event because of the failure of sacrificial religion to stand consistently with the victim. In our Christendom and secular imaginaries, both church and government have been trapped in patterns that are destructive of our ability to sustain stable national identities and liberal-democratic republics. We desire inclusion but, as the discussion of migration illustrates, we struggle to bind together our motley crew of the undifferentiated into a new community. According to a Girardian perspective, there is no foundation for inclusion other than that of the global community under Christ. In the absence of this, it is easier to fall back on theistic and atheistic totalitarianisms. The dragon and the beasts appear to be emerging from the indispensable powers as imitative desire creates new patterns of acquisition and competition. Perhaps this is visible in how the social media mob emerges from our supposed "choice," Mutual Assured Destruction (MAD) emerges from national security, structural inequality from the free market, or autonomous weapons from the marvel of artificial intelligence.

Girard's work implies that a post-Christendom political theology is needed to break this cycle. A post-Christendom theology of migration necessitates moving beyond the national and temporal to a global and eternal

---

rather than doctrinal approach and argue that the texts reflect both the allure of sacrificial religion and the love of a nonviolent God. See Neufeld, *Jesus and the Subversion of Violence*, ch. 5.

65. Girard, *Battling to the End*, xv.

spiritual terrain consistent with the universality of the kingdom of God.[66] Such theology demands a political ecclesiology that places moral and practical limits on the state's right to install borders against the movement of people for the purpose of the order-keeping function of the powers. Megoran labels this "an anarchist vocational ethics" emerging from the critique of the state contained in powers theology.[67] *If* we accept that the apocalypse approaches, and the powers are increasingly beastly, then Augustine's "two cities" are increasingly difficult to differentiate from one another. Milbank's critical summary of Girard's political theology is worth recalling here.

> Girard does not, in fact, really present us with a theology of two cities, but instead with a story of one city, and its final rejection by a unique individual. This means that while his metanarrative does, indeed, have politically critical implications, these are too undiscriminating, because every culture is automatically sacrificial and "bad." At the same time, criticism cannot really be used to promote an alternative practice taking a collective, political form.[68]

There is truth in this critique, which reminds us we need to go beyond Girard to discriminate between powers and develop alternatives. However, the truth of Girard's analysis, which Milbank cannot accept, is that the sacrificial religion, which was prominent in the West throughout the modern era, is increasingly becoming untenable. The two cities were always "commingled," as Augustine declared and as the Christian realist Niebuhr later restated.[69]

After Christendom, such commingling appears to have entered a new stage. States increasingly seek their own sacralization while churches face a choice between passive co-optation, as in the churches that participate in anti-migrant rhetoric and/or limited legal opportunities to offer hospitality, or resistance, as in those churches participating in the Sanctuary Movement and other pro-refugee actions that challenge the border-making practices of governments and risk being declared illegal by national governments. There is a very fine line between these two positions where Christian witness to the state can take place. If we accept Girard's claims, we see that this witness is not of one city or kingdom to another of equal standing but rather the proclamation of hope from the one true city to the powers and authorities of the lesser city's warring hinterlands. If the kingdoms of these

66. Groody, "Migration: A Theological Vision."
67. Megoran, "Go Anywhere I Damn Well Please?"
68. Milbank, *Theology and Social Theory*, 398.
69. Niebuhr, "Augustine's Political Realism."

disorderly hinterlands are metaphorically no more than rebellious suzerain powers, then the ordering principle of "two kingdoms" breaks down. With the capacity to witness to these idolatrous suzerains constrained, how can the post-Christendom church, other religious institutions, or secular civil society help constrain violence? Does their work necessarily involve martyrdom and the dismissal of security as a substantive value? Or can a prophetic practice regarding the ways and means of protection in a violent world be found for the church? These are the questions that animate the next chapter.

CHAPTER 11

Nonviolent Protection

They dress the wound of my people as though it were not serious. "Peace, peace" they say when there is no peace.

JEREMIAH 6:14

The cross is not a detour or a hurdle on the way to the kingdom, nor is it even the way to the kingdom; it is the kingdom come.

JOHN HOWARD YODER[1]

At the beginning of January 2022, the world's attention was briefly drawn to the Central Asian state of Kazakhstan, a post-Soviet and Muslim-majority country in which more than a quarter of the population identifies as Christian, largely ethnic Russian Orthodox believers. As the state responded to peaceful protestors with recalcitrance, order broke down, a greater variety of actors became involved, including factions within the state and organized criminal groups. Reflecting the pattern of post-Soviet political violence, state actors were involved on both sides as elites fought for power amidst the violence. According to official figures, over two hundred people were killed and almost ten thousand arrested.[2] During the early hours of the morning of 6 January, three thousand Russian troops were deployed under the banner of the Collective Security Treaty Organization (CSTO), the first ever

---

1. Yoder, *The Politics of Jesus*, 51.
2. RFE/RL, "Kazakh President Announces CSTO Troop Withdrawal."

such mission by the Russian-led body. The potential for diffusion to nearby states as in the colored revolutions of the early 2000s and the Arab Spring of a decade before was doubtless in the minds of the region's kleptocratic elites, especially Vladimir Putin. The deployment of the "peacekeepers" effectively deterred potential rebels, but, at the time of proof reading (February 2023), Kazakhstan remained unstable with the prospect that rising prices and competition between political factions might lead to further nonviolent protests and violent reprisals.

Whether these protests were successful depends on what we assess to be their objectives. The nonviolent campaign began over price hikes for Liquid Petroleum Gas (LPG) and its was successful in reversing the raising of price caps in a matter of days. However, the evidence that the protests were about much broader issues of kleptocracy is abundant. From 2018 to 2021, there was a fifteen-fold increase in recorded protests, according to one independent academic body, the Oxus Society for Central Asian Affairs, with most of the rise attributable to protests over "livelihoods" and "political issues."[3] In January 2022, local protest groups complained of corruption in the state and its private sector partners in the mineral sectors. They shouted *Shal Ket* (Old Man Out!) against eighty-one-year-old former President Nazarbayev, his family, and allies—a network of elites who continued to dominate the economy. Kazakhstan is a country where just 162 people—all of them from among the former president's family and associates—own 55 percent of the wealth.[4] Protestors demanded rises in child benefit and pensions for the poor in a country where the ruling elite have become millionaires and billionaires. They even pointed to the billions of dollars of wealth overseas in property empires and offshore tax havens across the Western world. In the years following the end of the Soviet Union, £530 million was invested by the Kazakh elites in property in London and the South-East of England alone.[5] Success in these terms is more difficult to assess. However, shortly after the protests, the relatively new and apparently less wealthy President Kassym-Jomart Tokayev began a process of pensions reform and launched a campaign to remove the kleptocrats and oligarchs of the Nazarbayev regime from their positions of power.

These kinds of episodes are increasingly commonplace, especially in the postcolonies of what once were European empires. They often begin with nonviolent protests before being hijacked by criminal groups and struggles between factions within the state. Many postcolonial orders have

3. RFE/RL, "Kazakh President."
4. KPMG, "Private Equity Market in Kazakhstan."
5. Heathershaw et al., *UK's Kleptocracy Problem*, 18.

been beset by political chaos and resource theft; and we might expect this to be especially so in a post-Soviet setting where political conflicts and huge gaps between rich and poor accompanied the collapse of the atheistic Soviet Union in the 1990s. Moreover, the apocalyptic breakdown of order into a world of mimetic desire and beastly power is garishly recalled in post-Soviet states whose leaders pay millions for pop stars to perform at their birthday parties and children's weddings while millions of their citizens remain in abject poverty. For example, Kanye West was reportedly paid $3 million to play at the wedding of Nazarbayev's grandson in 2013.[6] It was for these reasons, that I joined other researchers of Kazakhstan's political economy in providing the evidence and analysis for Margaret Hodge MP to name in parliament twenty-nine individuals, Kazakh elites and their foreign business partners, who may be considered for UK sanctions. My colleague and I subsequently published a report, *Criminality Notwithstanding*, which explained how the former president's family were able to evade UK anti-corruption measures and protect their London properties.[7]

As we have seen throughout this book, the post-Christendom political order is beset by forms of violence that are structural and global, spanning East and West. These forms of violence make a mockery of the liberal international order and may even reach its very centers. One year before Kazakhstan's rebellion, the United States faced its own uprising in which hundreds of armed protestors—many of them self-identifying Christians and "a disturbing number of veterans and active-duty members of the military"[8]—stormed the Capitol building on January 6, 2021. The motivations for the Capitol riot were different with Christendom-inflected white nationalism and "great replacement theory" inspiring protestors, many of whom were wealthy rather than deprived.[9] The Capitol riot demonstrated that those that seek to hold on to a Christendom order may use violence to do so. The events led three retired generals to write a commentary for the *Washington Post* to warn of the risks in 2024 and announce that they were "chilled to [their] bones at the thought of a coup succeeding next time."[10] Following the riot, evangelical leaders who supported President Trump's lie that the election was stolen sought to explain or, more encouragingly, repent of their statements. For example, Samuel Rodriguez, president of

---

6. Calamur, "Dancing with the Dictators."

7. Mayne and Heathershaw, *Criminality Notwithstanding*.

8. Eaton, Taguba, and Anderson, "The Military Must Prepare Now for a 2024 Insurrection."

9. Pape, "The Jan. 6 Insurrectionists."

10. Eaton et al., "The Military Must Prepare."

the National Hispanic Christian Leadership Conference, who prayed at the president's inauguration, spoke from the pulpit that "we must repent for making the person who occupies the White House more important than the one who occupies our hearts."[11]

These comparable yet contrasting January 6ths tell us something of the precarity of order in both East and West. Any credible theory of security after Christendom must be able to improve our understanding of political violence across the worlds, both in places like the USA where Christians remain in the majority and instigate disorder and in places like Kazakhstan where they are in the minority and sit on the sidelines of protests. We have argued that the post-Christendom shift is politically fraught, and, in this period, the church often faces a choice between tacitly legitimizing official security policies or openly resisting state violence. We have thus questioned a "two kingdoms" political theology, where the state is imagined as taking responsibility for security and the church merely asks a series of ethical questions that seek to hold it to account. We have suggested that this clear bifurcation of responsibilities no longer holds, especially in states with Christian minorities but also in those with majorities and enduring imaginaries of Christendom. All states, including the United States and Kazakhstan, seek their own security first, and many require their citizens' sacrifice for the sake of the state. But so often, as in the Capitol riot, it is members of the church who are participating in violence and idolatry and sacralizing the powers. This chapter seeks to elaborate a political mission for the church after Christendom: to imitate not one another but the eternal Christ—to stand up for victims, resist idolatry, and avoid the conflicts of government and market. How can the confessing church refute such apostasy and minister to a world that often associates it with violence?

Violence and protection

Protection from physical attack is widely considered to be the main task of security. But what does it mean to protect? At a basic level, protection may mean a "negative peace" (absence of war), which is contrasted to "positive peace" (presence of peace-*shalom*) by Christian activists and thinkers, including Martin Luther King and Herbert Butterfield. This kind of protection is from direct violence, while structural and cultural violence persist. This threefold understanding of violence was pioneered by the Swedish social scientist Johan Galtung, drawing on King. In 1969, Galtung argued:

---

11. Associated Press, "These Church Leaders Support Trump."

We shall refer to the type of violence where there is an actor that commits the violence as *personal* or *direct*, and to violence where there is no such actor as *structural* or *indirect*. In both cases individuals may be killed or mutilated, hit or hurt in both senses of these words, and manipulated by means of stick or carrot strategies. But whereas in the first case these consequences can be traced back to concrete persons as actors, in the second case this is no longer meaningful. There may not be any person who directly harms another person in the structure. The violence is built into the structure and shows up as unequal power and consequently as unequal life chances.[12]

Galtung later defined cultural violence, concomitant with direct and structural violence, as: "aspects of culture and social life—exemplified by religion, ideology, language, art, law and science—that can be used to justify or legitimize direct or structural violence, making direct and structural violence look, or even feel, right—or at least not wrong."[13] It is this kind of wider violence that is prosecuted by the powers, often in the name of security or even peace. State, civil society, and private companies practice "negative peace" when they reduce or contain direct violence by institutions of structural and cultural violence, such as systems of formal and informal racial, gender-based, or social segregation. They practice "positive peace" when they invest in education, pool resources to fund healthcare and shared infrastructures, and provide social security, seeking to reduce social conflict and promote integration.

In this context there has been a debate about the nature of peace, its forms, its magnitude, and whether the rise of the secular state has decreased or increased violence. In the medium term, the state appears to be doing a good job of protection as, since the mid-twentieth century, the number of large-scale wars and deaths in battle has gone down quite dramatically. But, when we consider armed conflict, what are we counting? Many non-experts think of war as primarily between states, yet civil conflict within a polity has historically been far more prevalent. More Americans died in the country's civil war than in First and Second World Wars, Korea, Vietnam, Afghanistan, and Iraq combined. According to one leading research project, armed conflict may be defined as "a contested incompatibility that concerns government and/or territory."[14] But since the end of the Cold War deaths in armed conflicts around the world have declined dramatically.[15] Scholars

---

12. Galtung, "Violence, Peace, and Peace Research," 70.
13. Galtung, "Cultural Violence," 291.
14. Uppsala Conflict Data Program, "Definitions."
15. Mack et al., *Human Security Report*, 15.

such as Steven Pinker, Joshua Goldstein, and Ted Gurr interpret the data in a similar way and predict that this decline will continue. However, a closer look at the data suggests that such an optimistic conclusion is only warranted with respect to battle deaths. And even here the picture is inconsistent on a global scale. Although there has been a sustained decline since 1945, regional figures show a big spike in sub-Saharan Africa as late as the 1990s and 2000s due to the civil wars in West Africa and the Congo regions.[16]

There are two further and major caveats to place on this promising global picture. First, these data are not good at picking up death of noncombatants. Research shows that these have been steadily rising. According to one summary,

> around a million of the 10 million deaths due to the first world war were of non-combatants, whereas around half of the more than 50 million casualties of the second world war and over 90% of the millions who have perished in the violence that has wracked the Congo for decades belong in that category.[17]

While these figures are very difficult to verify, the claim that 90 percent of deaths in armed conflict today are civilian is frequently repeated by the United Nations.[18] The trend toward civilians, especially children and the most vulnerable, suffering the greatest in armed conflict is clear. Second, the picture is very different if we look at the trajectory over the long run of six hundred years (see figure 1).

FIGURE 1

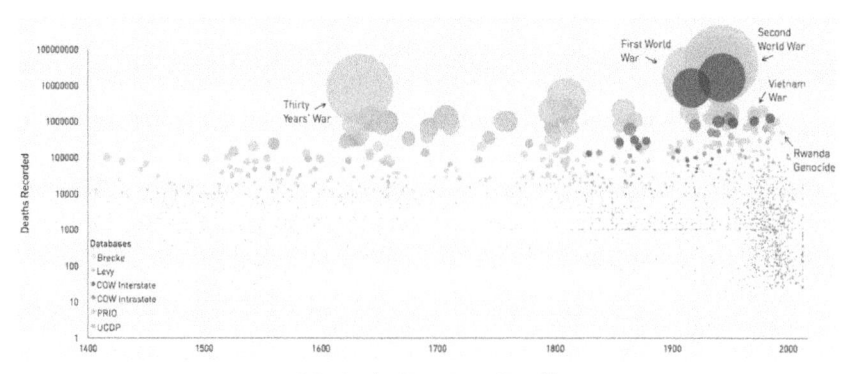

War in the Very Long Run[19]

16. Roser, "War and Peace after 1945."
17. Gray, "Steven Pinker Is Wrong about Violence and War."
18. United Nations, "Ninety Per Cent of War-Time Casualties Are Civilians."
19. Roser, "War and Peace after 1945."

This is a more appropriate perspective if one wants to consider security dynamics during the decline of Christendom and the emergence of the secular age. These data report that, in contrast to the period from 1400 to 1800, the nineteenth and twentieth centuries were especially violent. In the early modern period there was a large increase in battle deaths from the Thirty Years Wars (1618–48) onward.[20] But the world wars of the twentieth century, where the protagonists were fascists, communists, and liberal democrats, have been far more costly with the last century famously being the costliest in terms of battle deaths in human history.

Many of these wars are what the Lebanese-American social scientist Edward Azar has labeled protracted social conflict (PSC).[21] Arguably, Kazakhstan's unrest and even some urban areas of the United States may be considered in these terms. These armed conflicts are protracted as they may last for decades, leading to thousands of lives being lost over many years. They are social as they speak to communal divides between ethnic or religious groups and unmet basic human needs, such as those for land or water, education, or cultural rights. As one leading research group concluded: "collectively felt grievances result from structural inequalities and may produce violent conflict under specific conditions."[22] Conflict occurs due to an utter failure of governance where the state has picked sides, supporting its faction and its allies over others; often all groups suffer as an elite becomes wealthy from capturing the economy during the war itself. These conflicts and thefts become more intense as foreign state backers fund and arm governments and rebels while all sides use overseas professionals to launder their ill-gotten gains and retain control via struggles in foreign court rooms. In the Central Asian state of Tajikistan, the civil war began in 1992 and formally ended in 1997, but the elite fought over its major industrial assets until 2005. Rather than professional armies, it was warlord groups that fought this conflict with untold civilian casualties. The battle over lucrative assets continued in the court in London and New York for a further decade, while outbreaks of armed conflict occasionally break out in the country's mountainous regions, which sided with the opposition.[23] In May 2022, between forty and two hundred were reported killed in a secretive security operation in the Badakhshon region. Herfried Münkler identified these as "new wars," given their preponderance of civilian deaths and connections to the global

---

20. Brecke, "Violent Conflicts 1400 A.D. to the Present."
21. Azar, "Protracted International Conflicts."
22. Cederman, Gleditsch, and Buhaug, *Inequality, Grievances, and Civil War*, 6.
23. Cooley and Heathershaw, *Dictators without Borders*, 80–111.

economy, but others see them as fundamentally similar to modern wars for centuries.[24]

What may be new is that the causes of armed conflict and the means of protection from them are now globalized to a degree that was unimaginable even when the first globe-spanning empires arose in the seventeenth and eighteenth centuries. In response to the rising number of armed conflicts and civilian deaths in the twentieth century there was a major public effort to mediate armed conflicts and keep the peace through new intergovernmental organizations. The League of Nations, founded after the First World War, lacked teeth and was famously unsuccessful. But the United Nations with its Security Council (UNSC) and Department of Peacekeeping operations (UNDPKO) had some success during the Cold War and saw its role expand dramatically after 1989. While there had been fifteen UNDPKO missions prior to 1989, there were thirty-three from 1989 to 1999, with chapter 7 of the UN charter invoked at times to allow for intervention for the purposes of "international peace and security," imitating the Roman slogan, without the consent of the parties to the conflict. In 1992, the UN redefined peacekeeping as "the deployment of a United Nations presence in the field, hitherto with the consent of all the parties concerned." It also coined a new term, peace enforcement, to denote missions that were "more heavily armed than peace-keeping forces."[25] Despite being heavily armed, such missions were designed to enforce a liberal peace and post-conflict states where democracy may be built.

How successful were these attempts to protect *both* human security *and* international security in the globalization era? The record has been mixed, at best. In 1992, the mandate of the UN mission in Somalia was expanded under US leadership, ordering it "to take responsibility for the consolidation, expansion, and maintenance of a secure environment throughout Somalia." Within months, the pre-eminent global power of the age had met its match in a Mogadishu warlord, faced the very public deaths of eighteen US ranger troops, presided over war crimes by American, Canadian, and Belgian forces, and was driven out of the country by rag-tag rebels with the crucial advantage of local knowledge.[26] In Tajikistan, where a much more modest UN mission was deployed, it took decades for violence to be gradually reduced and for an "authoritarian peace" to emerge under a new dictator, Emomoli Rahmon, now in power for almost thirty years.[27]

24. Münkler, *The New Wars*.
25. Boutros Boutros-Ghali, *An Agenda for Peace*.
26. De Waal, "US War Crimes in Somalia."
27. Heathershaw, *Post-Conflict Tajikistan*.

These two examples are emblematic of wider patterns in the data. On the one hand, UN interventions and negotiated settlements generally lead to greater likelihood of civil war recurrence than decisive military victories.[28] On the other hand, in the minority of cases where UN peacekeeping is well resourced and well sustained there is greater likelihood of civil war termination.[29] But, even where civil war ends, a more democratic future is unlikely with research showing that UN peace operations lead to an initial appearance of "liberal peace" followed by authoritarian retrenchment under former warlords, dictators, and wannabe kleptocrats.[30]

NONVIOLENT PROTECTION

The very general takeaway from this broad overview of the track record of protection in the secular age—if we understand such an age as preponderant from the late-eighteenth century—is one of failure: dramatically increased violence. Even over the last half century, when battle deaths themselves have been in decline, we have seen increasing numbers of armed conflict, an increasing proportion of civilian deaths, and the globalization of armed conflict. Acts of protection by nation-states—including liberal democracies—are fraught by the security dilemma: in seeking to protect themselves they very easily threaten others. International protection from the UN and other bodies has been attempted but is only successful at ending armed conflict when it is heavily resourced and the armed conflict relatively small. Moreover, even peacekeeping is violent in both theory and practice. UN peacekeepers have been widely criticized for their lack of discipline and the many cases of sexual predation associated with their interventions in civil wars.[31]

Is there an alternative to protection from violence by violent means (which exacerbate the very problem they seek to solve)? Can the Christian peace tradition provide resource for the more modest security goal of protection? These are tough questions, especially when nonviolence is so difficult to define and sometimes unhelpfully equated with nonresistance.[32] Social scientists have begun to study unarmed civilian protection and

---

28. Toft, "Ending Civil Wars."

29. Doyle and Sambanis, *Making War and Building Peace*; Regan, Frank, and Aydin, "Diplomatic Interventions and Civil War."

30. Glassmyer and Sambanis, "Rebel—Military Integration and Civil War Termination"; Toft, "Ending Civil Wars."

31. Chenoweth and Stephan, *Why Civil Resistance Works*.

32. Cramer and Werntz, *A Field Guide to Christian Nonviolence*, 2.

nonviolent resistance but comparing these techniques to those of violence is fiendishly difficult. However, in the largest study of this kind, Erica Chenoweth and Maria J. Stephan argue that nonviolence (which they define as "civil resistance," a forceful but nonviolent use of civilian techniques) is more successful than violence as a form or resistance to armed conflict and economic exploitation because it has a "participation advantage." That is, "nonviolent campaigns facilitate the active participation of many more people than violent campaigns."[33] Chenoweth and Stephan's data show that between 1900 and 2006 nonviolent resistance movements *were twice as likely to achieve success in their aims than violent insurgencies and campaigns.* These data concur with other studies such as *A Force More Powerful* and the writing of secular thinkers such as Gene Sharp and the oft-cited historical examples of the movements of Gandhi and Martin Luther King.

But all these studies raise serious concerns of selection bias—whether they are comparing like with like. Are nonviolent campaigns only observable, and only take place, where they have higher chances of success? No. Chenoweth and Stephan show that the comparative advantage of nonviolence over violent resistance holds up in authoritarian regimes, strong states, and in the face of increases in repression.[34] Does nonviolence only succeed in achieving limited goals? The results here are mixed. Nonviolence is shown to remain more effective than violence at achieving regime change and ending imperial occupation (that is, reducing injustice) but less effective with respect to achieving secession (forming a new political community).[35] Where it takes place in contexts where violent struggles are also active, or at least threatened, is the parallel use or threat of force a casual factor in why they are effective? The result here is a categorical *no*. Chenoweth and Stephan conclude that "violent resistance has a consistently negative and statistically significant effect" on the success of nonviolent movements.[36]

These questions at the level of a campaign are important. But the question at the level of practice is more fundamental. In keeping with the wider tradition of "just peacemaking,"[37] what is now called "unarmed civilian protection" (UCP) or simply "accompaniment," has been pioneered by Christians and secularized. The classic text, *Unarmed Bodyguards*, defines accompaniment as "the physical presence of foreign volunteers with the dual purpose of protecting civilian activists or organizations from violent

33. Chenoweth and Stephan, *Why Civil Resistance Works*, 11–12, 10.
34. Chenoweth and Stephan, *Why Civil Resistance Works*, 66–69.
35. Chenoweth and Stephan, *Why Civil Resistance Works*, 69–73.
36. Chenoweth and Stephan, *Why Civil Resistance Works*, 81.
37. Stassen, *Just Peacemaking*.

politically motivated attacks, and encouraging them to proceed with their democratic activities."[38] In the more recent edition of the UCP manual of the Nonviolent Peaceforce, a less interventionist definition is offered: "the practice of civilians protecting other civilians in situations of imminent, ongoing, or recent violent conflict. It involves trained international civilians, protecting local civilians, local civilians protecting each other, and even local civilians protecting international or non-local civilians."[39] According to the tagline of a research network that studies and supports UCP, "states don't build peace—people do."[40]

Christian Peacemaker Teams, now known as Community Peacemaker Teams (CPT) is an international group that was a pioneer of UCP and began with a controversial interventionist model. CPT have been heavily criticized for their supposed naivete, particularly after four of their members were kidnapped in Iraq in 2005, one of whom was killed, while the three remaining were freed in a British special forces' operation in March 2006. Critics attacked CPT for failing to cooperate with the British special forces and continuing throughout the crisis to highlight that it was the foreign occupation that had led to thousands of kidnappings, mainly of Iraqis.[41] Such criticism is misplaced, as CPT has always sought *shalom*, not military victory, as it is only through shalom that wars will end. For Ron Sider, whose address to the Mennonite World Conference in 1984 prompted the creation of CPT, accompaniers must embrace the Anabaptist practice of martyrdom and "prepare to die by the thousands."[42] It is little wonder that such apocalyptic realism clashes with secular liberal and realist approaches to security.

However, there is some empirical evidence to suggest that at the practical level UCP is "making space for peace" amidst war.[43] One excellent example of UCP is narrated by the feminist political geographer Sara Koopman.[44] Koopman spent years studying FOR, the Fellowship of Reconciliation, which places accompaniers in San José de Apartadó, Colombia, in a region affected by the country's brutal civil war. The village had declared itself a peace community following two massacres by the Colombian armed forces in the 1990s. Despite this declaration, it faced 186 recorded

38. Mahony and Eguren, *Unarmed Bodyguards*, 2.
39. Huibert Oldenhuis et al., *Unarmed Civilian Protection*.
40. Creating Safer Space, "What Is Unarmed Civilian Protection?"
41. For the CPT's multi-vocal account of the crisis, see Gates-Brown, *118 Days*.
42. Sider, "God's People Reconciling."
43. For a discussion of the nature of space in accompaniment, see Eguren, "The Notion of Space in International Accompaniment."
44. Koopman, "Alter-Geopolitics."

assassinations by the military, paramilitaries, and insurgents in the period from 2000 to 2010.[45] But such violence is rare when villagers are accompanied. As Koopman summarizes,

> Accompaniment keeps growing because it seems to work. Of course, it is hard to know exactly why actors choose not to attack, but a peace community member told me that even after having FOR there for several years, when he runs into armed actors on paths further up the mountains they ask him, "are those internationals still there with you?" Since FOR has been in La Union the attacks have happened away from the hamlet, away from the internationals.[46]

Koopman frames this engagement, in contrast to traditional geopolitics, as alter-geopolitics, that is, "feminist geopolitics as done through action."[47] The fact that the authors on nonviolence and unarmed civilian protection, which we have covered in this section, are overwhelmingly female—whereas most of those studying and practicing military strategy are male—is surely significant. It is consistent with the fact that armed conflict is significantly more likely in societies fractured by gender inequality.[48] This fact points to how fields from political realism to political theology are highly masculinized, both in the representation of authors and in the underlying assumptions in their work. The gendered nature of the question of violence and protection requires further consideration.

John Howard Yoder's questionable commitment to nonviolence

Much of the theory and practice of nonviolence also has Christian theological, and specifically Mennonite, underpinnings. This book is not another in the library of studies of the just war versus pacifism debate, as its subject of security is broader in scope and analytically prior to that of war. However, for us to address the question of protection in a secular age we must consider the theological claims of perhaps the foremost thinker of nonviolence after Christendom and author of *The Politics of Jesus* (1972), John Howard Yoder (1927–97). As we consider Yoder, the church's comparative advantage is not its relative strength vis-à-vis state violence or its ability to deter violent

---

45. Koopman, "Alter-Geopolitics," 279.
46. Koopman, "Alter-Geopolitics," 279.
47. Koopman, "Alter-Geopolitics," 280.
48. Melander, "Gender Equality and Intrastate Armed Conflict."

actors (the *threat power* of war) but its realistic alternative to violence and ability to draw violent actors into new partnerships (the *integrative power* of nonviolence). This alternative is not pristinely nonviolent, and certainly neither pure nor infallible. Yoder's thought is not entirely logical and consistent, as recent scholarship has shown;[49] no strategy or philosophy in history is or could be either infallible or entirely consistent. Arguments for and against nonviolence on absolute grounds easily become polemical. Yet despite these limits, nonviolence is an alternative that is altogether more realistic in the post-Christendom age.

But there is a further problem specifically related to gender and sex. Before considering the theologian's work we must consider a period of sin in his life that only came to light after his death. Yoder himself painfully demonstrates that moral purity is not found in any earthly creed, person, or institution, regardless of their public commitment to nonviolence. From the 1970s, he engaged in a campaign—what he considered to be a theological experiment—of sexual abuse. More than one hundred women are thought to have been subject to a range of abuse, from suggestive comments and harassment to intercourse. Yoder was "methodically perpetrating sexual violence" on female students and other women in the various churches, campuses, seminaries, and conferences where he taught and presented.[50] Many of these episodes of sexual violence were known at the time and subject to successive but largely ineffective investigations, formal and informal, from 1979 to his death in 1997 by the Mennonite seminaries of northern Indiana.[51] The University of Notre Dame, where he taught, did not launch such an inquiry and indeed kept his name on the Kroc Institute's dialogues for Nonviolence, Religion, and Peace until they were made public beyond the Mennonite churches and seminaries.[52] It was not until 2014/15, more than forty years after the abuse began, that a public reckoning on Yoder's sexual violence came to fruition with the publication of Rachel Waltner Goossen's "'Defanging the Beast': Mennonite Responses to John Howard Yoder's Sexual Abuse," in the *Mennonite Quarterly Review*.

John Howard Yoder's theology of nonviolence remains insightful and must be central to a study of security after Christendom from a free church

---

49. Martens, *The Heterodox Yoder*.
50. Goossen, "Defanging the Beast."
51. Goossen, "Defanging the Beast."

52. I attended the "Yoder dialogues" in 2006, while a faculty fellow at Notre Dame, completely unaware of his sexual abuse. In 2015, there was a reckoning at Notre Dame too, with graduate students at the university presenting a paper arguing that Yoder's sexual abuse must be considered in any analysis of all his theological writings, including those of nonviolence. Salgado, "Why Write the Story of the Allegations."

perspective. Equally, it can no longer be introduced and analyzed without reference to his own violence. His abuse was specifically theological in that he framed it, whether instrumentally or sincerely, as an experiment to achieve the perfection that Christ achieved in his relations with women, including them in his ministry in ways that were otherwise unthinkable at the time. In a 1974 call in which he appealed to women, he stated, "only thanks to your friendship, sisterhood, can I do the theology." Yoder also claimed, according to Goossen, that "he was working from theological premises that included certain interpretations of the writings of Paul and the life of Jesus."[53] In his self-justificatory 1979 memo he sought to justify his work as "defanging the beast."[54] Goossen shows how this claim was taken seriously and was a "theological idea carried along by Mennonite interests for far too long."[55] It is reasonable and troubling to conclude that Yoder's theological notion of power as integrative was entirely consistent with his patriarchal power over the "sisterhood." Moreover, it was the self-governing and intimate nature of Mennonite churches and seminaries that apparently allowed the abuse to continue for so long. Sadly, Yoder's own violence risks undermining his own model of the church-as-polis, the peaceable kingdom, the *ecclesia*.

The church must submit itself to secular laws to prevent and investigate sexual abuse. No longer can it be the privileged chaplain, a source of ethics, and the conscience for the state. As we have argued, this option is slipping away in the post-Christendom age as the state loses its coherence, capacity, and authority. The route to a new understanding of the relationship between church and world is one that must be eschatological and, to some extent, apocalyptic. Yoder understood this more clearly than most and it is for this reason that we must continue to work (critically and conscientiously) with his ideas. Like Girard and Bulgakov, for Yoder, "the work of Jesus Christ on the cross has the effect of revealing the assumed sovereignty of the powers to be an illusion, a skewed vision of the way things really are."[56] In what follows we consider Yoder's perspective on nonviolence and question to what extent it offers more than a let-the-church-be-church stance of the martyr and bystander. Put more acutely, we consider the extent to which his specifically anti-Constantinian nonviolence offers a credible perspective on security. Does the integrative power of nonviolence, we ask, offer protection

53. Goossen, "Defanging the Beast," 8.

54. This appears to be a metaphorical use for putatively pastoral-theological purposes, where the "beast" refers to prior experiences of sex rather than being a biblical reference to the books of Daniel or Revelation. Goossen, "Defanging the Beast," 12–13.

55. Goossen, "Defanging the Beast," 80.

56. Gingerich-Hiebert, *Architectonics of Hope*, 142.

for the church and wider society (including women) against all forms of armed conflict and direct violence (including sexual abuse)? This question is simultaneously one of theological politics *and* political theology.

Yoder's "Middle Axioms" and "Two Orders"

In chapter 10, we concluded that Girard's diagnosis of the cultural and historical significance of the Christ is a post-Christendom argument for a single truly inclusive kingdom of Christ. According to Girard, during Christendom both the kingdoms of cross and sword relied on ideologies of representative death, of sacrifice, to create order; and this ideology is now losing its cultural resonance. The correlations noted in this chapter between the increasing number of intrastate wars with the end of Christendom, and the rise of nonviolence in the secular age, provides suggestive evidence to support this thesis. They also imply that the decline of two kingdoms heralds both fear of disorder and hope for a new order. Neo-Christendom nationalist movements and armed insurgents and terrorists of various faiths seek the fusing of religion and politics, which they would impose by force of arms. These imaginaries of new centered Christendom are politically and theologically comparable to those of other religions: the Muslim Caliphate, Buddhist nationalism, political Zionism, etc.

John Howard Yoder recognized this obvious problem and sought to refute the charge of sectarianism that was associated with it. According to one of his interpreters, he sought to maintain a "duality that does not fall into either a dualism (absolute separation of church and state) or monism (unity of church and state)."[57] His practical and ethical strategy for duality was that of "middle axioms" or, in his later work, "semantic frames." In *The Christian Witness to the State* (1964), the work in which he used middle axioms most extensively, he defined them as concepts that "mediate between the general principles of Christological ethics [which are in the purview of the church] and the concrete problems of political application [in the state and world]."[58] In this sense they are dialectically produced syntheses and successors to the Christendom dialectic of cross and sword discussed in chapter 1. Middle axioms are consistent with Yoder's partially realized eschatology and peace church ecclesiology, which are in turn central to his entire political theology.[59] Yoder takes the position that the old age of the powers is passing away and the new age of the kingdom is coming; but in

57. Marten, *The Heterodox Yoder*, 74.
58. Yoder, *Christian Witness to the State*, 32–33.
59. Carter, *The Politics of the Cross*, ch. 5.

the now-but-not yet sense of the period from the Pentecost to the parousia, the powers are commanded with political authority to keep order for a temporary period.[60] He holds them to be "roughly equivalent of the modern term 'structures', . . . the dimensions of cohesiveness and purposefulness which hold together human affairs beyond the strictly personal level"; "the powers govern that realm which the bible refers to as the world."[61]

For Yoder, to afford the powers a second kingdom and make them some kind secular antecedent of the kingdom of God, as in the dualist Christendom imaginary, is a false equivalence and an error of Augustine's Constantinian theology (cf. Rev 11:15; Dan 7). Yoder's directional and salvation-historical approach suggests that the powers have been relegated by the coming of the kingdom.[62] *The cross is triumphing over the sword.* However, "the powers cannot simply be destroyed or set aside or ignored," he argues, as "their sovereignty must be broken."[63] Israel was once suzerain under the powers of Egypt and the Assyrians, while today their sovereignty has been broken and the church has triumphed over the powers. But if the Lord has bequeathed the powers limited suzerainty, and we must witness to them through middle axioms, how might we characterize the old order's relationship to the new in dialectical terms distinct from those imagined and practiced in Christendom? The answer to this requires refrain to Yoder's ecclesiology. For Yoder, the church is the bride of the King and an *ecclesia*, a community whose citizens are both in heaven and on earth, whose heavenly purpose directs their earthly goals to "the social manifestation of the ultimately triumphant reign of God."[64] Instead of two kingdoms, he posits two orders:

> an "*order* of providence," where Christ reigns over man's disobedience, through the "powers" including the state, side by side with the "order of redemption" where Christ rules in and through the obedience of His disciples.[65]

This is a superseding of the dialectic between cross and sword to that of ultimate redemption and temporal providence. It is not that the church cannot disobey or that the world is not subject to grace.[66] But the state itself

---

60. Yoder, *Christian Witness to the State*, 9.
61. Yoder, *Christian Witness to the State*, 8.
62. Nugent, *The Politics of Yahweh*, 188–89.
63. Yoder, *Politics of Jesus*, 142.
64. Yoder, *Christian Witness to the State*, 10.
65. Yoder, *Christian Witness to the State*, 12.
66. Yoder argues, from the New Testament, that "the state has within the divine plan a function, modest but nevertheless essential, constantly shifting but nevertheless

does not redeem, that is the work of Christ and the prophetic ministry of the church to all authorities of the world. This raises various questions of the dialectical relationship between the eschatological power of redemptive nonviolence and historical function of providential violence.

THE POST-CHRISTENDOM DIALECTIC

Is nonviolence how to live peacefully in the church while the violence of the state is what's required to deter attack? This mainline Protestant answer is yes. But this is a dualistic rather than dialectical understanding and, as we have seen, the historical record of nonviolence and violence suggests otherwise. *The Christian Witness to the State* (1964) was written in response to Niebuhr's essay "Why the Christian Church Is Not Pacifist" and begins by arguing against the Christian realist argument that the Christian pacifist is a "gadfly," either a principled onlooker or dangerous activist.[67] However, such realism lacks an understanding of the codependent relationship between violence and nonviolence. The latter is naturally a negation of the former, which, in the present age, remains constrained by the conditions of violence against which it rebels. The role of the church is not merely to question earthly powers but to establish the kingdom power—protective and ultimately redemptive—of nonviolence. While "it is wise not to judge those who take up violence out of desperation"—including, I would argue, last resort uses of lethal force by police operating under the rule of law in a democracy—it is unquestionable that "Christians are called to a nonviolent life in imitation of Christ."[68] The force of such nonviolence rests on a different practice of power to that deployed by Christian realists, not merely, as Sykes frames it, the rejection of power.[69] While classical Christian realist thinking recognizes the power of the Christendom dialectic to generate responsible political authority—the merger of sword and the cross in Martin's terms—the post-Christendom position dialectic works to expose violence and make nonviolent political community possible. Here, providential "middle axioms" and prophetic witnesses do not seek closeness to power but distance. At the same time, they do not withdraw from questions of security. This tension between power and resistance, the now and the

---

fundamentally definable, distinct from that of the church yet within the redemptive plan." Yoder, *Christian Witness to the State*, 13.
  67. Yoder, *Christian Witness to the State*, 7.
  68. Wright, *Theology of the Dark Side*, 246–47.
  69. Sykes, *Power and Christian Theology*, ch. 4.

not yet, must be maintained rather than be overcome according to a post-Christendom imaginary of security.

As we have seen, Yoder sees a progression of dispensations in the eons and across the biblical testaments; this is reflected in his theology of nonviolence as much as in any other limb of his corpus. His nonviolence is "constitutive of the apocalyptic politics of Jesus [to defeat the powers]" not an unnecessary addition for needless martyrdom.[70] In "A Theological Critique of Violence" he argues:

> The gospel is not about legitimizing violence so much as about overcoming it. We overcome it partly by demythologizing its moral pretensions, partly by refusing to meet it on its own terms, partly by replacing it with other more humane strategies and tactics of moral struggle, partly by innocent suffering, and partly by virtue of the special restorative practices of forgiveness and community. Yet all these coping resources are derivative. At the bottom violence is judged—*critiqued* in the deep sense of the verb—because of the passion events.[71]

Yoder concurs with Girard that it is the cross of Christ that breaks the cycle of violence and its mimetic and sacrificial processes; an act foreshadowed in the Hebrew scriptures where "Yahweh intervenes to protect Cain's life from the universally threatening vengeance."[72] The Christian church *is* pacifist in the sense of refusing the protection of violence; again, this is modeled in the Old Testament, where "confidence in Yahweh is an alternative to the self-determining use of Israel's own military resources in defense of their existence as God's people."[73] Although there are times in the Hebrew scriptures when such confidence means following Yahweh's instructions for "holy war" (Josh 6 & 10; 1 Sam 15), this becomes a spiritual battle after Christ's victory on the cross (Eph 5:1–9; 6:10–18).[74] This spiritualization of warfare does not make the church apolitical. Rather, it is the mechanism by which difference from, and dialectical relations with, the world are maintained.

In Yoder's own terms, the church's witness of nonviolence is Spirit-led and political rather than being spiritualized. While the witness is structured in dialectical terms, it is ad hoc in political engagement and irreducible to a settled ideology of the Left or Right of interventionism or isolationism.

70. Gingerich-Hiebert, *Architectonics of Hope*, 166.
71. Yoder, "A Theological Critique of Violence," 41.
72. Yoder, "A Theological Critique of Violence," 28.
73. Yoder, *Politics of Jesus*, 83.
74. Thomas, "The Old Testament, 'Holy War' and Christian Morality."

Carter helpfully notes that it is an ad hoc witness in four ways: "in the sense of not being systematic," as it lacked a positive concept of the state, for the reasons discussed above; "in the sense of dealing with only one issue at a time," reflecting, of course, the nature of Yoder's own theology, which was often produced with respect to specific questions asked of him by the Mennonite church; "in the sense of usually taking a negative form"; and, "in the sense of arising out of its own life as example."[75] In the context of contemporary discussions of security such an ad hoc witness seems insufficient. However, Yoder is clear that the church's ask of the state is not for a "perfect society," but for "available, or at least conceivable, alternatives."[76] Carter concludes that such an ad hoc witness "need not be without power and effect."[77] In order to support that modest claim we need to recognize that what is meant by "power" and "effect" in Yoder is rather different from what is typically meant by national security advisors. There are, in fact, specific differences in *where* and *how* power is exercised. "The two cities," Cavanaugh argues, in a manner that is consistent with the post-Christendom dialectic elaborated here, "are not two institutions but two performances, two practices of space and time."[78] Similarly, for Yoder, the two orders connote two different spatiotemporal practices. The order of providence supports security insofar as its practices are held to account by church and civil society operating according to an order of redemption. At the same time, these security practices will cease to be providential if power is either fully concentrated (a monism, as in centered Christendom) or entirely separated (a dualism, as in decentered Christendom).

In Yoder and especially Hauerwas, a church-as-polis model, in accordance with the order of redemption, represents a kind of counter-power to the security order of the day. For Nathan Kerr, one of Yoder's leading interpreters, certain risks arise from this position: "the *ontologization* of the church" and "a concomitant *instrumentalization* of worship"—in short, "the danger of intensifying the Christian community's concern for its own interior *identity* over and against the world."[79] This is the danger of monism and is analogous to that of centered Christendom. Such a danger is visible both in the neo-Christendom claims of new political kingdom and in some post-Christendom imaginaries of exile and martyrdom. It arises from the premise that the church exists "*in advance* of encounter with 'the

---

75. Carter, *The Politics of the Cross*, 209.
76. Yoder, *Christian Witness to the State*, 38.
77. Carter, *The Politics of the Cross*, 212.
78. Cavanaugh, *Migrations*, 49.
79. Kerr, *Christ, History and Apocalyptic*, 169, 171.

world.'"⁸⁰ And yet the church was formed in Christ's encounter with the world in the Gospels and its own subsequent encounters as narrated in Acts, the Epistles, the early church fathers, and onward, often under the forces of "Constantinianism." Being the inaugurated community of God does mean the church is before the world; it remains entwined with it. In Kerr's conception the church engages with the world in terms of "an *apocalyptic politics of mission*," whereby "there is no 'church,' no real Christian existence even, prior to or apart from this mission."⁸¹ However, despite this radically social constructivist account of the church in the world—and thereby a variety of different positions from the center to the margins of politics—Kerr returns to the norm of Hauerwas and Yoder to frame the place of the church as being that of "exile" and "diaspora," which exercises power in "doxology" and "liturgy."⁸² While a traditional Anabaptist stance, this framing seems to ignore the prophetic work of the church envisioned in Revelation (a point to which we will return below).

In sum, the church's power is constituted in the world through a radical politics of mission from the margins against Christendom imaginaries and in the post-Christendom dialectic. As such, the eschatological work of the church in history, especially with regard to questions of security, takes place with respect to both orders, of providence and of redemption. Middle axioms take place in actual historical contexts and demand the exercise of judgment as to both providential and redemptive work. In chapter 5 of *Christian Witness to the State*, Yoder establishes the criteria for these judgments. The first five criteria appear to be most crucial: (a) the state exists, "for the sake of the work of the church and not vice-versa"; (b) the fundamental concept of the state is that of order (Rom 13), which he relates to "peace" (1 Tim 2); (c) the danger is that the state will "overdo" its ordering role and become demonic by seeking sovereign power, which belongs to God;⁸³ (d) the Christian social critique is derived from the approximation of the kingdom of God in terms of "conceivable alternatives" to the present order;⁸⁴ (e) "there exists a level of human values, not specifically Christian but somehow subject to Christian formative influences, where

---

80. Kerr, *Christ, History and Apocalyptic*, 173.
81. Kerr, *Christ, History and Apocalyptic*, 173–74.
82. Kerr, *Christ, History and Apocalyptic*, 175, 181.
83. Yoder, *Christian Witness to the State*, 36–37.

84. Yoder notes that the danger here is that the Christian imagines the achievement of the standard of the Kingdom of God in the state. But this "not an available possibility, lying beyond both the capacities and intentions of a fallen society" and, as such, "there is a very real sense in which the [Niebuhrian] lesser-evil mentality is correct." Yoder, *Christian Witness to the State*, 38–39.

the real movement of history takes place," and within which the church is dialectically participative.[85] With these criteria in mind we may sketch how the church works both redemptively and providentially with respect to the question of protection. We may outline three modes of witness and action.

BEING, DOING, PROCLAIMING

A first way the church acts is by *being* a community of nonviolent protection, as in the San Jose community and countless other peace communities. Despite the title of Yoder's pamphlet, the church's primary witness is not to the state as such, but the world.[86] It does this simply by *being ecclesia*, a non-hierarchical body, "which casts light beyond the borders of the church." This casting of light is firstly normative. Yoder gives the example of the development of human rights as an example of how the rights extended to individuals within Christian community have been transposed into the wider world via national constitutional orders and international law.[87] Such structural change has emerged in a secular age under the hope of justice but the structuring logic of economic liberalism—human rights thus exist alongside a return to inequality.[88] Each generation has its historian who plausibly traces the genealogy of modern human rights, social security, and democracy in ecclesial practices—and yet each of these achievements is subject to the power relations of the world.[89] There appears to be a post-Christendom pattern here. The secular age frees the church to witness across and beyond civilizational boundaries. However, the increased power of capital and structural violence in this secular age limit both the form and substance of redemptive projects like human rights. They may easily be coopted by the powers, become mythologized, and therefore lose their redemptive potential. If the church participates in such processes, it is no longer being a community of redemption but meekly participating in an order of providence.

---

85. The subsequent four "criteria" are derivative of the previous five, and appear to be criteria of nonconformism to assuage Yoder's Mennonite readers. They include: (f) the Christian position is likely to be unpopular; (g) to concede that violence is irremovable from state practice is not to approve it; (h) there are no objective criteria for "legitimacy" other than those of the kingdom; (i) virtue ethics over consequentialist ethics. Yoder, *Christian Witness to the State*, 40–44.

86. Marten, *Heterodox Yoder*, 72.

87. Yoder, *Christian Witness to the State*, 18.

88. Moyn, *Not Enough*.

89. For example, Siedentop, *Inventing the individual*.

A second way the church provides witness is by *doing* nonviolent protection, as in the practice of CPT and other nonviolent resistance and accompaniment activities. Here the church is called to be self-denying. Yoder summarizes its practice as such:

> When he called his society together Jesus gave its members a new way of life to live. He gave them a new way to deal with offenders—by forgiving them. He gave them a new way to deal with violence—by suffering. He gave him a new way to deal with money—by sharing it. He gave them a new way to deal with problems of leadership—by drawing upon the gift of every member, even the most humble. He gave them a new way to deal with a corrupt society—by building a new order not smashing the old. He gave them a new pattern of relationships between man and woman, between parent and child, between master and slave, in which was made concrete a radical new vision of what it means to be a human person. He gave him a new attitude towards the state and toward the "enemy nation."[90]

In Christendom, the church provided the first hospitals and schools, long before state or public provision occurred. At the same time, in Christendom, the church's cosy relationship with the state diluted this "new way of life" and made it more likely to take on its imperial, commercial, and racialized agendas concerning whom to educate and for what purpose. By contrast, after Christendom these practices are global and non-sectarian. Martin Luther King was inspired by Gandhi who was inspired by Tolstoy and English Baptists; all, according to Yoder, were converted to "universal love."[91] It is thus hard to argue that the church offers a unique functional model to the world when there are so many analogues in other faiths. Thus, the basis of Christian nonviolence is a witness to the world. Nonviolence is part of the Christian faith story and God's grace is common to all.

Therefore, a third form of witness is the prophetic: that of *proclaiming* the value of nonviolent protection to the security establishment. This requires standing against violence in ways that are heard and not merely dismissed. The direct witness is to the state, although this could be extended to corporations, international organizations, and NGOs. All should, in Cavanaugh's memorable phrase, be treated "like the telephone company, a large bureaucratic provider of goods and services that never quite provides

---

90. Yoder, *For the Nations*, 176; see also Gingerich-Hiebert, *The Architectonics of Hope*, 168.

91. Yoder, "The Political Meaning of Hope," 56–57.

value for money."⁹² This requires engaged and sustained attempts to develop and communicate prophetic critique and "middle axioms" in a fashion that is dialogic. Here is where there appears to be a weakness in Yoder's thought arising from his positionality as a Mennonite in America. The charge is not that of "gadfly" but simply that of the limited influence of the self-imposed "outsider." Yoder, however, makes a strong case for a pragmatic approach to the state. "The Christian speaks not of how to describe, and then to seek to create the ideal society, but of how the state can best fulfil its responsibilities in a fallen society," he argues in a passage that is almost Niebuhrian.⁹³ At the same time, secular scholarship appears to have a role in shaping the Christian witness, as he argues, "the application of these middle axioms should correspond with the most accurate and impartial descriptions of historical reality," and gives the example of the Christian realist Herbert Butterfield.⁹⁴ Here Yoder's critics argue he "grants too much 'epistemological sovereignty' to the wider world."⁹⁵ But surely the risk to be avoided is epistemological monism. The argument that by making a bridge to a particular context the ethicist is conceding ground, disregards the fact that *any* ethical practice from the basis of a sacred text must translate its precepts to context or fall foul of didacticism. Moreover, such duality allows for the possibility of integration, not toward an established church, theocracy, or some other institutional entwinement, but a normative integration where it becomes impossible for the state or any other religious or secular actor to legitimize war as just. Yoder welcomed "nuclear pacifism" and the use of "just war" criteria to normatively invalidate war for all but the most limited "policing" circumstances.⁹⁶ Far from being irrelevant, as Niebuhr charged, these positions have been taken on by more political movements during and after the Cold War.

The exact forms that being, doing, and proclaiming nonviolent protection take are necessarily of their time and place. For Yoder, this was Cold War USA and the nuclear era. He expounds: (a) an argument for mutual recognition of states according to an agreed international standard; (b) against world government and international military action, which he deems "idealistic," but for the early UN and cultural internationalism; (c) caveated support for international human rights and laws in the sense "less

---

92. Cavanaugh, *Migrations*, 42.
93. Yoder, *Christian Witness to the State*, 32.
94. Yoder, *Christian Witness to the State*, 34–35.
95. Yoder, *Christian Witness to the State*, 79.
96. However, the list of states that forbid offensive military capacity is short and includes states like Japan whose pacifism is not likely due to norm transfer from the church.

of general obligations than of specific injustices which visibly deserve the harmony and unity of society"; (d) for a "police conception of limited war"; (e) support for the use of just war criteria to delimit "the cases in which the use of violence is the least illegitimate."[97] What is striking about these stances is how broadly liberal-internationalist and in keeping with the normative standard of the day they are; the first three were entirely uncontroversial and consistent with Kennedy-Johnson era positions. The second two were and are mainstream ethical positions in the church and would be consistent with most Catholic and mainline Protestant thinking, although controversial for many of his fellow Anabaptists. Yoder's subsequent discussions are longer and more equivocal, including an unsurprising hesitancy to be directly involved in the security infrastructure along with a notable skepticism toward "radical pacifism."[98] Together, Yoder's examples suggest potential for ecumenism with respect to positions and the potential for being, doing, and proclaiming realistic nonviolent protection.

The power of nonviolence

It has been the purpose of this chapter to demonstrate that nonviolence is not merely the opposite of security—a manifesto for martyrdom in apocalyptic age—but a mode of civilian protection and a political-theological form of security after Christendom. The chapter has not sought to establish the effectiveness of nonviolence conclusively, and we have only summarized a fraction of the voluminous literature that provides powerful evidence that nonviolence is both strategically effective and constitutive of new community spaces.[99] Two of the most suggestive findings are implicit in this literature and provide important caveats to the argument of this book. First, the gender difference between violence and nonviolence is telling. Violence is more likely in gender-unequal societies and security studies as a field of inquiry has been dominated by men—and it is these men who make up the majority of authors cited in this book. Nonviolence, by contrast, is more likely to be written about and practiced by women. A second interesting finding relates to the regions of Christendom. Chenoweth and Stephan note that nonviolent campaigns have been most likely to succeed in the former Soviet Union and the Americas (arguably the two regions outside of Europe

---

97. Yoder, *Christian Witness to the State*, 45–49.
98. Yoder, *Christian Witness to the State*, 51–59.
99. One recent survey argues that "Christian nonviolence has never been monolithic but has always included merging and diverging streams," of which it identifies eight. Cramer and Werntz, *A Field Guide*, 2.

to be most affected by Christendom imaginaries) and least effective in the Middle East and Asia (the two regions where other religions, especially Islam, are typically majority faiths and Christendom is least imagined).[100] This is provisional evidence that a prehistory of Christendom and a current context of Judeo-Christian secularism may have a positive effect on the "participation advantage" of nonviolence.

In sum, both gender and faith matter in explaining if and how protection works in theory and in practice. Both point to a new order—to an "alter-geopolitics" or "pacific geopolitics"—a more hopeful and less masculine way of thinking about security and protection.[101] Even nonviolence, as painfully personified in the abuses committed by Yoder, has blind spots to gender and sexual violence, leading fifteen Anabaptist women to call for "Christian *anti*-violence."[102] However, notwithstanding the inviolable kingdom principle of nonviolence, it would be facile to dismiss all applications of the use of force in our interim times. Despite the best efforts of analysts, it is extraordinarily difficult to extricate the effects of nonviolent actions from those of violent ones. The apocalyptic realist position is to recognize that, in times of increasing violence and rising powers, the dominance of one power is only briefly and partially withheld by the violence of another. This chapter has suggested that mass participation and nonviolent resistance do not always achieve security in the short term by preventing violence—although sometimes they do—but gain it in the long-term by winning victories in their campaigns and thereby exposing and delegitimizing violence. In this light, policing actions and UCP in which violence is disallowed or strictly constrained, and Christian participation therein, are surely admissible to defend against violence. In addressing security, we need to push beyond the standard post-Christendom position with respect to participation in the world and the state. But what Christians must never do is sacralize, place hope in, or participate in the warfare of leviathans.

What we have done in this chapter is establish the theological and political basis of a post-Christendom approach to protection. Theologically, we have shown the biblical, eschatological, and ecclesiological underpinnings of the principles of nonviolent protection: for the church to live peacefully and model this to the world in ways that expose the myths of national security and violent protection. Although this hope is born in theology it quickly becomes political. In this, as in its wider mission to humankind, the church must imitate Jesus, expose the powers, and love them to death. At times

100. Chenoweth and Stephan, *Why Civil Resistance Works*, 74.
101. Koopman, "Alter-Geopolitics"; Megoran, "Towards a Geography of Peace."
102. Cramer and Werntz, *A Field Guide*, 127.

this involves martyrdom and nonviolent resistance, which "are the key to reading and performing history eschatologically."[103] At other times, allies in the saeculum will make providential policing or peace-making proposals to which the church may join. As the action of protection and the quest for security is no more than secondary to the Christian mission, we should not expect to find a single logic held consistently in all Christian security practice but be prepared to discern contextual and practical solutions. At the same time, we must never forget that the logos does not point to the compatibility of cross and sword but to the triumph of the nonviolent Christ over the violence of the powers. Empirically, there is considerable evidence that nonviolence works. Theologically, this alternative "logic" of this logos is, in Kerr's summary of Yoder, "concrete obedience of a singular human being to the inbreaking of God's Kingdom into the world as the way of suffering love."[104] The net effect of this way is apocalyptic: "to interrupt and to challenge the governing powers' universalist presumptions."[105] The promise of this victory is of a world where radical inclusion, nonviolent protection, and abundant provision are being inaugurated in our time.

103. Cavanaugh, *Migrations*, 63.
104. Kerr, *Christ, History and Apocalyptic*, 141.
105. Kerr, *Christ, History and Apocalyptic*, 141.

CHAPTER 12

Abundant Provision

A society incapable of giving God his due fails to give its citizens their due—as human beings made for the quest and enjoyment of God. Where there is no *jus* towards God, there is no commonsense of what is due to human beings, no *juris consensus*.

ROWAN WILLIAMS[1]

The creation waits with eager longing for the revealing of the children of God.

ROMANS 8:19

On 10 March 2022—on the day Russian businessman and Kremlin confidant Roman Abramovitch was sanctioned by his hitherto very obliging hosts in the UK—I visited a movie theatre in London's West End. *The Batman*, the latest superhero film from DC, had just been released. However, it was not this stylistically violent thriller that we had come to see. Promoted on the big screen in the foyer was the premiere of the film of the Global Integrity Anti-Corruption Evidence (GI-ACE) initiative, an international research program funded by UK Aid. Rather than seeing Batman fight the Riddler across fictional Gotham, we had the more cerebral experience of listening to academics discuss their research subjects, including, for example, the nature of corruption in public-sector procurement across the globe and how new data analytics might help officials spot red flags. No superpowers

---

1. Williams, "The Politics of the Soul," 736.

were needed in this struggle, merely the painstaking accrual of evidence and its timely and appropriate communication to policy makers.

From 2019 to 2022, I had the privilege of being part of GI-ACE, a research program with the stated aim, "to help researchers communicate and share findings in ways that support practitioners designing and implementing more effective anti-corruption interventions."[2] Our projects ranged from the study of cross-border trade in Africa to—in the case of my project—checks against money laundering by London-based professionals when handling wealth with origins in post-Soviet kleptocratic states. In the GI-ACE theory of change, researchers feed evidence on corruption and effective anti-corruption measures to policy-makers with whom relationships are built over many years. Practitioners thereby have greater capacity to design and implement policies and achieve the theory of change's stated outcome that: "Practitioner solves corruption problem."[3] In our conferences, the telos of ending corruption was rarely doubted but all acknowledged that the bumps in the road were considerable. The debates were about whether a "big bang" (requiring a political revolution) or incremental approaches were best, and whether the whole world needed to change or just particular individuals and groups if we are to defeat corruption. Despite all the evidence accrued, there remained something faith-based in our community; at times, I felt I was in church, a global community of shared practice and purpose, with its own patron saints, doctrines, and worshipful practices.

Such an observation may seem trite. Anti-corruption research often engages at the meeting point between the self-evident and the unsaid. The GI-ACE program was a worthy initiative with all the trappings of a modern influencing campaign: savvy social and visual media, branded merchandise, including hoodies, and high-profile events accruing millions of air miles. It supported some of the best researchers from some of the world's poorest countries and places most afflicted by corruption. In many ways, it was precisely the kind of civil society initiative that pointed to the means of redemption from the corruption of our age. Some of our carbon-intensive globe-trotting was tempered by the coronavirus pandemic but, almost like superheroes, researchers fought on to collect and analyze data and place it into the public sphere.

At the time of the movie premiere, the war in Ukraine was entering its third week and our project team was handling multiple requests on sanctions and the effectiveness of the UK's anti-money-laundering system against suspicious wealth from Russia. We accumulated yet more evidence to demonstrate what we already knew: post-Soviet wealth had harmed the

2. Global Integrity, "Our Programme."
3. Global Integrity, "Theory of Change."

rule of law in the UK due to long-standing conflicts of interest and financial opacity. Abramovitch himself was emblematic of this truth. The corrupt sources of his wealth from the Sibneft and Slavneft sales, and his close ties to the Kremlin, were well known, not just among researchers but among activists, officials, politicians, and in the world of football. Equally, the system of enablers and apologists that had kept this truth unsaid had existed for decades. Only three months before, London lawyers succeeded in extracting an apology from the publishers of the journalist Catherine Belton, whose excellent *Putin's People* had repeated the allegation that Vladimir Putin asked Abramovitch to buy Chelsea FC. One difficult-to-prove allegation grabbed the headlines and distracted from the wider truth of a six-hundred-page book.

The failure to make these wider truths matters of public consensus is one example of political vice found both inside and outside the church, as identified by Rowan Williams. On the one hand, our societies are atomistic and, in a fundamental sense, corrupt; across society, economy, and environment, interest groups scramble over power, wealth, and status. Governments lurch from one crisis to the next, eventually dealing with an individual Abramovitch but barely addressing the structural issues that allowed a person whose wealth has such corrupt sources to launder their reputation for so long. This is a tragedy of provision where concentrations of wealth in the hands of a few rule-breakers harm the capacity of the collective to provide for all. Modern liberal democracies suppose they have the sovereign power to end this tragedy, this scarcity, but in fact preside over economies of profound injustice. The Christian hope is that we are in transition away from this tragedy: we are aware of the tragic form, and we know its arbitrary victims, as in Christ and since Christ they have been revealed to us. We strive to enact forms of transition as "the creation waits with eager longing for the revealing of the children of God" (Rom 8:19). This final chapter explores the pre-history of that end: the tragedy of the commons, its form in the climate-change catastrophe, and, via Northcott and Gorringe, the political means and theological directions by which the tragedy may be overcome. These means are found in civil society, but we must be constantly self-critical of our attempts to achieve these ends or risk falling into the realm of mythology and becoming part of the problem.

The tragedy of provision

Students of security explicitly or implicitly recognize that the question of provision is a tragic one. Definitions of societal, economic, and environmental security are typically constrained—just as in military and political security—by the atomistic Schmittian distinction of friend/enemy, or included/excluded. Ole Waever, who was one of the founders of the influential Copenhagen School of Security Studies (as we saw in chapter 5), defines societal security as "the ability of *a society* to persist in its essential character under changing conditions and possible or actual threats."[4] Similarly, a common definition of economic security identifies it as "safeguarding the structural integrity and prosperity-generating capabilities and interests *of a politico-economic entity.*"[5] Not only are these definitions exclusively focused on the threat to a specified human community or communities from a distinct threat (whether it is another community or an external threat), they are clearly distinct from one another. What is good for economic security (in the extraction industries) may be bad for environmental security. A possible solution to environmental security (migration of people or the surrendering of land to the sea) may cause societal insecurity. Here is a broader truth about the scarcity- and insecurity-inducing practices of all market economics and the pursuit of trade. Homo economicus, in the face of scarcity, and wherever possible, consumes relentlessly and thereby reproduces the very problem she seeks to overcome.[6] "The result," Daniel Bell argues, "is desire driven by fear of loss into a frenetic search for security in the face of both our hostile environment and other humans, who are likewise scrambling to secure what they can under conditions of scarcity."[7]

Security theorists have picked apart this gloomy prognosis conceptually. They have shown how security professionals rely on static conceptions of the referent object (the society, the business) when their nature shift all the time.[8] They have pointed out that we have an anthropomorphic bias (why environmental security for *people* and not ecological security more broadly?).[9] In quite neoliberal terms, they have argued that securing an economic actor is, at a basic level, a violation of the principles of the market economy.[10] In fact, long-term inequalities between the owners of capital and labor denote structural conflict between classes that is endogenous to the system, i.e., generated by the market itself. Piketty's *Capital in the Twenty-First Century* argues that return on capital for the rich in the form of profits, rents, or interest income is around 5 percent per annum. By contrast, real

4. Wæver et al., *Identity, Migration and the New Security Agenda*, 23.
5. Dent, "Economic Security," 244.
6. Cavanaugh, *Being Consumed*, 91.
7. Bell, *The Economy of Desire*, 115.
8. McSweeney, *Security, Identity, and Interests*.
9. McDonald, "Climate Change and Security."
10. Buzan et al., *Security*.

wages for the majority have stagnated since the inflation of the 1970s and subsequent weakening of the unions and deregulation in the 1980s. The mid-twentieth century—when this was not the case—was a historical exception. We are returning to the global norm of very high wealth inequality.[11] As an editorial in the business-friendly magazine the *Economist* argued in 2013,

> The scale and breadth of this squeeze are striking. And the consequences are ugly. Since capital tends to be owned by richer households, a rising share of national income going to capital worsens inequality. . . . Politically, that is dangerous, and is producing a lot of particularly polarized debate. The left blames fat-cat firms and the weakness of unions for workers' declining share. Those on the right, if they acknowledge the problem at all, argue that the fault lies with big government and high taxes.[12]

The evidence of the significance of inequality is vast. Everything from the prevalence of teenage pregnancy to access to clean water are shaped by structural inequality.[13]

This dynamic of inequality is present across societal, economic, and environmental security concerns at a truly global scale. It is particularly acute if our reference point is that period after the Second World War, which Piketty identifies as the exception. Rising inequality correlates with rising household debt, which in turn puts banks at risk and causes the systemic financial crisis we saw in 2007–9, the worst since that around the Wall Street Crash of 1929. It is the very rich that deploy offshore companies for the purpose of tax avoidance by big corporates in democracies and the acquisition of enormous secret fortunes in kleptocracies. Trillions of dollars are held offshore and, consequently, hundreds of billions of dollars are lost from the public finances every year.[14] At the same time, the risk-based system for identifying money laundering through shell companies and banks is entirely risk-insensitive, being unable to identify suspicious transactions[15] and being manipulated by effective "enablers" who protect kleptocrats from foreign regulators and investigators.[16] Such findings suggest the systemic and enduring nature of inequality in the global economy.

11. Piketty, *Capital in the Twenty-First Century*.
12. The Economist, "A Shrinking Slice."
13. Pickett and Wilkinson, *The Spirit Level*.
14. Tax Justice Network, "Tax Avoidance and Evasion."
15. Findley, Nielson, and Sharman, *Global Shell Games*.
16. Heathershaw et al., *The UK's Kleptocracy Problem*.

These inequalities are particularly visible in humanity's relationship to the environment. In Hurricane Katrina, New Orleans, August 2005, "age- and race-associated poverty may have increased the vulnerability of these populations or limited their ability to evacuate."[17] However, annual deaths due to poor water quality in the world's wealthiest countries are negligible while in low- and middle-income countries there are an estimated 842,000 due to preventable problems of hygiene and poor sanitation, including 361,000 preventable deaths in under-fives.[18] This stress in the human and physical ecosystem creates lines of conflict. Regarding global heating, its causes are also shaped by inequality. The wealthiest 10 percent produce around 50 percent of the CO_2 emissions, while the poorest 50 percent just about 10 percent of CO_2 emissions.[19] While so-called "water wars" are rare and frequently exaggerated by politicians and experts,[20] longitudinal data shows that each degree of warmer temperature and more extreme rainfall increases the median frequency of interpersonal violence by 4 percent and intergroup conflict by 14 percent.[21]

In these figures the link between inequality and insecurity is indisputable. The core security problem then is neither the threat to a specific economic group nor the general lack of resources for a growing population but is a matter of provision: the failure of the common or public good. The form this takes is the politically constructed wealth of the few and poverty of the many; in the middle, billions compete to be winners. This problem was first conceptualized in William Forster Lloyd's *Two Lectures on the Checks to Population* of 1832, and more recently framed as "the Tragedy of the Commons."[22] In the tragedy, each personal gain creates the loss of common-pool resources. It is not a matter of privatization versus nationalization, as the political economy is far more complicated than that. Any system of regulated cooperation risks abuse (free riders). However, failing to establish any such credible system creates a panoply of local solutions and non-solutions. This is where we have arrived regarding the premier political problem of our age.

17. Brunkard, Namulanda, and Ratard, "Hurricane Katrina Deaths, Louisiana, 2005."
18. Prüss-Ustün, Annette, et al., "Burden of Disease from Inadequate Water."
19. Oxfam, "World's Richest 10% Produce Half of Carbon Emissions."
20. Katz, "Hydro-Political Hyperbole."
21. Hsiang, Burke, and Miguel, "Quantifying the Influence of Climate on Human Conflict."
22. Hardin, "The Tragedy of the Commons."

The climate-change catastrophe

The tragedy of the commons is now seeing its nadir in climate change—widely regarded as the greatest security threat the planet has ever faced. Theories of global warning began to be mooted in the early twentieth century. Advancements in data collection and modeling in the 1970s led to dire projections and eventually warnings to policy-makers, such as those of NASA's James Hanson in his 1988 testimony to the US Congress. Yet progress to reduce carbon dependency has been painfully slow; in the industrial era, more carbon has been emitted in the thirty+ years since Hanson's warning than in the two hundred+ years preceding it. The latest projections of climate change (AR6) suggests that catastrophic warming of more than 2 degrees is more likely than not to be reached in the period 2041–60, even if atmospheric concentration of carbon is kept at current levels.[23] To do this, emissions would need to be dramatically reduced, even below the estimated 8 percent drop for 2020 during the COVID-19 pandemic.[24] In 2021, emissions grew again. If emissions return to their historical growth trajectory, global heating that threatens the survival of the human species will occur before the end of the twenty-first century, perhaps by the early 2060s.[25] This means a temperature increase of 3°C above preindustrial, which will result in an additional one to four billion people facing water shortages, and 150 to 550 million additional people being at risk of hunger.[26]

But there is a great deal of uncertainty in such figures. The situation could get much worse much quicker. Already, thirty-three mainly Middle Eastern and Asian states are predicated by the World Resources Institute to face extremely high water stress by 2040—meaning they will have insufficient water to sustain their populations—while many other countries including China, India, and the United States will face high-water stress leading to significant internal migration within the next two decades.[27] Some research suggests that a series of "tipping points"—such as the loss of arctic sea ice and the melting of northern permafrost—may already be leading to a point of no return for the Anthropocene.[28] Even if such "tipping points" have yet to be reached, and even if UN FPCC magically leads to binding commitments about extraction (keeping coal, oil, and gas in the

---

23. IPCC, *Climate Change 2021*.
24. Lucas, "Risking the Earth Part 1," 3.
25. Betts et al., "When Could Global Warming Reach 4° C?"
26. Lucas, "Risking the Earth," 7.
27. Maddocks et al., "Ranking the World's Most Water-Stressed Countries."
28. Lenton, "Beyond 2°C: Redefining Dangerous Climate Change."

ground) not just emissions (how much and how they are consumed), a huge degradation of the earth's ability to provide for itself and for humankind is already underway. Other climate scientists argue that "the earth's climate is fast approaching a large-scale state transition, if indeed it has not already crossed the critical threshold" and that stabilizing "at 1.5°C or 2°C will not be sufficient to avert the possibility of catastrophic climate change by the end of the century."[29] Stabilizing at 1.5°C or 2°C is simply impossible without dramatic and immediate action.[30]

Those solutions that are proposed remain within the framework of the market. In this vein, the UN FPCC conferences have long attempted to address the tragedy of the commons directly by introducing nationally determined contributions—with agreement on the principle affirmed in the Paris Climate Accords of 2015. However, market-based solutions, such as carbon trading as a response to climate change, have been shown to have a small effect on emissions in the absence of a strict ceiling of carbon usage and mechanisms of enforcement that might hypothetically overcome the free-rider problem.[31] These are yet to be widely introduced. Nor are they likely to be when we consider that many states—including the middle-income countries and oil and gas producers like Nigeria, Russia, and Kazakhstan—are run by wealthy elites benefitting from their extraction economies. The national oil companies of these and other petro-states control over 60 percent of the world's oil reserves—compared to less than 20 percent that is controlled by the multinational oil majors such as Exxon-Mobil and Shell—and they are committed to extracting every last drop from the ground.[32] Politically, these states and their companies function as kleptocracies, vividly described by Oliver Bullough as governments of "greedy politicians at the top and pyramids of underlings beneath them, with each layer stealing in turn."[33]

In this "geopolitics of a slow catastrophe,"[34] political elites have tended to fall back on the techno-optimism of carbon capture, super-efficient renewable energy and storage, and the new mantra of "net zero." By these means, we are told, economies will thrive, elites or wannabe elites may aspire to the trappings of the wealthy, and environments can still be protected. At the same time, an increasing number of Western secular voices fall into

29. Lucas, "Risking the Earth," 5.
30. *Economist*, "Nationally Determined Contributors," 47.
31. Bayer and Aklin, "The European Union Emissions Trading System."
32. *Economist*, "Nationally Determined Contributors," 47–49.
33. Bullough, *Moneyland*, 26.
34. Northcott, *A Political Theology of Climate Change*, 1.

the eco-pessimism symbolized by Hollywood movies from *The Day After Tomorrow* (2004) to *Don't Look Up* (2022), the post-apocalyptic visions of novels such as Cormac McCarthy's *The Road* (2006) and John Lanchester's *The Wall* (2019), or the increasingly alarming warnings from the nonagenarian David Attenborough and teenage Greta Thunberg. There is currently little place for theology in these global debates, although many theologians, including both Northcott and Gorringe, count as eco-pessimists (or what Michael Budde calls the "We're f***ed brigade").[35] There is no eschaton in the naturalism of either techno-optimism or eco-pessimism. The Revelation of St. John's vision of a new heaven and new earth is seen by many as a supernatural departure from reality that can only be visited upon us by an act of God. Conversely, it is this apocalypticism that leads some in evangelical and Pentecostal churches to welcome global heating as heralding the second coming of Christ. But both techno-optimists and eco-pessimists, both scientists and Pentecostals share one thing in common: a natural/supernatural dualism that holds back our understanding of what's at stake in environmental security.

Michael Northcott's post-Christendom climate apocalypse

By contrast, most theologians avoid the dualisms of natural/supernatural and replace them with an alternative apocalyptic of Christ/Antichrist. Michael Northcott has addressed the science and politics of climate change directly for more than thirty years. He is one of the world's most pre-eminent theologian of environmental security.[36] In his first major book on the topic, *The Environment and Christian Ethics* (1996), he identified the tragedy of the commons not as a constant but as a function of secular modernity, scientific naturalism, and industrialization. Let us remind ourselves again, with Taylor, that such secular modernity grew out of Christendom. Features that were emergent in late-Christendom intensified in post-Christendom. They have freed mankind from the limits imposed by being under God—the law, the prophets, and the notion of a covenantal polity—to exploit the environment and become "detached" from the land. "Israel's poets and prophets read Israel's relationship with God through her experience

---

35. Budde, *Foolishness to Gentiles*, 24.

36. While he does not use the term "security," his work is clear that the job of Christian ethics is not merely to identify and undertake virtuous practice but to witness to the world about the causes and solutions to this existential threat to the planet.

of climate," Northcott remarks.[37] While recognizing that the pre-cursors of climate change—deforestation and agriculture—began much earlier, climate change itself is most directly a product of the secular economy and its mantra of personal choice. "The rise of individualism," he notes, "is closely associated with the quest for material fulfilment through ecologically damaging consumerism."[38] It is clear to Northcott that a new ethic of ecology cannot be established without a moral foundation; by the time such an ethic becomes a material necessity, it will be too late.

Northcott's work on the environment culminated in *The Political Theology of Climate Change* (2013). This book is especially important to us as it traverses history and political theory to establish climate change as a pre-eminent problem of security after Christendom. Northcott takes the journey from the Hebrew and New Testament scriptures to contemporary ecclesial form and practice, as all political theology must do. But he charts a rather different course, that flirts with Schmitt and apocalypticism thereby dismissing the secular and the liberal in entirety. Our route from the same biblical beginnings has taken in Girard and Yoder, whose insights allow us to identify both salvation history and sinful rebellion, both hope and disorder, in the emergence of the secular liberalism. But the reasons to go along the route we have followed are not merely to make us all sleep better at night. By comparing our route to Northcott's extant Christendom thinking we will see that post-Christendom thought offers a more compelling account of our secular predicament and security challenges.

For Northcott, the church's politics are necessarily eschatological in that "the political theology of the New Testament and the early Church involved no geopolitical claims other than apocalyptic ones about the end of the world and the revelation of who is really Lord instead of the emperor."[39] The church offers less a solution to the crisis of climate change than it's ultimate ecological end: the restoration of the created order, revealed in the risen body of Christ, and experienced politically through the church.[40] The modern nation-state as the premier actor of politics and the entity most responsible for climate change is, by contrast, "a cultural and secular, rather than created and providential, agency in human and earth history."[41] Without heavenly as well as earthly responsibilities, we cannot expect states to

---

37. Northcott, *A Political Theology*, 33.
38. Northcott *The Environment and Christian Ethics*, 41.
39. Northcott, *A Political Theology*, 35.
40. Northcott, *A Political Theology*, 38.
41. Northcott, *A Political Theology*, 48.

take ecological duties seriously. They simply lack the perspective of the created order and the ultimate purpose of its restoration.

For Schmitt, we may recall from chapter 3, such perspective is found in *nomos* ("a bounded space of political cohabitation")[42] and its purpose found in *katechon* (the restrainer of empires and powers that holds back the end of the world).[43] Schmitt's interpretation of Catholic natural law, which Northcott draws upon heavily, emerges from this perspective and purpose. While Christendom's *katechon* was the Holy Roman Empire, in the secular age it might be Nazi Germany, as Schmitt once thought, or the United States, as Schmitt came to believe along with conservative American Catholics in the post-war period. Northcott notes,

> For Schmitt, the United States was the only global power after the Second World War capable of donning the mantle of the *katechon* and restraining the tensions arising from the post-Christendom borderless condition; and, on the dominant reading of the history of the Cold War, *he was right*.[44]

As such, the US is also, "on Schmitt's account, the one nation whose influence on the globe is capable of generating a coherent and collective response to the problem of global climate change."[45]

Northcott's affirmation of Schmitt and US leadership here is odd given the obviously Christendom framing in terms of the *katechon* and the nation. From the perspective of the post-Cold War era of rising carbon emissions and rising Russian and Chinese power, neither the United States nor any other state has fulfilled this hope of a national restrainer emerging. But the problem here is not the lack of fulfilment but the false hope. What Northcott identifies as "the post-Christendom borderless condition" appears tragic—the tragedy of great power politics of which political realists constantly warn. Northcott agrees with Schmitt and the realists that the geopolitics of climate change tend toward destruction insofar as they require "a fearful Leviathan or *katechon* restraining the contest for the earth's last habitable lands and potable water."[46] And yet this Leviathan fails because of the fundamental misconception—a late-Christendom myth perhaps—that the state might ever adopt ethics of ecological security.

---

42. Northcott, *A Political Theology*, 224.
43. Northcott, *A Political Theology*, 221; Schmitt, *Nomos*, 60.
44. Northcott, *A Political Theology*, 237.
45. Northcott, *A Political Theology*, 230.
46. Northcott, *A Political Theology*, 241.

The failure of the nations to act for the global common good of a stable climate, and for the interests of future generations, is a powerful instance of the failure of political judgement conceived in economic stick terms as a means of deliberation on costs and benefits where, in the absence of an overarching biological and/or religious narrative of human origins and destiny, no larger agreement about moral or political ends can be assumed.[47]

This leaves us with the fundamental problem of security after Christendom. There is no covenant, no wider agreement, and no basis to attain one.

Northcott finds himself in a double bind. On the one hand, there is little historical basis and no foundation for such a covenant outside of reconciliation through Christ in the new aeon. Such a diagnosis inevitably leads Northcott to an apocalyptic reading of climate change. He turns to MacIntyre to argue convincingly that the modern state is incapable of inculcating virtues as the classical polis did because it fails to recognize biospheric constraints on consumption. There are "no sacrifices the state can ask of its corporations or citizens for these common goods other than their preparedness where necessary to defend the security of the state."[48] Moreover, as we have seen with Girard, the basis of this sacrificial order is breaking down in the conditions of the secular age. On the other hand, Northcott turns to Jürgen Moltmann's critique of Schmitt's pagan desire for Leviathan and for a covenantal politics. The emergence since the sixteenth century of a generalized right to resist the Leviathan ('the mortal God"), which Moltmann identifies with the Calvinist theology of covenant,[49] points us toward new political and theological grounds for human security without a security state.[50] However, human security is an ontologically-individualist rights-based narrative that cannot overcome the tragedy of the commons. The peril of Leviathan's failure can only be met in a new covenant formed of a shared global faith.

This is, in essence, the politics without state sovereignty that is the promise of the liberal constitutional state, which itself arose out of, in Moltmann's claim, "Jewish and Christian existence in the modern body politic" and is thereby a secular product of late-Christendom.[51] A political theology fit for purpose is one that rejects both extremes: on the one hand, the unity of church and state (a new one-kingdom Leviathan) and, on the other, the

---

47. Northcott, *A Political Theology*, 252.
48. Northcott, *A Political Theology*, 264.
49. Moltmann, "Covenant or Leviathan?"
50. Moltmann, "Covenant or Leviathan?," 28.
51. Moltmann, "Covenant or Leviathan?," 43.

privatization of faith (the secularist variant of two-kingdoms theology). The post-Christendom position is that the security of provision is impossible without what Moltmann identifies as "the impact of Christianity on politics, which means the desacralization of the state, the relativization of forms of political order, and the democratization of political decisions."[52] And to address climate change, all this must be advanced at the global scale and in short order. Representative democracy of the liberal-constitutional state is not sufficient in itself; direct democracy is required.[53] Northcott concludes "that there is a messianic alternative to the imperial *katechon*, and that it may yet draw the nations from the Babylon of fossil fueled economic growth and heedless consumerism to a new covenant or community between creatures, humans, and the heavenly realms."[54] However, caught between the idolatries of Schmitt and the market, he only begins to sketch out what form this messianic alternative might take (see below). Philosophically, we remain stuck between the opposing predicaments of secular individualism and a Christendom order.

Tim Gorringe and the "world turned upside down"

Perhaps one of those thinkers and practitioners who has thought hardest about what this means in practice is Tim Gorringe. Through theology and praxis, Gorringe has come to understand acutely that any messianic alternative to a politics of sovereignty must eschew individualism, but that this places countercultural demands on the contemporary individual. In the urgent and excoriating *The World Made Otherwise* (2018), inspired by the work of the Dutch theologian Ton Veerkamp, *Die Welt Anders*,[55] Gorringe surveys an extraordinary range of social science and political philosophy, but he begins by railing against the incapacity of today's expressive individuals to respond to the climate apocalypse. On the exemplar of hypocrisy that is airmiles he notes:

> The suggestion that one ought perhaps not to fly is regarded as absurd. [The British journalist and activist] George Monbiot spoke of the "love miles" people incurred to visit distant relatives. But in the academic community, at least, we have to speak of "ego miles," as tens of thousands of academics, including those who specialize in warning about the problems of climate

52. Moltmann, "Covenant or Leviathan?," 43–44.
53. Moltmann, "Covenant or Leviathan?," 45.
54. Northcott, *A Political Theology*, 267.
55. Gorringe, *The World Made Otherwise*, 3.

change, jet off annually to vast conferences which are not primarily about the exchange of ideas but about establishing and maintaining reputations and providing the "esteem indicators" universities demand. Middle class families take weddings in the West Indies, or foreign holidays, not simply for granted but as a basic human right.[56]

As an academic whose career has formed since the 1990s, the era of academic "internationalization," this author is not immune to the hypocrisy of "ego miles." Gorringe is from an earlier generation and this work stands as the culmination of theological thought and political praxis. His fire is aimed at those experts, corporations, and governments that preach market-based solutions—with little evidence that they can possibly achieve the radical reductions in consumption needed—as if such individual sacrifices are unnecessary.

For Gorringe, as with Northcott, responses to the climate apocalypse cannot be individualist—and thus require a very different polity to the market economy and democracy of the liberal secular imaginary. A transitional world toward a new heaven and new earth is necessarily one where energy will be more expensive. In the current context this suggests not an amelioration of the crisis of provision but its exacerbation, as our rampant inequality will cause fuel poverty for the many while the rich will continue to use in excess. Scarcity makes neighbors into potential enemies as subsistence farmers compete over depleted water flows—a common cause of localized violence across the Global South—while tensions emerge in the global North between those who can afford to be virtuous and those who can't. The logic of mimetic desire suggests that the future without mediating institutions of provision will look increasingly like the pagan war of all against all that Hobbes' Leviathan was imagined to prevent, but in reality exacerbates. The messianic alternative eschews the false anthropology on which Hobbes and Schmitt rest their claims. "The true apocalyptic way is the refusal to resist the enemy," Northcott remarks, "and instead to recognize a friend in the enemy by loving one's neighbor as oneself."[57] This covenantal promise "is fulfilled in an ecclesia which stays true to the suffering Messiah, and not the ecclesia which becomes a state or an empire."[58]

However, the practical challenges that such hope for new communities of democracy face are immense. With this political model, on current trends, civilizational collapse of some form is probable. "The question,"

---

56. Gorringe, *The World Made Otherwise*, 33.
57. Northcott, *A Political Theology*, 284.
58. Northcott, *A Political Theology*, 287.

Gorringe argues, "is how we manage politically without a regression into barbarism."[59] The academic literature on the topic suggests the three most-likely scenarios: "warlordism, authoritarian governmental response, and a reversion to simpler societies."[60] The first two of these options are prevalent, as discussed across chapters 6 and 7. In the context of climate apocalypse, they are imaginatively captured by George Miller and Byron Kennedy's *Mad Max* films and the P. D James novel *Children of Men*, set in Australia and the UK respectively. As both scenarios are clearly undesirable, the "messianic alternative" is to move toward simpler societies tied to the land and looking up to God. However, this does not mean a return to established governance and imperial economies of Christendom and other models of organized religion. Gorringe cites the final paragraph of *After Virtue*, where MacIntyre advocates "the construction of local forms of community within which civility and the intellectual and moral life can be sustained through the new dark ages which are already upon us."[61] But decent forms of community that avoid the temptation to demagoguery and dictatorship—and thus the security of the few—"involve maintaining, and in fact deepening, forms of democracy."[62]

The question arises as to whether there is either a secular or sacred foundation for such deepened democracy. Most states are not (and never have been) democracies. Today, autocracy has been advancing for two decades. Most states that are categorized as democracies are semi-democracies, and some of these are dominated by kleptocratic cabals and are effectively electoral dictatorships. In the private sector, democracy is even less common and is highly restricted to shareholder meetings in public companies or employee-ownership models, which are extremely rare. Democracy is fragile and rare because to be sustained it requires a fundamental commitment to human equality—not merely assent to a nominal "equality of opportunity"—which most governments and businesses lack. For Gorringe, the origins of this commitment are not secular—in Rousseau and other Enlightenment philosophers—but sacred, and specifically Christian and biblical. In Gorringe's telling, this commitment was neutered by the ideas of Augustine and Aquinas about order and hierarchy, leading to a delay in the emergence of democracy until Christendom declined.[63] Not until "post-

---

59. Gorringe, *The World Made Otherwise*, 118.
60. Gorringe, *The World Made Otherwise*, 28.
61. Gorringe, *The World Made Otherwise*, 31–32.
62. Gorringe, *The World Made Otherwise*, 155.
63. Gorringe, *The World Made Otherwise*, 170–73. This is comparable to Girard's argument about "sacrificial Christianity" (see chapter 10).

Christendom" imaginaries emerged in the thought and practice of Reformation figures like John Wycliffe, William Tyndale, and Gerald Winstanley did true equality reemerge as sacrificial and established church broke down. This is the radical model of equality (Acts 2:44–45) deployed by dissenting Christians since the first century, most especially the True Levellers, whose ballad of "world turned upside down" (Acts 17:5) was sang out in the English revolution. Gorringe argues,

> Although the Church has, probably from the beginning, compromised, and sometimes inverted, the gospel, the texts rise up against it. It is questionable whether there is a secular argument for equality which is as powerful as the theological. What I call "the gospel of equality" is, in fact, implicit in each article of the creed, itself a kind of thumbnail sketch of the biblical narrative.[64]

While the church of European empires inverted the gospel, faithful missions unshackled from the imaginaries of Christendom preached equality to transform societies in Africa and India and establish the seeds of democracy.[65] It is therefore misleading to assert the exclusivity of the biblical message as some neo-Christendom ideologues do or dismiss Christian mission as unequivocally imperial as some post-Christendom thinkers do. The reality is more complex because the impact of and resistance to Christendom has varied.

Given that such variation is an enduring feature of political practice, we should not fetishize any model of democracy, especially participative or direct democracy, which Gorringe recognizes has long been considered a form of anarchism and a route to fanaticism.[66] Unlike secular models of the anarchist movements, the democracy and community of ecclesia is nested within the global church and its sense that the temporal is provisional and the eternal beyond human grasp. However, Christian anarchism's history suggests it has often found itself pitted against the church.[67] The great Russian author and anarchist Lev Tolstoy, perhaps the most influential modern Christian anarchist, who had a great influence on nonviolent resistance after Christendom, was famously excommunicated by the Russian Orthodox church—which cleaved to Christendom thought—for rejecting both church and state.[68] His project in Russia was stillborn and overcome by Bolshevism.

64. Gorringe, *The World Made Otherwise*, 162.

65. Comaroff and Comaroff, *Of Revelation and Revolution*; Gorringe, *The World Made Otherwise*, 163.

66. Gorringe, *The World Made Otherwise*, 181.

67. Marshall, *Demanding the Impossible*, 74–85.

68. Marshall, *Demanding the Impossible*, 82.

To avoid these concerns with direct democracy, Gorringe argues that size is crucial and the principle of subsidiarity—where all things that can be are done locally—is essential.[69] This then leads to the familiar discussion about whether forms of "deliberative democracy," political education, and the reformation of virtues are necessary for such local units to avoid factionalism on the one hand and the trivialities of parochialism on the other.[70] In short, a transition economy must be practical and local while grounded in the metaphysical and global. The pathway of the emergence of such an economy is not, however, the instantiation of an ecclesia that defeats kleptocrats and disregards consumers. Rather, kleptocrats and consumers inevitably pass away as the conditions for their theft and consumption cease to exist. It is the modeling of alternative economies that is the task of the church in transition. But complete transition—the defeat of the beastly powers—is the work of *Christ*, not the action of the faithful community. The ecclesia must prophetically discern that political change and be ready to inaugurate a new world.

Providential Transition or the Ark of Redemption?

Both Northcott and Gorringe finish their books on how new political communities may form in response to climate change with the *Transition town movement* (TTM), an example of the messianic alternative, desacralized and democratic. TTM is focused on the emergence of local economies and even currencies that are tied to the land and far less resource-intensive than the global economy through green start-ups and the transition of existing businesses. It began in Totnes, near Exeter, UK, after its founder Rob Hopkins moved from Ireland, and quickly spread so that by 2013 there were more than four hundred groups in the UK and nine hundred worldwide.[71] Hopkins framed the TTM as "the foundation for one of the most important social, political, and cultural movements of the 21st century" and the basis for "an extraordinary renaissance—economic, cultural and spiritual."[72] Gorringe was a key figure in the movement in Totnes. He and his co-author Rosie Beckham, in their manual for churches, present the Transition movement as offering "a course between the apocalyptic (social chaos, warlordism) and the starry eyed (a hi tech, zero carbon future)."[73] By 2023, TTM

---

69. Gorringe, *The World Made Otherwise*, 182–83.
70. Gorringe, *The World Made Otherwise*, 183–91.
71. Gorringe and Beckham, *The Transition Movement*, 1.
72. Boudinot and LeVasseur, "'Grow the Scorched Ground Green.'"
73. Gorringe and Beckham, *The Transition Movement*, 9.

seems to have lost a great deal of its early enthusiasm and has increasingly fallen back on partnerships with and grants from the state rather than genuinely local initiatives. Many of its members now put their energies into the anarchist movement Extinction Rebellion.[74] We might ask how we avoid falling back on the framework of late-Christendom where we outsource our ecological security to the state. Even Northcott seems to doubt, as he remarks toward the end of *A Political Theology of Climate Change* that "only the nations acting together in a concerted fashion" can restrain the corporations of consumption.[75]

As an active member of TTM for years, and a theologian who does not entertain Schmittian thought, Gorringe has no time for residual Christendom ideas. However, he remains sanguine about what TTM can achieve, based on his experience as a participant.

> How far [TTM] changes mass perceptions of political culture is another matter however: in my experience it largely remains the domain of a small group of highly committed activists. Even in Totnes, the center of the movement, full of highly talented and engaged people working at Transition full time, ordinary citizens can be completely vague about what Transition stands for.[76]

Such anecdotes demonstrate that even the most intense experiments in participatory democracy are not necessarily much more participative than representative democracy. For transition to succeed in the world, it is implied, an *inner* transition must occur. Gorringe and Beckham ask: "What are the spiritual resources of the Transition process? How do we keep going when the challenges seem so immense? How do we avoid despair?"[77] These questions are acute for a political movement "which does not identify an adversary, does not think in terms of conflict, and for which the local community is the primary referent."[78] The endurance and success of such a movement would refute findings from the social movement theory that suggests they require elite buy-in and resources to be sustainable. In the absence of resources and sovereignties, transition demands *cultural* and *spiritual* transformation. Gorringe identifies this in Christian and realist terms: "dimensions of resilience—solidarity, compassion, an ability to cope

---

74. This observation is based on a personal communication from Tim Gorringe.
75. Northcott, *A Political Theology*, 312.
76. Gorringe, *The World Made Otherwise*, 324–25.
77. Gorringe and Beckham, *The Transition Movement for Churches*, 11.
78. Gorringe, *The World Made Otherwise*, 331.

with tragedy, a sense of purpose, and an understanding of faith, hope and agape."[79]

Transition then is both rational and revelational, both evidence- and faith-based. The evidence must relate both to the effectiveness of transition and the role of Christian faith in bringing that about. Participant-observational studies and even a cursory glance of documents from the Totnes TTM indicate that engagement by its participants is active, affective, and normative.[80] Boudinot and LeVasseur's study of Totnes TTM found, "a myriad of both spiritual and religious beliefs and practices, ranging from Tibetan Buddhist to Pagan to Quaker," but "a shared set of religious values and ethics" underlying that diversity.[81] "All participants," they argue, "showed a personal motivation to be a steward of the Earth."[82] Such views are not necessarily sub-Christian but are universalist in ways that would challenge much orthodox Christian theology. Nevertheless, churches are major actors in TTM. In my own church's participation in Exeter Community Energy, a neighboring and TTM-linked movement to Totnes, a stewardship rationale was frequently cited. Transition, Boudinot and LeVasseur argue, "is asking earth citizens to eschew secular, industrial lifeways based on views of an inert, desecrated natural world and replace them with vibrant, reskilled community-based lifestyles that situate human communities within a sacralized landscape."[83] A call to faith is *integral* to a radical response to the climate emergency.

The church is in essence a transition movement, much of which long forgot the fact and became a movement for retrenchment. In post-Christendom terms, it must be prepared to work with other movements of all faiths and none under an order of providence. However, in our apocalyptic times, we must also be aware that the church's primary place remains in the order of redemption. "My sense is that our energy should go into Transition type initiatives," Gorringe notes, "but at the same time we should 'dare to form communes,' because arks might be needed."[84] The metaphor of the ark is an obvious but helpful one in the context of climate change. "Forming communities which can carry people through really dark times cannot be accomplished by optimism," he remarks, "but only by a disciplined collective effort centered on a sober but hopeful spirituality, or as Christians would

---

79. Gorringe, *The World Made Otherwise*, 337.
80. Boudinot and LeVasseur, "Grow the Scorched Ground Green."
81. Boudinot and LeVasseur, "Grow the Scorched Ground Green," 390.
82. Boudinot and LeVasseur, "Grow the Scorched Ground Green," 390.
83. Boudinot and LeVasseur, "Grow the Scorched Ground Green," 397.
84. Gorringe, *The World Made Otherwise*, 373.

say, on a spirituality of cross and resurrection."[85] The challenge of provision after Christendom is to extricate our churches from reliance on the state and private sector for our economic and ecological security and recapture the vision of ecclesia given by Christ and the prophets.

From humanitarianism to hope

As with inclusion and protection, the advanced industrial powers that set the model for our secular age offer no more than a false promise of provision. The oft-stated goal of equality of opportunity remains far off. By contrast, the Torah and the New Testament combine to offer a very different model, one of abundance and equality. Tim Gorringe summarizes "the radicalization of the Deuteronomic imperatives" in the ecclesia of the New Testament and the early church. In this radicalization, "the program of Deuteronomy was deepened and extended to cover all people; it was no longer a program for Israel, but for all nations." What we need, argues Gorringe, is not the chimera of equality of opportunity, but "an attempt to structure the world economy around equality of outcome."[86] That surely requires nothing less than the utter transformation (that is, redemption) of the powers by the Lord of history. It is not for the church to initiate that process but to discern it and act according to the gospel hope. "The Christian," Cavanaugh argues, "is called not to replace one universal system with another, but to attempt to 'realize' the universal body of Christ in every particular exchange."[87] The metaphor he has recently offered for this role is that of "field hospital."[88]

However, such a framing rather understates the challenge for the church. From an eschatological perspective, there is little point engaging in practical political discussion of humanitarian trade-offs if the inclusion of migrants must take second place to the need to strengthen the border, or sustainable provision must sometimes be compromised due to the need for immediate protection from fuel poverty or food insecurity. For Moltmann, these domains are linked:

> The politics with which, if need be, justice and constitution are abolished in many countries, human rights are infringed and large parts of the poor are impoverished to safeguard the rich, and which in terms of Realpolitik are called "politics of national security," have become the politics of modern apocalyptic. The

---

85. Gorringe, *The World Made Otherwise*, 375.
86. Gorringe, *Capital and the Kingdom*, x, xi.
87. Cavanaugh, *Being Consumed*, 88.
88. Cavanaugh, *Field Hospital*.

hopeful start for "new frontiers" of social justice has given place to the resigned acceptance of the imminent, unavoidable final battle with the "kingdom of evil" in Armageddon.[89]

Speaking in the 1980s, Moltmann critically invokes the popular books of Hal Lindsay and the apocalyptic rhetoric of Ronald Reagan as emblematic of this national security apocalyptic (see chapter 9). Such chiliastic dogma of fear and dread lacks the hope of a faithfully Christian apocalyptic.

By contrast, this chapter has suggested that the church can participate in new models of security that are more than just martyrdom in the face of apocalyptic powers or a "field hospital" to those dying and wounded. Martyrdom and charity are necessary and of eschatological import, pointing to an alternative and beckoning its future, but they are not sufficient as practices of security that include, protect, and provide. Scholars like Northcott and Gorringe advocate a common treasury, as envisioned in Deuteronomy, and have sought to practice this through movements like TTM in response to the climate catastrophe for more than thirty years.[90] It is reasonable to conclude that they and others of all faiths and none are planting seeds of movements—locally based but globally connected—that may become the remaining basis for life in the world as dramatic climate change takes hold in the second half of this century. The state and the corporation will not only be unable to offer adequate provision to humanity, but they will also not be able to offer hope. And having known what was to come and having failed to act against the principal security threat of our time for generations, these institutions will increasingly face civil disobedience. As the climate-apocalyptic literature promises, humankind will search for meaning in sects and militant movements, including those of neo-Christendom. But it will be those who have faith in the restoration of creation after Christendom that will restore abundant provision in a new heaven and a new earth.

89. Moltmann, *Creating a Just Future*, 18.
90. Cavanaugh, *Being Consumed*, 87.

Conclusions

A Post-Christendom Approach to Security

The "questions" and "problems" of dissolving Christendom can now be seen for what they are, as judgments. They are judgments taking the form of demonic perversions: judgement on war, which is no longer a purposive and preservative activity governed by the doctrine of the just war, but has become an indiscriminate social convulsion; judgement on the state, in the form of an impending world state which may well be a more frightful concentration of tyrannical power than any we have yet experienced; judgement on nationalism, which has long been again a form of idolatry that was denounced by the prophets of the Old Testament; judgement on revolution, which has been swollen into the decisive factor of contemporary secular history and has produced a giant debased substitute for the church.

MARTIN WIGHT[1]

The church's first task is not to make the nation state system work, but rather to remind us that the nation, especially as we know it today, is not an ontological necessity for human living. The church, as an international society, is a sign that God, not nations, rules this world.

STANLEY HAUERWAS[2]

Where there is no vision, the people perish.

PROVERBS 29:18 (KJV)

---

1. Wight, "The Church, Russia and the West," 43.
2. Hauerwas, "The Church," 75.

On the Sunday of Orthodoxy, March 13, 2022, the "Declaration of the Orthodox Theologians on the Russian World" (hereafter the Declaration)[3] was issued, explicitly modeled on the Barmen declaration that opposed the Nazi worldview almost a century before. It was published in twenty languages, quickly collected almost 1,500 ecclesiastical and academic signatures, prompted ecumenical support from church leaders and theologians,[4] and accelerated an extant debate within the Orthodox world. The Declaration was against the "Russian World" and all forms of "ethnophyletism," a term used in the Orthodox world to denote a form of tribalism entailing the conflation between church and nation. The declaration notes the entwining of church and state, theology and international politics, stating, "Putin and Patriarch Kirill have used Russian World ideology as a principal justification for the invasion." Its authors note that the "Russian World" is articulated against an enemy, the West, "which has [according to the ideology] capitulated to 'liberalism,' 'globalization,' 'Christianophobia,' 'homosexual rights' promoted in gay parades, and 'militant secularism.'"[5] It is the prophetic role of the church to call out the heresy of such neo-Christendom ideology by reasserting gospel truths that security is not in Russia or Ukraine but in Christ. As the declaration states,

> We therefore condemn as non-Orthodox and reject any teaching which would subordinate the Kingdom of God, manifested in the One Holy Church of God, to any kingdom of this world seeking other churchly or secular lords who can justify and redeem us.[6]

The declaration gave moral and intellectual support to the moves to isolate the Moscow Patriarchate within the church. However, even some signatories subsequently sought to disassociate themselves from the explicitly post-Christendom framing of the Declaration, with the scholar Andrey Shishkov arguing "the idea of a 'symphony of authorities' is not criminal in itself as long as the church does not begin to support the morally unacceptable actions of the political regime."[7] Christendom dies hard.

3. Abatzidis et al., "A Declaration on the 'Russian World.'"
4. Hovorun, van der Tol, et al., "A Statement of Solidarity with the Orthodox Declaration."
5. Abatzidis et al., "A Declaration on the 'Russian World.'"
6. Abatzidis et al., "A Declaration on the 'Russian World.'"
7. Shishkov argues, "the introduction of the heresy of ethnophyletism into theological circulation is a stab in the back to Orthodox Ukrainians who are defending their lives and freedom with weapons in their hands." Shishkov, "Some Reflections on the Declaration."

The point here is that both legitimate Ukrainian resistance and demonic Russian aggression have ethnophyletist rationales that are commonplace across all autocephalous Orthodox churches. However, reducing the question of "symphony of authorities" to a matter of moral judgment rather sidesteps the theological problem of security after Christendom that faces the entire world. As the director of the Volos Academy for Theological Studies, Dr. Pantelis Kalaitzidis, argued in a lecture of May 2022, "the real challenge for Orthodoxy today is to formulate a theology of otherness and identity and to take seriously into account the consequences arising from it."[8] The security of ourselves and others, we might add, is not the security of Christendom *against the world*, but the security of *the world*, which is radically *included*, nonviolently *protected*, and abundantly *provisioned* by those acting in imitation of Christ according to his universal and eschatological purpose. As the powers are defeated, the attendant disorder becomes a problem for *all*. The states that raise boundaries against inclusion are those of neo-Christendom *and* of other faiths *and* secular nationalisms. The failure of war to protect, its increased incidence, and the modern rise in civilian deaths effects *everyone*. The tragedy of provision is truly global and *universal*.

A NEO-CHRISTENDOM SECURITY CRISIS

Russia's impending and then enacted invasion of Ukraine dominated the months in which this book was completed. This shattering war within the heartland of what was once Eastern Christendom has led to vociferous debate about how and why it happened, against the expectations of many. Liberals in International Relations decried Russia's unprovoked attack and favored the strongest military and economic measures in support of Ukraine on moral grounds. Some felt that the breakdown of NATO-Russia relations over many years were a harbinger to the conflict but argued optimistically that the crisis may galvanize the rules-based order.[9] By contrast, the secular realist John Mearsheimer has long argued that the expansion of NATO would always lead to a backlash by Russia as it disrupted the balance of power and thereby threatened the Kremlin's core security interests.[10] Classical Christian realists may too have recognized the instability of the balance but pointed to the failure of a holder of the balance—the United States—to

---

8. Volos Academy for Theological Studies, "The War in Ukraine."
9. Way, "The Rebirth of the Liberal World Order?"
10. Mearsheimer, "Why the Ukraine Crisis is the West's Fault."

providentially restrain Russia by judicious force of arms. However, all miss a truth that is clear to regional specialists: that Putin's strategic rationale of "great-powerness" (*velikaderzhavnost*) is primordialist and rooted in a perverted neo-Christendom theology.[11] For Vera Shevzov, Orthodox constructions of the Western other in Russia have ebbed and flowed in the Russian church-state since at least the thirteenth century and are "an ancient preoccupation."[12] Putin embarks very much from this preoccupation and while he miscalculated strategically, his strategy is consistent. Wars had been launched twice before, in Georgia (2008) and Ukraine (2014), with a similar rationale invoked.[13] The Kremlin's post-Soviet, post-secular, and neo-imperial ideology of itself—it's creed, culture, society, economy, and therefore its security—came up against Ukraine's own self-image and its unanticipated capacity to resist. The "Russian World" imaginary did not allow for a sovereign Ukrainian state and autocephalous church. Something had to give. In this sense, this is a war of neo-Christendom.

According to the framework elaborated in parts 1 and 2 of this book, the Christendom character of the war is clear. The "judgments" and "demonic perversions" after Christendom—of war, of the state, of nationalism, etc.[14]—are also judgments on Christendom and its extant ideologies. In 2022, some pointed to the instrumental adoption of theological language by the craven Russian political elite,[15] while others note the fertile ground for re-enchantment in a society traumatized by post-Soviet chaos and post-imperial decline.[16] Either way, the Russian Orthodox church participates in the Russian war machine via its priests and its convoluted rationales of a just war for civilization.[17] Vladimir Putin deploys explicitly religious language in his articulation of the "Russian World" that he claims to be securing. During Gorbachev's policy of openness (*glasnost*) and especially after 1991, there was an extraordinary re-enchantment of Russian life, the rediscovery of Russian Orthodox spirituality and heritage, and the return to ideas of "greater Russia."[18] The fracturing and decentering of the post-Soviet state and the emergence of a globalized Russian kleptocracy under Boris Yeltsin

---

11. Marten, "President Putin's Rationality and Escalation."
12. Shevzov, "Orthodox Constructions of the West in Russia."
13. Radnitz, "Vladimir Putin's Casus Belli for Invading Ukraine."
14. Wight, "The Church, Russia and the West," 43.
15. Shishkov, "Some Reflections on the Declaration."
16. Stoeckl, "The Russian Orthodox Church."
17. Adamsky, *Russian Nuclear Orthodoxy*.
18. Richters, *The Post-Soviet Russian Orthodox Church*.

and Vladimir Putin,[19] sustained by financial and legal services in the West,[20] was a powerful force fueling imaginaries of a centered and enchanted "Russian World." The church did not cause the war in Ukraine, but neo-Christendom ideology has provided motivation and legitimation.

Part 3 of this book sketched out the basis for resistance to such neo-Christendom ideology. Such resistance must begin with a recognition that "Russian World" is not a means to security under God but a beastly power in the service of Satan. The point here is not, in Niebuhrian vein, that the evil "Russian World" is relatively worse than benign "US-led international order" (although it is), but that the ideologies of both are idolatrous, and Christian worship in the name of either is *heretical*. Post-Christendom alternatives to such heresies are emerging and are being proclaimed. With respect to inclusion, Christians in Ukraine have worked across denominational boundaries to offer relief.[21] Anecdotally, the church elsewhere in Europe appears to have been disproportionately represented in the offering of homes and services to Ukrainian refugees and in proclaiming the need for open borders.[22] With respect to provision, Christian relief organizations, working alongside secular organizations, have been central in the humanitarian response, as they always are in emergency situations.[23] With respect to protection, the questions are most acute. Nonviolent resistance in Ukraine has been under-reported as it so often is in situations of armed conflict. Yurii Sheliazhenko, leader of the Ukrainian Pacifist Movement, observed in the violent early stages of the conflict that "Ukrainian civilians are changing street signs and blocking streets and blocking tanks, just staying in their way without weapons."[24] In Russia, nonviolent protests, including many dissenting Orthodox priests, led to fifteen thousand arrests in the first weeks of the invasion,[25] undermining the legitimate claim to a "special military operation," before a state crackdown slowed protests and arrests down to a trickle.

---

19. Belton, *Putin's People*.

20. Heathershaw et al., *The UK's Kleptocracy Problem*.

21. For example, the Dnipro Hope Mission, to which I am an international advisory board member.

22. In the UK, all major churches were quick to join government and relevant civil society organizations in offering to participate. CTBI, "Church Response to Russian Invasion of Ukraine."

23. Pope Francis' metaphor and William Cavanaugh's portrayal of the church as "field hospital" is illustrative here. Cavanaugh, *Field Hospital*.

24. Hill, "As a Christian Pacifist I Can't Encourage Ukrainians to Take up Arms."

25. OVD-Info, "Persecution for Anti-War Views."

Given the urgency of the crisis, these efforts are largely palliative and humanitarian. Classical Christian realism appears to offer a more effective and political response to the Ukraine crisis. Its authors may make the obvious remark that the protests of pacifists will not withstand Russian artillery and bombing. Nigel Biggar argues that Ukraine is fighting a just war and thus arming the Ukrainian state is right according to this "Christian teaching." And yet the points Biggar makes in support of this position—the Ukrainian state is better than the Russian one, it is for Ukrainians to decide whether to join Russia, etc.—are not distinctively *Christian* at all but simply morally instinctive and politically realist. A military response is just, Biggar tells us, insofar as "armed resistance by Ukraine intends to stop and reverse the grave injustice being perpetrated by Putin." External involvement by NATO must be limited: "it would be prudent to avoid direct conflict with Russian forces—and prudence is a Christian virtue."[26] It is more accurate to say that prudence is a *Christendom* virtue, with Aristotelian origins, that was developed by Augustine, Aquinas, and others to guide statecraft in the Christian empire. And such an empire no longer exists.

All the weaknesses of the just war position (see chapter 4) are reprised in Biggar's argument about Ukraine, most especially the moral and descriptive oversimplification and the failure to understand the beastly cycles of violence that occur in *all* wars, be they "just" or unjust. Twenty years on from the Western wars in Afghanistan and Iraq, which Biggar also defends as just, many hundreds of thousands of civilians have died, there is more and more evidence of Western forces torturing and executing prisoners,[27] and both countries have reverted to brutal dictatorships. Modern war simply *cannot* be limited in the way the just war theorists imagine. Those that support arming Ukraine in 2022 do so without strategy for conflict resolution and fail to acknowledge that *ceteris paribus* arms to Ukraine comes with devastating human costs and traumatic geopolitical consequences. They do so in the hope that advanced technology and economic support from the West, alongside Ukrainian patriotism and morale, will make the difference. The difference is primarily for the defense of the state not the protection of the people, especially males up to the age of sixty-five, who are legally required to remain in the country and be ready to fight. These are plausible positions, but they are not *Christian* ones.

26. Biggar, "This Christian Teaching."

27. An official Australian government inquiry found a practice of executions by their special forces. The US and UK have refused to conduct full inquiries, but a BBC investigation found fifty-four executions of prisoners by one unit in one six-month tour. O'Grady and Gunter, "SAS Unit Repeatedly Killed Afghan Detainees."

On the other hand, Christian pacifists must honestly recognize that, without such arms, Ukraine is likely to have lost the war by now and still many civilians would have died. For one Orthodox scholar, a more plausible and ecumenical response engages just peacemaking on the one hand and Christian realism on the other.[28] However, a properly Christian response must recognize that the work of Christ and his church in history is not to protect the sovereignty of one somewhat morally better state from the aggression of another. The Christian purpose of "peace among nations" does not equate to achieving victory in the wars of states. As Hauerwas remarks, *the work of the church is to be, do, and proclaim the gospel of peace for the nations*. The Christian security witness seeks to protect *the diversity of peoples* not the survival of individual states and regimes of power.[29] At the same time, examples such as the murder and torture of over a thousand civilians in Bucha in March 2022 provide an almost unanswerable case for the use of force to protect a people from genocide or other crimes against humanity.[30]

How we got here

A post-Christendom approach to security is a long-term project that works to delegitimize ideological-political institutions and present a practical vision of a future order that is just and sustainable. In this book we have merely sketched a prologue to this project of reconstructing an evangelical vision of global security after Christendom. While ubiquitous in modern political and academic International Relations discourse, security is little more than a derivative or even pejorative term in most theological studies. It is derivative of a political theology of Christendom in that classical Christian realists identify just wars and balances of powers by which security may be attained for brief periods before the next armed conflict, which is often worse than the last. Security is also derivative of the secular in that such putatively "Christian" reasoning retains little that is distinctively Christian at all. For post-Christendom thinkers and the peace church, meanwhile, "security" is a pejorative associated with secular realists and with little biblical basis. A peace witness, from such a perspective, is the opposite of security, requiring that true church willingly forego security and accept suffering.

However, both social science and theology, both evidence and logic, helped this book make the case that security is no chimera after Christendom

---

28. Hamalis, "Just Peacemaking and Christian Realism."
29. Hauerwas, "The Church," 75.
30. Williams and Caldwell, "Jus Post Bellum."

but can be practiced from a Christocentric view of the world. The case has been made across three moves. First, we have established that the historical circumstances known as "after Christendom" have had a considerable import for security and global politics. Christendom is not a Western affair, and, as an imagined community, it is not exclusively a matter of the past. The dialectical process of the centering and decentering of church and world, of eternal and temporal, which characterized Christendom for a millennium, was the engine for the emergence of the secular age and its security dynamics. It is still visible today in the artefacts of JWT and Christian realism and the resurgence of religion in international affairs. But that these secularized and ethnocentric Christian visions of inclusion, protection, and provision are losing ground to new visions of post-Christendom should not cause dismay. Highly decentered forms of Christendom that developed in the twentieth century—where the church remains formally privileged in places like the UK but in practice has little influence on culture, politics, and security—are not in themselves evidence of decline or concession to "liberalism." Rather, they are steps on the path back to proper relations between faith and government, where the church's role is *prophecy, not partnership*.

Second, we have offered a new analysis of the contemporary security environment that has emerged after Christendom. The secularization thesis and the revised theory of modernization are too linear to grasp the ebbs and flows of the secular age. There is a rhythm to the world today that is an echo of the drumbeat of the Christendom dialectic. A world recentered on the secular security state is necessarily decentered by the economic forces of capitalism and the cultural forces of postmodernity, which are the driving forces of the so-called "liberal international order" today. At the same time, people and communities who feel insecure due to security states, capital forces, and changing values strike back with neo-Christendom imaginaries, such as those offered sincerely or insincerely by a Trump or a Putin. Most fascinatingly, and beyond the scope of this book, there are cognates in other faiths—Islam and Judaism, Hinduism and Buddhism—where religious nationalisms are rife. Normative secular dismissals of God cannot explain these resurgences. Postmodern accounts explain neo-Christendom and cognate movements as artefacts, dismissing arguments about why they persistently return in new forms, some emancipatory and some regressive. The secular age has not overcome "religious violence." Violence is a constant across the secular and religious, taking different forms depending on whether and how the security order is more disenchanted or re-enchanted, recentered or decentered. Secular modes of security, be they realist or liberal, merely change the forms that violence takes.

Third, this book has suggested a new theory to account for these developments. This is a new Christian realism based on the person of Christ and the purpose of the powers. It is "new"—some might say foolhardy—in being overtly *Christo*-centric rather than state- and Euro-centric. Yet it remains a Christian realist account in that it sits within the logic of an Augustinian "two cities" theology. This book has not challenged the notion of two cities—for such a notion has a strong biblical basis. Rather, it has argued against any notion of a clear *separation* of church and world and/or an *equivalence* between church and government. The problem with imaginaries of Christendom is not that they envisage a relationship between the two but the harmonious and "civilizationist" character they ascribe to that relationship. By contrast, this book has argued that all the religious and secular authorities in history—from Babylon to Beijing—are powers that are established in tension with God and with one another, and are symbolically and spiritually defeated by Christ on the cross. Defeated by their own capacity for violence and excess, they are passing away. Powers theology provides an alternative ontology of ideological-political entities competing in International Relations; insofar as powers accept these tensions and their own temporality, their practices may be providential (Rom 13), but when they seek to overcome these tensions, deny their defeat, and resist their passing, they are beastly actors (Rev 13). Such acceptance can only occur where theological hope generates prophetic political insight. The order of providence is dialectically related to the order of redemption founded in Christ; without it, the order of providence breaks down. When the powers are highly disenchanted and/or decentered, they generate violence and insecurity because they are not held in check by the message of love, grace, and redemption. When the powers are re-enchanted and/or recentered, they violently impose their own order of "love" and "grace." The first danger for government is to *disregard* Christ while the second is to *displace* him. The first error of the church is to *defer* to government in a post-Christian concession, as some Lutherans do, while the second is to *refer* to government in neo-Christendom terms, as some Calvinists do. This is the post-Christendom dialectic with its eschatological implications. New Christian realism's account of history is *apocalyptic* and *redemptive* in that it presents the transformation of the world by Christ as being partially realized, facing resistance, and yet ultimately triumphant. Table 3 summarizes its key elements and compares them to early Christian realism and the dominant secular approaches of realism and liberalism.

TABLE 3: CHRISTIAN AND SECULAR APPROACHES TO SECURITY

APPROACH	Christian realism (Christendom security) Chapter 3	Secular realism (national security) Chapter 6	Secular liberalism (human security) Chapter 7	New Christian realism (post-Christendom security) Chapters 9–12
Manifest actors of security	States as self-interested and moralizing actors	States, especially great powers, as instrumental actors	States and civil society as normative and instrumental actors	"Powers and authorities" of church (*ecclesia*) and world
Root causes of insecurity	*Animus dominandi*—personal sin and pride writ large in the state	Anarchy—self-help demands aggression and relentless pursuit of power	Deprivation and isolation—economic, political, and institutional failures	"Dragon and beasts"—fallen Powers (agents and structures) which disregard or displace Christ
Understanding of history	Tragic and ultimately apocalyptic	Tragic and cyclical	Normative and progressive	Apocalyptic and ultimately redemptive
Means of inclusion	*Civilizational:* sovereign recognition of selves on cultural grounds; scapegoating of others	*National:* recognition, alliance structures, military strength	*Liberal International Order:* recognition, economic interdependence, and international institutions	*Global:* The defeat of scapegoat mechanisms (undifferentiation); asylum and sanctuary for migrants
Means of protection	The *katechon*, the balance of power, and the limited use of force	National defense, the balance of power, and the potentially unlimited use of force	International law, intervention, and "peace enforcement"	Nonviolent resistance and civilian protection; limited "policing" uses of force
Means of provision	Order, justice, and *caritas* of the state and church together	National economic growth and industry; hegemony in global trade and finance by great powers	Global free trade for all; international aid and market-based solutions for the poor	Local and globally networked communities of sharing and redistribution; internationally agreed limits on consumption.

The contrasts between the Christian realism of the twentieth century and the new version proposed here are pronounced. The former's history is tragic as it imperialistically adopted a "standard of civilization" from the precepts of Christendom, implicitly presented those beyond this Eurocentric order as inferior, and assumed that the sacrifice of Christendom's subjects for its powers was necessary for security. By contrast, from a post-Christendom perspective, new Christian realism presents the violence associated with these powers as apocalyptic. As their sacrificial orders break down so undifferentiation creates the partial and disorderly liberations on a global scale of those hitherto made victims—a process most clearly seen in hospitality offered to minorities and migrants. The original Christian realists understood protection in terms of the balance of power, with the holder (*katechon*) of that balance typically being a person or entity of Western Christendom. Going with and beyond Yoder, a post-Christendom security standpoint is not merely that of martyrdom from the margins but a prophetic witness of unarmed civilian protection for the world that is relatively effective at achieving protection and non-domination. Finally, the early Christian realists often held a left-liberal approach to provision where the church and civil society prompt the state to act as a "field hospital." With Northcott and Gorringe, a new Christian realist approach starts from the considerable evidence that the state's provision of goods is tragic and sometimes kleptocratic in that it institutionalizes a world of inequalities between excess consumption and scarcity; therefore, hope is found in new communities formed out of the world and spreading across the world by the inbreaking of new-covenant practices of sharing. It is Wight in his apocalyptic vein who came closest to recognizing the hope of a Christian approach to security. However, shackled by a hard distinction between theology and politics, he failed to bring this to fruition in his work on International Relations.

Realistic hope?

As Wight understood, the Christian's hope is found in a Lord of History who providentially restrains evil *and* redeems the world. As Proverbs 29:18 notes, no such hope is possible without prophetic insight and the law of love. It may seem idiosyncratic to speak of peril in a time in which hundreds of millions have been dragged out of poverty and the toll of warfare appears to have reduced. However, the absence of restraint in a secular world without limits is beckoning a climate apocalypse, increasing the incidence of political violence, and intensifying struggles over migration and borders between rich and poor. A new and explicitly apocalyptic Christian realist analysis of International Relations identifies these traumas as security problems arising after Christendom. But these traumas are freighted with hope insofar as they expose the arbitrariness of scapegoating, as revealed by Christ on the cross, and elicit protection and provision for the innocent victim, as modeled by his ministry and by his church. Prophetic work from an apocalyptic realist perspective is that which exposes scapegoating and witnesses a hopeful message for the victim.

The tragic message of the Christian realists of the twentieth century lacked such hope even if it allowed Christendom's empires fleeting moments of providence. Niebuhr advised "a generation which finds its communities imperiled" to take Augustine's counsel and weep at the biblical rivers of Babylon. "Ultimately," he argues, "we cannot find peace if we are merely tossed down the river of time. We must find security in that which is not carried down the river."[31] For Niebuhr, Wight, and the Christian realists, hope was theological not political. Theology outlines redemption while politics is simply tragic. By contrast, the apocalyptic Christian realism sketched in this book envisions *both* a providential witness *and* an ultimate redemption and renewal of the world. In Moltmann's terms, it imagines "hope against danger."[32] That is, post-Christendom's prophets "anticipate the future of the new creation, the Kingdom of justice and freedom, not because they are optimists but because they trust in the faithfulness of God."[33] In the shadow of mutual assured destruction, Moltmann argued that it is "only the *protest* of the apocalyptic hope for God against all the Powers which makes possible and prepares for that annihilation of the world."[34]

Unlike earlier Christian realism, this book has argued that this ecclesial "protest" is the basis for a realistic approach to security both in its own terms and in its dialectical relations with the sword. We do not need to rely on states but must look first to the church as the anticipation of God's hope for the earth, while recognizing that many of the sins of states—of greed and egoism—seep into the church too. At the same time, apocalyptic Christian realism does not pit a new idealistic martyrdom against the power of the state. This would be a fundamentally flawed theology of security confining the church to the role of insurgent. Certainly, the standard of loving the enemy found in Anabaptist and other radical political theology is indeed otherworldly. However, removing the enemy's enmity is not just a matter

---

31. Niebuhr, "Augustine's Political Realism," 141, 139.
32. Moltmann, *Creating a Just Future*, 37.
33. Moltmann, *Creating a Just Future*, 8.
34. Moltmann, *Creating a Just Future*, 38, emphasis added.

of protest and martyrdom—although generations of the poor have eroded enmity this way.[35] It is also a matter of creating new security communities locally and globally, in the manner of transition towns, unarmed defense groups, and sanctuary movements in partnership with other faith groups in accordance with a universalist vision. These movements expose the defeat of the beastly powers; and they demonstrate that the tasks of inclusion, protection, and provision are dispersing to a greater variety of actors whose security practices are not determined by national borders. Work to understand this emergent apocalyptic politics of our time may be developed by further comparisons of Bulgakov, Girard, and Yoder given that the intertextual and genealogical ties between their works have only begun to be explored here. This book merely sketches the historical circumstances and eternal perspective by which this change is occurring across what was formerly Eastern and Western Christendom. Perhaps there are cognate debates that may be fleshed out within the narratives of other faiths. It is for a future study to elaborate a political theology of the apocalyptic and take this forward in discourse that advances theology in conversation with the social sciences.

Such a conversation must extend beyond the Western authors and debates that have composed the majority in this book to a greater variety of scholars of the Eastern Orthodox world and Global South. It is not for any author from a particular stance to write a singular vision of security after Christendom. The former Christian realism was dominated by Western white males that shared a tragic perspective on the decline of Christendom. By contrast, a new Christian realism must be pluralistic in its hopeful account of the security of the kingdom of God. Such plurality is both more biblical and more realistic (Gen 11:1–9). It is necessary to capture the character of security, "decolonize" the debate, and generate a post-Christendom imaginary through discourse. However, while acknowledging the privileges afforded to certain voices, and seeking out diversity, we must not lose sight of the universal point of reference for any Christian political theology: the life, death, and resurrection of Jesus Christ. For hope is a theological *and therefore* a political virtue.

---

35. Moltmann, *Creating a Just Future*, 43.

Bibliography

Abatzidis, Theofilos, et al. "A Declaration on the 'Russian World' (*Russkii Mir*) Teaching." *Public Orthodoxy*, March 13, 3022. https://publicorthodoxy.org/2022/03/13/a-declaration-on-the-russian-world-russkii-mir-teaching/.

Abrahamsen, Rita, and Michael C. Williams. "Security beyond the State: Global Security Assemblages in International Politics." *International Political Sociology* 3.1 (2009) 1–17.

Abrams, Philip. "Notes on the Difficulty of Studying the State (1977)." *Journal of Historical Sociology* 1.1 (1988) 58–89.

Acharya, Amitav. "Global International Relations and Regional Worlds: A New Agenda for International Studies." *International Studies Quarterly* 58 (2014) 647–59.

———. "The Myth of the 'Civilization State': Rising Powers and the Cultural Challenge to World Order." *Ethics & International Affairs* 34.2 (2020) 139–56.

Ackerman, Peter, and Jack DuVall. *A Force More Powerful*. Basingstoke, UK: Palgrave Macmillan, 2000.

Adamsky, Dmitry. *Russian Nuclear Orthodoxy: Religion, Politics, and Strategy*. Stanford, CA: Stanford University Press, 2019.

Adamson, Fiona B. "Crossing Borders: International Migration and National Security." *International security* 31.1 (2006) 165–99.

Adler, Emanuel. "Imagined (Security) Communities: Cognitive Regions in International Relations." *Millennium* 26.2 (1997) 249–77.

Agensky, Jonathan C. "Recognizing Religion: Politics, History, and the 'Long 19th Century.'" *European Journal of International Relations* 23.4 (2017) 729–55.

Alexander, Laura E. "Christian Realism and the State as Idol: Feminist and Postcolonial Critique and Christian Realist Theology in an Interdependent World." *Political Theology* 22.8 (2021) 680–98.

Alkopher, Tal Dingott. "The Social (and Religious) Meanings That Constitute War: The Crusades as Realpolitik vs. Socialpolitik." *International Studies Quarterly* 49.4 (2005) 715–37.

Ames, Christine Caldwell. *Righteous Persecution: Inquisition, Dominicans, and Christianity in the Middle Ages*. Philadelphia: University of Pennsylvania Press, 2009.

Anderson, Benedict. *Imagined Communities: Reflections on the Origin and Spread of Nationalism*. London: Verso, 2006.

Anderson, Bernhard W. *From Creation to New Creation: Old Testament Perspectives*. OBT. Minneapolis: Fortress, 1994.

Aquinas, Thomas. "Suma Theologiae, 1a 2ae." In *Thomas Aquinas: Selected Philosophical Writings*, edited by Timothy McDermott, 90–91. Oxford: Oxford University Press, 1993.

Aradau, Claudia. "Security and the Democratic Scene: Desecuritization and Emancipation." *Journal of International Relations and Development* 7.4 (2004) 388–413.

Asad, Talal. *Formations of the Secular*. Stanford, CA: Stanford University Press, 2003.

Associated Press. "These Church Leaders Support Trump. What Did They Say from the Pulpit Sunday?" *LA Times*, January 11, 2021. https://www.latimes.com/world-nation/story/2021-01-11/pro-trump-church-leaders-sunday-sermons-capitol-riot.

Augustine, Saint. *De Civitate Dei*. Aris and Phillips Classical Texts. Oxford Oxford University Press, 2005.

Ayoob, Mohammed. "Inequality and Theorizing in International Relations: The Case for Subaltern Realism." *International Studies Review* 4.3 (2002) 27–48.

Azar, Edward E. "Protracted International Conflicts: Ten Propositions." In *Conflict: Readings in Management and Resolution*, 145–55. London: Palgrave Macmillan, 1990.

Bader-Saye, Scott. *Church and Israel after Christendom: The Politics of Election*. Reprint, Eugene, OR: Wipf and Stock, 1999.

Bain, William. *Political Theology of International Order*. Oxford: Oxford University Press, 2020.

Baldwin, David A. "The Concept of Security." *Review of International Studies* 23.1 (1997) 5–26.

Balzacq, Thierry. "A Theory of Securitization: Origins, Core Assumptions, and Variants." In *Securitization Theory: How Security Problems Emerge and Dissolve*, edited by Thierry Balzacq, 15–44. London: Routledge, 2011.

Barkawi, Tarak, and Mark Laffey. "The Postcolonial Moment in Security Studies." *Review of International Studies* 32.2 (2006) 329–35.

Barker, M. *The Revelation of Jesus Christ*. Edinburgh: T. & T. Clark, 2000.

Barth, Karl. *Epistle to the Romans*, Oxford: Oxford University Pres, 1968.

Bauckham, Richard. *The Bible in Politics: How to Read the Bible Politically*. London: SPCK, 1989.

———. *The Theology of the Book of Revelation*. Cambridge: Cambridge University Press, 1993.

Baudrillard, Jean. *Simulacra and Simulation*. Ann Arbor: University of Michigan Press, 1994.

Bayer, Patrick, and Michaël Aklin. "The European Union Emissions Trading System Reduced CO_2 Emissions Despite Low Prices." *Proceedings of the National Academy of Sciences* 117.16 (2020) 8804–12.

BBC News. "Dorset Veteran's Wife Wants More Help for Veterans with PTSD." January 17, 2020. https://www.bbc.co.uk/news/av/uk-england-dorset-51148313.

———. "SAS Death Squads Exposed: A British War Crime?" *Panorama*, July 12, 2022. https://www.bbc.co.uk/programmes/m0019707.

———. "Today Programme." BBC Radio 4, December 6, 2017, 08:10.

Beale, G. K. *Revelation*. Grand Rapids: Eerdmans, 1999.

Beasley-Murray, G. R. *The Book of Revelation*. New Century Bible. London: Marshall, Morgan, and Scott, 1974.
Beetham, David. *The Legitimation of Power*. Cambridge: Cambridge University Press, 1991.
Behera, N. C. "Re-Imagining IR in India." *International Relations of the Asia-Pacific* 7 (2007) 341–68.
Bell, Daniel M. *Divinations: Theopolitics in an Age of Terror*. Eugene, OR: Cascade, 2017.
———. *The Economy of Desire: Christianity and Capitalism in a Postmodern World*. Ada, MI: Baker Academic, 2012.
Belton, Catherine. *Putin's People: How the KGB Took Back Russia and Then Took on the West*. London: Harper Collins, 2020.
Berger, Peter. "The Desecularization of the World: A Global Overview." In *The Desecularization of the World: Resurgent Religion and World Politics*, edited by Peter Berger, 1–18. Grand Rapids, Eerdmans, 1999.
———. "A Sociological View of the Secularization of Theology." *Journal for the Scientific Study of Religion* 6.1 (1967) 3–16.
Berger Peter L., and Thomas Luckmann. *The Social Construction of Reality: A Treatise in the Sociology of Knowledge*. Harmondsworth, UK: Penguin, 1971.
Berkhof, H. *Christ and the Powers*. Goshen, NY: Herald, 1962.
Besley, Timothy, and Torsten Persson. "The Causes and Consequences of Development Clusters: State Capacity, Peace, and Income." *Annual Review of Economics* 6.1 (2014) 927–49.
Bettiza, Gregorio. *Finding Faith in Foreign Policy: Religion and American Diplomacy in a Postsecular World*. Oxford: Oxford University Press, 2019.
———. "How Do Religious Norms Diffuse? Institutional Translation and International Change in a Post-Secular World Society." *European Journal of International Relations* 21.3 (2015) 621–46.
Bettiza, Gregorio, Dereck Bolton, Katerina Dalacoura, and David Lewis. "Civilizationism as Counter-Hegemonic Ideology: Contesting the Liberal International Order's Ontological Trap." Draft paper presented to the University of Exeter Centre for Advanced International Studies, October 2021.
Betts, Richard A., et al. "When Could Global Warming Reach 4° C?" *Philosophical Transactions of the Royal Society A: Mathematical, Physical and Engineering Sciences* 369.1934 (2011) 67–84.
Bevir, Mark. "Decentring Security Governance." *Global Crime* 17.3–4 (2016) 227–39.
Bevir, Mark, and Rod A. W. Rhodes. *The State as Cultural Practice*. Oxford: Oxford University Press, 2010.
Bielefeldt, Heiner. "Misperceptions of Freedom of Religion or Belief." *Human Rights Quarterly* 35.1 (2013) 33–68.
Biggar, Nigel. *Between Kin and Cosmopolis: An Ethic of the Nation*. Didsbury Lectures. Eugene, OR: Cascade, 2014.
———. *In Defence of War*. Oxford: Oxford University Press, 2013.
———. "This Christian Teaching Suggests It's Ethical for Ukraine to Fight (and for Us to Arm Them)." *Premier Christianity*, March 29, 2022. https://www.premierchristianity.com/opinion/this-christian-teaching-suggests-its-ethical-for-ukraine-to-fight-and-for-us-to-arm-them/12765.article.
Bilgin, Pinar. "The Securityness of Secularism? The Case of Turkey." *Security Dialogue* 39.6 (2008) 593–614.

Boesak, Alan. *Comfort and Protest.* Edinburgh: St. Andrew, 1986.
Bogdanor, Vernon. "The Scott Report." *Public Administration* 74 (1996) 593–611.
Bonhoeffer, Dietrich. *The Cost of Discipleship.* New York: Simon and Schuster, 2012.
Boudinot, F. Garrett, and Todd LeVasseur. "'Grow the Scorched Ground Green': Values and Ethics in the Transition Movement." *Journal for the Study of Religion, Nature & Culture* 10.3 (2016) 379–404.
Bourne, Mike. *Understanding Security.* London: Bloomsbury, 2013.
Bousquet, Antoine. *The Eye of War: Military Perception from the Telescope to the Drone.* St. Paul: University of Minnesota Press, 2018.
Boutros-Ghali, Boutros. *An Agenda for Peace.* New York: UN, 1992.
Bowen, John R. *Why the French Don't Like Headscarves: Islam, the State, and Public Space.* Princeton, NJ: University of Princeton Press, 2007.
Boyd, Gregory A. *The Myth of a Christian Nation: How the Quest for Political Power Is Destroying the Church.* Grand Rapids: Zondervan, 2007.
Brahm, George. "Douglas Murray Cherishes Christianity. What Would It Take for Him to Believe?" *Premier Christianity*, January 14, 2020. https://www.premierchristianity.com/home/douglas-murray-cherishes-christianity-what-would-it-take-for-him-to-believe/1510.article.
Braun, Christian Nikolaus. "Quo Vadis? On the Role of Just Peace within Just War." *International Theory* online first (2022) 1–23.
Brecke, Peter. "Violent Conflicts 1400 A.D. to the Present in Different Regions of the World." Paper prepared for the 1999 Meeting of the Peace Science Society (International) on October 8–10, 1999, Ann Arbor, MI. https://cpn-us-w2.wpmucdn.com/sites.gatech.edu/dist/1/19/files/2018/09/Brecke-PSS-1999-paper-Violent-Conflicts-1400-AD-to-the-Present.pdf.
Brent, Allen. *A Political History of Early Christianity.* London: Black, 2009.
Bretherton, Luke. *Christianity and Contemporary Politics: The Conditions and Possibilities of Faithful Witness.* Chichester, UK: Wiley, 2011.
Brown, Chris. *Understanding International Relations.* 5th ed. London: Bloomsbury, 2019.
Brown, Peter. *The Rise of Western Christendom: Triumph and Diversity, AD 200–1000.* Vol. 3. Chichester, UK: Wiley, 2012.
Brown, Garrett Wallace, and Alexandra Bohm. "Introducing Jus ante Bellum as a Cosmopolitan Approach to Humanitarian Intervention." *European Journal of International Relations* 22.4 (2016) 897–919.
Brown University. "Costs of War." Watson Institute of International Affairs, September 2021. https://watson.brown.edu/costsofwar/figures/2021/WarDeathToll.
Bruce, Steve, ed. *Religion and Modernization: Sociologists and Historians Debate the Secularization Thesis.* Oxford: Clarendon, 1999.
———. *Secularization: In Defense of an Unfashionable Theory.* New York: Oxford University Press, 2013.
Bruckner, Pascal. *The Tyranny of Guilt.* Princeton, NJ: Princeton University Press, 2010.
Brunkard, Joan, Gonza Namulanda, and Raoult Ratard. "Hurricane Katrina Deaths, Louisiana, 2005." *Disaster Medicine and Public Health Preparedness* 2.4 (2008) 215–23.
Budde, Michael L. *Foolishness to Gentiles: Essays on Empire, Nationalism, and Discipleship.* Eugene, OR: Cascade, 2022.

Bulgakov, Sergius. *The Apocalypse of John: An Essay in Dogmatic Interpretation*. Translated by Mike Whitton. Revised by Michael Miller. Münster, Germany: Aschendorff Verlag, 2019.

———. *The Sophiology of Death: Essays on Eschatology: Personal, Political, Universal*. Eugene, OR: Cascade, 2021.

———. "The Unfading Light (1917)." In *Sergii Bulgakov: Towards a Russian Political Theology*, edited by Rowan Williams, 113–62. London: Black, 1999.

Bull, Hedley. *The Anarchical Society: A Study of Order in World Politics*. 2nd ed. Basingstoke, UK: Palgrave, 2002.

Bullough, Oliver. *Moneyland: Why Thieves and Crooks Now Rule the World and How to Take It Back*. London: Profile, 2018.

Burgis, Tom. *Kleptopia: How Dirty Money Is Conquering the World*. London: HarperCollins, 2021.

Burton, John. *Conflict: Human Needs Theory*. New York: Springer, 1990.

Butterfield, Herbert. *Christianity and History*. London: Bell, 1949.

Buzan, Barry. "Peace, Power, and Security: Contending Concepts in the Study of International Relations." *Journal of Peace Research* 21.2 (1984) 109–25.

Buzan, Barry, and George Lawson. *The Global Transformation: History, Modernity and the Making of International Relations*. Cambridge: Cambridge University Press, 2015.

Buzan, Barry, Ole Wæver, and Jaap De Wilde. *Security: A New Framework for Analysis*. Boulder, CO: Rienner, 1998.

Caird, G. B. *Principalities and Powers: A Study in Pauline Theology*. Oxford: Clarendon, 1956.

———. *The Revelation of St. John*. Peabody, MA: Hendrickson, 1966.

Calamur, Krishnadev. "Dancing with the Dictators: Kanye West Joins the Club." September 5, 2013. https://www.npr.org/sections/parallels/2013/09/05/219238748/dancing-with-the-dictators-kanye-west-joins-the-club.

Caldentey, Esteban Pérez. "The Concept and Evolution of the Developmental State." *International Journal of Political Economy* 37.3 (2008) 27–53.

Campbell, David. *National Deconstruction: Violence, Identity and Justice in Bosnia*. Minneapolis: University of Minnesota Press, 1998.

———. *Writing Security: United States Foreign Policy and the Politics of Identity*. Minneapolis: University of Minnesota Press, 1992.

Carr, W. *Angels and Principalities*. Cambridge: Cambridge University Press, 1981.

Carroll, James. *Constantine's Sword: The Church and the Jews, a History*. Boston: Houghton Mifflin Harcourt, 2002.

Carter, Craig A. *The Politics of the Cross: The Theology and Social Ethics of John Howard Yoder*. Grand Rapids: Brazos, 2001.

Casanova, Jose. *Public Religions in the Modern World*. Chicago: Chicago University Press, 1994.

Cavanaugh, William T. *Field Hospital: The Church's Engagement with a Wounded World*. Grand Rapids: Eerdmans, 2016.

———. "From One City to Two: Christian Reimagining of Political Space." *Political Theology* 7.3 (2006) 299–321.

———. "Girard and the Myth of Religious Violence." In *Does Religion Cause Violence? Multidisciplinary Perspectives on Violence and Religion in the Modern World*, edited by Scott Cowdell, Chris Fleming, Joel Hodge, and Carly Osborn, 7–24. London: Bloomsbury Academic, 2018.

———. *The Myth of Religious Violence: Secular Ideology and the Roots of Modern Conflict*. Oxford: Oxford University Press, 2009.

———. *Theopolitical Imagination: Christian Practices of Space and Time*. London: Black, 2002.

Cavanaugh, William T., Jeffrey W. Bailey, and Craig Hovey, eds. *An Eerdmans Reader in Contemporary Political Theology*. Grand Rapids: Eerdmans, 2011.

Cederman, Lars-Erik, Kristian Skrede Gleditsch, and Halvard Buhaug. *Inequality, Grievances, and Civil War*. Cambridge: Cambridge University Press, 2013.

Center for Disease Control. "Leading Causes of Death in Males, United States." Last reviewed March 3, 2022. https://www.cdc.gov/healthequity/lcod/index.htm.

Center for the Study of Global Christianity. "Christianity in Africa." 2015. Accessed July 17, 2022. https://www.gordonconwell.edu/wp-content/uploads/sites/13/2019/04/ChristianityinAfricaFINAL.pdf.

Cesari, Jocelyne. "Civilization as Disciplinization and the Consequences for Religion and World Politics." *Review of Faith & International Affairs* 17.1 (2019) 24–33.

Chabol, Patrick, and Jean-Francois Daloz. *Africa Works: Disorder as Political Instrument*. Oxford: Currey, 1999.

Chanaa, Jane. *Security Sector Reform: Issues, Challenges and Prospects*. Adelphi Paper 344. Oxford: Oxford University Press for the International Institute for Strategic Studies, 2002.

Chatham House. "Foreign Secretary Liz Truss and the UK's Foreign Policy Priorities." Event transcript, December 8, 2021. https://chathamhouse.soutron.net/Portal/DownloadImageFile.ashx?fieldValueId=6400.

Chayes, Sarah. *Thieves of State: Why Corruption Threatens Global Security*. New York: Norton, 2015.

Chenoweth, Erica, and Maria J. Stephan. *Why Civil Resistance Works: The Strategic Logic of Nonviolent Conflict*. New York: Columbia University Press, 2011.

Chislett, William. "The UK and Brexit: A Failed or a Failing State?" *Real Institute Elcano Blog*, September 6, 2019. https://www.realinstitutoelcano.org/en/the-uk-and-brexit-a-failed-or-a-failing-state/.

Clarke, John, and Janet Newman. *The Managerial State: Power, Politics and Ideology in the Remaking of Social Welfare*. London: Sage, 1997.

Clausewitz, Carl von. *On War*. London: Penguin, 2003.

Cohn, N. *The Pursuit of the Millennium*. London: Pimlico, 1956.

Coker, Christopher. *The Rise of the Civilizational State*. Cambridge: Polity, 2019.

Cole, Jonathan. "Political Theology and Political Authority: Evaluating Oliver O'Donovan's Christian Liberalism." *ABC Religion and Ethics*, June 21, 2021. https://www.abc.net.au/religion/political-theology-oliver-odonovans-christian-liberalism/13401594.

Comaroff, Jean, and John L. Comaroff. *Of Revelation and Revolution*. Vol. 1, *Christianity, Colonialism, and Consciousness in South Africa*. Chicago: University of Chicago Press, 1991.

Cooley, Alexander. *Great Games, Local Rules: The New Power Contest in Central Asia*. Oxford: Oxford University Press, 2012.

Cooley, Alexander A., and John Heathershaw. *Dictators without Borders: Power and Money in Central Asia*. New Haven, CT: Yale University Press, 2017.

Cooley, Alexander, David Lewis, and Graeme P. Herd. "Russia and China in Central Asia." *In Moscow's Shadows*, July 19, 2022. https://inmoscowsshadows.wordpress.com/2022/07/21/scss10-19-july-2022-russia-and-china-in-central-asia/.

Cox, Robert W. "Social Forces, States and World Orders: Beyond International Relations Theory." *Millennium* 10.2 (1981) 126–55.

Cramer, David C., and Myles Werntz. *A Field Guide to Christian Nonviolence: Key Thinkers, Activists, and Movements for the Gospel of Peace*. Ada, MI: Baker Academic, 2022.

Creating Safer Space. "What Is Unarmed Civilian Protection (UCP)?" Department of International Politics, Aberystwyth University. Last accessed August 22, 2022. https://creating-safer-space.com/what-is-unarmed-civilian-protection-ucp/.

Crombie, Noelle. "No Mercy." *Oregonian/OregonLive*, October 8, 2019. https://projects.oregonlive.com/no-mercy/.

Cross, F. L., and E. A. Livingstone, eds. *The Oxford Dictionary of the Christian Church*. 2nd ed. Oxford: Oxford University Press, 1985.

CTBI. "Church Response to Russian Invasion of Ukraine." August 25, 2022. https://ctbi.org.uk/church-response-to-russian-invasion-of-ukraine/.

Cullman, O. *The State in the New Testament*. London: Scribners, 1956.

Curtis, Mark. *The Good, the Bad and the Ugly: A Decade of Labour's Arms Exports*. Report for Saferworld. London: Saferworld, May 2007.

Dambeck, Robert. "The Late Great Planet Earth (1978) Part 4." YouTube, May 11, 2012, 2:01. https://www.youtube.com/watch?v=zqkxRojexMc&list=PL918C55849FD8F729&index=4.

Darwin, J. *After Tamerlane: The Rise and Fall of Global Empires, 1400–2000*. London: Bloomsbury, 2008.

Dawes, James. "UN Fails to Agree on 'Killer Robot' Ban as Nations Pour Billions into Autonomous Weapons Research." *The Conversation*, December 20, 2021. https://theconversation.com/un-fails-to-agree-on-killer-robot-ban-as-nations-pour-billions-into-autonomous-weapons-research-173616.

Debrix, François. *Re-envisioning Peacekeeping: The United Nations and the Mobilization of Ideology*. Minneapolis: University of Minnesota Press, 1999.

Demacopoulos, George E., and Aristotle Papanikolaou, eds. *Orthodox Constructions of the West*. New York: Fordham University Press, 2013.

Dent, Christopher M. "Economic Security." In *Contemporary Security Studies*, edited by Alan Collins, 243–59. 3rd ed. Oxford: Oxford University Press, 2010.

Department for International Development (DfID). *Eliminating World Poverty: Making Governance Work for the Poor*. White Paper of the UK Government, July 2006.

Deudney, Daniel, and G. John Ikenberry. "The Nature and Sources of Liberal International Order." *Review of International Studies* 25.2 (1999) 179–96.

De Waal, Alex. "US War Crimes in Somalia." *New Left Review* 230.July/August (1998) 131–44.

Deyermond, Ruth. "Matrioshka Hegemony? Multi-Levelled Hegemonic Competition and Security in Post-Soviet Central Asia." *Review of International Studies* 35.1 (2009) 151–73.

Diggins, John P. *Why Niebuhr Now?* Chicago: University of Chicago Press, 2011.

Dillon, Michael. "Underwriting Security." *Security Dialogue* 39.2–3 (2008) 309–32.

Dincecco, Mark. "The Rise of Effective States in Europe." *Journal of Economic History* 75.3 (2015) 901–18.

Dombrowski, David A. "The Death of the Just War Theory." *Peace Research* 13.3 (1981) 135–44.

Doyle, Michael W., and Nicholas Sambanis. *Making War and Building Peace: United Nations Peace Operations*. Princeton, NJ: Princeton University Press, 2006.

Driver, J. *How Christians Made Peace with War: Early Christian Understandings of War*. Scottsdale, PA: Herald, 1988.

Druzenko, Gennadii. "Geopolitics from the Patriarch: The Heavenly Kingdom Versus the 'Russian World.'" *Russian Politics & Law* 49.1 (2011) 65–73.

Duffield, Mark. *Global Governance and the New Wars: The Merging of Development and Security*. London: Zed, 2002.

Dunne, Tim. *Inventing International Society: A History of the English School*. New York: Springer, 1998.

Dunne, Tim, Lene Hansen, and Colin Wight. "The End of International Relations Theory?" *European Journal of International Relations* 19.3 (2013) 405–25.

DW. "Two Years since Germany Opened Its Borders to Refugees: A Chronology." September 4, 2017. https://www.dw.com/en/two-years-since-germany-opened-its-borders-to-refugees-a-chronology/a-40327634.

Eaton, Paul D., Antonio M. Taguba, and Steven M. Anderson. "The Military Must Prepare Now for a 2024 Insurrection." *Washington Post*, December 17, 2021. https://www.washingtonpost.com/opinions/2021/12/17/eaton-taguba-anderson-generals-military/.

Economist. "Nationally Determined Contributors." *The Economist*, July 30, 2022.

———. "A Shrinking Slice." *The Economist*, November 2, 2013.

Eguren, Luis Enrique. "The Notion of Space in International Accompaniment." *Peace Review* 27.1 (2015) 18–24.

Eisenhower, Dwight D. "President's Farewell Address." National Archives, January 17, 1961. https://www.archives.gov/milestone-documents/president-dwight-d-eisenhowers-farewell-address.

Elbe, Stefan. "AIDS, Security, Biopolitics." *International Relations* 19.4 (2005) 403–19.

Eller, Vernon. *War and Peace from Genesis to Revelation*. Goshen, NY: Herald, 1973.

Elshtain, Jean Bethke. "The Just War Tradition and Natural Law." *Fordham International Law Journal* 28 (2004) 742–55.

———. "The Third Annual Grotius Lecture: Just War and Humanitarian Intervention." In *Proceedings of the ASIL Annual Meeting*, 95:1–12. Cambridge: Cambridge University Press, 2001.

Enloe, Cynthia. *The Morning After: Sexual Politics at the End of the Cold War*. Berkeley: University of California Press, 1993.

Epp, Roger. "The 'Augustinian Moment' in International Politics: Niebuhr, Butterfield, Wight and the Reclaiming of a Tradition." *International Politics Research Paper* 10. Aberystwyth, UK: Department of International Politics, 1991.

Fairey, Jack. *The Great Powers and Orthodox Christendom: The Crisis over the Eastern Church in the Era of the Crimean War*. New York: Springer, 2015.

Federal Vision. "The Federal Vision on the 'Next' or 'Global' Christendom." Last updated May 3, 2019. http://federal-vision.com/ecclesiology/joint-federal-vision-statement/.

Feldman, Gregory. "Estranged States: Diplomacy and the Containment of National Minorities in Europe." *Anthropological Theory* 5.3 (2005) 219–45.

Ferrarotti, F. "Toward the End of Constantinian Christendom." *International Journal of Politics, Culture, and Society* 3.4 (1990) 433–61.
Finamore, Stephen. *God, Order and Chaos*. PTMS. Carlisle, UK: Paternoster, 2009.
———. "Hope: Prophetic Vision and the Lie of the Land." In *Mission in Marginal Places: The Theory*, edited by Paul Cloke and Mike Pears, 220–38. Milton Keynes, UK: Paternoster, 2016.
———. "A Kinder, Gentler Apocalypse? René Girard, the Book of Revelation and the 'Bottomless Abyss of the Unforgettable Victim.'" In *Compassionate Eschatology*, edited by Ted Grimsrud and Michael Hardin, 196–217. Eugene, OR: Cascade, 2011.
———. "Wright, Wrong and Wrath: Apocalypse in Paul and Girard." In *Mimesis and Atonement: René Girard and the Doctrine of Salvation*, edited by Michael Kirwan and Sheelah T. Hidden, 47–70. London: Bloomsbury, 2017.
Finamore, Stephen, and John Heathershaw. "Mimesis, Market and Mission: René Girard and the Christian Witness to the World." In *Attending to the Margins: Essays in Honour of Stephen Finamore*, edited by Helen Paynter and Peter Hatton, 11–30. Oxford: Regent's Park College, 2022.
Financial Conduct Authority. "Finalised Guidance: FG 17/6 The treatment of politically exposed persons for anti-money laundering purposes." July 6, 2017, 9. https://www.fca.org.uk/publications/finalised-guidance/fg17-6-treatment-politically-exposed-persons-peps-money-laundering.
Findley, Michael G., Daniel L. Nielson, and Jason Campbell Sharman. *Global Shell Games: Experiments in Transnational Relations, Crime, and Terrorism*. Cambridge: Cambridge University Press, 2014.
Fisher, David, and Nigel Biggar. "Was Iraq an Unjust War? A Debate on the Iraq War and Reflections on Libya." *International Affairs* 87.3 (2011) 687–707.
Fischer, Markus. "Feudal Europe, 800–1300: Communal Discourse and Conflictual Practices." *International Organization* 46.2 (1992) 427–66.
Fletcher, P. "The Political Theology of the Empire to Come." *Cambridge Review of International Affairs* 17.1 (2004) 49–61.
Folz, Richard. *The Concept of Empire in Western Europe: From the Fifth to the Fourteenth Century*. London: Arnold, 1969.
Forceswatch. "Armed Forces Report Reveals MPs' Confusion over Recruitment of Under-18s." Press release, March 18, 2013. https://www.forceswatch.net/news/armed-forces-report-reveals-mps-confusion-over-recruitment-under-18s.
Foreign Affairs Committee of the House of Commons. *Moscow's Gold: Russian Corruption in the UK*. House of Commons, UK Parliament, 2018. https://publications.parliament.uk/pa/cm201719/cmselect/cmfaff/932/93202.htm.
Francis, Andrew. *Dorothee Sölle: Life and Work*, Bristol: Imagier, 2014.
Freedom House. *Freedom in the World: The Global Expansion of Authoritarian Rule*. Washington, DC: Freedom House, 2022. https://freedomhouse.org/sites/default/files/2022-02/FIW_2022_PDF_Booklet_Digital_Final_Web.pdf.
Freud, Sigmund. *Civilization and Its Discontents*. Peterborough, ON: Broadview, 2015.
Gallaher, Brandon. "Eschatological Anarchism: Eschatology and Politics in Contemporary Greek Theology." In *Political Theologies in Orthodox Christianity: Common Challenges-Divergent Positions*, edited by Stoeckl, Kristina, Ingeborg Gabriel, and Aristotle Papanikolaou, 135–49. London: Bloomsbury, 2017.

———. "A Secularism of the Royal Doors." In *Fundamentalism or Tradition: Christianity after Secularism*, edited by George E Demacopoulos, 108–30. New York: Fordham University Press, 2019.
Gallie, William. "Essentially Contested Concepts." In *The Importance of Language*, edited by Max Black, 121–46. Englewood Cliffs, NJ: Prentice-Hall, 1962.
Galtung, Johan. "Cultural Violence." *Journal of Peace Research* 27.3 (1990) 291–305.
———. "Violence, Peace, and Peace Research." *Journal of Peace Research* 6.3 (1969) 167–91.
Garškaitė, Rosita. "Threats and Safeguards: Political Reasoning about the EU by Lithuanian Catholics." Paper presented to the conference Christian Identity in National, Transnational and Local Space, New College, University of Oxford, April 4–5, 2022.
Gates-Brown, Tricia. *118 Days: Christian Peacemaker Teams Held Hostage in Iraq*. Chicago: Christian Peacemaker Teams, 2008.
Gault, Matthew. "Russia's Church Blesses Nuclear Weapons, Some Clergy Want to Stop." Vice, February 6, 2020. https://www.vice.com/en/article/akwky4/russias-church-blesses-nuclear-weapons-some-clergy-want-to-stop.
Gentry, Caroline E. "Feminist Christian Realism." *International Feminist Journal of Politics*. 18.3 (2016) 449–67.
George, Charles H. "Puritanism as History and Historiography." *Past & Present* 41 (1968) 77–104.
Ghani, Ashraf, and Clare Lockhart. *Fixing Failed States: A Framework for Rebuilding a Fractured World*. Oxford: Oxford University Press, 2009.
Gifford, Paul. "Chiluba's Christian Nation: Christianity as a Factor in Zambian Politics, 1991–1996." *Journal of Contemporary Religion* 13.3 (1998) 363–81.
Gingerich Hiebert, Kyle. *The architectonics of hope: violence, apocalyptic, and the transformation of political theology*. Eugene OR: Wipf and Stock Publishers, 2017.
Girard, René. *Battling to the End: Conversations with Benoît Chantre*. Translated by Mary Baker. East Lansing: Michigan State University Press, 2010.
———. *I See Satan Fall like Lightning*. Leominster, UK: Gracewing, 2001.
———. *The Scapegoat*. Translated by Yvonne Freccero. Baltimore: Johns Hopkins University Press, 1986.
———. *Violence and the Sacred*. Translated by Patrick Gregory. London: Bloomsbury, 1977.
Girard, René, Jean-Michel Oughourlian, and Guy Lefort. *Things Hidden since the Foundation of the World*. London: Bloomsbury, 1978.
Givens, Tommy. *We the People: Israel and the Catholicity of Jesus*. Augsburg: Fortress, 2014.
Glassmyer, Katherine, and Nicholas Sambanis. "Rebel—Military Integration and Civil War Termination." *Journal of Peace Research* 45.3 (2008) 365–84.
Global Integrity. "Our Programme." Anti-Corruption Evidence Programme. Last accessed September 14, 2022. https://ace.globalintegrity.org/about/.
———. "Theory of Change." Anti-Corruption Evidence Programme. Last accessed September 14, 2022. https://ace.globalintegrity.org/wp-content/uploads/2019/09/TOC_rev.pdf.
Goffman, Alice. *On the Run: Fugitive Life in an American City*. New York: Picador, 2015.
Goodman, Jack. "Has China Lifted 100 Million People out of Poverty?" BBC, February 28, 2021. https://www.bbc.co.uk/news/56213271.

Goossen, Rachel Waltner. "'Defanging the Beast': Mennonite Responses to John Howard Yoder's Sexual Abuse." *Mennonite Quarterly Review* 89 (January 2015). Available at https://www.bishop-accountability.org/news5/2015_01_Goossen_Defanging_the_Beast.pdf.

Gopal, Anand. *No Good Men among the Living: America, the Taliban, and the War through Afghan Eyes*. New York: Metropolitan, 2014.

Gorringe, Timothy. *Capital and the Kingdom: Theological Ethics and Economic Order*. New York: Orbis, 1994.

———. *God's Theatre: A Theology of Providence*. London: SCM, 1991.

———. *Karl Barth: Against Hegemony*, Oxford: Clarendon, 1999.

———. *Redeeming Time: Atonement through Education*. London: Darton, Longman and Todd, 1986.

———. *The World Made Otherwise: Sustaining Humanity in a Threatened World*. Eugene, OR: Cascade, 2018.

Gorringe, Timothy, and Rosie Beckham. *The Transition Movement for Churches: A Prophetic Imperative for Today*. Canterbury: Canterbury Press, 2013.

Gower, Melanie, and Patrick Butchard. *UK-Rwanda Migration and Economic Development Partnership*. House of Commons Research Briefing, June 28, 2022. https://commonslibrary.parliament.uk/research-briefings/cbp-9568/.

Gray, John. *Black Mass: Apocalyptic Religion and the Death of Utopia*. London: Macmillan, 2007.

———. "Steven Pinker Is Wrong about Violence and War." *The Guardian*, March 13, 2015. https://www.theguardian.com/books/2015/mar/13/john-gray-steven-pinker-wrong-violence-war-declining.

Gray, William Glenn. "Floating the System: Germany, the United States, and the Breakdown of Bretton Woods, 1969–1973." *Diplomatic History* 31.2 (2007) 295–323.

Greitens, Sheena Chestnut, Myunghee Lee, and Emir Yazici. "Counterterrorism and Preventive Repression: China's Changing Strategy in Xinjiang." *International Security* 44.3 (2019) 9–47.

Groody, Daniel G. "Migration: A Theological Vision." In *Intersections of Religion and Migration*, edited by Jennifer Beth Saunders, Elena Fiddian-Qasmiyeh, and Susanna Snyder, 225–40. New York: Palgrave Macmillan, 2016.

Grozdanov, Zoran. "Christian Identity between Nation and the Christ." Paper presented to the conference Christian Identity in National, Transnational and Local Space, organized by the Protestant Political Thought Network at New College, University of Oxford, April 4–5, 2022.

Guilhot, Nicolas. *After the Enlightenment: Political Realism and International Relations in the Mid-Twentieth Century*. Cambridge: Cambridge University Press, 2017.

———. "American Katechon: When Political Theology Became International Relations Theory." *Constellations* 17.2 (2010) 224–53.

———. *The Invention of International Relations Theory: Realism, the Rockefeller Foundation, and the 1954 Conference on Theory*. New York: Columbia University Press, 2011.

Gusciute, Egle, Peter Mühlau, and Richard Layte. "All Welcome Here? Attitudes Towards Muslim Migrants in Europe." *International Migration* 59.5 (2021) 149–65.

Gutkowski, Stacey. "Misreading Islam in Iraq: Secular Misconceptions and British Foreign Policy." *Security Studies* 20.4 (2011) 592–623.

———. "Secularism and the Politics of Risk: Britain's Prevent Agenda, 2005–2009." *International Relations* 25.3 (2011) 346–62.
Habermas, Jürgen. "Notes on a Post-Secular Society." *New Perspectives Quarterly* 25.4 (2008) 17–29.
Hagevi, Magnus. "Are Christian Values Religious or Political? The Case of Sweden." Paper presented to the conference Christian Identity in National, Transnational and Local Space, New College, University of Oxford, April 4–5, 2022.
Hall, Ian. *The International Thought of Martin Wight*. New York: Palgrave Macmillan, 2006.
Hall, Rodney Bruce. "Moral Authority as a Power Resource." *International Organization* 51.4 (1997) 591–622.
Hamalis, Perry T. "Just Peacemaking and Christian Realism: Possibilities for Moving beyond the Impasse in Orthodox Christian War Ethics." In *Orthodox Christian Perspectives on War*, edited by Perry T. Hamalis and Valerie A. Karras, 335–59. Notre Dame, IN: University of Notre Dame Press, 2017.
Hameiri, Shahar, and Lee Jones. *Governing Borderless Threats: Non-Traditional Security and the Politics of State Transformation*. Cambridge: Cambridge University Press, 2015.
———. "Rising Powers and State Transformation: The Case of China." *European Journal of International Relations* 22.1 (2016) 72–98.
Hameiri, Shahar, Lee Jones, and John Heathershaw. "Reframing the Rising Powers Debate: State Transformation and Foreign Policy." *Third World Quarterly* 40.8 (2019) 1397–414.
Hamerton-Kelly, Robert G., ed. *Violent Origins: Walter Burkert, René Girard, and Jonathan Z. Smith on Ritual Killing and Social Formation*. Stanford, CA: Stanford University Press, 1987.
Hanciles, Jehu J. "Beyond Christendom: African Migration and Transformations in Global Christianity." *Studies in World Christianity* 10.1 (2004) 93–113.
———. *Migration and the Making of Global Christianity*. Grand Rapids: Eerdmans, 2021.
Hansard. *UK Parliament*. Last accessed May 23, 2022. https://hansard.parliament.uk/.
Hansen, Lene. "Gender, Nation, Rape: Bosnia and the Construction of Security." *International Feminist Journal of Politics* 3.1 (2000) 55–75.
———. "Reconstructing Resecuritisation: The Normative-Political in the Copenhagen School and Directions for How to Apply It." *Review of International Studies* 38.3 (2012) 525–46.
Hanson, Stephen E., and Jeffrey S. Kopstein. "Understanding the Global Patrimonial Wave." *Perspectives on Politics* 20.1 (2022) 237–49.
Hardin, Grant. "The Tragedy of the Commons." *Science* 162 (1968) 1243–48.
Hardt, Michael, and Antonio Negri. *Empire*. Cambridge: Harvard University Press, 2000.
———. *Multitude: War and Democracy in the Age of Empire*. London: Penguin, 2005.
Hardy, Elle. *Beyond Belief: How Pentecostal Christianity Is Taking Over the World*. Oxford: Oxford University Press, 2022.
Hauerwas, Stanley. *After Christendom*. Nashville: Abingdon, 1991.
Hauerwas, Stanley. "The Church in a Divided World. The Interpretative Power of the Christian Story." *The Journal of Religious Ethics* 8, no. 1 (1980): 55–82.

Hauerwas, Stanley, and James Fodor. "Remaining in Babylon: Oliver O'Donovan's Defense of Christendom." *Studies in Christian Ethics* 11.2 (1998) 30–55.

Haven, Cynthia L. *Evolution of Desire: A Life of René Girard*. East Lansing: Michigan State University Press, 2018.

Hayes, Andy. "Kathleen Stock: Professor Who Resigned over Trans Rights 'Witch-Hunt' Joins New US University." *Sky News*, November 8, 2021. https://news.sky.com/story/kathleen-stock-professor-who-resigned-over-trans-rights-witch-hunt-joins-new-us-university-12464140.

Haymes, Brian, and Kyle Gingerich Hiebert. *God After Christendom? After Christendom*. Eugene, OR: Cascade, 2017.

Haynes, Jeffrey. "Donald Trump, 'Judeo-Christian Values,' and the 'Clash of Civilizations.'" *Review of Faith & International Affairs* 15.3 (2017) 66–75.

Heathershaw, John. *Post-Conflict Tajikistan: The Politics of Peacebuilding and the Emergence of Legitimate Order*. London: Routledge, 2009.

———. "Unpacking the Liberal Peace: The Dividing and Merging of Peacebuilding Discourses." *Millennium* 36.3 (2008) 597–621.

Heathershaw, John, Alexander Cooley, Tom Mayne, Casey Michel, Tena Prelec, Jason Sharman, and R. Soares De Oliveira. *The UK's Kleptocracy Problem: How Servicing Post-Soviet Elites Weakens the Rule of Law*. London: Chatham House, 2021.

Herz, John H. "Idealist Internationalism and the Security Dilemma." *World Politics* 2.2 (1950) 157–80.

Herzog, Donald E. *Happy Slaves*. Chicago: University of Chicago Press, 1989.

Hiebert, Theodore. "The Tower of Babel and the Origin of the World's Cultures." *Journal of Biblical Literature* 126.1 (2007) 29–58.

Higgs, Robert. "Government Growth." *Econlib*. Last accessed March 10, 2022. https://www.econlib.org/library/Enc/GovernmentGrowth.html.

Hill, Symon. "As a Christian Pacifist I Can't Encourage Ukrainians to Take Up Arms. But Neither Will I Condemn Them." *Premier Christianity*, March 25, 2022. https://www.premierchristianity.com/opinion/as-a-christian-pacifist-i-cant-encourage-ukrainians-to-take-up-arms-but-neither-will-i-condemn-them/12749.article/.

HM Government. Economic Crime (Transparency and Enforcement) Act 2022. https://www.legislation.gov.uk/ukpga/2022/10/contents/enacted.

———. *Global Britain in a Competitive Age: The Integrated Review of Security, Defence, Development and Foreign Policy*. Policy paper, March 16, 2021. https://www.gov.uk/government/publications/global-britain-in-a-competitive-age-the-integrated-review-of-security-defence-development-and-foreign-policy.

Hobson, John M. *The Eastern Origins of Western Civilization*. Cambridge: Cambridge University Press, 2004.

Hobson, John M., and Jason C. Sharman. "The Enduring Place of Hierarchy in World Politics: Tracing the Social Logics of Hierarchy and Political Change." *European Journal of International Relations* 11.1 (2005) 63–98.

Hochschild, A. *To End All Wars: A Story of Loyalty and Rebellion, 1914–1918*. London: Mariner, 2011.

Holland, Tom. *Millennium: The End of the World and the Forging of Christendom*. London: Abacus, 2011.

Horowitz, Michael C. "Long Time Going: Religion and the Duration of Crusading." *International Security* 34.2 (2009) 162–93.

Hovorun, Cyril. "Orthodox Political Theology between National Identity and Empire." Transcript of presentation at the conference Christian Identity in National, Transnational and Local Space, Oxford, April 4–5, 2022.

Hovorun, Cyril, Marietta van der Tol, et al. "A Statement of Solidarity with the Orthodox Declaration on the 'Russian World.'" *Religion in Praxis*, April 4, 2022. https://religioninpraxis.com/a-statement-of-solidarity-with-the-orthodox-declaration-on-the-russian-world-russkii-mir-teaching-and-against-christian-nationalism-and-new-totalitarianism/.

Howard-Brook, Wes. *Empire Baptized: How the Church Embraced What Jesus Rejected 2nd–5th Centuries*. Maryknoll, NY: Orbis, 2016.

Howard-Brook, Wes, and Anthony Gwyther. *Unveiling Empire: Reading Revelation Then and Now*. Maryknoll, NY: Orbis, 1999.

Howell, Alison, and Melanie Richter-Montpetit. "Is Securitization Theory Racist? Civilizationism, Methodological Whiteness, and Antiblack Thought in the Copenhagen School." *Security Dialogue* 51.1 (2020) 3–22.

Hsiang, Solomon M., Marshall Burke, and Edward Miguel. "Quantifying the Influence of Climate on Human Conflict." *Science* 341.6151 (2013) 1–14.

Huntingdon, Samuel P. *The Clash of Civilizations and the Remaking of World Order*. London: Touchstone, 1996.

Hurd, Elizabeth Shakman. "International Politics after Secularism." *Review of International Studies* 38.5 (2012) 943–61.

———. *The Politics of Secularism in International Relations*. Princeton, NJ: Princeton University Press, 2007.

———. "The Political Authority of Secularism in International Relations." *European Journal of International Relations* 10.2 (2004) 235–62.

Hutchinson, John. "Warfare and the Sacralisation of Nations: The Meanings, Rituals and Politics of National Remembrance." *Millennium* 38.2 (2009) 401–17.

Huysmans, Jef. "The European Union and the Securitization of Migration." *JCMS: Journal of Common Market Studies* 38.5 (2000) 751–77.

Huysmans, Jef, and Vicki Squire. "Migration and Security." In *Handbook of Security Studies*, edited by Myriam Dunn Cavelty, and Victor Mauer, 161–71. London: Routledge, 2009.

Inglehart, Ronald F. *Religion's Sudden Decline: What's Causing It, and What Comes Next?* Oxford: Oxford University Press, 2020.

Intelligence and Security Committee of Parliament. *Russia*. London: UK Parliament, 2020. https://isc.independent.gov.uk/wp-content/uploads/2021/03/CCS207_CCS0221966010-001_Russia-Report-v02-Web_Accessible.pdf.

International Organization for Migration [IOM]. *World Migration Report 2020*. Accessed March 10, 2022. https://worldmigrationreport.iom.int/.

IPCC. *Climate Change 2021: Summary for Policymakers*, 14. Last accessed April 10, 2022. https://www.ipcc.ch/report/ar6/wg1/downloads/report/IPCC_AR6_WGI_SPM_final.pdf.

Iraq Inquiry. "Section 17: Civilian Casualties." *National Archives* (UK), November 23, 2017. https://www.iraqinquiry.org.uk/media/246676/the-report-of-the-iraq-inquiry_section-170.pdf.

Isachenko, Daria. *The Making of Informal States: Statebuilding in Northern Cyprus and Transdniestria*. Basingstoke, UK: Palgrave Macmillan, 2012.

Isbister, Roy. *An Independent Audit of the 2000 UK Annual Report on Strategic Export Controls: Report*. London: Saferworld, 2000.
Jackson, Robert H. *Quasi-States: Sovereignty, International Relations and the Third World*. Cambridge: Cambridge University Press, 1993.
Jeffrey, Alex. *The Improvised State: Sovereignty, Performance and Agency in Dayton Bosnia*. London: Wiley, 2012.
Jenkins, Philip. *The Next Christendom: The Coming of Global Christianity*. New York: Oxford University Press, 2002.
Jenkings, K. Neil, Nick Megoran, Rachel Woodward, and Daniel Bos. "Wootton Bassett and the Political Spaces of Remembrance and Mourning." *Area* 44.3 (2012) 356–63.
Jervis, Robert. "Cooperation under the Security Dilemma." *World Politics* 30.2 (1978) 167–214.
Johnston, Alastair Iain. *Cultural Realism: Strategic Culture and Grand Strategy in Ming China*. Princeton, NJ: Princeton University Press, 1995.
Jones, Charles A. "Christian Realism and the Foundations of the English School." *International Relations* 17.3 (2003) 371–87.
Joustra, R. J. "The Religious Problem with Religious Freedom: Why International Theory Needs Political Theology." PhD diss., University of Bath, 2013.
Juergensmeyer, M. "Religion as a Cause of Terrorism." *Roots of Terrorism* 1 (2006) 133–44.
Kalaitzidis, Pantelis. *Orthodoxy and Political Theology*. Geneva: World Council of Churches, 2012.
———. "Toward and Orthodox Political Theology." In *Political Theologies in Orthodox Christianity: Common Challenges-Divergent Positions*, edited by Kristina Stoeckl, Ingeborg Gabriel, and Aristotle Papanikolaou, 151–78. London: Bloomsbury, 2017.
Katongole, Emmanuel. "Postmodern Illusions and the Challenges of African Theology." In *An Eerdmans Reader in Contemporary Political Theology*, edited by William T. Cavanaugh, Jeffrey W. Bailey, and Craig Hovey, 503–24. Grand Rapids: Eerdmans, 2011.
———. *The Sacrifice of Africa: A Political Theology for Africa*. Grand Rapids: Eerdmans, 2011.
Katz, David. "Hydro-Political Hyperbole: Examining Incentives for Overemphasizing the Risks of Water Wars." *Global Environmental Politics* 11.1 (2011) 12–35.
Kassenova, Togzhan. *Atomic Steppe: How Kazakhstan Gave up the Bomb*. Stanford, CA: Stanford University Press, 2022.
Kaunda, C. J. *The Nation That Fears God Prospers: A Critique of Zambian Pentecostal Theopolitical Imagination*. Minneapolis: Fortress, 2018.
Kelly, Robert E. "A 'Confucian Long Peace' in Pre-Western East Asia?" *European Journal of International Relations* 18.3 (2012) 407–30.
Kelso, Paul. "UK Response to Salisbury Poisonings 'Indulged' Russia, Says Irish PM." Sky News, May 25, 2022. https://news.sky.com/story/uk-response-to-salisbury-poisonings-indulged-russia-says-irish-pm-12621088.
Kerr, Nathan R. *Christ, History and Apocalyptic: The Politics of Christian Mission*. Eugene, OR: Cascade, 2008.
Keys, Mary M. *Aquinas, Aristotle, and the Promise of the Common Good*. Cambridge: Cambridge University Press, 2006.

Khalid, Adeeb. *Islam after Communism: Religion and Politics in Central Asia*. Berkeley: University of California, 2007.

Khamidov, Alisher, Nick Megoran, and John Heathershaw. "Bottom-Up Peacekeeping in Southern Kyrgyzstan: How Local Actors Managed to Prevent the Spread of Violence from Osh/Jalal-Abad to Aravan, June 2010." *Nationalities Papers* 45.6 (2017) 1118–34.

Khodour, David. "Is Migration Good for Development? Wrong Question!" OECD Development Centre, October 8, 2015. https://www.oecd.org/dev/development-posts-migration-development.htm.

King, John Edward. *A History of Post Keynesian Economics Since 1936*. Cheltenham, UK: Edward Elgar, 2002.

Kinnvall, Catarina. "Globalization and Religious Nationalism: Self, Identity, and the Search for Ontological Security." *Political Psychology* 25.5 (2004) 741–67.

Klusmeyer, Douglas. "Beyond Tragedy: Hannah Arendt and Hans Morgenthau on Responsibility, Evil and Political Ethics." *International Studies Review* 11.2 (2009) 332–51.

Koch, A. "The New Crusaders: Contemporary Extreme Right Symbolism and Rhetoric." *Perspectives on Terrorism* 11.5 (2017) 13–24.

Koehler, J. O. *Stasi: The Untold Story of The East German Secret Police*. New York: Basic, 2008.

Kolpinskaya, Ekaterina, and Stuart Fox. "Praying on Brexit? Unpicking the Effect of Religion on Support for European Union Integration and Membership." *JCMS: Journal of Common Market Studies* 57.3 (2019) 580–98.

Kommersant. "The Nuclear Center in Sarov Will Buy Icons and Panels for 2.3 Million Rubles" (*Yaderniy Tsentr v Sarove zakupitikoniy I planno na 2.3 mln rublei*). May 24, 2019. https://www.kommersant.ru/doc/3977792?fbclid=IwAR1UpLztLM8W DBC_lygFAXRl3ftBJozOEiTIoJk7JHeNilqLYomde7Z8r5w.

Koopman, Sara. "Alter-Geopolitics: Other Securities Are Happening." *Geoforum* 42.3 (2011) 274–84.

KPMG. "Private Equity Market in Kazakhstan." May 2019. Accessed September 3, 2021. https://assets.kpmg/content/dam/kpmg/kz/pdf/2019/09/KPMG-Private-Equity-Market-in-Kazakhstan-ENG-2019.pdf.

Krauthammer, Charles. "The Unipolar Moment Revisited." *National Interest* 70 (2002) 5–18.

Kreider, Alan. *Journey towards Holiness: A Way of Living for God's Nation*. Scottsdale, PA: Herald, 1986.

Kritsiotis, Dino. "When States Use Armed Force." In *The Politics of International Law*, edited by Christian Reus-Smit, 45–79. Cambridge Studies in International Relations. Cambridge: Cambridge University Press, 2004.

Kroeker, P. Travis. *Messianic Political Theology and Diaspora Ethics: Essays in Exile*. Eugene, OR: Cascade, 2017.

Kubálková, Vendulka. "Toward an International Political Theology." In *Religion in International Relations: The Return from Exile*, edited by P. Hatzopoulos and F. Petito, 79–105. Basingstoke, UK: Palgrave Macmillan, 2003.

Kunhiyop, Samuel W. *African Christian Ethics*. Nairobi: Hippo, 2008.

Kuru, Ahmet T. "Passive and Assertive Secularism: Historical Conditions, Ideological Struggles and State Policies towards Religion." *World Politics* 59.4 (2007) 568–94.

Latham, Andrew. "Theorizing the Crusades: Identity, Institutions, and Religious War in Medieval Latin Christendom." *International Studies Quarterly* 55.1 (2011) 223–43.
Lazaridis, Gabriella, ed. *Security, Insecurity and Migration in Europe*. London: Routledge, 2016.
Lee, Ji-Young. *China's Hegemony: Four Hundred Years of East Asian Domination*. New York: Columbia University Press, 2016.
Leithart, Peter J. *Defending Constantine: The Twilight of an Empire and the Dawn of Christendom*. Downers Grove: InterVarsity, 2010.
Lenton, Tim M. "Beyond 2° C: Redefining Dangerous Climate Change for Physical Systems." *Interdisciplinary Review of Climate Change* 2.3 (2011) 451–61.
Lewis, David G. *Russia's New Authoritarianism: Putin and the Politics of Order*. Edinburgh: Edinburgh University Press, 2020.
Lindsay, Hal. *The Late Great Planet Earth*. Grand Rapids: Zondervan, 1970.
Ling, L. H. M. "Worlds beyond Westphalia: Daoist Dialectics and the 'China Threat.'" *Review of International Studies* 39.3 (2013) 549–68.
Lopez, Julia Costa. "Political Authority in International Relations: Revisiting the Medieval Debate." *International Organization* 74.2 (2020) 222–52.
Lopez, Julia Costa. "Beyond Eurocentrism and Orientalism: Revisiting the Othering of Jews and Muslims through Medieval Canon Law." *Review of International Studies* 42.3 (2016) 450–70.
Lucas, Adam. "Risking the Earth Part 1: Reassessing Dangerous Anthropogenic Interference and Climate Risk in IPCC Processes." *Climate Risk Management* 31 (2021) 100257.
Luehrmann, Sonja. *Secularism Soviet Style: Teaching Atheism and Religion in a Volga Republic*. Bloomington: Indiana University Press, 2011.
Mabee, Bryan. "Security Studies and the Security State: Security Provision in Historical Context." *International Relations* 17.2 (2003) 135–51.
MacDonald, Paul K., and Joseph M. Parent. "The Status of Status in World Politics." *World Politics* 73.2 (2021) 358–91.
Mack, Andrew, et al. *Human Security Report*. Vancouver: Liu Institute for Global Issues, University of British Columbia, 2005.
Maddison, Angus. *Development Centre Studies: The World Economy Historical Statistics*. Paris: OECD, 2003.
Maddocks, Andrew, et al. "Ranking the World's Most Water-Stressed Countries in 2040." World Resources Institute, August 26, 2015. https://www.wri.org/insights/ranking-worlds-most-water-stressed-countries-2040.
Mahony, Liam, and Luis Enrique Eguren. *Unarmed Bodyguards: International Accompaniment for the Protection of Human Rights*. West Hartford, CT: Kumarian, 1997.
Maloney, Sean M., and Scot Robertson. "The Revolution in Military Affairs: Possible Implications for Canada." *International Journal* 54.3 (1999) 443–62.
Mann, Michael. "The Autonomous Power of the State: Its Origins, Mechanisms and Results." *European Journal of Sociology/Archives Européennes de Sociologie* 25.2 (1984) 185–213.
———. *The Dark Side of Democracy: Explaining Ethnic Cleansing*. Cambridge: Cambridge University Press, 2005.
———. *The Sources of Social Power*. Vol. 1, *A History of Power From the Beginning to AD 1760*. Cambridge: Cambridge University Press, 2012.

Marranci, G. "Multiculturalism, Islam and the Clash of Civilisations Theory: Rethinking Islamophobia." *Culture and Religion* 5.1 (2004) 105–17.

Marsh, Christopher, and Daniel Payne. "Religion, Culture, and Conflict in the 'Other' Christendom." *Nationalities Papers* 35.5 (2007) 807–10.

Marshall, Peter. *Demanding the Impossible: A History of Anarchism*. San Francisco: PM, 2009.

Marten, Kimberly. "President Putin's Rationality and Escalation in Russia's Invasion of Ukraine." *PONARS Eurasia Policy Memo.756* (March 2022). https://www.ponarseurasia.org/wp-content/uploads/2022/03/Pepm756_Marten_March2022.pdf.

Martens, Paul. *The Heterodox Yoder*. Eugene OR: Wipf and Stock Publishers, 2012.

Martin, David. *The Breaking of the Image: A Sociology of Christian Theory and Practice*. Oxford: Blackwell, 1980.

———. *On Secularization: Towards a Revised General Theory*. London: Routledge, 2005.

———. *Reflections on Sociology and Theology*. Oxford: Oxford University Press, 1997.

Mavelli, Luca. "Security and Secularization in International Relations." *European Journal of International Relations* 18.1 (2012) 177–99.

Mavelli, Luca, and Erin Wilson, eds. *The Refugee Crisis and Religion: Secularism, Security and Hospitality in Question*. Lanham, MD: Rowman & Littlefield, 2016.

Mayne, Tom, and John Heathershaw. *Criminality Notwithstanding: The Use of Unexplained Wealth Orders in Anti-Corruption Cases*. Global Integrity: Anti Corruption Evidence Project, March 2022. https://ace.globalintegrity.org/wp-content/uploads/2022/03/CriminalityNotwithstanding.pdf.

McAlister, Melani. *The Kingdom of God Has No Borders: A Global History of American Evangelicals*. Oxford: Oxford University Press, 2018.

McAlpine, T. H. *Facing the Powers: What Are the Options?* Eugene, OR: Wipf and Stock, 1991.

McDonald, Matt. "Climate Change and Security: Towards Ecological Security?" *International Theory* 10.2 (2018) 153–80.

McIntyre, A. *After Virtue: A Study in Moral Theology*. 2nd ed. Notre Dame, IN: University of Notre Dame Press, 1984.

McQueen, Alison. *Political Realism in Apocalyptic Times*. Cambridge: Cambridge University Press, 2017.

McSweeney, Bill. *Security, Identity and Interests*. Cambridge: Cambridge University Press, 1999.

Mearsheimer, John J. "Back to the Future: Instability in Europe After the Cold War." *International Security* 15.1 (1990) 5–56.

———. *The Tragedy of Great Power Politics*. New York: Norton, 2001.

———. "Why the Ukraine Crisis Is the West's Fault: The Liberal Delusions That Provoked Putin." *Foreign Affairs* 93 (2014) 77–89.

Megoran, Nick. "'Go Anywhere I Damn Well Please?' Towards an Anarchist Vocational Ethics of International Borders." In *A Research Agenda for Border Studies*, edited by James Scott, 183–200. Cheltenham, UK: Edward Elgar, 2020.

———. "Towards a Geography of Peace: Pacific Geopolitics and Evangelical Christian Crusade Apologies." *Transactions of the Institute of British Geographers* 35.3 (2010) 382–98.

———. *Warlike Christians in an Age of Violence*. Eugene, OR: Cascade, 2018.

Melander, Erik. "Gender Equality and Intrastate Armed Conflict." *International Studies Quarterly* 49.4 (2005) 695–714.

Mignolo, Walter. *The Darker Side of Western Modernity: Global Futures, Decolonial Options*. Chapel Hill, NC: Duke University Press, 2011.

Milbank, John. *Theology and Social Theory*. 2nd ed. Oxford: Blackwell, 2006.

Milbank, John, and Adrian Pabst. *The Politics of Virtue: Post-Liberalism and the Human Future*. Lanham, MD: Rowman & Littlefield, 2016.

Missing Migrants Project. "Deaths during Migration." Last accessed March 10, 2022. https://missingmigrants.iom.int/data.

Mitchell, Timothy. "Society, Economy and the State Effect." In *State/Culture: State Formation after the Cultural Turn*, edited by G. Steinmetz, 76–97. Ithaca, NY: Cornell University Press, 1999.

Mitchell, Chris. "'I See Us in the Middle of Prophecy!' Mike Evans Has 30M Evangelicals Praying for Jerusalem." *CBN News*, October 12, 2017. https://www1.cbn.com/cbnnews/israel/2017/december/mike-evans-we-rsquo-re-in-the-middle-of-prophecy.

Mitzen, Jennifer. "Ontological Security in World Politics: State Identity and the Security Dilemma." *European Journal of International Relations* 12.3 (2006) 341–70.

Moltmann, Jürgen. "Covenant or Leviathan? Political Theology for Modern Times." *Scottish Journal of Theology* 47.1 (1994) 19–42.

———. *Creating a Just Future: The Politics of Peace and the Ethics of Creation in a Threatened World*. London: SCM, 1989.

Morgenthau, Hans J. *Politics among Nations: The Struggle for Power and Peace*. 5th ed. New York: Knopf, 1985.

Morkevičius, Valerie. *Realist Ethics: Just War Traditions as Power Politics*. Cambridge: Cambridge University Press, 2018.

Moses, R. E. *Practices of Power: Revisiting the Principalities and Powers in the Pauline Letters*. Minneapolis: Fortress, 2014.

Moyn, Samuel. *Not Enough: Human Rights in an Unequal World*. Cambridge: Harvard University Press, 2018.

Muggeridge, Malcolm. *The End of Christendom*. Grand Rapids: Eerdmans, 1980.

Münkler, Herfried. *The New Wars*. London: Polity, 2005.

Murray Williams, Stuart. *Post-Christendom*. Milton Keynes, UK: Paternoster, 2011.

Myers, Ched. *Binding the Strongman*. New York: Orbis, 2008.

National Statistics. "UK Armed Forces Biannual Diversity Statistics." April 1, 2018. https://assets.publishing.service.gov.uk/government/uploads/system/uploads/attachment_data/file/712124/Biannual_Diversity_Statistics_Apr18.pdf.

Neufeld, Thomas Yoder. *Jesus and the Subversion of Violence: Wrestling with the New Testament Evidence*. London: SPCK, 2011.

Nichols, Aidan. *Christendom Awake: On Re-Energising the Church in Culture*. London: Black, 1999.

Niebuhr, Rheinhold. "Augustine's Political Realism." In *The Essential Reinhold Niebuhr*, edited by Robert McAfee Brown, 123–41. New Haven, CT: Yale University Press, 1986.

———. *The Nature and Destiny of Man: A Christian Interpretation*. Vol. 1, *Human Nature*. Louisville: Westminster John Knox, 1996.

———. "Why the Christian Church Is Not Pacifist." In *The Essential Rheinhold Niebuhr*, edited by Robert McAfee Brown, 102–19. New Haven, CT: Yale University Press, 1986.
Norris, Pippa, and Ronald Inglehart. *Sacred and Secular: Religion and Politics Worldwide*. 2nd ed. Cambridge: Cambridge University Press, 2011.
Northcott, Michael S. *An Angel Directs the Storm: Apocalyptic Religion and American Empire*. London: IB Tauris, 2004.
———. *The Environment and Christian Ethics*. Cambridge: Cambridge University Press, 1996.
———. *A Political Theology of Climate Change*. Grand Rapids: Eerdmans, 2013.
Nugent, John C. "A Yoderian Rejoinder to Peter J. Leithart's Defending Constantine." *Mennonite Quarterly Review* 85.4 (2011) 551+. Gale Academic OneFile. Accessed June 2, 2022. https://link.gale.com/apps/doc/A271514877/.
Nyberg–Sørensen, Ninna, Nicholas Van Hear, and Poul Engberg-Pedersen. "The Migration–Development Nexus: Evidence and Policy Options." *International Migration* 40.5 (2002) 49–73.
O'Donovan, Oliver. *The Desire of the Nations: Rediscovering the Roots of Political Theology*. Cambridge: Cambridge University Press, 1996.
———. *The Just War Revisited*. Cambridge: Cambridge University Press, 2003.
———. "Response to Respondents: Behold, the Lamb!" *Studies in Christian Ethics* 11.2 (1998) 91–110.
O'Grady, Hannah, and Joel Gunter. "SAS Unit Repeatedly Killed Afghan Detainees, BBC Finds." BBC *Panorama*, July 12, 2022. https://www.bbc.co.uk/news/uk-62083196.
Oh, Rebecca S. "Apocalyptic Realism: 'A New Category of the Event.'" *ISLE: Interdisciplinary Studies in Literature and Environment* 29.4 (2022) 1–20.
Oldenhuis, Huibert, et al. *Unarmed Civilian Protection*. Nonviolent Peaceforce. 2nd ed. 2021. https://www.nonviolentpeaceforce.org/images/UCPManual/2021_Course_Manual Full.pdf.
Osiander, A. "Sovereignty, International Relations, and the Westphalian Myth." *International Organization* 55.2 (2001) 251–87.
Ó Tuathail, Gearóid, and John Agnew. "Geopolitics and Discourse: Practical Geopolitical Reasoning in American Foreign Policy." *Political Geography* 11.2 (1992) 190–204.
OVD-Info. "Persecution for Anti-War Views." Last accessed August, 22, 2022. https://ovdinfo.org/.
Owen, Catherine, John Heathershaw, and Igor Savin. "How Postcolonial Is Post-Western IR? Mimicry and Mētis in the International Politics of Russia and Central Asia." *Review of International Studies* 44.2 (2018) 279–300.
Ozyakar, Ahmet Furkan. "A Constructivist Interpretation of Status-Seeking Cultural Diplomacy in Iran's Foreign Policy during the Era of Khatami and Ahmadinejad, 1997–2013." PhD diss., University of Exeter, August 2022.
Pabst, Adrian. "The Secularism of Post-Secularity: Religion, Realism, and the Revival of Grand Theory in IR." *Review of International Studies* 38.5 (2012) 995–1017.
Paipais, Vassillios. "Necessary Fiction: Realism's Tragic Theology." *International Politics* 50.6 (2013) 846–62.
———. "Reinhold Niebuhr and the Christian Realist Pendulum." *Journal of International Political Theory* 17.2 (2021) 185–202.

Pape, Robert A. "The Jan. 6 Insurrectionists Aren't Who You Think They Are." *Foreign Policy*, January 6, 2022. https://foreignpolicy.com/2022/01/06/trump-capitol-insurrection-january-6-insurrectionists-great-replacement-white-nationalism/.
Papkova, Irina, and Dmitry P. Gorenburg. "The Russian Orthodox Church and Russian Politics: Editors' Introduction." *Russian Politics & Law* 49.1 (2011) 3–7.
Pasha, Mustapha K. "Fractured Worlds: Islam, Identity, and International Relations." *Global Society* 17.2 (2003) 111–20.
Patriarch Kirill. "Letter to the General Secretary of the World Council of Churches." March 10, 2022. https://www.oikoumene.org/sites/default/files/2022-03/Scan%20of%20the%20official%20letter.pdf.
Patterson, Eric, ed. *The Christian Realists: Reassessing the Contributions of Niebuhr and His Contemporaries*. Lanham, MD: University Press of America, 2003.
Pavlischek, Keith. "Reinhold Niebuhr, Christian Realism, and Just War Theory: A Critique." In *Christianity and Power Politics Today*, edited by Eris Patterson, 53–71. New York: Palgrave Macmillan, 2008.
Perry, John. "Grandpa Milbank." *Marginalia*, October 13, 2017. https://themarginaliareview.com/grandpa-milbank/.
Peterson, Matt. "Did Iraq Ever Become A Just War?" *Atlantic*, March 24, 2018. https://www.theatlantic.com/international/archive/2018/03/iraq-war-ethics/556448/.
Petito, Fabio, and Pavlos Hatzopoulos. *Religion in International Relations: The Return from Exile*. New York: Springer, 2003.
Pew Research. "Country's Economic Situation: United States." Global Indicators Database, Updated in March 2022 with polling data from Spring 2021 Global Attitudes Survey. https://www.pewresearch.org/global/database/indicator/5/country/US.
———. "The Future of World Religions: Population Growth Projections 2010–2050." April 2, 2015. https://assets.pewresearch.org/wp-content/uploads/sites/11/2015/03/PF_15.04.02_ProjectionsFullReport.pdf.
Phillips, Andrew. "Global IR Meets Global History: Sovereignty, Modernity, and the International System's Expansion in the Indian Ocean Region." *International Studies Review* 18.1 (2016) 62–77.
———. "The Global Transformation, Multiple Early Modernities, and International Systems Change." *International Theory* 8.3 (2016) 481–91.
———. "Saving Civilization from Empire: Belligerency, Pacifism and the Two Faces of Civilization during the Second Opium War." *European Journal of International Relations* 18.1 (2012) 5–27.
———. *War, Religion, and Empire: The Transformation of International Orders*. Cambridge: Cambridge University Press, 2010.
Phillips, Andrew, and Jason Campbell Sharman. *Outsourcing Empire*. Princeton, NJ: Princeton University Press, 2020.
Philpott, Daniel. "Explaining the Political Ambivalence of Religion." *American Political Science Review* 101.3 (2007) 505–25.
———. "The Religious Roots of Modern International Relations." *World Politics* 52.2 (2000) 206–45.
Phiri, I. "President Frederick J. T. Chiluba of Zambia: The Christian Nation and Democracy." *Journal of Religion in Africa* 33.4 (2003) 401–28.
Pickett, Kate, and Richard Wilkinson. *The Spirit Level: Why Equality Is Better for Everyone*. London: Penguin, 2010.

Piketty, Thomas. *Capital in the Twenty-First Century*. Translated by Arthur Goldhammer. Cambridge: Belknap, 2014.
Piven, W., and S. Cloward. *Poor People's Movements*. New York: Vintage, 1977.
Pocock, John Greville Agard. *The Machiavellian Moment: Florentine Political Thought and the Atlantic Republican Tradition*. Princeton, NJ: Princeton University Press, 2016.
Polimédio, Chayenne. "The Rise of the Brazilian Evangelicals." *Atlantic*, January 24, 2018. https://www.theatlantic.com/international/archive/2018/01/the-evangelical-takeover-of-brazilian-politics/551423/.
Porter, Brian. "David Davies: A Hunter after Peace." *Review of International Studies* 15.1 (1989) 27–36.
Porter, Patrick. *Blunder: Britain's War in Iraq*. New York: Oxford University Press, 2018.
———. *The False Promise of Liberal Order: Nostalgia, Delusion and the Rise of Trump*. Cambridge: Polity, 2020.
Prichard, Alex. "What Can the Absence of Anarchism Tell Us about the History and Purpose of International Relations?" *Review of International Studies* 37.4 (2011) 1647–69.
Prüss-Üstün, Annette, et al. "Burden of Disease from Inadequate Water, Sanitation and Hygiene in Low- and Middle-Income Settings: A Retrospective Analysis of Data From 145 Countries." *Tropical Medicine & International Health* 19.8 (2014) 894–905.
Putin, Vladimir. *On the Historical Unity of Russians and Ukrainians*. July 12, 2021. https://en.kremlin.ru/events/president/news/66181.
Qin, Y. "Why Is There No Chinese International Relations Theory?" *International Relations of the Asia-Pacific* 7 (2007) 313–40.
Quijano, Anibal. "Coloniality of Power, Eurocentrism and Latin America." *Nepantla: Views from South* 1.3 (2000) 533–80.
Rachman, Gideon. *The Age of the Strongman: How the Cult of the Leader Threatens Democracy around the World*. London: Vintage 2022.
Radnitz, Scott. "Vladimir Putin's Casus Belli for Invading Ukraine." *PONARS Eurasia Policy Memo* 762, March 2022. https://www.ponarseurasia.org/wp-content/uploads/2022/03/Pepm762_Radnitz_March2022-1.pdf.
Ramsey, Paul. *The Just War: Force and Political Responsibility*. New York: Scribner, 1968.
Ranger, T. "Evangelical Christianity and Democracy in Africa: A Continental Comparison." *Journal of Religion in Africa* 33.1 (2003) 112–17.
Rapoport, Anatol, Albert M. Chammah, and Carol J. Orwant. *Prisoner's Dilemma: A Study in Conflict and Cooperation*. Vol. 165. Ann Arbor: University of Michigan Press, 1965.
Redress. "UK Anti-Corruption Sanctions: A Year in Review." May 2, 2022. https://redress.org/news/uk-anti-corruption-sanctions-a-year-in-review/.
Reed, Esther D. "Ecclesial Life and Political Practice: Re-Appropriating Augustine's Political Rhetoric in Contexts of Risk and Counter-Terrorism Strategy." In *Internationale Gerechtigkeit und Institutionelle Verantwortung*, Proceedings of the Berlin-Brandenburg Academy of Sciences and Humanities Symposium, December 21, 2017, edited by Julian Nida-Rümelin, 407–24. Berlin: de Gruyter 2019.
———. *Theology for International Law*. London: Bloomsbury, 2013.

Regan, Patrick M., Richard W. Frank, and Aysegul Aydin. "Diplomatic Interventions and Civil War: A New Dataset." *Journal of Peace Research* 46.1 (2009) 135–46.
Rengger, Nicholas. "The Exorcist? John Gray, Apocalyptic Religion and the Return to Realism in World Politics." *International Affairs* 83.5 (2007) 951–59.
———. *Just War and International Order: The Uncivil Condition in World Politics*. Cambridge: Cambridge University Press, 2013.
Reno, William. *Warlord Politics and African States*. Boulder, CO: Rienner, 1998.
RFE/RL. "Kazakh President Announces CSTO Troop Withdrawal, Criticizes Predecessor." January 11, 2022. https://www.rferl.org/a/kazakhstan-detains-10000-unrest/31648618.html.
Richters, Katja. *The Post-Soviet Russian Orthodox Church: Politics, Culture and Greater Russia*. London: Routledge, 2012.
Ringen, Stein. *The Perfect Dictatorship: China in the 21st Century*. Hong Kong: Hong Kong University Press, 2016.
Ritchie, Hannah. "Climate Change and Flying: What Share of Global CO_2 Emissions Come from Aviation?" *Our World in Data*, October 22, 2020. https://ourworldindata.org/co2-emissions-from-aviation.
Rosenberg, Emma. "Taking the 'Race' out of Master Race: The Evolving Role of the Jew in White Supremacist Discourse." Paper presented to the conference Christian Identity in National, Transnational and Local Space, New College, University of Oxford, April 4–5, 2022.
Roser, Max. "War and Peace after 1945." OurWorldInData.org. Accessed July 25, 2022. http://ourworldindata.org/data/war-peace/war-and-peace-after-1945/.
Rowland, Christopher. "Response to *Desire of the Nations*." *Studies in Christian Ethics* 11.2 (1998) 77–85.
Rubinstein, William D. "Genocide and Historical Debate." *History Today* 54.4 (2004) 36–38.
Rumer, Eugene, and Andrew S. Weiss. "Ukraine: Putin's Unfinished Business." *Carnegie Endowment for International Peace*, November 12, 2021. https://carnegieendowment.org/2021/11/12/ukraine-putin-s-unfinished-business-pub-85771.
Rummel, R. J. *Death by Government*. University of Hawaii, 2002. Last accessed March 10, 2022. https://www.hawaii.edu/powerkills/DBG.CHAP1.HTM.
Russell, Stuart. "Lecture 2: The Future Role of AI in Warfare—Transcript." The Reith Lectures 2021, recorded at the BBC, December 2021. https://downloads.bbc.co.uk/radio4/reith2021/BBC_Reith_Lectures_2021_2.pdf.
Russian Orthodox Church. "Archpastors—Participants of the Local Council Attended a Reception in the St. George Hall of the Grand Kremlin Palace" (Arkhipastyri — Uchastniki Pomestnogo Sobora Prisutstvovali Na Priyeme v Georgiyevskom Zale Bol'shogo Kremlevskogo Dvortsa) February 2, 2009. http://www.patriarchia.ru/db/text/548365.html.
Salgado, Soli. "Why Write the Story of the Allegations against John Howard Yoder?" *National Catholic Reporter*, June 25, 2015. https://www.ncronline.org/blogs/ncr-today/why-write-story-allegations-against-john-howard-yoder.
Sandal, N. A., and P. James. "Religion and International Relations Theory: Towards a Mutual Understanding." *European Journal of International Relations* 17.1 (2010) 3–25.

Sanneh, Lamin. *Whose Religion Is Christianity? The Gospel beyond the West*. Grand Rapids: Eerdmans, 2003.
Schipani, Daniel S. *Freedom and Discipleship: Liberation Theology in an Anabaptist Perspective*. Maryknoll, NY: Orbis, 1989.
Schlabach, Gerald W. "Just Policing, Responsibility to Protect, and Anabaptist Two-Kingdom Theology." *Conrad Grebel Review* 28.3 (2010) 73–88.
Schmitt, Carl. *The Concept of the Political: Expanded Edition*. Chicago: University of Chicago Press, 2008.
———. *The Nomos of the Earth*. 1950. Reprint, New York: Telos, 2003.
———. *Political Theology: Four Chapters on the Concept of Sovereignty*. Chicago: University of Chicago Press, 2005.
Schüssler-Fiorenza, Elizabeth. *The Book of Revelation: Justice and Judgment*. Philadelphia: Fortress, 1989.
Scott, James C. *Domination and the Arts of Resistance: Hidden Transcripts*. New Haven, CT: Yale University Press, 1990.
———. *Seeing Like a State: How Certain Schemes to Improve the Human Condition Have Failed*. New Haven, CT: Yale University Press, 1998.
Searle, Joshua T. *Theology After Christendom: Forming Prophets for a Post-Christian World*. After Christendom. Eugene, OR: Cascade, 2018.
Searle, Joshua T., and Mikhail Cherenkov. *A Future and a Hope: Mission, Theological Education, and the Transformation of Post-Soviet Society*. Eugene, OR: Wipf and Stock, 2014.
Seiple, Robert A., and Dennis R. Hoover, eds. *Religion and Security: The New Nexus in International Relations*. Lanham, MD: Rowman and Littlefield, 2004.
Shahi, D. "Introducing Sufism to International Relations Theory: A Preliminary Inquiry into Epistemological, Ontological, and Methodological Pathways." *European Journal of International Relations* 25.1 (2019) 250–75.
Shani, Giorgio. *Religion, Identity and Human Security*. London: Routledge, 2014.
———. "Towards a Post-Western IR: The Umma, Khalsa Panth, and Critical International Relations Theory." *International Studies Review* 10 (2008) 722–34.
Shevzov, Vera. "Orthodox Constructions of the West in Russia." In *Orthodox Constructions of the West*, edited by George E. Demacopoulos and Aristotle Papanikolaou, 83–101. New York: Fordham University Press, 2013.
Shishkov, Andrey. "Some Reflections on the Declaration of the 'Russian World' Teaching." *Public Orthodoxy*, April 13, 2022. https://publicorthodoxy.org/2022/04/13/some-reflections-on-the-declaration-on-the-russian-world-teaching/.
Sibley, Nate, and Ben Judah. *Countering Global Kleptocracy: A New US Strategy for Fighting Authoritarian Corruption*. Washington, DC: Hudson Institute, 2020. http://media.hudson.org.s3.amazonaws.com/Countering%20Global%20Kleptocracy%20(002).pdf.
Sider, Ronald J. "God's People Reconciling." CPT. Last accessed August 22, 2022. https://cpt.org/sider.
Siedentop, Larry. *Inventing the Individual: The Origins of Western Liberalism*. Cambridge: Harvard University Press, 2014.
Sledge, Benjamin. "The Decline of the American Church." *Medium*, September 21, 2021. https://gen.medium.com/the-decline-of-the-american-church-689386914491.
Smith, Graeme. *A Short History of Secularism*. London: Bloomsbury, 2007.

Smith, James K. A. *Awaiting the King: Reforming Public Theology*. Grand Rapids: Baker Academic, 2017.

Smith Finley, Joanne. "Why Scholars and Activists Increasingly Fear a Uyghur Genocide in Xinjiang." *Journal of Genocide Research* 23.3 (2021) 348–70.

Social Science Research Council. "The Immanent Frame." Last accessed September 1, 2022. https://tif.ssrc.org/.

Sölle, Dorothee. "Fatherhood, Power, and Barbarism: Feminist Challenges to Authoritarian Religion." In *An Eerdmans Reader in Contemporary Political Theology*, edited by Cavanaugh, William T., Jeffrey W. Bailey, and Craig Hovey, 327–34. Grand Rapids: Eerdmans, 2011.

Spillsbury, P. *The Throne, the Lamb and the Dragon*. Downers Grove: InterVarsity, 2002.

Stassen, Glen Harold. *Just Peacemaking: Transforming Initiatives for Justice and Peace*. Louisville: Westminster John Knox, 1992.

———. "Just Peacemaking as the New Paradigm for the Ethics of Peace and War." In *Formation for Life: Just Peacemaking and Twenty-First-Century Discipleship*, edited by Glen Stassen, Rodney L. Petersen, and Timothy A. Norton, 137–46. Eugene, OR: Pickwick, 2013.

Statista. "Number of Scheduled Passengers Boarded by the Global Airline Industry from 2004 to 2022." Accessed July 9, 2022. https://www.statista.com/statistics/564717/airline-industry-passenger-traffic-globally/.

Stavrianakis, Anna. "Playing with Words while Yemen Burns: Managing Criticism of UK Arms Sales to Saudi Arabia." *Global Policy* 8.4 (2017) 563–68.

Stewart, Katherine. "Eighty-One Percent of White Evangelicals Voted for Donald Trump. Why?" *The Nation*, November 17, 2016. https://www.thenation.com/article/archive/eighty-one-percent-of-white-evangelicals-voted-for-donald-trump-why/.

Stiglitz, Joseph E. "Some Lessons from the East Asian Miracle." *World Bank Research Observer* 11.2 (1996) 151–77.

Stoeckl, Kristina. "The Russian Orthodox Church's Conservative Crusade." *Current History* 116.792 (2017) 271–76.

Stolarski, Piotr Tadeusz. "Dominican-Jesuit Rivalry and the Politics of Catholic Renewal in Poland 1564–1648." *Journal of Ecclesiastical History* 62.2 (2011) 255–72.

Stringfellow, William. *Conscience and Obedience*. Waco, TX: Word, 1977.

Swaine, Jon, et al. "Young Black Men Killed by US Police at Highest Rate in Year of 1,134 Deaths." *Guardian*, December 31, 2015. https://www.theguardian.com/us-news/2015/dec/31/the-counted-police-killings-2015-young-black-men.

Sykes, Stephen. *Power and Christian Theology*. London: Bloomsbury, 2006.

Syse, Henrik. "The Platonic Roots of Just War Doctrine: A Reading of Plato's *Republic*." *Diametros* 7.23 (2010) 104–23.

Taylor, Charles. *A Secular Age*. Cambridge: Harvard University Press, 2009.

Tax Justice Network. "Tax Avoidance and Evasion—The Scale of the Problem." Briefing, November 2017. https://taxjustice.net/wp-content/uploads/2017/11/Tax-dodging-the-scale-of-the-problem-TJN-Briefing.pdf.

Teschke, Benno. "Theorizing the Westphalian System of States: International Relations from Absolutism to Capitalism." *European Journal of International Relations* 8.1 (2002) 5–48.

Thomas, Heath. "The Old Testament, 'Holy War' and Christian Morality." *Comment*, November 21, 2021. https://comment.org/the-old-testament-holy-war-and-christian-morality/.
Thomas, Scott. *The Global Resurgence of Religion and the Transformation of International Relations: The Struggle for the Soul of the Twenty-First Century.* New York: Palgrave Macmillan, 2005.
Tilly, Charles. "War Making and State Making as Organized Crime." In *Collective Violence, Contentious Politics, and Social Change*, edited by E. Castaneda and Cathy Schneider, 121–39. London: Routledge, 2017.
Tin-Bor Hui, Victoria. *War and State Formation in Ancient China and Early Modern Europe.* New York: Cambridge University Press, 2005.
Tobin, Sam. "Students at University of Kent Must Take 'White Privilege' Course." *Times*, September 28, 2021. https://www.thetimes.co.uk/article/students-at-university-of-kent-must-take-white-privilege-course-clc9zm6nl.
Toft, Monica Duffy. "Ending Civil Wars: A Case for Rebel Victory?" *International Security* 34.4 (2010) 7–36.
Transition Town Totnes. "How to Create a People's Climate Emergency Action Plan." July 2019. https://www.transitiontowntotnes.org/resources-3/.
Transparency International. "What Is Grand Corruption and How Can We Stop It?" September 21, 2016. https://www.transparency.org/en/news/what-is-grand-corruption-and-how-can-we-stop-it.
———. "Who Is Opening the Gates for Kleptocrats?" June 11, 2020. Accessed August 4, 2021. https://www.transparency.org/en/news/who-is-opening-the-gates-for-kleptocrats.
Troy, Jodok. *Christian Approaches to International Affairs.* Basingstoke, UK: Palgrave Macmillan, 2012.
Truss, Elizabeth. "Building the Network of Liberty: Foreign Secretary's Speech." Speech to Chatham House. Gov.UK, December 8, 2021. https://www.gov.uk/government/speeches/foreign-secretary-liz-truss-building-the-network-of-liberty.
Turner, Camilla. "Russell Group University Accused of Soviet-Style Censorship." *Telegraph*, May 15, 2021. https://www.telegraph.co.uk/news/2021/05/15/russell-group-university-accused-soviet-style-censorship2/.
UAWire. "France's Far-Right National Front Asks Russia for €27 Million Loan." February 19, 2016. https://www.uawire.org/news/france-s-far-right-national-front-asks-russia-for-27-million-loan.
UNHCR. "Figures at a Glance." Last accessed March 10, 2022. https://www.unhcr.org/uk/figures-at-a-glance.html.
United Nations. "Growth in United Nations Membership." Accessed May 31, 2022. https://www.un.org/en/about-us/growth-in-un-membership.
———. "Ninety Per Cent of War-Time Casualties Are Civilians." Press Release, May 25, 2022. https://www.un.org/press/en/2022/sc14904.doc.htm.
United Nations Development Programme. *Human Development Report.* New York: Oxford University Press, 1994. https://hdr.undp.org/system/files/documents//hdr1994encompletenostatspdf.pdf.
———. "Special Report on Human Security." February 8, 2022. https://hcss.nl/wp-content/uploads/2014/01/Peace_and_conflict_across_time.pdf.
United States of America. *National Security Strategy.* Washington, DC: White House, 2002.

Uppsala Conflict Data Program. "Definitions." Accessed September 19, 2018. http://www.pcr.uu.se/research/ucdp/definitions/.
Valk, John-Harmen. "Poetics and Politics: Rengger, Weber and the *Virtuosi* of Religion." In *The Civil Condition in World Politics: Beyond Tragedy and Utopianism*, edited by Vassilios Paipais, 53–74. Bristol, UK: Bristol University Press, 2022.
———. "Religiosity with/out Religion: Hans J. Morgenthau, Disenchantment and International Politics." In *Theology and World Politics*, edited by Vassilios Paipais, 315–43. London: Palgrave Macmillan, 2020.
Van Rythoven, Eric. "Learning to Feel, Learning to Fear? Emotions, Imaginaries, and Limits in the Politics of Securitization." *Security Dialogue* 46.5 (2015) 458–75.
Veković, Marko. "Belonging without Attending? National Identity and Contemporary Religious Pattern in Serbia." Paper presented to the conference Christian Identity in National, Transnational and Local Space, New College, University of Oxford, April 4–5, 2022.
Venkatesh, Sudhir Alladi. "The Social Organization of Street Gang Activity in an Urban Ghetto." *American Journal of Sociology* 103.1 (1997) 82–111.
Volos Academy for Theological Studies. "The War in Ukraine and the Emergence of a New Theological Agenda in Orthodoxy." May 11, 2022. https://mailchi.mp/8fbfb55daa1c/lecture-by-the-director-of-the-volos-academy-in-geneva-the-war-in-ukraine-the-emergence-of-a-new-theological-agenda-in-eastern-orthodoxy?e=bded5df083.
Wæver, Ole, Barry Buzan, Morten Kelstrup, and Pierre Lemaitre. *Identity, Migration and the New Security Agenda in Europe*. New York: St. Martin's, 1993.
Walker, Christopher, and Melissa Aten. "The Rise of Kleptocracy: A Challenge for Democracy." *Journal of Democracy* 29.1 (2018) 20–24.
Walker, Robert B. J. "The Subject of Security." In *Critical Security Studies*, edited by Keith Krause and Michael C. Williams, 61–81. Minneapolis: Minnesota University Press, 1997.
Wallis, Jim. *Agenda for Biblical People: A New Focus for Developing a Lifestyle of Discipleship*, New York: Harper and Row, 1976.
Walsh, Brian, and Sylvia Kessmat. *Colossians Remixed: Subverting the Empire*. Downers Grove: InterVarsity, 2004.
Walters, James. *Loving Your Neighbour in an Age of Religious Conflict: A New Agenda for Interfaith Relations*. London: Kingsley, 2019.
Waltz, Kenneth N. *Man, the State, and War: A Theoretical Analysis*. New York: Columbia University Press, 2001.
———. *Theory of International Politics*. New York: Random House, 1979.
Walzer, Michael. *Arguing about War*. New Haven, CT: Yale University Press, 2008.
Ward, Graham. *The Politics of Discipleship*. The Church and Postmodern Culture. Becoming Postmaterial Citizens. Grand Rapids: Baker Academic, 2009.
Way, Lucan Ahmad. "The Rebirth of the Liberal World Order?" *Journal of Democracy* 33.2 (2022) 5–17.
Weaver, J. Denny. *The Nonviolent God*. Grand Rapids: Eerdmans, 2013.
Weber, C. *Simulating Sovereignty*. Cambridge: Cambridge University Press, 1995.
Wedeman, Andrew. "The Rise of Kleptocracy: Does China Fit the Model?" *Journal of Democracy* 29.1 (2018) 86–95.
Weima, Jeffrey A. D. "'Peace and Security' (1 Thessalonians 5.3) Prophetic Warning or Political Propaganda?" *New Testament Studies* 58.3 (2012) 331–59.

Weiner, Myron. "Security, Stability, and International Migration." *International Security* 17.3 (1992) 91–126.
Wendt, Alexander. "Anarchy Is What States Make of It: The Social Construction of Power Politics." *International Organization* 46.2 (1992) 391–425.
———. "Constructing International Politics." *International Security* 20.1 (1995) 71–81.
———. *Social Theory of International Relations*. Cambridge: Cambridge University Press, 1999.
Wheeler, Nicholas, and Ken Booth. *The Security Dilemma: Fear, Cooperation, and Trust in World Politics*. London: Palgrave Macmillan, 2008.
White, Joel R. "'Peace and Security' (1 Thessalonians 5.3): Is It Really a Roman Slogan?" *New Testament Studies* 59.3 (2013) 382–95.
Wight, Colin. *Agents and Structures in International Relations*. Cambridge: Cambridge University Press, 2007.
Wight, Martin. "The Church, Russia and the West." *Ecumenical Review* 1.1 (1949) 25–45.
———. *Power Politics*. London: Black, 2002.
———. "Why Is There No International Theory?" *International Relations* 2.1 (1960) 35–48.
Williams, Michael C. "Identity and the Politics of Security." *European Journal of International Relations* 4.2 (1998) 204–25.
———. "Securitization as Political Theory: The Politics of the Extraordinary." *International Relations* 29.1 (2015) 114–20.
———. "Why Ideas Matter in International Relations: Hans Morgenthau, Classical Realism, and the Moral Construction of Power Politics." *International Organization* 58.4 (2004) 633–65.
Williams, Robert E., Jr., and Dan Caldwell. "Just Post Bellum: Just War Theory and the Principles of Just Peace." *International Studies Perspectives* 7.4 (2006) 309–20.
Williams, Rowan. "John Mere's Commemoration Sermon." Archbishop of Canterbury, April 20, 2004. http://rowanwilliams.archbishopofcanterbury.org/articles.php/1645/john-meres-commemoration-sermon.html.
———. "Politics and the Soul: A Reading of the City of God." In *An Eerdmans Reader in Contemporary Political Theology*, edited by William T. Cavanaugh, Jeffrey W. Bailey, and Craig Hovey, 731–49. Grand Rapids: Eerdmans, 2011.
———, ed. *Sergii Bulgakov: Towards a Russian Political Theology*. London: Black, 1999.
Wink, Walter. *Engaging the Powers: Discernment and Resistance in a World of Domination*. Philadelphia: Fortress, 1992.
———. *Unmasking the Powers: The Invisible Forces That Determine Human Existence*. Philadelphia: Fortress, 1984.
Wolfers, Arnold. "'National Security' as an Ambiguous Symbol." *Political Science Quarterly* 67.4. (1952) 481–502.
Womack, Jess. "The Rise and Fall of Liberal Evangelicalism in the United States." *Retrospect Journal*, April 25, 2021. https://retrospectjournal.com/2021/04/25/the-rise-and-fall-of-liberal-evangelicalism-in-the-united-states/.
Woodman, Simon. *The Book of Revelation*. London: SCM, 2008.
Woolcock, Nicola. "St Andrews University Sets Bias Test for Entry." *Times*, October 1, 2021 https://www.thetimes.co.uk/article/pass-bias-test-to-enter-st-andrews-rgcvcglx3.
Wordsworth, William. *Ecclesiastical Sonnets*. 1821–22.

World Bank. "Personal Remittances Received." Last accessed March 10, 2022. https://data.worldbank.org/indicator/BX.TRF.PWKR.DT.GD.ZS?most_recent_value_desc=true.
World Values Survey. "Findings and Insights." Accessed August 30, 2022. https://www.worldvaluessurvey.org/WVSContents.jsp?CMSID=Findings.
Wright, N. T. *Revelation for Everyone*. London: SPCK, 2012.
Wright, Nigel G. *Free Church, Free State: The Positive Baptist Vision*. Reprint, Eugene, OR: Wipf and Stock, 2011.
———. *A Theology of the Dark Side: Putting the Power of Evil in Its Place*. Carlisle,UK: Paternoster, 2003.
Yabro Collins, Adela. *Crisis and Catharsis: The Power of the Apocalypse*. Louisville: Westminster John Knox, 1984.
Yoder, John Howard. *Christian Witness to the State*. Scottsdale, PA: Herald, 2007.
———. *For the Nations: Essays Public and Evangelical*. Grand Rapids: Eerdmans, 1997.
———. *Original Revolution: Essays on Christian Pacifism*. Scottsdale, PA: Herald, 2003.
———. "Peace without Eschatology?" In *The Royal Priesthood: Essays Ecclesiological and Ecumenical*, edited by Michael G. Cartwright, 143–67. Scottsdale, PA: Herald, 1998.
———. *The Politics of Jesus*. Grand Rapids: Eerdmans, 1972.
———. "A Theological Critique of Violence." In *The War of the Lamb: The Ethics of Nonviolence and Peacemaking*, edited by Glen Stassen, Mark Thiessen Nation, and Matt Hamsher, 27–42. Grand Rapids: Brazos, 2009.
Young, Daniel. "Martin Wight: Politics in the Era of the Leviathan." In *The Christian Realists*, edited by Eric Paterson, 103–36. Lanham, MD: University Press of America, 2003.
Zembylas, Loukaidis, M. "Greek-Cypriot Teachers' Perceptions of Religion and Its Contribution to Peace: Perspectives of (In)compatibility in a Divided Society." *Journal of Peace Education* 14.2 (2017) 176–94.

Index

Aquinas, Thomas, 57, 73–75, 287, 300
Adamsky, Dmitry, 55, 298
Africa,
    Christianity in, 6–7, 11, 14, 57, 188 fn 33, 194
    European empire in, 39, 50, 68, 143, 169, 288
    war in, 252
Apocalyptic (see also apocalyptic realism), 4
    age, 18, 24, 79, 163, 238
    genre, 9, 21, 80, 206, 206 fn 12
    social movement (apocalypticism), 92–93, 182–83, 204–5, 210
Apocalyptic realism, 22–25, 184, 198–99, 230–31, 265–66, 271–72
Anabaptism, 23, 49, 257, 266
    Münster and, 43, 56–57, 70
Armenian Kingdom of Cilicia, 43, 56, 63, 70
Asad, Talal, 7, 123 n 34
Augsberg, Peace of, 34, 49
Augustine of Hippo, 57,
    Christendom thought of, 37–38, 287, 300
    influence on Christian realism of, 78, 197–98
    just war theory and, 97, 111
    "two cities" concept of, 26–27, 36, 73–75, 245

Bauckham, Richard, 23–24, 217–18, 221
Bell, Daniel M. Jr, 7, 171–72, 205, 225, 276
Biggar, Nigel, 7
    just war theory of, 96, 101–6
Brazil, 51, 186
Bulgakov, Sergius, 65, 195, 206, 260, 307
    The Apocalypse of John of, 209–10, 215–19, 221–22
Butterfield, Herbert, 18, 77, 81–82, 250

Cavanaugh, William T., 7, 21, 35, 59, 124, 231, 233–34, 265, 292, 299 fn 23
China, 3, 142–43, 170
    authoritarianism of, 157–58, 174, 176
    religion in, 4, 43
    security affairs of, 14, 67, 143–44, 279
Christendom
    centered, 11, 45–49, 56–62, 70, 85–86, 86 fn 55, 97 fn 10
    conditions of, 43–44
    crusades and,
    decentered, 11, 27, 45, 46–53, 62–71, 82, 97, 100, 121
    definition, xi, 10–11, 33, 40, 51–53, 85
    dialectic of, 45–51

Christendom (*continued*)
  eastern, 38, 63, 194–95 (see also Justinian)
  end of, 6, 39, 41–42, 92–93, 104, 169, 261
  global, 9, 19, 44, 184–87
  late-, 18, 67, 133, 281–85, 290
  micro-, 11, 33, 50, 56
  minorities and, 65–67
  origins of, 9–10, 36–37
  trade and, 68–69
  war and, 67–68
  Western, 33, 71–72
Christian nationalism (see also nationalism), 89, 190–92
  antisemitism and, 121 fn 22, 191–92, 239
  as neo-Christendom ideology, 11, 25, 39, 51, 191
Christian Peacemaker Teams (CPT), 257
Christian realism (see also Apocalyptic realism), 18, 77–83
  inadequacies of old, xii-xiii, 90–93
  possibilities for new, xiv, 5, 22–28, 132, 196–99
Christocentrism, xi, 23–24, 53, 301–3
  necessity of, 2–3, 8
Church, xi (see also eccelsia)
  establishment of, 9, 46, 69, 192
  evangelical (see evangelicalism)
  Orthodox (see Orthodox church)
  polis (ecclesia) of, 12, 212, 260, 262, 267, 286, 288–89, 292, 304
  Protestant, 3, 10, 48–49, 188
  Roman Catholic, 34–35, 65–66, 71, 185–86, 189, 192
  state and, 3, 33–37, 45–47, 50–51, 57–58, 70, 133, 284–85
The Clash of Civilizations, 187–90, 232–23
climate change, 2, 148, 150
  apocalyptic thought and, 280–81, 282–85, 287, 293
  UN assessment of, 279–80
Collective Security Treaty Organization (CSTO), 247–48
Constantinian, emperor and empire, 37, 41, 52, 119, 209–10, 217, 221, 262
corruption (see also kleptocracy), 108, 137–39, 174–75, 273–74
Costa-Lopez, Julia, 60–61, 65–66, 68–69
Croatia, 189–90, 192

Decentering (see also decentering Christendom), 26–27, 50–51, 70, 163, 175–79
  Taylor's use of, 121–22, 134
decolonial thought, 41–42, 71–72, 193
decolonization, 1, 12–13, 50-1, 81, 145–46

economy,
  globalization of (see globalization),
  growth of, 13–14, 148, 156–57, 183, 304
  inequality in, 157, 183, 276–77
  political control of, 13, 155, 278
economic security, 276
Elshtain, Jean Bethke, 99–100, 103
empire, 8, 169–70
  church and, 36–39, 41–42, 288
  end of, 12–13, 62–65, 170–72
Enloe, Cynthia, 108
Environmental security, 148–49, 164, 207, 275–76
Equality, Diversity, and Inclusivity (EDI), 2, 108, 226–28, 230
Eschatology, 2, 4, 27, 91–92, 210–11 (see also apocalyptic)
Eurasia 38, 50, 65, 71, 119, 189–90, 233
European Union (EU), 39, 127, 161, 192

Index   341

Evangelical Church, 48–49, 50
　political engagement of, 64,
　　185–86, 190–91, 203
evangelical thought, 22–23, 48, 84,
　　193–94

Failed states, 166–69
Finamore, Stephen, 211–12, 229,
　　238–39
France, 32 fn 4, 57, 68, 119, 236
Freedom of Religion and Belief
　　(FoRB), 44

Gallaher, Brandon, 126, 195
Galtung, Johan, 250–51
Gingerich-Hiebert, Kyle, xiii, 33, 80
Girard, Rene, 228, 229–30
　Anabaptists/Yoder and, 242, 243
　　fn 64, 260–61, 264, 282
　apocalyptic thought of, 238–40,
　　244–45
　concept of *indifférenciation* of,
　　240–42
　criticism of, 7, 213, 243
　"sacrificial Christianity" and,
　　228, 238–39, 243 fn 64, 244,
　　287 fn 63
　scapegoat mechanism of, 237–
　　39, 242–43
Givens, Tommy, 41–42
Globalization, 13–14, 18–19, 155,
　　276–77
　security and, 172–75, 244–45
　Christianity and, 184–87, 204,
　　233, 240
Gorringe, Timothy, 203, 206
　on Barth, 192, 208
　as eco-pessimist, 281, 285–86
　apocalyptic hope of, 291–92,
　　293, 305
　Transition Town Movement and,
　　289–91
　The World Turned Upside Down
　　of, 285–89
Gray, John, 4, 227
Grotius, Hugo, 77, 87, 98
Guilhot, Nicolas, 91–92

Hanciles, Jehu, 12, 193
Hauerwas, Stanley,
　as Western "after Christendom"
　　thinker, 9, 23 fn 84, 72, 119
　and church as political actor, 85,
　　102, 265–66, 301
Hobbes, Thomas, 2, 17, 77, 218 fn
　　78, 226, 286
　and Girard, 229, 241
Hovorun, Cyril, 64–65
Hungary, 51, 57, 189–90, 192
Hurd, Elizabeth Shakman, 19, 118,
　　121, 121 fn 22, 197

Imperium Christianum (see also
　　Christendom), 10, 38, 58, 76
　and relationship to
　　Christendom, 39, 57, 64, 65
Inclusion, 1, 15, 304
　Christendom and, 59
　EDI and, 226–30
　Girardian conception of, 241–
　　42, 244, 307
　human security as, 164–65
　post-Christendom and, 223,
　　230–34, 238, 299, 302
　security and, 15, 16, 25, 75, 141,
　　151
India, 123 fn 34, 156, 169–70, 170 fn
　　37, 279, 288
International Relations (IR), 5 fn 15
　Balance of power and, 77
　Christian realism in, 77–83, 90,
　　196–99
　Christendom and, 5, 34, 38–39,
　　76, 180
　concept of anarchy in, 17, 47
　contemporary theories of,
　　141–46
　dialogue with theology of, 5–6,
　　7, 22, 170
　English school of, 5, 81–83
　"religious turn" of, 21, 124
　Schmitt's influence on, 80, 91
　Secularization of, 4, 18, 140–42,
　　180
　secular realism in, 90, 103, 145

Islam and Muslims, 68, 71, 96, 178, 271
  Christendom and, 25, 60–61, 66–69, 70, 71
  neo-Christendom imaginaries against, 42, 187–88, 190, 232, 236
  secularist perceptions of, 20, 21, 95, 119
Israel, (see also Judaism and jews)
  American evangelicals and, 44, 181–82, 191, 204
  Hebrew scriptures of, 155, 217, 223–24, 264, 281, 292
  Christendom idea of "new", 40–42, 46, 88, 224
  Palestinian conflict and, 182, 204

Jenkins, Phillip, 186–87
Judaism and jews,
  antisemitism towards, 121 fn 22, 191–92, 239
  Christendom and, 60, 66, 69, 70, 231, 237
  Christian supercessionism and, 43 fn 46, 191
Just War, 8, 25
  as artefact of Christendom, 97–98
  Christian realism and, 99–100
  critique of, 96, 104–11
  defence of, 100–104
  pacifism/nonviolence and, 26, 105, 168–69, 269–70
  recent applications of, 98–99, 104–5, 135, 298
  theory of, 96, 97–101, 103, 110–11, 131–32, 302
  as contested tradition, 99–101
Justinian, emperor, 38, 49, 56–57, 70

Kalaitzidis, Pantelis, 7, 131 fn 65, 196, 297
Kant, Immanuel, 77, 90 fn 69
Katongole, Emmanuel, 194, 196
Kazakhstan, 138, 143, 247–48
  as kleptocracy, 232, 248–50, 280

King, Martin Luther, 250, 256, 268
Kyrgyzstan, 7, 74, 171, 178,
Kleptocracy (see also corruption), 155–56
  in Kazakhstan, 248–50
  in Russia, 138–39, 174, 298–99
  in UK, 137–40, 174

Leithart, Peter, 9, 11, 35, 37
Liberal democracy, 84, 87–88, 255, 275, 284–85
Liberal individualism, 123, 163–64, 183, 244–45
Liberal international order, 1, 3, 133, 160–80, 304
  membership of, 83, 127, 233
  false promise of, 163–65, 179, 183, 302
  violence of, 143, 154, 169–72
Liberal peace, 163–65, 254
Liberalism, 3, 15, 17
  neo-liberalism and, 133, 180, 183, 244, 276
  post-liberalism and, 5, 8, 180, 183
  secularism and, 3, 8, 87, 89–90, 119–20, 282
  realism and, 17, 23, 75–77, 83–87, 234
Luther, Martin, and Lutheranism, 70, 86, 99
  "two kingdoms" of, 11, 35, 46, 64, 103, 229–30

McAllister, Melani, 188, 193
Mann, Michael, 41
  Christendom dialectic of, 47–51, 63–64, 180
Martin, David, xiii
  Christian dialectic of, 48–51
Marxism, 15–16, 147, 172, 194
Mavelli, Luca, 124–25, 152, 153–54, 158
Mearsheimer, John, 90–91, 142–43, 145, 297
Megoran, Nick, 97 fn 7, 245,
Mercy Corps, 73–74, 115–17

Migration
    climate change and, 276, 279
    development value of, 234–35
    post-Christendom church and, 244–45, 305–6
    spread of church and, 12
    securitization and perceived threat of, 125, 143–44, 149, 166, 235–36
Millbank, John, 13, 16, 93, 138, 180, 183, 213–14, 245
Moltmann, Jürgen, 130, 136–37, 284–85, 292–93, 306
Morgenthau, Hans, 77–78, 80–82, 90–91, 98
Mutual Assured Destruction, 17, 142, 244, 306
Myers, Ched, 52 fn 74, 205–6

Nationalism (see also Christian nationalism), 40, 127, 222
    civilizational politics and, 133, 232–33, 250–51
    neo-Christendom, 11, 128, 133, 184, 186
    apocalypticism in, 204, 206, 210–20, 233, 293
    relationship to Christian nationalism, 11, 133–34, 182, 191, 261
    cognate ideologies in other faiths, 302
    Russian and Eurasian forms of, 189–90, 296–99
Niebuhr, Reinhold, xiii, 24
    Christian realism of, 18, 78–79, 105, 197–98, 245, 306
    Just War Theory of, 99–100, 105
    John Howard Yoder and, 92, 263, 266 fn 84, 269
Nonviolence (see also protection), 23, 255
    Christ and, 238
    post-Christendom church and, 263–64, 268, 270–71
    effectiveness of, 256–58, 271–72
    relationship to violence of, 168

John Howard Yoder and, 258–63, 264–65
North Atlantic Treaty Organization (NATO), 3, 61, 94, 143, 171, 297, 300
Northcott, Michael, 23, 204
    as eco-pessimist, 281–82
    as apocalyptic realist, 286, 293, 305
    A Political Theology of Climate Change of, 282–85
    Katechon in work of, 283, 285, 290
Nuclear weapons (see weapons)

O'Donovan, Oliver, 22–23, 83–84
    Christendom definition of, 85
    Christocentrism of, xiii
    Desire of the Nations of, 83–90, 188
    Just war thinking of, 98, 100–101, 103–4
    political liberalism of, 87–88, 91, 123
Orthodox Church (see also Russian Orthodox Church), 63, 88, 184
    Crimean war and, 68
    ecumenical patriarchate of, 64
    modern theology of, 64–65, 126, 195–96, 296–98
    Ukrainian, 194–95

Phillips, Andrew, 34, 35, 36, 38, 177
Philpott, Daniel, 34, 35, 36, 63, 66, 186
Poland, 39, 51, 66, 192
Porter, Patrick, 179, 182
post-Christendom, xi, 133
    dialectic of, 263–67
    ecclesia and, 119, 132, 197–98, 267–68
    as age, 3, 4–6, 11–15, 24–25, 34, 50, 64, 117
    the secular age as, 123–26, 134–35, 166, 180, 196–97, 227–28

344   Index

post-Christendom (*continued*)
  security as problem of, 3, 15–19, 223, 281–82
  as theology, xiii, 12, 27–28, 67, 192–96, 206–8, 244–45
  relationship to neo-Christendom of, 44, 86
powers, theological concept of, 206, 210–11
  Bulgakov's approach to, 209–10, 215–19, 221–22
  Suzerains as, 223–35
  theological approaches to, 206–8, 211–12, 219–23
  Wink's approach to, 208–9, 212–14, 215–19
Protection, xii-xiii, 5, 15–16, 223, 304
  Christendom and, 46, 58
  Christian nonviolence and, 255–56
  human security and, 164
  R2P and, 168–69
  relationship to inclusion and provision of, 228–29, 241–42, 272
  relationship to violence of, 141, 143, 147, 153, 250–54
  unarmed civilian (UCP), 256–58
Protestantism (see church)
Provision, xiv, 304
  Christendom and, 46, 268
  Christian theology of, 264–65, 291–93
  definition of, 5, 15, 16
  human security and, 164–65
  inequality and, 243, 275–78, 286, 297
  post-Christendom practice of, 289–92, 299, 304
  relationship to inclusion and protection of, 228–29, 241–42, 272
  security theory and, xiii, 5, 151, 275–76
Putin, Vladimir,
  war against Ukraine of, 31–32, 68, 298–99

Russian neo-Christendom and, 51, 55, 57, 128, 133–34, 189, 296, 302
Russia's kleptocracy and, 174, 275, 298–99
as strong man, 51, 182, 232

Reed, Esther, 131–32, 132 fn 69
Rengger, Nick, 104–5, 160
Responsibility to Protect (R2P), 168–69
  relationship to just war theory of, 98, 168
Roman Empire, 2
  scriptural references to, 213, 216, 218
  Christianity and, 9–10, 14, 36, 37, 42, 52 fn 74, 221
  Decline of, 6, 37–38
  Eastern and Western forms, 14, 34, 49, 56–57, 63, 70
Russia
  Kleptocracy of, 174, 275, 298–99
  "Russian World" (*Russkii Mir*), 51, 55, 57, 128, 133–34, 189, 296, 302
  War against Ukraine of, 31–32, 68, 298–99
Russian Orthodox Church, 184–85, 189, 194–95
  Orthodox declaration against, 295–97

Sanneh, Lamin, 193
Saudi Arabia, 108, 161 fn 5
Schmitt, Carl, 79
  idea of katechon of, 79–80, 283
  influence on theology of, 80, 196, 282–83
  influence on IR of, 80, 111
Secular, the, 133
  defined as "secular age" (see Taylor)
  disenchantment and, 18, 27, 118, 120–23, 133, 172
  post-Christendom and, 134–35

re-enchantment and, 27, 118, 121, 133, 180, 183–84, 192, 197, 219, 298
relationship to religion of, 20–21, 26–27
secularization and, 118–21
the state and, 124–26, 152–58
varieties of, 132–34
Securitization, concept of, 147–52
Security (see also Securitization)
concept and definition of, 2–3, 15–16
crisis of, 2
dilemma of, 17–18
human, 163–65
national, 152–54, 158–59
objective condition of, 15
private, 172–73
questions of, 8
relationship to Christendom of, 2–3, 15
secularization and, 118–21
subjective condition of, 15
theological conception of, 16–17, 27–28
Sierra Leone, 12, 94–96
Smith, James K. A., 7, 10, 11, 16 fn 51, 121
Sölle, Dorothee, 184
Soviet Union, xii, 43, 51 fn 71, 144, 145, 215
State, the,
emergence under Christendom, 51, 84–85, 87
failure of, 166–69
theory of, 175–78
secular form of, 72, 87–88, 109, 124–26, 52–58
transformation of, 173–75

Tajikistan, 74, 115–16, 235, 253, 254
Tilly, Charles, 105, 153
Taylor, Charles, 6
The Secular Age of, 121–30
"expressive individualism" of, 122, 164, 285
Transition town movement (TTM), 289–93

Trump, Donald,
Evangelical support for, 25, 32, 249–50, 182
Israel and, 32, 181–82
as strongman, 51, 302

Ukraine
Orthodox church of, 55, 61, 189, 194–95
pacifist movement of, 194–95, 299, 301
Russian war against, xii, 10, 32, 140, 172, 297–300
United Kingdom
post-Christian character of, 45, 192, 302
remembrance in, 109, 110–11
security affairs of, 95–96, 107–9, 138–40, 160–62, 166, 174, 300 fn 27
kleptocracy problem of, 137–39, 146, 155, 155 fn 78, 249
United Nations, 13, 95, 132, 135, 146, 235,
Development Programme (UNDP) of, 164, 165
Department of Peacekeeping Operations (UNDPKO) of, 254, 255, 269
Intergovernmental Panel on Climate Change (IPCC) of, 279–80
Security Council of, 94, 179, 254
United States of America, 2, 107, 167, 171, 185, 253, 279, 283
Conservative evangelicals in, 44, 185, 188, 203–4, 249–50
church and state in, 11, 39, 43, 64, 120, 127–28, 236
as holder of the balance of power, 80, 142
Uzbekistan, 73

Valk, John-Harmen, 230–31

Waltz, Kenneth N., 90, 141–42
War and armed conflict, 251–54

Weapons,
    autonomous, 2, 107–9, 130–31
        135, 244
    nuclear, 1, 54–55, 77, 98, 130,
        143, 144
    trade in, 108, 135, 161–62
Wendt, Alexander, 146, 212 fn 46
Westphalian, peace of, 21, 34
    end of Christendom and, 36, 39,
        63–64, 81
    foundation of IR and, 35–36
Wight, Martin,
    as apocalyptic thinker, 198–99,
        305
    Christian realism and, 82–83,
        147, 199
    criticism of secularization of,
        90 fn 69
    "The Church, Russia and the
        West" of, vi, xi–xiii, 1 97–98,
        295
Wink, Water, 206, 208–14, 218–21
Williams, Michael C., 124, 151
Williams, Rowan, 75, 94, 105–6,
    111, 195, 273
World Council of Churches (WCC),
    xi
Wright, Nigel G., 23 fn 87, 212–13

Yabro-Collins, 218 fn 75, 222
Yoder, John Howard
    Christian Witness to the State of,
        261–63, 266–67, 269–70
    Christocentrism of, 268
    critical analysis of, 263–66, 269
    sexual abuse scandal of, 258–61,
        271